Corporate Governance Models and Applications in Developing Economies

Otuo Serebour Agyemang
University of Cape Coast, Ghana

Abraham Ansong
University of Cape Coast, Ghana

Ben Kwame Agyei-Mensah
Solbridge International School of Business, South Korea

A volume in the Advances in Human Resources Management and Organizational Development (AHRMOD) Book Series

IGI Global
DISSEMINATOR OF KNOWLEDGE

Published in the United States of America by
IGI Global
Business Science Reference (an imprint of IGI Global)
701 E. Chocolate Avenue
Hershey PA, USA 17033
Tel: 717-533-8845
Fax: 717-533-8661
E-mail: cust@igi-global.com
Web site: http://www.igi-global.com

Library of Congress Cataloging-in-Publication Data

Names: Agyemang, Otuo Serebour, 1983- editor. | Ansong, Abraham, 1981- editor. | Agyei-Mensah, Ben Kwame, 1962- editor.
Title: Corporate governance models and applications in developing economies / Otuo Serebour Agyemang, Abraham Ansong, and Ben Kwame Agyei-Mensah, editors.
Description: Hershey, PA : Business Science Reference, [2019]
Identifiers: LCCN 2019005250| ISBN 9781522596073 (hardcover) | ISBN 9781522596097 (ebook) | ISBN 9781522596080 (softcover)
Subjects: LCSH: Corporate governance--Developing countries.
Classification: LCC HD2741 .C776516 2019 | DDC 338.609172/4--dc23 LC record available at https://lccn.loc.gov/2019005250

This book is published in the IGI Global book series Advances in Human Resources Management and Organizational Development (AHRMOD) (ISSN: 2327-3372; eISSN: 2327-3380)

British Cataloguing in Publication Data
A Cataloguing in Publication record for this book is available from the British Library.

All work contributed to this book is new, previously-unpublished material.
The views expressed in this book are those of the authors, but not necessarily of the publisher.

For electronic access to this publication, please contact: eresources@igi-global.com.

Advances in Human Resources Management and Organizational Development (AHRMOD) Book Series

ISSN:2327-3372
EISSN:2327-3380

Editor-in-Chief: Patricia Ordóñez de Pablos, Universidad de Oviedo, Spain

MISSION

A solid foundation is essential to the development and success of any organization and can be accomplished through the effective and careful management of an organization's human capital. Research in human resources management and organizational development is necessary in providing business leaders with the tools and methodologies which will assist in the development and maintenance of their organizational structure.

The **Advances in Human Resources Management and Organizational Development (AHRMOD) Book Series** aims to publish the latest research on all aspects of human resources as well as the latest methodologies, tools, and theories regarding organizational development and sustainability. The **AHRMOD Book Series** intends to provide business professionals, managers, researchers, and students with the necessary resources to effectively develop and implement organizational strategies.

COVERAGE

- Process Improvement
- Employee Evaluation
- Talent Identification and Management
- Compliance
- Corporate Governance
- Skills Management
- Organizational Behavior
- Executive Education
- E-Human Resources Management
- Workplace Discrimination

IGI Global is currently accepting manuscripts for publication within this series. To submit a proposal for a volume in this series, please contact our Acquisition Editors at Acquisitions@igi-global.com or visit: http://www.igi-global.com/publish/.

The Advances in Human Resources Management and Organizational Development (AHRMOD) Book Series (ISSN 2327-3372) is published by IGI Global, 701 E. Chocolate Avenue, Hershey, PA 17033-1240, USA, www.igi-global.com. This series is composed of titles available for purchase individually; each title is edited to be contextually exclusive from any other title within the series. For pricing and ordering information please visit http://www.igi-global.com/book-series/advances-human-resources-management-organizational/73670. Postmaster: Send all address changes to above address.

Titles in this Series

For a list of additional titles in this series, please visit:
https://www.igi-global.com/book-series/advances-human-resources-management-organizational/73670

Macro and Micro-Level Issues Surrounding Women in the Workforce Emerging Research and Opportunities
Başak Uçanok Tan (Istanbul Bilgi University, Turkey)
Business Science Reference • ©2020 • 309pp • H/C (ISBN: 9781522591634) • US $195.00

Cases on Learning Design and Human Performance Technology
Jill Stefaniak (University of Georgia, USA)
Business Science Reference • ©2020 • 362pp • H/C (ISBN: 9781799800545) • US $195.00

Organizational Culture and Achieving Business Excellence Emerging Research and Opportunities
Rassel Kassem (Abu Dhabi Judicial Department, UAE) and Mian M. Ajmal (Abu Dhabi University, UAE)
Business Science Reference • ©2019 • 143pp • H/C (ISBN: 9781522584131) • US $165.00

Workforce Coaching, Mentoring, and Counseling Emerging Research and Opportunities
Jayaranjani Sutha (Eastern University, Sri Lanka)
Business Science Reference • ©2019 • 226pp • H/C (ISBN: 9781522592358) • US $195.00

Corporate Standardization Management and Innovation
Kai Jakobs (RWTH Aachen University, Germany)
Business Science Reference • ©2019 • 362pp • H/C (ISBN: 9781522590088) • US $225.00

Handbook of Research on Metaheuristics for Order Picking Optimization in Warehouses to Smart Cities
Alberto Ochoa Ortiz-Zezzatti (Autonomous University of Juarez City, Mexico) Gilberto Rivera (Autonomous University of Juarez City, Mexico) Claudia Gómez-Santillán (National Institute of Technology of Mexico, Mexico & Technological Institute of Ciudad Madero, Mexico) and Benito Sánchez–Lara (National Autonomous University of Mexico, Mexico)
Business Science Reference • ©2019 • 498pp • H/C (ISBN: 9781522581314) • US $345.00

For an entire list of titles in this series, please visit:
https://www.igi-global.com/book-series/advances-human-resources-management-organizational/73670

IGI Global
DISSEMINATOR OF KNOWLEDGE

701 East Chocolate Avenue, Hershey, PA 17033, USA
Tel: 717-533-8845 x100 • Fax: 717-533-8661
E-Mail: cust@igi-global.com • www.igi-global.com

Editorial Advisory Board

Table of Contents

Section 2
Governance and Financial Institutions

Detailed Table of Contents

in large, systemic banks' management board structure and 2) whether systemic banks' financial performance is determined by the management board's features (board size, number of women in the board, number of independent members). The empirical approach relies on several complementary methods (descriptive statistics, cluster analysis, panel regression) to reveal dominant board features in a sample of 29 European systemic banks, over a time frame of 11 years.

People's IPO is a project that aims at distribution shares of state-owned entities to members of the public. Three Russian state-owned enterprises, VTB, SBERBANK, and ROSNEFT, conducted People's IPO between 2006 and 2007. The aim of these IPOs was to offer the general public an opportunity to own shares in state-owned enterprises. Such an investment opportunity would give ordinary citizens a stake in Russia's biggest state enterprises. Authors investigated the success or otherwise of these IPOs in distributing shares of government enterprises to ordinary citizens and gave recommendations on possible ways of improving public participation in People's IPOs. The aim of this chapter is to propose People's IPO as one of the ways of ensuring proper wealth distribution and eradicating injustice in the financial system. Authors recommend adoption of offer prices that friendly to small investors, creation of credit lines that would avail funds for investing in the IPOs. Companies going public should also adherer to the world's best to ensure growth in shareholders wealth.

The failure of top firms in the world who once represented the icon of their industries has renewed the interest of research scholars, practitioners, policymakers, and academics on the subject matter of financial distress. A firm is financially distressed when the operating cash flow is not sufficient for meeting the current obligation of the firm. It also involves a situation where the firm constantly experiences loss, breach loan contract, and find it difficult in honouring organisational commitment.

Foreword

Corporate governance has been amplified over the past two decades due significant effects of ethical, financial, accounting and regulatory failures in developed countries. These corporate governance failures as being described have global transmission effects. The scale of integration of global corporate governance reforms into corporations and, national financial and corporate sector regulations in developing economies is very fast.

This book is apt, timely and broad as it is useful for all categories of sectors and professionals interested in good corporate governance. The book discusses relevant legal, historical, contextual, accounting, finance and ethical aspects of corporate governance. Students of management, developments studies, accounting, finance and public policy as well as policy makers will benefit greatly from reading this book.

John Gartchie Gatsi
University of Cape Coast, Ghana

Preface

INTRODUCTION

Corporate governance has its roots from the emergence of capitalism and modern stock organisations, the development of international trade and the enormous growth of multinational corporations during the "industrial revolution" in the early part of the nineteenth century. It has recently received much attention as a result of the incidence of corporate frauds, accounting scandals, excessive compensation packages, insider trading, self-dealing, misleading disclosures and possible civil and criminal liabilities of corporate organisations. Accordingly, these have alerted both internal and external stakeholders to intensify their inspection of the unassailability of corporate governance practices within corporations. In addition, many economies are incrementally making reforms to corporate governance practices to raise the entire standards of corporate governance and to offer corporate organisations possible financial and investment benefits. However, there has been a spate of arguments about the "essential" principles of effective corporate governance in the sense that this concept develops and expands, and it changes in accordance with new insights and challenges in the corporate world. Thus, works on corporate governance should seek to examine the relevant principles of sound corporate governance and contribute to both theory and practice.

RATIONALE AND GOAL OF THE BOOK

Issues of corporate governance are germane to developing countries, in view of the assertion that these economies lack vibrant, long-established institutions to address matters pertaining to corporate governance. The widespread existence of small enterprises that do not have their shares listed, and of large family-owned, foreign-owned and or state-owned enterprises whose stocks are also not widely listed locally, is argued to be the obvious logic behind the absence of good corporate governance issues in these economies. However, the view that issues of corporate governance are less relevant to countries with insignificant amount of large corporate organizations with widely traded stocks is flawed. Just as good public governance allows the citizenry to effectively ascertain whether their interests are being served, corporate organisations, irrespective of their sizes and locations, must also strive to strengthen their governance practices so that their shareholders can make reasonable investment decisions. Currently, virtually all developing, transition and emerging-market economies are faced with one pressing concern; how to establish the groundwork for long-term economic performance and competitiveness in diverse ways. But the setting up of such foundation to embark on such tasks cannot be materialized without the existence of good corporate governance in these economies. This has currently, prompted governments, directors, corporate owners, corporate managers and other stakeholders in these economies to realize the indispensability of effective corporate governance practice. Thus, this book intends to come up with chapters that will suggest models of corporate governance and their application in developing economies.

Our target audience of this book was primarily composed of researchers and professionals working in the field of corporate governance in developing economies. Moreover, the book will provide theoretical and practical insights and support corporate executives concerned with the governance of their corporations.

SUMMARY OF THE BOOK THEMES AND CHAPTERS

"Audit Committee Effectiveness, Audit Quality, and Internal Control Information Disclosures: An Empirical Study": This chapter examined the linkages between audit committees' effectiveness, audit quality and internal control information disclosure. Empirical evidence on the effect of audit committee effectiveness and audit quality on internal control information disclosure is scanty. Using a 210 firm-year sample of firms listed on the Ghana Stock Exchange for the period, 2013-2017, the paper tried to fill the research gap. After controlling for board size, proportion of independent directors and leverage, the results from univariate and multivariate analyses indicated that effective audit committee and audit firm size play complimentary and substitution roles in ensuring internal control information disclosure. Board size and proportion of independent directors were also found to influence the disclosure of quality voluntary information.

"Audit Committee Characteristics and Earnings Quality: Evidence From Bahrain Bourse": The aim of this study at investigates the relationship of the audit committee and earnings quality of listed companies in Bahrain bourse and to examine whether those companies comply with the obligatory code of corporate governance. The sample of this study includes 40 companies listed in Bahrain Bourse for the period

2013-2017. The model of the study tested the relationship between the independent variables of audit committee characteristics and the dependents variable of earnings quality using pooled data regression. The findings of the study showed that the Bahraini listed companies comply and follow the code of corporate governance and some audit committee characteristics have an impact on earnings quality.

"Corporate Governance Role of the Board Committees in India": The establishment of board sub-committees has been strongly recommended as a suitable mechanism for improving corporate governance, by delegating specific tasks from the main board to a smaller group and harnessing the contribution of non-executive directors. This chapter discusses the constitution of board committees in Indian context, their composition, processes and their role in promoting good corporate governance. India has constantly made efforts to update its corporate governance regulations in line with the international best practices. This chapter will help the readers to understand the corporate governance scenario in India with special reference to the board committees and will have implications for the regulators, policy makers, corporate governance practitioners, researchers and academicians in the developing countries.

"Systemic Financial Institutions' Corporate Governance Features: Comparative Insights": Several international and European regulatory and supervisory authorities, such as the Basel Committee for Banking Supervision, the European Banking Authority or the European Central Bank are increasingly emphasizing that the structure of banks' managing bodies is a key driver of future financial stability and ask for reviews of existing skills, competencies and expertise in order to cope with the newest economic, social and technological challenges. The chapter subscribes to these views and aims at investigating two research directions: i) whether there are resemblances in large, systemic banks' management board structure; and ii) whether systemic banks' financial performance is determined by the management board's features (board size, number of women in the board, number of independent members). The empirical approach relies on several complementary methods (descriptive statistics, cluster analysis, panel regression) to reveal dominant board features in a sample of 29 European systemic banks, over a time frame of eleven years.

"Effects of People's IPO on the Russian Financial Market and Corporate Governance Praxis": People's IPO is a project that aims at distribution shares of state-owned entities to members of the public. Three Russian state-owned enterprises, VTB, SBERBANK, and ROSNEFT conducted People's IPO between 2006 and 2007. The aim of these IPOs was to offer the general public an opportunity to own shares in state-owned enterprises. Such an investment opportunity would give ordinary citizens a stake in Russia's biggest state enterprises. Authors investigated the success or otherwise of these IPOs in distributing shares of government enterprises to ordinary citizens and gave recommendations on possible ways of improving public participation in people's IPOs. The aim of this paper is to propose People's IPO as one of the ways of ensuring proper wealth distribution and eradicating injustice in the financial system. Authors recommend adoption of offer prices that friendly to small investors, creation of credit lines that would avail funds for investing in the IPOs. Companies going public should also adherer to the world's best to ensure growth in shareholders' wealth.

"Financial Distress Overview: Determinants and Sustainable Remedial Measures": In recent times, the failure of top firms in the world who once represent the icon of their industries has renewed the interest of research scholars, practitioners, policy-makers and academics on the subject matter of financial distress. A firm is financially distressed when the operating cash flow is not sufficient for meeting the current obligation of the firm. It also involves a situation where the firm constantly experiences loss, breach loan contract and find it difficult in honouring organisational commitment. This chapter is set out to synthesize the recent development in the topics of financial distress and corporate recovery. This chapter primarily focuses on financial distress, its determinants and the way forward on how firms can recover from financial distress. The chapter also discussed the financial distress theories as well as sustainable remedial measures of financial distress. Finally, the chapter provides the concluding remarks and policy implications.

"Equilibrium in Corporate Governance: Effects in Developing Countries": Corporate governance systems around the world are shaped by legal traditions, but the most important determinant of their effectiveness is law enforcement. Developing countries tend to have weak institutional structures and contracting environments. In this context, markets are inefficient and ownership concentration becomes the main corporate governance mechanism in order to protect property rights. How can developing countries design an optimal corporate governance system in their poor business environments? Corporate governance mechanisms are interdependent, and each country needs to search for a set of mechanisms in equilibrium—that is, an optimal combination of control and incentives—that solves its own agency problems. But another problem in developing countries is the lack of public enforcement. Just as internal mechanisms may substitute for ineffective external mechanisms, private initiatives may reinforce weak public enforcement.

"Cash Holdings and Corporate Governance: Evidence From Turkey": This paper investigates the empirical factors affecting corporate cash holdings with special emphasis on corporate governance variables for a sample of Turkish-listed nonfinancial firms over the period 2006 to 2010. The findings reveal a significant non-linear relation between family ownership and cash holdings. In addition, while board structure does not significantly affect the level of cash holdings, tunneling increases cash reserves of firms. Furthermore, the results indicate that cash flow, leverage, other liquid assets that can be used as cash substitutes, the degree of tangibility of assets and firm size are important in determining cash holdings among Turkish companies.

"Corporate Governance and Performance": The purpose of the present study is to evaluate the current state of the linkage between corporate governance and performance. Corporate governance is by far the most important subject that should be studied due to its role and significance. Accordingly, there is intensive literature on corporate governance and its possible impact on performance. By conducting a systematic literature review, we provide the results of frequently used variables that supposed to reflect the character of corporate governance on firm performance. The study covers the findings of empirical papers that analyze the impact of "Board Size", "Percentage of Independent Directors", "CEO Duality", "Ownership Concentration", "Audit Committee and Auditor Reputation", "Board Meetings", and "Firm Size". The examination of the reviewed studies indicates that there is a need to explain the competing findings observed among firms, markets and countries by developing theoretical based explanation.

"The Promotion of Partnership Value Through Employee Share Ownership and Customer Share Ownership": Our research proposes an enriched analysis of value creation seeking to integrate all the stakeholders. To this end, we suggest two practices that counterbalance the power of shareholders and managers by allowing other stakeholders to exercise political and financial power. We are interested in employee share ownership and customer shareholding, in fact, the property allows to grant customers and employees the superior status of the shareholder in order to enjoy a higher power likely to limit the attempts of managerial entrenchment and shareholders supremacy.

"Ethics and CSR Practices for Enduring Corporate Governance Culture": The studies in corporate governance have explained different motives responsible for adoption of corporate governance. This chapter provides answers to why business should be morally responsible and practice CSR. We shed light on crucial areas of corporate responsibilities of business and various theoretical justification advanced in previous studies in CSR. We look at the relationship between CSR and corporate governance – their crucial points of divergence and convergence. We also look at ethics and responsibilities for unethical behaviours and ethical theories with their limitations. Finally, we evaluate CSR and ethics from African perspective – how CSR in Africa is framed from by sociocultural influences, like communalism, ethnic-religious beliefs and charitable tradition (ubuntu Philosophy).

"How Credit Portfolio Diversification Affects the Profitability of Vietnamese Commercial Banks": This study analyzed the impact of credit portfolio diversification on the profitability by using the data of 20 Vietnam commercial banks from 2009 to 2015. The results from Feasible Generalized Least Squares (FGLS) estimation show that the strategy of diversifying the credit portfolio increased the profitability of commercial banks. In addition, the study also indicates that the positive correlation of the ratio of owners' equity, credit growth, liquidity, assets, inflation rate with the profitability; while the increase in non-performing loan decreased the profitability of these commercial banks.

"System Dynamics Modelling for Policy Design: A Case Study in Turkey": The system dynamics model was developed in the Vensim software. The model was developed based on the Yamaguchi study. The construct and behavioral validity of the model were addressed. Construct validity means that the correlations that construct the model, that is, the "rationale" of the model, are consistent with the correlations in the real system. There were five sub-models in the model. These were manufacturers and consumers sub-model, banks sub-model, central bank sub-model, balance of payments sub-model, exchange rate market sub-model. Five sub models included in the model developed with the VENSIM software are included in the appendices.

Section 1

Operations of Board Committees

Chapter 1
Audit Committee Effectiveness, Audit Quality, and Internal Control Information Disclosures:
An Empirical Study

Ben Kwame Agyei-Mensah
https://orcid.org/0000-0002-5652-1628
Solbridge International School of Business, South Korea

Otuo Serebour Agyemang
University of Cape Coast, Ghana

Abraham Ansong
University of Cape Coast, Ghana

ABSTRACT

This chapter examined the linkages between audit committees' effectiveness, audit quality, and internal control information disclosure. Empirical evidence on the effect of audit committee effectiveness and audit quality on internal control information disclosure is scanty. Using a 210 firm-year sample of firms listed on the Ghana Stock Exchange for the period 2013-2017, the chapter tried to fill the research gap. After controlling for board size, proportion of independent directors, and leverage, the results from univariate and multivariate analyses indicated that effective audit committee and audit firm size play complimentary and substitution roles in ensuring internal control information disclosure. Board size and proportion of independent directors were also found to influence the disclosure of quality voluntary information.

DOI: 10.4018/978-1-5225-9607-3.ch001

INTRODUCTION

The purpose of this paper is to investigate the influence of audit committee effectiveness and audit quality on disclosure of internal control information in corporate annual reports. The paper wants to test whether there is a substitute or complementary effect between the presence of Big Four auditor and effective audit committee in influencing disclosure of internal control information.

Establishment of proper corporate governance mechanisms is essential for the optimal application of resources, enhancement of responsiveness, transparency and protecting the rights of the stakeholders (Sun *et al.*, 2010; Grougiou *et al.*, 2014). According to Deumes, (2004) reporting on internal control improves the quality of financial reporting and reduces governance problems. Internal control also helps to ensure that information is reliable and that firms comply with laws and regulations (Beretta et al., 2010; Hunziker, 2013).

Lack of proper attention to proper internal controls could either result in a direct loss of earnings or may result in imposition of constraints on the firm's ability to meet its profit-making objectives. In the wake of recent corporate failures, the necessity of establishing audit committees and engaging quality audit in enhancing quality financial reports has been emphasized. A company that has an effective audit committee will have less likelihood of experiencing problems with internal control (Zhang et al., 2007; Krishnan, 2005). According to Ashbaugh-Skaife et al. (2007), lack of internal control disclosures raises shareholders' uncertainty about the reliability of the reported earnings and appear to elicit a significant negative market reaction. An effective internal control system can prevent large losses (Jaya et. al., 2016). The interaction among corporate governance actors is crucial to the issue of quality financial reports. This study focuses on two of these corporate governance actors, namely audit committee and external auditors. In particular, this study attempts to investigate the nature of relationship between audit committees and external auditor on internal control information disclosure. Zhang et al. (2007) posit that audit committees with financial expertise or accounting expertise have a smaller probability of experiencing internal control issues. Ho and Wong (2001) also argue that the presence of an audit committee influence the level of corporate disclosure. In emerging economies, where corporate governance mechanisms are typically weak to contain agency problems, external auditors provide assurance on the reliability of financial statements of listed companies (Fan and Wong, 2005). This study focused on the audit committee because it is one of the elements responsible for overseeing the interests of shareholders and supervising financial statements. The audit committee should be efficient and provide maximum transparency. This organ of control needs other mechanisms, such as the quality of external auditor, to mitigate annual report manipulation.

Based on the aforementioned and in order to ensure clarity, the main objectives of this paper are:

1. To measure the extent of internal control information disclosure in the listed firms' annual reports;
2. To study the interaction between an effective audit committee and the presence of an external audit function to promote the disclosure of internal control information.

After controlling for board size, proportion of independent directors and leverage, the results from univariate and multivariate analyses indicated that effective audit committee and audit firm size play complimentary and substitution roles in ensuring internal control information disclosure. Board size and proportion of independent directors were also found to influence the disclosure of quality voluntary information.

This study takes a step forward in the academic literature with contribution and implications that are both practical and academic. The study findings contribute to the corporate governance literature by shedding light on the role of external audit, and audit committee characteristics, such as accounting expertise, prior experience, size and number of meetings in the disclosure process. This paper is one of the few to examine the association between audit committee effectiveness and audit quality, and internal control information disclosure.

LITERATURE REVIEW

Audit Committee

The Ghana Corporate Governance guidelines on best practices issued by the Securities and Exchange Commission require all companies to establish audit committees. The audit committee

should comprise at least three directors, the majority of whom should be independent directors and the chairman should be an independent director. For quality presentation and disclosure of financial and non-financial information, companies in Ghana are required to comply with the International Financial Reporting Standards (IFRS) which have been adopted by the Institute of Chartered Accountants Ghana (ICAG).

The audit committee is one of the most important board sub-committees and its main responsibility is to oversee then effectiveness of internal control and financial reporting quality.

Prior research shows that financial experts within the audit committee curb internal control weaknesses (Krishnan, 2005; Zhang *et al.*, 2007) and ensure high financial reporting quality (Abbott *et al.*, 2004; Kang *et al.*, 2011; Lary and Taylor, 2012; Sun *et al.*, 2012).

Empirical evidence shows that audit committees' role is very important because it is responsible for oversight of the financial reporting process (Johl et al., 2012).

Prior studies provide mixed results on the role of audit committee size in ensuring financial reporting quality. While a number of studies found size to be a significant determinant of financial reporting quality (Lin *et al.*, 2006; Cornett *et al.*, 2009), other studies reported insignificant impact on the financial reporting process (Abbott *et al.*, 2004; Bedard *et al.*, 2004; Lary & Taylor, 2012). Alzoubi and Selamat (2012) stated that, audit committees with financial expertise will increase the capability of monitoring and in turn, increases the quality of financial reporting.

Krishnan (2005) provides evidence that an independent and large audit committee reduces the likelihood of material internal control weaknesses.

According to Shah and Butt (2009), the more independent the audit committee is, the higher quality the financial reporting. Razman and Iskandar (2004) conducted a research on Malaysian-listed companies studying the link between financial reporting and audit committee members' academic background. Their results show that high-quality financial reporting comes attached to the extent of how much the members serving on the committee are financially literate.

Bedard et al. (2004) observe that the best way to sustain a company's control function is by increasing the occurrence of audit committee meetings. According to Abbott et al. (2004), the more the audit committee meets and makes sure that its members are doing the job required of them for the best interest of the company, the less the possibility of fraud. Abbott *et al.* (2000) argue that the frequency of audit committee meetings shows their desire to fulfil their responsibilities. Audit committees who hold frequent meetings, despite their busy schedules, emerge as an effective committee in enhancing corporate financial reporting quality (Abbott *et al.*, 2000; Kang *et al.*, 2011).

Audit Quality

Knechel et al. (2013) defined audit quality as execution of a well-designed audit process by properly motivated and trained auditors who understand the inherent uncertainty of the audit and appropriately adjust to the unique conditions of the client. This paper in consonance with prior literature, (e.g. Bepari, & Mollik, 2015) used the size of the audit firm as a proxy for audit quality. It is assumed that Big-4 and non-Big-4 audit firms differ in terms of their audit qualities and enforcement abilities.

The literature suggests that firms with strong corporate governance tend to engage high quality auditors (Big-4 audit firms) and pay larger audit fees (DeFond & Zhang, 2014). Audit quality may also enhance the transparency of a report via higher voluntary disclosure (Barros et al., 2013). Audit firm size is highly associated with a greater level of disclosure, hence it can be hypothesized that audit quality can lead to greater level of internal control disclosure. Ashbaugh-Skaife, et a., (2007) posit that Big-4 audit firms have a reputation to protect and are motivated to perform high quality internal control quality and to ensure that companies disclose weaknesses in internal control.

Audit fees can be defined as the actual cost charged to the company by the auditor in return for their opinion regarding the financial statement of the latter (Coffee, 2005).

Internal Control Disclosure

Effective internal control system represents an adequate assessment of earnings quality and reliable financial reporting (Costello & Wittenberg-Moerman, 2011; Doyle et al., 2007). Internal control can also be viewed as the process put in place by management to provide reasonable assurance regarding the achievement of effective and efficient operations, reliable financial reporting, and compliance with laws and regulations.

In 1978, Cohen Commission (the Commission on Auditors' Responsibilities), (cited in Agyei-Mensah, 2016a), required that management should assess internal control systems. Internal control consists of all of the related methods and measures adopted within an organisation to:

- Safeguard assets from employee theft, robbery, and unauthorized use.
- Enhance the accuracy and reliability of its accounting records by reducing the risk of errors (unintentional mistakes) and irregularities (intentional mistakes and misrepresentations) in the accounting process.

The Committee of Sponsoring Organisations of the Treadway Commission (COSO) also defines internal control as:

A process, effected by an entity's board of directors, management and other personnel, designed to provide reasonable assurance regarding the achievement of objectives in the following categories: Effectiveness and efficiency of operations; Reliability of financial reporting; and Compliance with applicable laws and regulations.

Internal control according COSO consists of five interrelated components:

- Control environment
- Risk assessment
- Control activities
- Information and communication
- Monitoring.

Ismail and Rahman, (2011) argue that Information related to corporate governance such as internal control and risk management system could help the companies to fulfill the need of the investors. Verschoor (2002) suggests that the financial scandal of Enron was mainly caused by its weak internal control system. Internal control information has been cited as one of the most important non-financial information items to be included in the corporate reporting domains (Guthrie & Petty, 2000; Abeysekera, 2013). The underlying argument is that internal control resources represent a substantial amount of a firm's market value in the modern economy (Edvinsson, 2013), and therefore, disclosure of internal control information reveals "the 'true' value of a firm by identifying new or hidden relations between various forms of assets" (Liu & Wang, 2012, p. 37). Hermanson (2000) posits that despite importance of internal control investors cannot directly observe it and until the firm discloses it voluntarily, investors will remain unaware of the level and quality of the firm's internal control systems (Deumes & Knechel, 2008; Michelon et al., 2009).

Ashbaugh-Skaife, Collins, and Kinney (2007) find that firms reporting internal control deficiencies have more complex operations, greater exposure to accounting risk, fewer resources to invest in internal control, and a higher likelihood of using a dominant audit firm.

Poor corporate governance and low level of transparency in disclosing information by the companies are some of the reasons to the 1997-1998 Malaysia financial crisis, according to Norwani, Mohamad and Check, (2011).

Relationship Between Audit Committee Effectiveness, Audit Quality, and Internal Control Disclosure

Zhang *et al.* (2007) provide empirical evidence that the audit committee and the external auditor play an important role in reducing internal control weaknesses. Abbot et al. (2004), documented that completely independent and financial expertise of audit committee were positively related with a demand for higher audit quality.

According to Cohen et al., (2004) the interactions between the audit committee, the external auditors and the board of directors are crucial to improve the quality of financial reporting. Thus, supporting the argument that the interactions between effective audit committee and the external auditor will bring about good internal control in organisations.

Mitchell *et al.* (2008) showed that the relation between an audit committee and the quality of audit can potentially enhance the quality of financial statements published to the external stakeholders.

As noted by Xie et al. (2003), the audit committee has the responsibility to oversee ICFR, communicating with management, internal and external auditors, and the board of directors to assure that appropriate controls are in place and reporting processes are effective.

The corporate governance literature suggests that audit committee effectiveness is positively associated with firms' financial reporting quality (Carcello *et al.*, 2006; Klein, 2002) and negatively associated with the incidence of management fraud (Carcello *et al.*, 2009; Abbott *et al.*, 2004). Carcello *et al.* (2006), Abbott *et al.* (2003) declare that the existence of an independent audit committee equipped with financial expertise is positively related with audit quality. Zhang et al. (2007) find that internal control disclosure is negatively associated with audit committee financial expertise, but do not find an association with other audit committee characteristics.

Based on the objectives of the study the following hypotheses would be tested:

H1. Firms with an effective audit committee and a Big Four auditor, are likely to disclose internal control information

H2. Firms with an effective audit committee and disclose audit fee charged, are likely to disclose internal control information

H3. Firms with an effective audit committee and a long auditor tenure are likely to disclose internal control information

Method

The data to be used in the empirical analysis will be derived from the financial statements of all the listed firms on the GSE during a five-year period, 2013-2017. Five years were selected, because these were the latest financial statements. Data for these years were selected because firms' disclosures tend to persist across years (Bushee et al. 2003, Skinner 2003, Graham et al. 2005). Once managers decide to disclose internal control information in the narrative sections of the annual report, it is unlikely that they would switch back to no disclosure.

A disclosure index consisting of eight reportable items were used to measure the extent of voluntary internal control reporting. This internal control disclosure evaluation criteria have been used by Jainfei Leng and Yiran Ding (2011). The Appendix shows the internal control disclosure evaluation criteria used in the study.

In all 210 firm-years reports for the period 2013 - 2017 were used. The annual reports were downloaded from Africanfianncials.com web site. Each annual report was individually examined and coded in order to obtain the disclosure of internal control information. For the purpose of this article, dummy variables are assigned to represent whether or not an item is used, if an item is used 1 is assigned to that item and zero if an item is not used. The values assigned are then summed up to represent the total score for each company. This is mathematically presented as follows:

The disclosure index = Total internal control items disclosed / Maximum (8) items disclosed for each company. This can mathematically be stated as follows:

$$Disclosure\,Index = \frac{Actual\,Disclosure}{Total\,Possible\,Disclosure} = \frac{\sum_{1}^{m} di}{\sum_{1}^{n} di}$$

Where:

d_i = 1 if the item *di* is disclosed (0 if not disclosed)
m = number of items disclosed;
n = maximum number of disclosure items possible

Measurement of Independent Variables

Following prior studies (Sultana, *et al.*, 2015; Ika & Ghazali, 2012; Nelson & Shukeri, 2011; Mohamad-Naimi et al., 2010; Lin et al., 2006; DeZoort et al., 2002) this study uses five audit committee variables best proxying audit committee effectiveness for analysis. These are; audit committee financial expertise, audit committee previous experience, audit committee size, independent audit committee, and audit committee meeting.

Measurement of Effectiveness of Audit Committee

The study model includes audit committee variables such as: ACPE, a dummy variable that is 1 where at least one director of the audit committee has prior audit committee experience and 0 otherwise. Additionally, ACSZ: the number of members forming the audit committee, and ACIND, a dummy variable that is 1 where companies have an independent audit committee, and 0 otherwise. An audit committee is independent when it is formed exclusively by external and independent members. ACFE; it is a dummy variable that takes the value1 if the audit committee includes at least one member with finance expertise in each year during the period 2013-2017, and 0 otherwise. ACMT is a variable that measures the number of meetings of the audit committee.

This study uses three proxy of measurement of audit quality; audit firm size (AUDFSZ), audit fees (AUDFEE), auditor tenure (TENURE). These measures have been used by Zgarni, Hlioui and Zehri (2016); Khlif and Samaha (2016) and Wahab et al. (2011). Furthermore, the study tests the interaction between effectiveness of audit committee and external auditor (ACSCORE×AUDFSZ+ACSCORE×AUD FEE+ACSCORE×TENURE).

- **ACSCORE×AUDFSZ**: It is a variable to measure the interaction of the ACSCORE and AUDFSZ and takes the value 1 if a firm-year observation has an external audit function (Big Four auditor) and an effective audit committee, 0 otherwise.
- **ACSCORE×AUDFEE**: It is a variable to measure the interaction of the ACSCORE and AUDFEE and takes the value 1 if a firm-year observation has disclosed an external audit fee and an effective audit committee, 0 otherwise.
- **ACSCORE×TENURE**: It is a variable to measure the interaction of the ACSCORE and TENURE and takes the value 1 if a firm-year observation has an external audit function (tenure of auditor) and an effective audit committee, 0 otherwise.

Finally, the empirical model of the study also includes four control variables. These control variables are; board size (BDS), profitability (ROA), proportion of independent directors (PNED), and leverage (LEV). Prior studies suggested that these company-specific characteristics may affect the level of internal control information disclosure (Alsaeed, 2006; Celik et al., 2006; Aljifri & Hussainey, 2007; Wang et al., 2008; Hassan et al., 2011; Uyar & Kilic, 2012; Orens et al., 2013; Alkhatib, 2014).

- Board size: Research by Chen and Jaggi, (2000) points out that board composition affects the effectiveness of control on top management increasing the quality of mandatory disclosure.
- Profitability: According Agyei-Mensah (2016b p. 85). There is a general belief that a firm's willingness to disclose information is related to its profitability. Companies of strong profitability have more financial resources

to establish and implement internal control system and are more likely to disclose information (Khlif & Samahak, 2016)

Proportion of independent directors (PNED):

- Leverage: Eng and Mark (2003) and Barako et al. (2006) provide evidence that leverage is positively related to the extent of voluntary disclosure. Xiaowen (2013) on the other hand posits that companies with high leverage are not willing to disclose internal control information.
- Independent directors: Gul and Leung (2004) document a negative relationship between board independence and disclosure. Haniffa and Cooke (2005) found that, board independence improves the quality of disclosures.

A linear-multiple regression analysis will be used to test the interaction between disclosure of internal control information (dependent variable) and effectiveness of audit committee and audit quality (independent variables).

To test the construct validity of the scores of the effectiveness of audit committee (ACSCORE), a factor analysis was performed on the items in their respective measure. The aim of the factor analysis is to limit the whole of the criteria selected to characterize various dimensions of the governance variable in a minimum number of factors. That is, the five individual data items of audit committee; audit committee prior experience, its size, the independence, expertise and the frequency of the meetings of the members of audit committee, were factor analyzed to determine if they loaded onto two factors as expected. Results given in Table 1, in the rotated component matrix, confirm a correct loading into two factors.

Table 1. Factor analysis of items in audit committee effectiveness

Rotated Component Matrix		
	Component	
	1	**2**
ACFE	.431	.540
ACSZ	.660	.051
ACIND	-.441	.702
ACPE	.733	.055
ACMT	-.129	-.541

Results

Descriptive Statistics

The descriptive statistics for the variables are presented in Table 2. The dependent variable ICID has a mean of 41 per cent, the minimum is 19 per cent, the maximum being 81 per cent with a standard deviation of 21 per cent. According to the results, internal control information disclosure level is not high among listed companies in Ghana. The findings are consistent with that of, Agyei-Mensah (2016), Cheng and Courtenay (2006), Pateli and Prencipe (2007), Lim *et al.* (2007), Donnelly and Mulcahy (2008), Chen and Jaggi (2000) and Fang *et al.* (2009), but is inconsistent with the findings of Eng and Mak (2000).

Univariate Analysis

To meet the requirements of the regression analysis assumptions, the correlation between the study variables and test for multicollinearity problems were examined. Table 3 presents the correlation results for the study variables. The correlation analysis shows that ICID has a significant relationship with AUDITOR at 0.05 level. TENURE has a significant relationship with AUDITSCORE and AUDITFEE at 0.05 level. BDS also has a significant relationship with AUDITOR at 0.01 level. These results indicate the need to pay attention to possible multi-co linearity problem in the regression analysis.

Table 2. Descriptive statistics

Descriptive Statistics				
	Mean	**Std. Deviation**	**Minimum**	**Maximum**
ICID	0.41	0.21	0.19	0.81
ACSCORE	7.02	7.40	0.00	24.00
AUDITOR	0.73	0.37	0.00	1.00
AUDFEE	0.80	0.30	0.00	1.00
TENURE	4.43	1.07	3.00	6.00
BDS	8.60	2.77	4.00	18.00
LEV	0.88	0.57	0.06	2.77
PROF	6.74	8.41	(8.00)	33.00
PNED	70.43	11.90	50.00	88.89
Valid N (listwise)	210			

Table 3. Spearman's rho correlation coefficient matrix

		Correlations								
		ICID	**ACSCORE**	**AUDITOR**	**AUDFEE**	**TENURE**	**BDS**	**LEV**	**PROF**	**PNED**
ICID	Correlation Coefficient	1.000								
	Sig. (2-tailed)									
ACSCORE	Correlation Coefficient	.013	1.000							
	Sig. (2-tailed)	.853								
AUDITOR	Correlation Coefficient	.205**	.047	1.000						
	Sig. (2-tailed)	.003	.496							
AUDFEE	Correlation Coefficient	-.080	.032	-.029	1.000					
	Sig. (2-tailed)	.247	.643	.681						
TENURE	Correlation Coefficient	.044	.180**	-.022	-.214**	1.000				
	Sig. (2-tailed)	.523	.009	.755	.002					
BDS	Correlation Coefficient	.180**	.165*	.153*	-.029	-.015	1.000			
	Sig. (2-tailed)	.009	.017	.026	.675	.833				
LEV	Correlation Coefficient	.058	.105	.249**	.027	.051	.026	1.000		
	Sig. (2-tailed)	.401	.129	.000	.694	.459	.706			
PROF	Correlation Coefficient	.100	.044	.248**	-.027	.025	-.029	-.481**	1.000	
	Sig. (2-tailed)	.150	.524	.000	.700	.717	.676	.000		
PNED	Correlation Coefficient	-.277**	-.245**	-.044	.075	-.127	-.153*	.200**	-.090	1.000
	Sig. (2-tailed)	.000	.000	.523	.277	.065	.027	.004	.194	
**. Correlation is significant at the 0.01 level (2-tailed).										
*. Correlation is significant at the 0.05 level (2-tailed).										

Multicollinearity and Autocorrelation Tests (Assessment of the Validity of the Model)

A regression analysis (Table 4) was performed on the dependent and independent variables to check on the existence of the multi-co linearity and serial or autocorrelation problems. The tolerance and Variable Inflation Factor (VIF) tests revealed no

Table 4. Interaction between the effectiveness of audit committee and audit quality on disclosure of internal control information

Regression Analysis Results							
Model	Unstandardized Coefficients		Standardized Coefficients	t	Sig.	Collinearity Statistics	
	B	Std. Error	Beta			Tolerance	VIF
(Constant)	.508	.141		3.602	.000		
ACSCORE	.004	.004	.141	.892	.037	.471	1.863
AUDITOR	.071	.052	.127	1.349	.179	.484	1.068
AUDFEE	.027	.038	.049	.719	.473	.929	1.077
TENURE	.003	.014	.016	.227	.821	.861	1.162
ACSCORE×AUDFSZ	.003	.005	.088	.526	.060	.511	1.616
ACSCORE×AUDFEE	.031	.039	.056	.795	.427	.847	1.181
ACSCORE×TENURE	.033	.032	.070	1.008	.003	.880	1.136
BDS	.011	.005	.151	2.205	.029	.914	1.094
LEV	.040	.028	.109	1.439	.152	.746	1.341
PROF	.003	.002	.137	1.935	.054	.847	1.181
PNED	-.006	.001	-.319	-4.525	.000	.859	1.164
R2 = 0.555; Adj. R2 = 0.509; F=3.314 (p=0.000), Durbin Watson =1.497; N=210							

harmful correlation. According to (Pallant, 2013; Field, 2009), if the largest VIF is greater than 10, there is cause for concern. However, the maximum VIF value in Table 5 is 1.863 and Durbin Watson value of 1.497. In addition, the tolerance is greater than 0.20 for the variables (the smallest tolerance is 0.471). Therefore, this study is not subject to high collinearity problems. Overall, there are no linearity, multicollinearity, and autocorrelation problems.

Main Findings

The table indicates R^2 of 0.555, and Adj. R^2 of 0. 509 (F=0.775, p = 0.000), which shows that a good percentage (50.9%) of the variation in ICID can be explained by variations in the whole set of independent variables.

There is a positive relationship between ICID and AUDSCORE (β=0.141) and significant at the 5% level (p= 0.037). Thus, H1 is supported, hence accepted. The results indicate that firms with independent audit committee, with financial expertise, prior experience and meeting frequently are likely to disclose more internal control information. This finding is consistent with Zhang *et al.* (2007) who provide empirical evidence that the audit committee and the external auditor play an important role in reducing internal control weaknesses.

There is a positive relationship between ICID and ACS x AUDFSZ (β=0.088) and significant at the 5% level (p= 0.060). Thus, H1 is supported, hence accepted. This result indicate that, firms with an effective audit committee and a Big Four auditor, are likely to disclose internal control information. The results also indicate complementary effect between the score of audit effectiveness and audit firm size in the disclosure of internal control information. This finding is consistent with Khlif and Samaha, (2016) who found that in Egypt the association between audit committee activity and internal control quality is more pronounced when an organisation is audited by a Big 4 audit firm.

There is a positive relationship between ICID and ACSORE x AUDFEE (β =0.056) but insignificant at the 5% level (p=0.427). Thus, H2 is not supported, hence rejected. This result indicate that, firms with an effective audit committee and disclose audit fee, are not likely to disclose internal control information.

There is a positive relationship between ICID and ACSORE x TENURE (β =0.068) and significant at the 1% level (p=0.003). Thus, H3 is supported hence accepted. This results indicate that, firms with an effective audit committee and long auditor tenure, are likely to disclose internal control information.

With regards to the control variables the findings are as follows:

There is a positive relationship between ICID and BDS (β=0.141) and significant at the 1% level (p=0.029). This result indicate that, board size influence disclosure of internal control information.

There is a positive relationship between ICID and LEV (β=0.109) but insignificant at the 1% level (p=0.152). This result indicate that, leverage does not influence disclosure of internal control information. This is consistent with Xiaowen (2013) who posits that companies with high leverage are not willing to disclose internal control information.

There is a negative relationship between ICID and PROF (β =0.137) and significant at the 1% level (p=0.054). This result indicate that, the higher a firm's profitability the lower the amount of internal control information disclosed. This finding is inconsistent with Xiaowen, (2013 p. 631), who posits that, "when a company reaches a certain level of profitability, the governance structure will be relatively complete and internal control will be correspondingly sound, so it will actively disclose internal control information".

There is a negative relationship between ICID and PNED (β =0.255) and significant at the 1% level (p=0.000). This result indicate that, firms with a higher proportion of non-executive (independent) directors are not likely to disclose internal control information.

CONCLUSION

This paper examined the linkages between audit committees' effectiveness, audit quality and internal control information disclosure. Empirical evidence on the effect of audit committee effectiveness and audit quality on internal control information disclosure is scanty. Using a 210 firm-year sample of firms listed on the Ghana Stock Exchange for the period, 2013-2017, the paper tried to fill the research gap. The dependent variable ICID has a mean of 41 per cent, the minimum is 19 per cent, the maximum being 81 per cent with a standard deviation of 21 per cent. The low level (41%) of internal control information disclosure makes it very difficult for the firms' stakeholders to determine future performance of the company. After controlling for board size, proportion of independent directors and leverage, the results from univariate and multivariate analyses indicated that effective audit committee and audit firm size play complimentary and substitution roles in ensuring internal control information disclosure. Board size and proportion of independent directors were also found to influence the disclosure of quality voluntary information.

This study makes several important contributions. The analysis fills a gap in the extant literature where very little research has examined the relationship between effective audit committee and audit quality on internal control information disclosure. The findings are consistent with agency theory, suggesting that effective audit committee and audit quality tend to support the disclosure of internal control information.

The results also have implication for managers and policy makers. With regard to managers, findings from the study emphasize audit committee that have finance and accounting expertise which meets regularly, cooperating with auditors from the Big Four auditing firms can help increase the disclosure of internal control information. With respect to policy makers, the results highlight that effective audit committee and audit quality help promote the disclosure of internal control information. Hence, they should encourage corporate boards to insist on audit committees having people with finance and accounting qualification and meeting regularly with their external auditor to ensure disclosure of voluntary information.

Despite the contributions and the implications of the findings, there are some limitations to this study. Whilst the independent and control variables included in the regression model are all validated by prior research, there may exist other factors influencing internal control information disclosure that were not addressed by this study. Further researchers may consider other corporate governance variables such as; audit committee gender, audit committee chair financial expertise and ownership concentration, etc., in order to provide an in-depth explanation to determine the relationship between audit committee effectiveness and audit quality on disclosure of internal control information.

Furthermore, the same methodology can be used by other researchers using data from other emerging markets where there is lack of evidence, to measure the effect of audit committee effectiveness and audit quality on disclosure of internal control information.

REFERENCES

Abbott, L. J., Park, Y., & Parker, S. (2000). The effects of audit committee activity and independence on corporate fraud. *Managerial Finance*, *26*(11), 55–67. doi:10.1108/03074350010766990

Abbott, L. J., Parker, S., & Peters, G. F. (2003). Audit committee characteristics and restatements: A study of the efficacy of certain Blue Ribbon Committee recommendations. *Auditing*, *23*(1), 69–87. doi:10.2308/aud.2004.23.1.69

Abbott, L. J., Parker, S., & Peters, G. F. (2004). Audit committee characteristics and restatements. *Auditing*, *23*(1), 69–87. doi:10.2308/aud.2004.23.1.69

Agyei-Mensah, B. K. (2016a). Accountability and internal control in religious organisations: A study of Methodist church Ghana, *African Journal of Accounting. Auditing and Finance*, *5*(2), 95–112.

Agyei-Mensah, B. K., (2016b). Internal control information disclosure and corporate governance: evidence from an emerging market. *Corporate Governance: The International Journal of Business in Society, 16*(1), 79-95.

Aljifri, K., & Hussainey, K. (2007). The determinants of forward-looking information in annual reports of UAE companies. *Managerial Auditing Journal*, *22*(9), 881–894. doi:10.1108/02686900710829390

Alkhatib, K. (2014). The determinants of forward-looking information disclosure. *Procedia: Social and Behavioral Sciences*, *109*, 858–864. doi:10.1016/j.sbspro.2013.12.554

Alsaeed, K. (2006). The Association Between Firm-specific Characteristics and Disclosure. *Managerial Auditing Journal*, *21*(5), 476–496. doi:10.1108/02686900610667256

Alzoubi, E. S. S., & Selamat, M. H. (2012). The effectiveness of corporate governance mechanisms on constraining earnings management: Literature review and proposed framework. *International Journal of Global Business*, *5*(1), 17–35.

Ashbaugh-Skaife, H., Collins, D., & Kinney, W. Jr. (2007). The discovery and reporting of internal control deficiencies prior to SOX-mandated audits. *Journal of Accounting and Economics, Vol.*, *44*(1-2), 166–192. doi:10.1016/j.jacceco.2006.10.001

Barako, D. G., Hancock, P., & Izan, H. Y. (2006). Factors influencing voluntary corporate disclosure by Kenyan companies. *Corporate Governance*, *14*(2), 107–125. doi:10.1111/j.1467-8683.2006.00491.x

Bedard, J. C., Chtourou, S. M., & Courteau, L. (2004). The effect of audit committee expertise, independence, and activity on aggressive earnings management. *Auditing*, *23*(2), 13–35. doi:10.2308/aud.2004.23.2.13

Bepari, M. K., & Mollik, A. T. (2015). Effect of audit quality and accounting and finance backgrounds of audit committee members on firms' compliance with IFRS for goodwill impairment testing. *Journal of Applied Accounting Research*, *16*(Issue: 2), 196–220. doi:10.1108/JAAR-05-2013-0038

Bushee, B., & Noe, C. (2003). Corporate Disclosure Practices, Institutional Investors, and Stock return Volatility. *Journal of Accounting Research*, *38*(Suppl.), 171–202. doi:10.2307/2672914

Carcello, J. V., Hollingsworth, C. W., Klein, A., & Neal, T. L. (2006). *Audit committee financial expertise, competing corporate governance mechanisms, and earnings management*. Available at: https://ssrn.com/abstract_887512

Carcello, J. V., Vanstraelen, A., & Willenborg, M. (2009). Rules rather than discretion in audit standards: Going-concern opinions in Belgium. *The Accounting Review*, *84*(5), 1395–1428. doi:10.2308/accr.2009.84.5.1395

Celik, O., & Ecer, A., & Karabacak. (2006). Disclosure of forward-looking information: Evidence from listed companies on Istanbul stock exchange. *Investment Management and Financial Innovations*, *3*(2), 197–216.

Chen, C. J. P., & Jaggi, B. (2000). Association between independent non-executive directors, family control and financial disclosures in Hong Kong. *Journal of Accounting and Public Policy*, *19*(, 4-5), 285–310. doi:10.1016/S0278-4254(00)00015-6

Coffee, J. C. (2005). A theory of corporate scandals: Why the USA and Europe differ. *Oxford Review of Economic Policy*, *21*(2), 198–211. doi:10.1093/oxrep/gri012

Cohen, J., Krishnamoorthy, G., & Wright, A. (2004). The corporate governance mosaic and financial reporting quality. *Journal of Accounting Literature*, *23*, 87–152.

Cornett, M. M., McNutt, J. J., & Tehranian, H. (2009). Corporate governance and earnings management at large US bank holding companies. *Journal of Corporate Finance*, *15*(4), 412–430. doi:10.1016/j.jcorpfin.2009.04.003

COSO. (1992). *Internal Control Integrated Framework*. Retrieved June 25 2015, from http://www.coso.org/publications/executive_summary_integrated_framework.htm

Costello, A., & Wittenberg-Moerman, R. (2011). The impact of financial reporting quality on debt contracting: Evidence from internal control weakness reports. *Journal of Accounting Research*, *49*(1), 97–136. doi:10.1111/j.1475-679X.2010.00388.x

Deumes, R. (2004). *Voluntary reporting on internal control by listed Dutch companies*. Working paper, Maastricht University, Maastricht, Faculty of economics and business administration.

Deumes, R., & Knechel, W. R. (2008). Economic incentives for voluntary reporting on internal risk management and control systems. *Auditing*, *27*(1), 35–66. doi:10.2308/aud.2008.27.1.35

Donnelly, R., & Mulcahy, M. (2008). Board structure, ownership and voluntary disclosure in Ireland. *Corporate Governance*, *16*(5), 416–429. doi:10.1111/j.1467-8683.2008.00692.x

Doyle, J., Ge, W., & McVay, S. (2007). Determinants of weaknesses in internal control over financial reporting. *Journal of Accounting and Economics*, *44*(1/2), 193–223. doi:10.1016/j.jacceco.2006.10.003

Eng, L., & Mak, Y. (2003). Corporate governance and voluntary disclosure. *Journal of Accounting and Public Policy*, *22*(4), 325–345. doi:10.1016/S0278-4254(03)00037-1

Fama, E., & Jensen, M. (1983). Separation of Ownership and Control. *The of Law and Economics*, *26*(2), 36–67.

Fan, J. P. H., & Wong, T. J. (2005). Do external auditors perform a corporate governance role in emerging markets? Evidence from East Asia. *Journal of Accounting Research*, *43*(1), 35–72. doi:10.1111/j.1475-679x.2004.00162.x

Fang, H., Sun, H., & Jin, Y. (2009). Corporate characteristics, external audit, and voluntary disclosure of internal control information: An empirical study based on annual reports of listed companies of Shanghai stock exchanges from 2003 to 2005. *Accountability in Research, 10*(1), 44–95.

Field, A. (2009). *Discovering Statistics Using SPSS for Windows* (3rd ed.). London: Sage Publications.

Graham, J. H., Harveya, C. R., & Rajgopal, S. (2005). The economic implications of corporate financial reporting. *Journal of Accounting and Economics, 40*(1-3), 3–73. doi:10.1016/j.jacceco.2005.01.002

Grougiou, V., Leventis, S., Dedoulis, E., & Owusu-Ansah, S. (2014). Corporate Social Responsibility and Earnings Management in U.S. Banks. *Accounting Forum, 38*(3), 155–169. doi:10.1016/j.accfor.2014.05.003

Gul, F. A., & Leung, S. (2004). Board leadership, outside directors' expertise and voluntary corporate disclosures. *Journal of Accounting and Public Policy, 23*(5), 351–379. doi:10.1016/j.jaccpubpol.2004.07.001

Haniffa, R. M., & Cooke, T. E. (2005). The impact of culture and governance on corporate social reporting. *Journal of Accounting and Public Policy, 24*(5), 391–430. doi:10.1016/j.jaccpubpol.2005.06.001

Hermanson, H. M. (2000). An analysis of the demand for reporting on internal control. *Accounting Horizons, 14*(3), 325–341. doi:10.2308/acch.2000.14.3.325

Ho, S. M. S., & Wong, K. R. (2001). A Study of the Relationship Between Corporate Governance Structures and the Extent of voluntary Disclosure. *Journal of International Accounting, Auditing & Taxation, Vol., 10*(2), 139–156. doi:10.1016/S1061-9518(01)00041-6

Hunziker, S. (2013). Efficiency of internal control: Evidence from Swiss non-financial companies. *The Journal of Management and Governance*, 401–433.

Johl, S. K., Johl, S. K., Subramaniam, N., & Cooper, B. (2013). Internal audit function, board quality and financial reporting quality: Evidence from Malaysia. *Managerial Auditing Journal, 28*(9), 780–814. doi:10.1108/MAJ-06-2013-0886

Khlif, H., & Samaha, K. (2016). Audit committee activity and internal control quality in Egypt: Does external auditor's size matter? *Managerial Auditing Journal, 31*(3), 269–289. doi:10.1108/MAJ-08-2014-1084

Knechel, W. R., Krishnan, G. V., Pevzner, M. B., Stefchik, L., & Velury, U. (2013). Audit quality: Insights from the academic literature. *Auditing*, *32*(1), 385–421. doi:10.2308/ajpt-50350

Krishnan, J. (2005). Audit Committee Financial Expertise and Internal Control: An Empirical Analysis. *The Accounting Review*, *80*(2), 649–675. doi:10.2308/accr.2005.80.2.649

Lary, A. M., & Taylor, D. W. (2012). Governance characteristics and role effectiveness of audit committees. *Managerial Auditing Journal*, *27*(4), 336–354. doi:10.1108/02686901211217969

Lim, S., Matolcsy, Z., & Chow, D. (2007). The association between board composition and different types of voluntary disclosure. *European Accounting Review*, *16*(3), 555–583. doi:10.1080/09638180701507155

Lin, J. W., Li, J. F., & Yang, J. S. (2006). The effect of audit committee performance on earning quality. *Managerial Auditing Journal*, *21*(9), 921–933. doi:10.1108/02686900610705019

Mitchell, V. Z., Singh, H., & Singh, I. (2008). Association between independent audit committee members' human-resource features and underpricing. The case of Singapore IPOs from 1997-2006. *Journal of Human Resource Costing & Accounting*, *12*(3), 179–212. doi:10.1108/14013380810919840

Norwani, N., Mohamad, Z. Z., & Chek, I. A. (2011). Corporate governance failure and its impact on financial reporting within selected companies. *International Journal of Business and Social Science, 2*, 205 – 213.

Pallant, Y. (2011). *SPSS Survival Manual: A Step by Step Guide to Data Analysis using SPSS for Windows* (3rd ed.). McGraw Hill Open University Press.

Patteli, L., & Prencipe, A. (2007). The Relationship Between Voluntary Disclosure and Independent Directors in the Presence of a Dominant Shareholder. *European Accounting Review*, *16*(1), 5–33. doi:10.1080/09638180701265820

Razman, S. R., & Iskandar, M. (2004). The effectiveness of audit committee in monitoring the quality of corporate reporting. In *Corporate Governance: An International Perspective* (pp. 154–175). Kuala Lumpur: Malaysian Institute of Corporate Governance.

Shah, A. S. Z., & Butt, S. A. (2009). The impact of corporate governance on the cost of equity: Empirical evidence from Pakistani listed companies. *The Lahore Journal of Economics*, *14*(1), 139–171. doi:10.35536/lje.2009.v14.i1.a6

Sun, F., Wei, X., & Xu, Y. (2012). Audit committee characteristics and loss reserve error. *Managerial Auditing Journal*, *27*(4), 355–377. doi:10.1108/02686901211217978

Verschoor, C. C. (2002). Reflections on the audit committee's role. *Internal Auditor*, *59*(April), 26–35.

Wahab, E. A., Mat Zain, M., & James, K. (2011). Political connections, corporate governance and audit fees in Malaysia. *Managerial Auditing Journal*, *26*(5), 393–418. doi:10.1108/02686901111129562

Wang, K., Sewon, O., & Claiborne, M. C. (2008). Determinants and consequences of voluntary disclosure in an emerging market: Evidence from China. *Journal of International Accounting, Auditing & Taxation*, *17*(1), 14–30. doi:10.1016/j.intaccaudtax.2008.01.001

Xiaowen, S. (2013). Corporate characteristics and internal control information disclosure – evidence from annual reports in 2009 of listed companies in Shenzhen stock exchange. *Physics Procedia*, *25*(1), 630–635.

Xie, B., Davidson, W. III, & DaDalt, P. (2003). Earnings management and corporate governance: The role of the board and the audit committee. *Journal of Corporate Finance*, *9*(3), 295–316. doi:10.1016/S0929-1199(02)00006-8

Zhang, Y., Zhou, J., & Zhou, N. (2007). Audit Committee Quality, Auditor Independence, and Internal Control Weaknesses. *Journal of Accounting and Public Policy*, *26*(3), 300–327. doi:10.1016/j.jaccpubpol.2007.03.001

APPENDIX

Table 5. Internal control evaluation sheet

Item	Content	Scores
Internal Environment	Corporate governance structure, human resources policies, corporate culture	Disclosing =1, Otherwise =0
Risk Evaluation	Identification of internal and external risk, risk analysis, risk responses	Disclosing =1, Otherwise =0
Control Activities	Internal control activities based on risk evaluation	Disclosing =1, Otherwise =0
Information and Communication	The establishment of information and communication system	Disclosing =1, Otherwise =0
Internal Supervision	Internal supervision from internal audit department	Disclosing =1, Otherwise =0
Internal control defects	The defects or abnormal items in internal control and the improvement methods	Disclosing =1, Otherwise =0
Internal assessment	Assessment from board of directors	Disclosing =1, Otherwise =0
External assessment	External auditor's assessment	Disclosing =1, Otherwise =0

Adapted from: Jainfei Leng and Yiran Ding (2011)

Chapter 2
Audit Committee Characteristics and Earnings Quality:
Evidence From Bahrain Bourse

Fatima Albedal
Ahlia University, Bahrain

Allam Mohammed Hamdan
Ahlia University, Bahrain

Qasim Zureigat
Sulaiman AlRajhi Colleges, Saudi Arabia

ABSTRACT

This chapter investigates the relationship between the audit committee and earnings quality of listed companies in Bahrain Bourse and to examine whether those companies comply with the obligatory code of corporate governance. The sample of this study includes 40 companies listed in Bahrain Bourse for the period 2013-2017. The model of the study tested the relationship between the independent variables of audit committee characteristics and the dependent variable of earnings quality using pooled data regression. The findings of the study showed that the Bahraini listed companies comply and follow the code of corporate governance and some audit committee characteristics have an impact on earnings quality.

DOI: 10.4018/978-1-5225-9607-3.ch002

INTRODUCTION

The advent of corporate governance has dramatically created some significant changes in business environments in general, and in the accounting and auditing works in specific. The organization for economic cooperation and development (OECD, 2015) stated, "Good corporate governance is not an end in itself. It is a means to create market confidence and business integrity, which in turn is essential for companies that need access to equity capital for long-term investment. Access to equity capital is particularly important for future oriented growth companies and to balance any increase in leveraging".

In the Middle East countries, the rules and regulation of corporate governance got consideration for two decades. The organization for economic cooperation and development (OECD) gave a great deal of attention to the Middle East and North Africa (MENA) countries through the initiatives which basically aims to adopt the procedures and implication of corporate governance in order to enhance the investment environment and policies (Miteva, 2005).

In the last few years the way people look at the function of audit committees as a mechanism of corporate governance has increased significantly; the audit committee's main goal is to increase the interrogative of the board of management and to increase the role of audit and its neutrality and independence (Hamdan et al, 2013). The organizational interest in the role of audit committee increased during the last years in preparing financial statements and reports (Martnez & Fuentes, 2007). Moreover, Martnez and Fuentes (2007) stated that the audit committee plays an important role in reducing and limiting the differences raised between external auditors and managers in addition to monitor financial statements; however, the chance of receiving a qualified opinion as a result of non- complying with the accounting standards and accounting errors is reduced.

As for Bahrain case, all listed companies in Bahrain Bourse (BHB) were operating in accordance to "Company Law". In late 2013, Ministry of Industry and Commerce (MOIC) with the collaboration of Central Bank of Bahrain (CBB) have launched the National Steering Committee in order to move Bahrain forward in reaching its objectives. This committee represents stakeholders and it is consisting of government agencies, academics, the banking and accounting sectors, business associations, and other members of the business community. Later on, the National Steering Committee has worked to issue corporate governance as a guide to be used by the listed companies enrolled in Bahrain Bourse (BHB) in order to defend the interest of the stockholders and to enhance the wheel of economic development in addition to help companies from private and public sector to implement the national practices in a better and enhanced way. The Code of Corporate Governance was published on January 2011, which means that all the companies enrolled in (BHB) were obliged to fully comply with this code by the end of 2011 CCG (2015).

Principle (3) of code of corporate governance issued in order to manage the work of audit committees in listed companies in Bahrain Bourse. This study examined the rules and regulation related to audit committee to ensure the implementation by Bahraini companies. Afterwards, the study investigated the role of the committee in improving and enhancing earnings quality CCG (2015). As for Bahrain, much rules and legislations supporting the advent of corporate governance were issued in order to manage the work of audit committee of listed companies in Bahrain Bourse (BHB) in order to protect the right and interest of the stockholders in addition to different parties in the company to ensure the financial and organizational transparency. The establishment of audit committee became mandatory in 2011 for listed companies enrolled in Bahrain Bourse (BHB). Moreover, Principle No. (3) from the Bahrain code of corporate governance stated that the company's Board should establish an audit committee, which comprises of at least three members of whom the majority should be independent involving the Chairman. Additionally, this committee should meet at least four times a year. The effectiveness of the audit committee based on three main characteristics (Audit committee size, audit committee independence and the number of audit committee meetings) Accordingly, the committee should be able to review the company's accounting and financial practices, assess the reliability of the company's financial and internal controls and financial statements, As well as reviewing if whether the company's comply the legal requirements. The committee recommends the appointment, compensation and oversees a company's outside auditor. Furthermore, the majority of the audit committee should hold financial qualifications and have a background in finance, accounting and related fields. CCG (2015). The area of the study is still unexplored in the Bahraini market, which adopted and implemented the code of corporate governance less than Five years ago. Therefore, the study shaded the light on the audit committee characteristics and legislations in addition to examine the extent of their application by listed companies in Bahrain bourse and then investigate the role of audit committee characteristics and its impact on earnings quality of listed companies in Bahrain bourse (BHB).

LITERATURE REVIEW

In 1991, some important recommendations were issued by the Blue-Ribbon Committee, which indicates the significance of audit committee and its characteristics such as, size, independence of the committee members and their financial proficiency and number of audit committee meetings BRC, (1999). Therefore, many previous literatures investigate the influence of audit committee characteristics in relation to earnings quality.

- **Independence**: The independence of audit committee members could be considered as the most important characteristic as it has a great impact on the efficiency of preparing and overseeing the financial statements (Baxter & Cotter, 2009). The independence of audit committee members considers a mean to control the process of financial reporting. Therefore, this characteristic can be used as an indicator to measure the earnings quality in previous relevant studies (Baxter & Cotter, 2009). While, the study conducted by Nimer, et al. (2012) revealed that the findings of multiple regressions showed that there is no association between the factors of efficiency audit committee and the policies of dividend payout in listed companies in Amman Stock Exchange.
- **Expertise**: The financial experience and knowledge could lead to improve the effectiveness of audit committee members. For an effective operation the financial expertise of the audit committee members considers the most important characteristic Baxter and Cotter (2009). According to Lisic, et al. (2011), the findings showed a negative relationship between the financial experience of audit committee members and occurrence of restatements controlled by CEO powerful. When the CEO power is low the financial experience of audit committee inversely related to the occurrence of restatements. Moreover, they propose that having a financial expertise does not necessarily mean that having an effective monitoring. Rather, an effective monitoring depends on the top management power (Baxter & Cotter, 2009).
- **Activity and Size**: The size of the audit committee and its activity has been recommended in order to increase and improve the quality of the earnings (Baxter and Cotter, 2009). Accordingly, the size of audit committee positively relates to earnings quality. The large size of the audit committee is more efficient and effective as it can add members with financial experience and knowledge whom perform controlling and monitoring functions of financial statements and reporting practices (Baxter & Cotter, 2009). According to the study conducted by Baxter and Cotter (2009) in Australian companies

in relation to the impact of formation audit committee and its characteristics in enhancing earnings quality before the mandatory requirement to form an audit committee in 2003. The findings of this study indicated that founding an audit committee led to moderate the practice of earnings management, however, this doesn't reduce the accrual error. Additionally, the study results showed that there is a significant relationship between audit committee' financial experience and the improvement of earnings quality. On the other hand, the other characteristics of the audit committee have no impact on improving the earnings quality.

The Regulations of Bahraini Listed Companies Audit Committees

Bahrain tried to adopt rules and regulation in order to support the advent of corporate governance, one of which is the essence of code if corporate governance in late 2013, this code obliges all listed companies in Bahrain Bourse (BHB) to launch an audit committee which composed of at least three members Who are non-executives and if the board chooses to appoint non-board members (experts) in the committee. These members should be independent, as it has been stated in Appendix (A) to the Code. Moreover, they should have no conflict of interest with any roles and tasks for the company. Additionally, Audi committee members should have recent financial information and relevant background in accounting and financial experience, which mainly includes; ability to read the company's financial statements and evaluating the complexity in those statements in addition to understand the international accounting practices and principles. The meeting schedule of the audit committee shall be associated with the company board and shall meet at minimum four times per year. CCG (2015). The code also explained the rules of forming the audit committee, and how it is responsible for the activities of the internal audit department and has responsibility for the appointment of company's auditors and agreeing their remuneration, oversees a company's audit process and internal accounting controls and ensure auditors observe independence requirements in the preparation of annual reports by Saleh and Millan (2002). The audit committee should accomplish different roles and tasks; one of these major tasks is reviewing the company financial statements, internal controls, financial practices and comply with legal and international requirements in addition to discuss the results of the external audit and any difficulties the auditors faced such as; difficulties in access to information or any disagreements with management of the company. Hence, the committee should adopt a charter, which basically describes the purposes, tasks and responsibilities of the committee. Moreover, the committee should, additionally, the committee shall make recommendations related to internal auditors such as; selection, determining appointments and termination when needed and appropriate, furthermore, it monitors and supervises if the companies comply with the rules and regulations or not. CCG (2015)

Earnings Quality

In the last decade, many international companies started to announce temporary earnings as a part in their quarterly financial reports, therefore, various definition raised regarding the increased investors' concerns, thus, investors became more aware about the net earnings of the companies. According to the study conducted by Qaraqish (2009) and Ohlson and Feltham (1995) the earnings quality defined as the ability of the investors to use recent data in order to predict abnormal earnings of the companies. The term earnings quality refers as the ability to draw a real and clear picture about the Company in addition to survive in the future Qaraqish (2009). Bagava, (2006) mentioned that the earnings quality use as an indicator for decision making as it is an important factor in the financial statements. According to (Schipper & Vincent, 2003), lower earnings quality of companies can lead to inappropriate management fortune. With the companies' earnings, quality can be used as an indicator to measure the dividends. Furthermore, the study conducted by Farinha (2007) showed that there is relationship between earnings quality and dividends: when the earnings quality is high that lead to increase the possibility of the company dividends, which ultimately increase the amount of the dividends. There are different studies regarding earnings quality. In order to measure earnings quality of the companies the continuity of quality used as a standard, which explain the relationship between the present and future earnings of the companies. Using different methods to measure the earnings quality might lead to different results and evaluations, where in the same company the earnings quality might be high or low depending on the method used to measure the earnings quality Abdelghany (2005). Givoly et al. (2013) examined earnings management practices by comparing public companies with the private ones, the results of this study showed that the public companies maintain high quality of the financial reports more than private ones by having less accruals, which indicates that the earnings quality of these companies is high compared to private companies, due to the desires of the public companies' directors to avoid and reduce the likelihood of litigation risk and agency costs. Regarding the study conducted by Teitel and Machuga (2013) the results showed that the corporate governance rules and regulations lead to the improvement of earnings quality. Additionally, the high-quality internal control can lead to improve earnings quality Altamuro and Beatty (2006). Furthermore, the results of the study conducted by Teitel and Machuga (2013) indicated that if the corporate governance rules and practices implemented by highly professional offices that could improve the earnings quality. Other study conducted by Hamdan and Abu Ijeila (2013) the relationship between audit quality and its role in improving earnings quality showed that the earnings management practices were not eliminated in Jordanian industrial companies although the auditing quality was performed and monitored by audit offices in Jordan. But these results differ from to the study conducted by Teitel and Balsam et al. (2003) which, found that the firms which hired and used professional specialized auditors in refer to discretionary accruals and management practices have a higher level of earning quality in comparison to the companies which used less professional specialized auditors.

RESEARCH METHODOLOGY

Study Sample

The sample of this study included all listed companies in Bahrain Bourse (BHB) which are (47) companies from different sectors which met the conditions of having all the data available and have never been suspended or merged with another company during the period of the study. There are several companies which met the conditions from 2013 -2017. The sample selection procedures are summarizing in Table 1.

Table 1. Sample selection

Sector	Listed Companies	Excluded Companies	Study Sample
Commercial Banks	7	0	7
Investment	12	3	9
Services	10	1	9
Insurance	5	0	5
Hotels and Tourism	5	0	5
Preferred Shares	1	1	0
Closed Companies	2	1	1
Non-Bahraini Co.	2	1	1
Industrial	3	0	3
Total	**47**	**7**	**40**

Measuring Variables

Audit Committee Characteristics

The characteristics of the audit committees have been studied and used in this study were based on many previous studies. Table 2 summarize the measuring of independent variables.

Measuring Earnings Quality

This study adopted one of the most common Model for measuring earnings quality for listed companies in Bahrain Bourse (BHB) which is the DeAngelo (1981) model to confirm the results of the study. The model of accrual accounting techniques is used as a proxy to measure the earnings quality, as earnings managements and earnings quality is a two-sided coin, this model consists of comparing the components of earnings in one year to the accruals of the previous year as an estimation of normal accruals and this model is presented below:

$AC_t = NPAT_t - CFO_t$

Where:

AC= the accruals component of earnings in year t;

Table 2. Measuring of audit committee characteristics

Independent Variable	Label	Measurement
Audit Committee Size	AC Size	This variable was measured through members of audit committee elected by the board of directors Hamdan & Mushtaha (2011).
Audit Committee Independence	AC Indp	With reference to the code of corporate governance of Bahrain, researcher found that Bahrain Bourse (BHB) requires that the majority of the audit committee should be independent including the chairman under appendix A in code of corporate governance. Therefore, the study adopt this quality to determine the independence of the audit committee. This committee that totality comprises independent members is given (1), but if not all the members were independent, it is given (0) Hamdan & Mushtaha (2011).
Number of Audit Committee Meetings	AC activity	According to the code of corporate governance of companies listed in (BHB), the audit committee must meet on a regular basis. These meetings should not be less than four meetings per year. Thus, this variable was measured through the number of annual meetings, holds by the committee Hamdan & Mushtaha (2011).

NPAT=net operating profit after interest and tax in year t;
CFO= cash flow from operating activities in year t.

And this model is calculated as the difference between the change in net operating profit after interest and tax and the change in cash flow from operating activities from year t-1 (the previous year) to year t (the current year); this is shown in the following model:

Δ Act= Ac t – Ac t-1

Measuring Control Variables

- **Big Four**: In order to achieve the goal of this study, the researcher determined the big four firms in Bahrain and accordingly assigned (1) to refer to the companies whose financial reports are audited by the large firms, and the value (0) to refer to the companies whose financial statements are audited by small firms.
- **Company Age**: The age of the companies listed in Bahrain bourse is considered one of the control variables the researcher used in this study, hence; this variable was measured by the operating years in the market for the company
- **Company Size**: This control variable of the company size was taken to examine the difference between the small and large companies with regard to earnings quality. The total assets were used as a measure to this variable.
- **Degree of Financial Leverage**: The percentage of financial leverage is used to evaluate the efficiency of financial policies adopted by the management of the listed companies in Bahrain bourse. This variable is considered one of the significant indicators that clarify and show how suitable and accurate the published financial reports of joint-stock companies are Matar (2006). As for the purpose of this Study, the overall ratio of percentage of debts to assets is used as an indication of financial leverage in the sample for this study.

The Study Model

The dependent variable (earnings quality) was measured by using DeAngelo (1981) model and expressed in the following Linear Regression Model by the continuous variable ($EQRCV_{i,t}$) as follows:

EQRCVi,t = β0 + β1 ACSizei,t + β2 ACIndepi,t + β3 ACActivityi,t

+β4Big4i,t +β5Sizei,t +β6FinLavi,t+β6Agei,t+εi,t

Where: $EQRCV_{i,t}$: is a continuous variable: dependent variable: earnings quality measured through (DeAngelo., 2005) model for the company (i) in the year (t). $ACSize_{i,t}$: is number of audit committee members for the company (i) in the year (t). $ACIndep_{i,t}$: is dummy variable, audit committee independence for the company (i) in the year (t). $ACActivity_{i,t}$: is number of audit committee meetings for the company (i) in the year (t). $Big4_{i,t}$: is control variable, dummy variable, size of the audit firm with the value of 1 if audited by Big four firms and 0 otherwise for the company (i) in the year (t). $Size_{i,t}$: is control variable, the company size measured by natural log of total assets for the company (i) in the year (t). $Age_{,t}$: is control variable, the company size measured by operating years in the market for the company (i) in the year (t). $FinLav_{i,t}$: control variable, financial leverage ratio, total debts/total assets of the company (i) in the year (t). $\varepsilon_{i,t}$: random error.

RESULTS AND DISCUSSION OF FINDINGS

Descriptive Statistics of Continuous Variables

Audit Committee Size

From Table 3 the study showed that the minimum size of the audit committee in Bahraini listed companies is one member, while the maximum committee members were eight in the same year. These results indicate that the size of the audit committee should not be big, because that might affect the performance of the committee and their duties (Martinez & Fuentes, 2007). As a result, the listed companies in Bahrain Bourse committed to decrease the number of audit committee members in order to comply with the code of corporate governance.

The Number of Audit Committee Annual Meetings

As stated in the code of corporate governance that the average of audit committee meetings is four times per year. The results of the study showed that the maximum number of meetings was ten times in the year 2017 and the minimum number of meetings was one in the same year. These findings indicate that the listed companies in Bahrain bourse comply with the rules and regulations of the code of corporate governance.

Company Age

The company age was one of the control variables used in the study, the findings of the study showed that the mean increased from the year 2013 to the year 2017. The maximum company age was 67 years in telecommunication sector, while the minimum was 11 years in the banking sector.

Company Size

The company size is one of the control variables used in the study, and as shown in Table 3 that the mean of the company size, which is measured by the total assets for the listed companies in Bahrain Bourse (BHB) is fluctuated from one year to another. The maximum total assets were BD 21,777,018 in Hotels & Tourism sector in the year 2012, while the minimum was BD 4797 in the same sector in 2011.

Financial Leverage

Another control variable is the financial leverage of the listed companies in Bahrain Bourse (BHB). The study showed that the maximum rate of financial leverage was analyzed to be 94%. The results also showed that there is a high variance between minimum and maximum rate of financial leverage. The standard deviation of the financial leverage of listed companies in Bahrain bourse is 30.760 in the year 2013 and decreased to be 29.252 in the year 2017. The mean of the study sample was found to be 42.694% in the year 2013.

Total Accruals

The study found that maximum total accruals was BD 11,165,000 in the year 2017 which, found in banking sector which indicated low earnings quality, while the minimum were BD 362.7973 in the year 2013 as it indicated high quality of earnings.

Descriptive Statistics of Dichotomous Variables

See Table 4.

Independence of Audit Committee Members

Table 3 showed that 32 listed companies out of 40 had 80% of their audit committee members whom are independent in the first year of the study, while 8 listed companies had 20% in the first year of the study. On the second year the independence of the

Table 3. Descriptive statistics for 40 Bahraini listed companies during 2013-2017

Panel A: Continuous Variables					
Variable	**Year**	**Minimum**	**Maximum**	**Mean**	**SD**
AC size	2013	2	6	3.450	0.783
	2011	2	6	3.620	0.952
	2012	2	7	3.580	0.903
	2013	2	5	3.580	0.712
	2017	1	8	3.940	1.413
Ac activity	2013	2	8	4.130	0.853
	2011	2	7	4.100	0.841
	2012	3	6	4.150	0.622
	2013	2	7	4.250	0.840
	2017	1	10	4.330	1.373
Company age	2013	4	63	27.070	13.753
	2011	5	64	28.100	13.758
	2012	6	65	29.100	13.758
	2013	7	66	30.100	13.758
	2017	8	67	31.110	13.932
Company size	2013	5033	16,319,987	1,656,153.550	3,474,204.849
	2011	4797	20,737,074	1,751,781.350	4,013,371.580
	2012	5163	21,777,018	1,836,315.450	4,215,060.570
	2013	5949	12,309,764	1,393,515.670	2,942,331.493
	2017	7955	12,608,723	1,569,424.970	3,214,238.814
Financial leverage	2013	3.79%	90%	42.694	30.760
	2011	4.30%	90%	44.017	28.812
	2012	4.69%	92%	42.967	29.096
	2013	3.63%	94%	41.633	28.995
	2017	3.52%	90%	41.161	29.252
Total accruals	2013	419.4961	9,140,300	891,486.100	2,108,793.100
	2011	504.2641	9,582,700	1,036,757.000	2,248,137.900
	2012	469.7224	10,070,000	1,066,879.000	2,342,293.300
	2013	362.7973	10,966,000	1,016,757.000	2,495,206.800
	2017	374.897	11,165,000	882,866.700	2,251,901.600

Table 4.

Panel B: Dichotomous Variables			
Variable	Year	Frequency of 1	Frequency of 0
	2013	32(80%)	8(20%)
	2011	30(75%)	10(25%)
	2012	33(82.5%)	7(17.5%)
	2013	33(82.5%)	7(17.5%)
	2017	31(79.5%)	9(12.8%)
	2013	39 (97.5%)	1(2.5%)
	2011	39 (97.5%)	1(2.5%)
	2012	39 (97.5%)	1(2.5%)
	2013	38(94.9%)	2(5.2%)
	2017	39(97.4%)	1(2.6%)

audit committee members is decreased to 75%. However, the third year of the study it increased up to 82.5% in 33 listed companies in Bahrain bourse. This percentage went down to 79.5% in the year 2017.

Big Four

Through the descriptive analysis, the findings showed that 97.5% of the study sample which is 39 listed companies in Bahrain Bourse (BHB), were audited by the big four auditing firms through most years of the study period. This indicates that the big audit firms have control over the companies listed on Bahrain Bourse.

Empirical Analysis and Testing Study Hypotheses

See Table 5.

Testing the Study Main Hypotheses

This study depends on De Angelo (1981) model to measure the relationship between audit committee characteristics and earnings quality in listed companies in Bahrain bourse (BHB). This model explains the relationship between the dependent variable "earnings quality" with the continuous and dichotomous variables of the study sample, thus, the data of (40) companies listed in Bahrain Bourse for the period 2013-2017 were used in a manner that is possible to apply the (Pooled Data Regression). The

Table 5. Pooled regression results to study model

Variable	Predicted Sign	T-Test	Sig.
Independent Variable			
AC members	+	2.6	0.01
Ac Independence	+	1.983	0.031
Ac Activity	-	0.758	0.449
Control Variable			
Big Four	+	2.055	0.003
Firm Age	-	0.765	0.446
Firm Size	-	18.038	0.000
Financial Leverage	-	8.856	0.000
F-statistic		8.456	
P-value		0.000	
R		0.871	
R-Square		0.758	
Adjusted R-Square		0.749	

main hypothesis is "There is no impact of Audit committee characteristics (the size of committee, independence of committee members, and number of annual meetings) on earnings quality of companies listed in at Bahrain Bourse. Table 5 showed that the R is 87.1%, which represent the percentage of correlation between the independent variables, dependent variables and control variables of the study sample. The audit committee characteristics (independent variables) in addition to the control variables have an impact on the earnings quality (dependent variables) of Bahraini listed companies by 75.8%, (R-Square), which is the degree of changes of dependent variables caused by the independent variables and control variables. When testing the main hypothesis, the audit committee characteristics' impact the earnings quality can be arithmetically explained as: null hypothesis (H_0: $\beta_1=\beta_2=\beta_3=0$) against the alternative hypothesis one at least from (H_a: $\beta_i \neq 0$). The study found that F-statistic is more in its critical value (8.456) and the p-value calculated is 0.000, which is less than 0.050, which indicated that the characteristics of audit committees affect earnings quality and the model of the study is acceptable and therefore, the study hypothesis can be concluded. However, this hypothesis led to another sub-hypothesis, which measure the impact of each characteristic of the audit committee on the improving and enhancing earnings quality. The following are tests of study sub-hypotheses.

Testing the First Sub-Hypothesis

This hypothesis aims to test the impact of the size of the audit committee on improvement of earnings quality. The first sub-hypotheses can be written as a null - form:

The first hypothesis tend to test the impact of audit committee size on the company's earnings quality, the null form of this sub-hypotheses can be expressed as follows:

H01 There is no impact on the audit committee's size on earnings quality at Bahrain Bourse.

According to the study implemented by Hamdan and Mushtaha (2011) Felo et al. (2003) there is a positive relationship between audit committee size and the dependent variable "earnings quality". Moreover, the size of audit committee members can reduce the risks and material misstatements arise in the financial statements (Huang, 2005). The larger audit committee can effectively help in the process of preparing the company financial statement that ultimately enhances earnings quality (Lin & Yang, 2006). As for the role of the size of the audit committee of Bahraini listed companies in enhancing and improving earnings quality, from Table 5 it was noticed that the size of the audit committee is positively related to earnings quality measured by De Angelo (1981) model and the Sig. Calculated equal to 0.001 showed that the hypothesis is significant as it is less than 0.050 and the size of the audit committee has an impact on the earnings quality of listed companies in Bahrain Bourse. This means that the study rejects the hypothesis, which stated that there is no impact on the audit committee's size on earnings quality at Bahrain Bourse. These results differ from the study conducted in Amman stock exchange by Qaraqish (2009) which stated that the audit committee size is not related to the earnings quality in Jordanian industrial companies. Most properly this different refer to the model used in this study and that of Qaraqish (2009). However, an inappropriate increase in the size of audit committee members might lead to undesired results and decrease the efficiency of the activity of the work of the audit committee as a result of waste in cost and confuse in work Al-Farah (2001).

Testing the Second Sub-Hypothesis

The second sub-hypothesis, try to answer whether or not the degree of independence of audit committee members has an impact on earnings quality of companies listed in Bahrain Bourse and it can be written as the following null-form:

H02 There is no impact of audit committee independence on earnings quality at Bahrain Bourse.

As an existence of the independence of audit committee members lead to improve the performance and enhancing earnings quality of the companies (Qaraqish, 2009)

And reduce the practice of earnings management (Saleh et al., 2007; Carcello et al., 2006). However, the results of this study showed a positive relationship between the degree of independence of the members of the audit committee and earnings quality of the companies listed in Bahrain Bourse (BHB) by using De Angelo, (1981) Model. The degree of independence of the audit committee members in Bahraini listed companies has a significant impact on the quality of the earnings. As Sig. Was equal to 0.031 which is less than 0.050; Such results differ from the findings of the study conducted by Lin & Yang, (2006), which indicated that there is no statistical significance relationship between the independence of committee member and earnings quality as well as financial reporting practices. Moreover, this study differ from the study conducted by Hamdan and Mushtaha (2011). Regarding the industrial companies listed in Amman Stock Exchange (ASE) which indicated that the independence of audit committee member not contributed in improving earnings quality of the companies and this refer to family connection and an apparent financial. For that reason, the degree of independence has no obvious impact on the earnings quality of the companies. This means that the study rejects the hypothesis, which stated that there is no impact of audit committee's independence on earnings quality at Bahrain Bourse and accept the alternative hypothesis, which determined that there is an impact of audit committee independence on earnings quality of listed companies in Bahrain Bourse.

Testing the Third Sub-Hypothesis

The third sub-hypothesis, try to answer whether or not the Number of meetings of the audit committee members has no impact on earnings quality of companies listed in Bahrain Bourse and it can be written as the following null-form:

H03 There is no impact of numbers of meetings of the audit committee on earnings quality at Bahrain Bourse.

Table 5 showed that the t-test is equal to -0.758which, indicated that the number of audit committee meetings in Bahraini listed companies had a negative relationship with earnings quality and the sig. equal to 0.449 which indicated that the number of audit committee meetings had no impact on earnings quality of Bahrain bourse. These results comply with the results of the study conducted by Hamdan and Mushtaha

(2011) in Jordanian industrial companies listed on the Amman Stock Exchange and the study conducted by Lin and Yang (2006) which confirmed that there is no impact of the number of audit committee annual meetings with the quality of the financial reports and statements. According to the ten recommendations of the Blue Ribbon Committee (BRC) regarding audit committee, it pays no attention to the number of audit committee meetings. This was disregarded because there was no impact of a number of the meetings on the financial reporting and companies' control (Hamdan & Mushtaha, 2011). This means that the study rejects the hypothesis, which stated that there is no impact on numbers of meetings of the audit committee on earnings quality at Bahrain Bourse. On the other words, the study rejects this hypothesis and accepts the alternative hypothesis.

Testing Control Variables

Large Audit Firms

The results of the study sample showed that when the listed companies in Bahrain Bourse audited by big four firms, this led to enhance the quality of earnings, because this committee are qualified and can oblige the listed companies to comply with international accounting standards. Therefore, a positive relationship exists between this big four and earnings quality of listed companies in Bahrain Bourse. However, the study appears to be significant with a sig. equal to 0.003 which is less than 0.050. The big audit firms help to increase the quality of financial reports (Hamdan & Mushtaha, 2011). Accordingly, when the companies audited by large firms this lead to reduce earnings management practices and issue a clean report (Johl, et al., 2007). In addition, the creditability of financial statements increased if the firm audited by external auditors through large firms (Becker et al., 1998).

Company Age

The size of the company used as an indicator to measure the relationship between the audit committee characteristics and earnings quality, the results of the study showed a negative impact on the earnings of listed companies in Bahrain Bourse (BHB) with t-test equal to -0.765 which is insignificant as Sig. equal to 0.0446 which is greater than 0.050.

Many previous studies stated the young companies are more able to organize the information and have an impact on earnings quality than those that been around for a while. Which indicates that the company age had statistically significant impact on earnings quality of companies listed in Bahrain Bourse.

Company Size

According to the studies conducted by Hamdan and Mushtaha (2011) and Change and Walter (1996) the quality of financial reports of the large companies is higher than the quality of smaller ones. In this study, the results indicated that there is a negative relationship between the control variable (company size) and earnings quality measured by De Angelo (1981) model. As shown in Table 4 the findings showed that sig. is 0.000 which is less than 0.050, which indicate that the company size had statistically significant impact on earnings quality of companies listed in Bahrain Bourse.

Financial Leverage

According to the study conducted by Qaraqish (2009) the findings indicated that the companies, which had minimum financial leverage, had high earnings quality. Moreover, the study conducted by Hamdan and Mushtaha (2011). found that the control variable (financial leverage) had a negative impact on the earnings quality when it was measured by Richardson et al. (2005). This result complies with the study conducted by Qaraqish (2009) which showed that the financial leverage in listed companies in Bahrain Bourse had a negative implication on the earnings quality with t-test equal to -8.856. However, the study indicated that the financial leverage appears to be statistically significant with Sig. 0.000 which is less than 0.050. According to (Clemente & Labat, 2009) the increased financial debt enforces the companies to maintain high quality financial information and records as the creditor demand, therefore, the higher the financial leverage the higher the quality of earnings.

CONCLUSION AND RECOMMENDATIONS

Conclusion

The audit committee as a mechanism of corporate governance, which main purpose is to harmonize the work of external auditors, management, monitor the performance of the company, increasing the financial statements transparency in addition to detect and report any material misstatements raised. Therefore, this main objective of this study is to examine the relationship between audit committee as a tool of corporate governance and the earnings quality of listed companies in Bahrain bourse after complying with the code of corporate governance.

This study also examined the formation and composition of audit committee in Bahraini listed companies. The sample size of the study was 40 companies listed in Bahrain Bourse with the exclusion of 2 investment companies, 1preffered shares, 1 non-Bahraini company and 3 companies which do not meet the condition of selection the study sample as their data were not available. The necessary data for this study were collected from the annual reports and financial statements for the period 2010 -2014 as the study was conducted in the year 2015 and not all the companies have published their annual report.

The audit committee as a mechanism of corporate governance mechanisms was measured as the independent variable using the variables related to audit committee characteristics; which are: audit committee size, independence, and the number of audit committee annual meetings. Moreover, the study took into consideration 4 different control variables in which they are: big four, company's size, company's age and the financial leverage of listed companies in Bahrain bourse.

Earnings quality was determined as the dependent variable of the study by using the total accruals for the companies as an indicator to measure the earnings quality, since the relationship between the total accruals and the earnings quality is like a two-sided coin. The lower total accruals the higher earnings quality and vice versa.

The results of the study showed that Bahraini listed companies complied with the practice of code of corporate governance regarding the formation of audit committee. When the impact of audit committee' characteristics were tested, the findings of the study showed that the size of audit committee positively related to earnings quality. Furthermore, increasing the size of the committee might affect the performance of this committee; the committee' size should be within the convenient number which specified in Bahrain code of corporate governance in order to perform perfectly.

After that, the study tested the degree of independence of audit committee' members and their role in improving earnings quality, the findings showed that the independence of audit committee' members related positively to the earnings quality of listed companies enrolled in Bahrain bourse.

The relationship between board of directors' members and audit committee' member is important, thus, the specialized authorities in Bahrain have focused on the degree of independence of the members of audit committee.

As for the activity and the numbers of annual meetings of the audit committee' members, the study showed that the annual meetings of audit committee' members related positively to the earnings quality.

Furthermore, the results showed that 87.1%, is the percentage of correlation between the independent variables, dependent and control variables of the study sample. Moreover, the audit committee characteristics (independent variables) in addition to the control variables have an impact on the earnings quality (dependent variables) of Bahraini listed companies equal to 75.8%which is the degree of changes of dependent variables caused by the independent variables and control variables.

It was noticed that the financial debt had a negative implication on the earnings quality of listed companies in Bahrain Bourse. Moreover, Companies which audited by big four auditing firms had a statistically significant impact and positive relationship with the earnings quality of listed companies in Bahrain bourse. However, the size of listed companies was negatively related to the earnings quality of listed companies in Bahrain bourse and had a statistically significant implications on earnings quality, while, the age of those companies had no impact on earnings quality of listed companies in Bahrain Bourse.

Recommendations

In general, it is recommended that central bank of Bahrain and ministry of industry and commerce which organize the work of Bahraini listed companies, to increase the attention and support the audit committee as a mechanism of corporate governance as this act will lead to eliminate earnings management practice, increase the disclosure transparency in order to improve the earnings quality. Furthermore, the code of corporate governance should be strictly regulated and implemented by all companies in Bahrain weather its listed or unlisted. On the other hand, the shareholders, investors, creditors and other related parties are recommended to gain more knowledge and increase their financial experiences in relation to audit committee and its importance when it come to make business decision and better investment.

The study recommends that the code of corporate governance should be controlled and directed by the ministry of industry and commerce rather than the central bank of Bahrain as the latter, is an authority which responsible for the regulating the banking sector as well as licensing and supervision of banks (both conventional and Islamic).

Future Studies

Many questions have been raised up which need future studies and investigation in the following areas: the audit committee characteristics and its impact on accounting conservatism and the audit committee as a tool of corporate governance and its effect on company financial and operational performance of listed companies in Bahrain Bourse.

Implication of The Study

This study conducted for the first time in Bahrain and the findings and statistical results of this study are to benefit managers, shareholders, investors, creditors and other related parties in order to make an enhanced business decision and to increase their knowledge about Bahrain bourse.

REFERENCES

Abdelghany, K. (2005). Measuring the Quality of Earnings. *Managerial Auditing Journal, 20*(9), 1001–1015. doi:10.1108/02686900510625334

Al-Farah, A. (2001). *The effectiveness of audit committees in the Jordanian public shareholding companies: empirical study* (Unpublished Master dissertation). University of Jordan.

Al-Malkawi, H. A. N., Pillai, R., & Bhatti, M. I. (2014). Corporate governance practices in emerging markets: The case of GCC countries. *Economic Modelling, 38*, 133–141. doi:10.1016/j.econmod.2013.12.019

Al-Saidi, M. T., Al-Shammari, B. A., & Page, M. (2014). Corporate governance disclosure in Kuwait. *Arab Journal of Administrative Sciences, 21*(1), 69–104.

Al-Thuneibat, A. (2006). *Audit in the light of the international auditing standards and regulations and local laws: the theory and application* (1st ed.). Amman: Jordan University publications.

Allam Mohammed Mousa, H., Sabri Maher Sabri, M., & Abd Almuttaleb Mohammed, A. (2013). The Audit Committee Characteristics and Earnings Quality: Evidence from Jordan. *Australasian Accounting Business & Finance Journal, 7*(4), 51–80. doi:10.14453/aabfj.v7i4.5

Altamuro, J., & Beatty, A. (2006). *Do Internal Control Reforms Improve Earnings Quality?* Working Paper. Retrieved from www.ssrn.com

Amba, S. M. (2014). Corpoate governance and firms' financial performance. Journal academic and business. *Ethics, 8*, 1–11.

Ameer, B (2013). Corporate governance – issues and challenges in Pikistan. *International Journal of Academic Research in Business and Social Sciences, 3*(4),79-96.

Arens, A. A., Elder, R. J., & Beasley, M. S. (2009). *Auditing and Assurance Services: An Integrated Approach* (13th ed.). Prentice Hall.

Bahrain Bourse. (2013). *Annual Report*. Retrieved from http://www.bahrainbourse.com.bh/

Bahrain Code of Corporate Governance. (2010). Ministry of Commerce and Industry, Kingdom of Bahrain. Retrieved from http://www.moic.gov.bh/

Bahrain Code of Corporate Governance. (2010). Retrieved 14 October 2015, from http://www.moic.gov.bh/Ar/Pages/Home.aspxSmallBusiness-Chron.com

Balhaj, S. (2006). *Factors affecting the voluntary disclosure of a practical study on public companies* (Unpublished PhD dissertation). Arab Academy for Banking and Financial Sciences.

Balsam, S., Krishnan, J., & Yang, J. (2003). Auditor Industry Specialization and Earnings Quality. *Auditing*, *22*(2), 71–97. doi:10.2308/aud.2003.22.2.71

Baxter, P., & Cotter, J. (2009). Audit committees and earnings quality. *Accounting and Finance*, *49*(2), 267–290. doi:10.1111/j.1467-629X.2008.00290.x

Beng, W. G. (2009). Audit committees, boards of directors, and remediation of material weaknesses in internal control. *Contemporary Accounting Research*, *26*(2), 7.

Bianco, M., Ciavarella, A., & Signoretti, R. (2015). Women on Corporate Boards in Italy: The Role of Family Connections. *Corporate Governance*, *23*(2), 129–144. doi:10.1111/corg.12097

Blue Ribbon Committee (BRC). (1999). *Report and recommendations of the Blue Ribbon Committee on improving the Effectiveness of Corporate Audit Committees*. Author.

Caneghem, T. V. (2004). The impact of audit quality on earnings rounding-up behaviour: Some UK evidence. *European Accounting Review*, *13*(4), 771–786.

Carcello, J., & Neal, T. (2003). Audit Committee Independence and Disclosure: Choice for Financially Distressed Firms. *Corporate Governance*, *11*(4), 289–299. doi:10.1111/1467-8683.00327

Carcello, J. V., Hollingsworth, C. W., Klein, A., & Neal, L. T. (2006). *Audit Committee Financial Expertise, Competing Corporate Governance Mechanisms, and Earnings Management*. Available at www. ssrn.com

Chung, R., Firth, M., & Kim, J. B. (2005). Earnings management, surplus free cash flow, and external monitoring. *Journal of Business Research*, *58*(6), 766–776. doi:10.1016/j.jbusres.2003.12.002

Clemente, A., & Labat, B. (2009). *Corporate Governance mechanism and Voluntary Disclosure. The role of independent directors in the boards of listed Spanish firms.* Retrieved from http://pendientedemigracion.ucm.es/

Crutchley, C. E., Jensen, M. R., & Marshall, B. B. (2007). Climate for scandal: Corporate environment that contribute to accounting fraud. *Financial Review*, *42*(1), 53–73. doi:10.1111/j.1540-6288.2007.00161.x

DeAngelo, L. (1981). Auditor size and audit quality. *Journal of Accounting and Economics*, *3*(December), 183–199. doi:10.1016/0165-4101(81)90002-1

Dechow, P., & Dichev, I. (2002). The Quality of Accruals and Earnings: The Role of Accrual Estimation Errors. *The Accounting Review*, *77*(September), 35–59. doi:10.2308/accr.2002.77.s-1.35

Dechow, P., & Schrand, C. (2004). *Earnings Quality*. The Research Foundation of CFA Institute.

Dechow, P., Sloan, R., & Sweeney, A. (1995). Detecting Earnings Management. *The Accounting Review*, *70*(2), 193–225.

DeFond, M. L., Raghunandan, K., & Subramanyam, K. R. (2002). Do non-audit service fees impair auditor independence? Evidence from going concern audit opinions. *Journal of Accounting Research*, *40*(4), 1247–1274. doi:10.1111/1475-679X.00088

Dezoort, F., & Salterio, S. (2001). *The Effect of Corporate Governance Experience and Financial Reporting and Audit Knowledge on Audit Committee Members Judgment*. Academic Press.

Dezoort, F., & Salterio, S. (2001). The Effect of Corporate Governance Experience and Financial Reporting and Audit Knowledge on Audit Committee Members Judgment. *Auditing*, *20*(2), 31–47. doi:10.2308/aud.2001.20.2.31

Fan, J. P. H., & Wong, T. J. (2005). Do external auditors perform a corporate governance role in emerging markets? Evidence from East Asia. *Journal of Accounting Research*, *43*(1), 35–72. doi:10.1111/j.1475-679x.2004.00162.x

Faraj, A. (2005). *Assess the level of disclosure in interim financial reports of public shareholding companies of Jordan in light of the disclosure requirements of the progress of local and international* (Unpublished PhD dissertation). Arab Academy for Banking and Financial Sciences.

Faraj, A. (2005). *Assess the level of disclosure in interim financial reports of public shareholding companies of Jordan in light of the disclosure requirements of the progress of local and international* (Unpublished PhD dissertation). Arab Academy for Banking and Financial Sciences.

Farinha, J., & Moreira, A. (2007). *Dividends and Earnings Quality: The Missing Link?* Working Paper, University of Porto.

Felo, A., Krishnamurthy, F., & Solieri, S. (2003). *Audit Committee Characteristics and the Perceived Quality of Financial Reporting an Empirical Analysis*. Working Paper, School of Graduate Professional Studies, Malven. Retrieved from www.ssrn.com

Givoly, D., Hayn, C., & Katz, S. (2010). Does Public Ownership of Equity Improve Earnings Quality? *The Accounting Review, 85*(1), 195–225. doi:10.2308/accr.2010.85.1.195

Gowthorpe, C., & Amat, O. (2005). Creative accounting: some ethical issues of macro- and micromanipulation. *Journal of Economic Literature Classification, 41*(1), 1-22.

Gujarati, D. (2003). *Basic Econometrics*. New York: McGraw Hill Book Co.

Hamdan, A., & Abu Ijela, I. (2010). Auditing Quality in Jordan and its Impact on Earnings Management and Earnings Quality. *The Arab Journal of Accounting*. Retrieved from http://www.bahrainedb.com/en/about/Documents/index.html#.VjcX8bzYpPN

Hamdan, A., & Mudshtaha, S. (2011). The Relationship Between Audit Committee Characteristics and Type of Auditor's Report: An Empirical Study on the Public Shareholding Industrial Companies Listed at Amman Bourse. *The Arab Journal of Accounting, 14*(1), 109–163. doi:10.12785/aja/140104

Huang, H. (2005). *The Effects of Audit Committee Characteristics on Investors Perception of Financial Reporting*. Working Paper, Florida International University.

Hussain, S., & Millan, C. (2002). Corporate Governance in Bahrain. *Corporate Governance: An International Review, 10*(3), 197-210.

Johl, S., Jubb, C., & Houghton, K. (2007). Earning Management and the Audit Opinion: Evidence from Malaysia. *Managerial Auditing Journal, 22*(7), 688-715. doi:10.1108/02686900710772591

Khan, M. (2015). *Program governance*. Boca Raton, FL: CRC Press.

Kim, J. B., Chung, R., & Firth, M. (2003). Auditor conservatism, asymmetric monitoring, and earnings management. *Contemporary Accounting Research*, *20*(2), 323–359. doi:10.1506/J29K-MRUA-0APP-YJ6V

Kukreja, G. (2013). Impact of new corporate governance on disclosure: Evidence from Bahrain Listed commercial Banks. *Advance in Management and Applied Economics*, *3*(3), 171–191.

Lee, P. (2015). Problems of Implementing Audit Committee and Supervisory Board Simultaneously in China. *Journal of Accounting, Auditing & Finance*, *30*(4), 509–528. doi:10.1177/0148558X15587649

Lin, J., & Yang, J. (2006). The Effect of Audit Committee Performance on Earnings Quality. *Managerial Auditing Journal*, *21*(9), 921–933. doi:10.1108/02686900610705019

Lisic, L., Neal, T., & Zhang, Y. (2011). *Audit committee financial expertise and restatements: The moderating effect of CEO power*. Fairfax, VA: School of Management, George Mason University.

Marilen, P., & Ana-Cristina, N. (2013). Corporate governance codes of best practice of top romanian banks. *Annals of the University of Oradea. Economic Science Series*, *22*(2), 390–397.

Matar, M. (2006). Recent trends in financial and credit analysis, methods, tools and practical uses (2nd ed.). Amman: Darwael for publication and distribution.

McMullen, D., & Raghunandan, K. (1996). Enhancing Audit Committee Effectiveness. *Journal of Accountancy*, *182*(2), 79–81.

Miteva, E. (2005). *Improving Corporate Governance in the Middle East and North Africa*. Paper presented at the MENA and OECD's Initiative on Governance for Investment and Development, MENA Regional Corporate Governance Forum, Amman, Jordan.

Mushtaha, S. (2009). *The Extent to Which the Characteristics of The Audit Committee Improves the Quality of Financial Reporting*. PHD Research.

Nimer, K., Warrad, L., & Khuraisat, O. (2012). The effect of audit committee's effectiveness on dividend payout policy: Evidence from the Jordanian firms. *International Journal of Business and Management, 7*(7), 172–179. doi:10.5539/ijbm.v7n7p172

Obay, L. A. (2009). Corporate governance & business ethics: A Dubai-based survey. *Journal of Legal. Ethical & Regulatory Issues, 12*(2), 29–47.

OECD Policy Brief. (2004). *The OECD Principles of Corporate Governance*. Available: http://www.oecd.org/corporate/corporateaffairs/corporategovern

Ohlson, J., & Feltham, J. (1995). Valuation and clean surplus accounting for operating and financial activities. *Contemporary Accounting Research, 11*(2), 689–731. doi:10.1111/j.1911-3846.1995.tb00462.x

Organization for Economic Co-operation and Development. (2004). *Corporate Governance: A Survey of OECD Countries*. OECD Publishing.

Pucheta-Martínez, M. C., & De Fuentes, C. (2007). The Impact of Audit Committee Characteristics on the Enhancement of the Quality of Financial Reporting: An empirical study in the Spanish context. *Corporate Governance, 15*(6), 1394–1412. doi:10.1111/j.1467-8683.2007.00653.x

Qaraqish, S. (2009). *The Effect of Audit Committee Characteristics on Earnings Quality An Empirical Study on the Industrial Sector Firms Listed at Amman Stock Exchange* (Unpublished dissertation). Arab Academy for Banking and Financial Sciences.

Saleh, N., Iskandar, T., & Rahmat, M. (2007). Audit Committee Characteristics and Earning Management: Evidence from Malaysia. *Asian Review of Accounting, 15*(2), 147–163. doi:10.1108/13217340710823369

Samaha, K., & Dahawy, K. (2010). Factors influencing corporate disclosure transparency in the active share trading firms: An explanatory study. *Research in Accounting in Emerging Economies, 10*, 87–118. doi:10.1108/S1479-3563(2010)0000010009

Samaha, K., Dahawy, K., Hussainey, K., & Stapleton, P. (2012). The extent of corporate governance disclosure and its determinants in a developing market: The case of Egypt. *Advances in Accounting, 28*(1), 168–178. doi:10.1016/j.adiac.2011.12.001

Schipper, K., & Vincent, L. (2003). Earnings Quality. *Accounting Horizons, 17*(s-1), 97–110. doi:10.2308/acch.2003.17.s-1.97

Securities and Exchange Commission. (2003). Final Rule: Standards Related to Listed Company Audit Committees (SEC Release Nos. 33-8330; 34-47654). Washington, DC: Author.

Stewart, J., & Munro, L. (2007). The Impact Of Audit Committee Existence and Audit Committee Meeting Frequency on the External Audit: Perceptions of Australian Auditors. *International Journal of Auditing*, *11*(1), 51–69. doi:10.1111/j.1099-1123.2007.00356.x

Teitel, K., & Machuga, S. (2010). The Interaction of Audit Firm Quality and the Mexican Code Of Best Corporate Practices On Earnings Quality. *Review of Business Research*, *10*(1), 32–40.

Thomson, C. (2009). *Knowledge Center for Students: Corporate governance theories and issues*. Retrieved 13 October 2016, from http://knowledgecenterforstudents.blogspot.com/2011/10/corporate-governance-theories-and.html

Tirole, J. (2001). Corporate governance. *Econometrica*, *69*(1), 2–18. doi:10.1111/1468-0262.00177

Veaco, K., & Sorokin, C. (2014). Corporate Governance Consultants: What to Look for When Hiring. *Corporate Governance Advisor*, *22*(4), 1–5.

Yang, J., & Krishnan, J. (2005). Audit Committee and Quarterly Earning Management. *International Journal of Auditing*, *9*(3), 201–219. doi:10.1111/j.1099-1123.2005.00278.x

Yoshikawa, T., & Rasheed, A. A. (2009). Convergence of Corporate Governance: CriticalReview and Future Directions. *Corporate Governance*, *17*(3), 388–404. doi:10.1111/j.1467-8683.2009.00745.x

Zeitoun, H., Osterloh, M., & Frey, B. S. (2015). Learning from ancient Athens: Demarchy and corporate governance. *Academy of Management Perspectives*, *3015*(1), 4-18. doi:10.5465/amp.2012.0105.test

Zureigat, Q. (2010). The Effect of Modified Auditors Opinions on Shares Prices: Evidence from Amman Stock Exchange. *Jordan Journal of Business Administration.*, *6*(2), 210–224.

Chapter 3
Corporate Governance Role of the Board Committees in India

Shinu Vig
https://orcid.org/0000-0002-0063-0470
TERI School of Advanced Studies, India

Manipadma Datta
TERI School of Advanced Studies, India

ABSTRACT

The establishment of board sub-committees has been strongly recommended as a suitable mechanism for improving corporate governance by delegating specific tasks from the main board to a smaller group and harnessing the contribution of non-executive directors. This chapter discusses the constitution of board committees in Indian context, their composition, processes, and their role in promoting good corporate governance. India has constantly made efforts to update its corporate governance regulations in line with the international best practices. This chapter will help the readers to understand the corporate governance scenario in India with special reference to the board committees and will have implications for the regulators, policymakers, corporate governance practitioners, researchers, and academicians in the developing countries.

DOI: 10.4018/978-1-5225-9607-3.ch003

INTRODUCTION

The establishment of board sub-committees has been strongly recommended as a suitable mechanism for improving corporate governance, by delegating specific tasks from the main board to a smaller group and harnessing the contribution of non-executive directors. The effectiveness of the board depends on its composition and size and also its internal administrative structure (John & Senbet, 1998). Constitution of board committees leads to the division of responsibilities within the board and shows a systematic approach to handle issues on the agenda. Board decisions initially originate in the board committees. Hence, it is expected that the effective use of committees by the board shall have a positive effect on firm performance (Vig & Datta, 2018). As each committee functions only for a specific issue and the expertise and professions of the independent directors on different committees are varied, they can contribute to the performance of the company from different dimensions. For a Board of Directors, its committee structure symbolizes its method of operation.

Harrison (1987) makes an analysis of the roles of board sub-committees and recognises them as strategic tools, fulfilling board responsibilities of maintaining corporate legitimacy, protecting directors from excessive exposure to liability and contributing to the formation of corporate strategy. He argued that audit and remuneration committees, with a monitoring and oversight brief, contributed to the first – establishing and maintaining organisational legitimacy in the eyes of external resource providers. Some other scholars identify a corporate strategy role for the board committees (Andrews, 1981).

The Anglo-Saxon model of governance (adopted by UK, USA and also India) has recognised the importance of the unitary board structure, while providing for boards sub-committees to focus on specific aspects of governance which have been identified as important but difficult, such as financial reporting quality, directors' remuneration and board appointments. The codes of governance all over the world have recommended the establishment of audit, remuneration and nomination committees for improving corporate governance standards. There is ample literature in the area of corporate governance where various researchers have conducted studies on these Board committees mainly required to be constituted by various corporate governance codes.

Role of Board Committees

Committees appointed by the Board focus on specific areas and are intended to take informed decisions within the framework of delegated authority. They enable better and more focused attention on the company affairs and review items in great detail before it is placed before the Board for its consideration. These committees prepare the groundwork for decision making and place their report at the subsequent board meeting. They make specific recommendations to the Board on matters in their areas or purview. However, all decisions and recommendations of the committees are placed before the Board for information or for approval. The committees are supposed to supplement the board decision making. Membership of each committee has different demands and requires a slightly different focus.

Harrison (1987) divides the board committees into two types- first, management support or operating committees and second, monitoring or oversight committee. The management committees are required to support management in their operation and examples can be executive committee and finance committee. On the other hand monitoring or oversight committees are supposed to protect shareholder interests by providing an objective, independent review of company affairs, especially with respect to the legality, integrity and ethical quality of corporate activities. Monitoring committees comprise majorly of outside directors, and include the audit, compensation, and nomination committees. These committees enhance corporate accountability and provide independent oversight of corporate activities. They are intended to serve as mechanisms for monitoring the management and protecting the interest of the shareholders. The committees can also have some strategic uses for the company like maintaining corporate legitimacy, protecting directors from excessive exposure to liability and helping in formulation of corporate strategy. Harrison further argued that audit and remuneration committees contributed to establishing and maintaining organisational legitimacy in the eyes of external resource providers. Stiles and Taylor (2001) in their research have identified three major roles for the board- strategic, control and institutional. Wherein, they place both audit and remuneration committees firmly in the control role. They also identify the role of these committees in the corporate strategy formulation.

The need for and importance of the major board committees for good corporate governance has been highlighted in the extant research in this area. The section hereafter summarises the same.

Audit Committee

Audit committees are very important in a company as the board "delegates the responsibility for the oversight of management's financial reporting to an audit committee" (Carcello et al., 2002), and the audit committee subsequently determines the quality and scope of the audit. The main responsibility of an audit committee is to supervise the transparency of financial reports and ensure the integrity of an external audit (Vicknair, Hickman, & Carnes, 1993). Audit Committees are expected to monitor the reliability of the company's accounting processes and compliance with corporate legal and ethical standards including the maintenance of preventive fraud controls. Any relationship between the audit committee and management would interfere with the independent judgment of the audit committee because inside directors appointed as audit committee members may be biased toward management. Companies with better governance mechanisms will appoint more independent directors on the audit committee (Klein, 2002). This view is supported in other studies also where it was found that board monitoring and financial performance improve after companies appoint more independent directors on their audit committees (Brick and Chidambaran, 2008; Chan & Li, 2008; Aggarwal et al., 2011).

Compensation Committee

Large companies are known to pay high compensation packages to their top executives and high level of pay brings with it a need for greater transparency and formal control mechanisms. (Rosen, 1990). Thus, there is a need for a Board sub-committee such as the remuneration committee to exert an influence on top executive pay. And this influence should be in the interests of the owners, i.e., the shareholders. An independent compensation committee is crucial for ensuring that the compensation packages better align the interests of managers and shareholders. High quality compensation committees set more efficient executive compensation to enhance the alignment of the interests of managers and shareholders and thus maximize firm value. Many researchers have investigated the impact of compensation committee quality on the association between CEO pay and firm performance where the measure of compensation committee quality is compensation committee independence (i.e. the percentage of independent directors on the compensation committee). Bryan and Klein (2004) hold that independent directors provide more effective monitoring, which reduces the need for equity-based compensation for directors. (also Sun, Cahan and Emanuel, 2009). On the other hand, the affiliated directors on the compensation committee will be more inclined and biased towards executives, resulting in extravagant or misaligned compensation packages (Newman & Mozes, 1999; Sun & Cahan, 2012). Anderson and Bizjak (2003) also examine whether greater independence of compensation committee promotes shareholder interests and whether the CEO's presence on the committee leads to opportunistic pay structure.

Nomination Committee

Corporate governance codes all over the world encourage the establishment of nomination committees for the purpose of identifying and selecting new members for the board. It is expected that these committees will enhance the effectiveness of the board by making it more independent and by raising directors' qualifications.

Despite of their importance, there is not much academic literature in this area. Some authors explain the importance of the nomination committees from a behavioural perspective. They say that in the absence of a nomination committee the current board of directors is more likely to appoint new board members who are similar to them and whose characteristics they understand. Nomination committees can lay down clear selection criterion and decision procedures and can thus serve as an important tool to overcome the limitations of the board selection process. These committees can also undertake activities like developing board member profiles, employing the services of search firms and interviewing candidates and ultimately contribute to improve new director selection procedures (Ruigrok et al, 2006). Agency theory (Jensen & Meckling, 1976; Fama & Jensen, 1983; Jensen, 1993) can be applied to explain governance-related factors which influence the adoption of nomination committees. In order to understand the effects of nomination committees on board composition, their purpose can be related to existing theories of board roles. Based on agency theory it can be explained that nomination committees play a role in enabling boards to perform their control function effectively. Based on the resource-dependence view (Pfeffer, 1972; Pfeffer & Salancik, 1978) it can be said that nomination committees' purpose is to adjust board composition as per the changes taking place in a firm's external environment.

The existence of nomination committee in a company depends upon several factors like- the existence of a large shareholder. If a company is directly monitored by a large shareholder, the importance of other control mechanisms such as boards of directors is reduced (Rediker & Seth, 1995). In this situation, this large shareholder may also have a role in selection of new board members, restraining the involvement of the CEO and inside directors in the director selection process. Hence, in the presence of a large shareholder it is less likely that boards will have a nomination committee. Another important factor in this regard, is the existing distribution of power between a board and the company CEO, which also a potential to affect the director nomination process (Hermalin & Weisbach, 1988; Finkelstein & Hambrick, 1996). Patton and Baker (1987) put forward that management may intrinsically dominate the boards through the nomination and election process. So, nomination committee can play an important role in enhancing board independence by selecting more outsiders who possess the necessary qualifications, skills and expertise. A higher ratio of outside directors will enable the board to act independently from the firm's management and to perform its monitoring role effectively (Zahra & Pearce, 1989). When there are more independent directors on the nomination committee, the board of directors is more capable of selecting higher qualified management and further monitoring the managers effectively.

Figure 1. Board committees in India

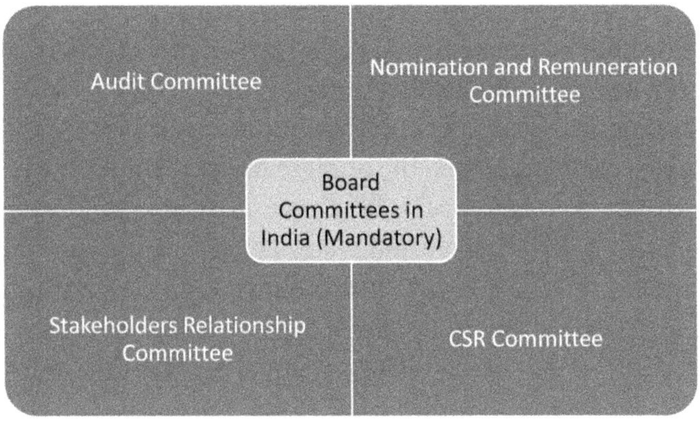

BOARD COMMITTEES IN INDIA

In India the companies are regulated by the Ministry of Corporate Affairs and the Securities and Exchange Board of India (SEBI). The basic framework of corporate governance in India is provided in the Companies Act 2013, SEBI Act, SEBI guidelines and the Listing Agreements of Bombay Stock Exchange and National Stock Exchange. Clause 49 of the standard listing agreement establishes the basic minimum compliance norms for corporate governance by listed companies in India. Clause 49 focuses on corporate boards and requirements of disclosure to shareholders and consists of mandatory as well as non-mandatory provisions for corporate governance by the listed companies in India.

As per the provisions of the Companies Act 2013 and the standard listing agreement, the committees which are required to be mandatorily constituted by the listed companies are- audit committee, nomination and remuneration committee, stakeholders' relationship (shareholders' grievance) committee and the CSR (corporate social responsibility) committee. Each of these committees has its own specified function and shall be comprised of majority of non-executive or independent directors. Apart from these committees, the Kotak Committee (constituted in 2017 to make recommendations on corporate governance in India) also suggests constitution of Risk Management committee for cyber security and Information Technology committee for digital and technological aspects.

Audit Committee in India

Section 177 of the Indian Companies Act 2013 lays down the provisions relating to constitution, composition and the roles and responsibilities of the Audit Committees. It is applicable to all listed companies and to public limited companies having paid up share capital of rupees 100 Crore or more or aggregate outstanding loans/borrowings/debentures/deposits exceeding rupees 200 Crore, as specified by the Rules.

Audit Committee shall comprise a minimum of three directors including a majority of Independent Directors. Majority of members of Audit Committee including its Chairperson must have the ability to read and understand the financial statements. The board of directors of the company shall lay down in writing the terms of reference for the Audit Committee.

The terms of reference of the audit committee shall include:

- Recommendation for appointment, remuneration and terms of appointment of the auditors;
- Review and monitor auditor's independence and performance and effectiveness of the audit process;
- Examination of the financial statement and auditor's report;
- Approval or modification of related party transactions;
- Scrutiny of inter corporate loans and investments;
- Valuation of assets;
- Evaluation of internal financial controls and risk management systems;
- Monitoring of end use of funds of the public offers;
- Vigil mechanism (whistle blower policy) and access to Audit Committee chairperson under vigil mechanism. Details of establishing the vigil mechanism have to be disclosed on the company's web site and in the Director's report.
- Discuss issues with internal and statutory auditors;

Audit Committee shall also call for comments of the auditors about internal control systems, scope of audit including the observations of the auditors and review of the financial statements before submission to the board. The auditors and the key management personnel will have a right to be present when the financial statements is considered by the Audit Committee but will not have a right to vote. Every Audit Committee to have an authority to investigate into any matter in relation to the items specified above or referred to it by the board and for this purpose the Audit Committee shall have power to obtain professional advice from external sources and have full access to information contained in the records of the company.

Nomination and Remuneration Committee in India

Provisions relating to composition of nomination and remuneration committee are covered under Section 178 of the Indian Companies Act 2013. It requires the constitution of a Nomination and Remuneration Committee consisting of minimum three non-executive directors with a majority of Independent Directors. It also lays down that the chairperson of the company cannot hold chairmanship of this committee. The policy of the committee shall be disclosed in the board's report. The functions of the committee are as follows:

- To formulate the criteria for determining qualifications, positive attributes and independence of a director and recommend to the board a policy, relating to the remuneration for the directors, key managerial personnel and other employees.
- To ensure that level and composition of remuneration is reasonable and sufficient, relationship of remuneration to performance is clear and meets performance benchmarks, and involves a balance between fixed and incentive pay.
- To identify persons who may be appointed in senior management in accordance with the criteria laid down.
- To carry out evaluation of every director's performance and recommend to the board his/her appointment and removal based on the performance.

Stakeholders Relationship Committee in India

As per Section 178 of the Companies Act 2013, listed companies or those that have more than one thousand shareholders, debenture-holders, deposit-holders and any other security holders at any time during a financial year shall constitute a Stakeholders Relationship Committee. The committee shall be chaired by a non-executive director and the board shall decide other members of the committee. The role of the committee is to consider and resolve the grievances of security holders of the company. The Chairperson is required to be present at the annual general meetings of the company to answer the queries of the security holders. The committee shall meet at least once in a year. The major functions of the committee are:

- To resolve the grievances of the security holders of the company including complaints regarding transfer/ transmission of shares, non-receipt of annual report, non-receipt of declared dividends, issue of new or duplicate share certificates, etc.

- To review the measures taken by the company for effective voting rights by shareholders.
- To review adherence to the service standards followed by the Registrar and Share Transfer agents of the company.
- To Review the measures taken by the company for reducing the amount of unclaimed dividends and ensuring timely receipt of dividend warrants/ annual reports/ statutory notices by the shareholders of the company.

Corporate Social Responsibility Committee in India

Indian Companies Act 2013, under section 135 has mandated listed companies to spend two percent of their average net profits of the previous three years, on corporate social responsibility. The companies covered under section 135 are the companies having net worth of rupees 500 Crore or more, or turnover of rupees 1000 Crore or more or a net profit of rupees 5 Crore or more during any financial year. These companies have to constitute a Corporate Social Responsibility (CSR) Committee, lay down a CSR policy and also explain with reasons if they fail to spend this mandatory amount. The companies are also compulsorily required to disclose the details of their CSR activities in the Directors' Report and on its website.

CSR committee shall comprise three or more directors, out of which at least one director must be an independent director. The committee shall formulate and recommend to the board, a CSR policy, which will list the activities to be undertaken by the company as well as the amount of expenditure to be incurred on the activities referred to in the CSR policy. The committee shall monitor CSR policy from time to time and shall prepare a transparent monitoring mechanism for ensuring implementation of the projects/programmes/activities proposed to be undertaken by the company.

Risk Management Committee in India

Securities and Exchange Board of India (SEBI) mandated the constitution of risk management committee by top 100 listed companies (based on their market capitalization) in 2015. The majority of the members of the committee shall be the board of directors and other members can be the senior executives of the company. The committee shall be expected to monitor and review the risk management plan of the company and make suggestions to the board of directors. The board may delegate any other function to the committee as deemed fit. Subsequently, SEBI constituted the Kotak Committee in June 2017 to look into the existing SEBI regulations on corporate governance and suggest changes. The Kotak Committee, apart from other recommendations also suggested constitution of a Risk Management committee for risk identification, mitigation and specifically for cyber security. SEBI has accepted this recommendation with some modifications and has extended its applicability from current top 100 listed entities to top 500 listed entities by their market capitalisation. This provision will become applicable from 1st April 2019. The functions of Risk Management Committee shall specifically include monitoring and reviewing of cyber security as a primary function. This recommendation is intended to overall strengthen the position of risk management committee as an institutional mechanism. Role of the Committee would be to provide the board of the company with quantified information on the total risk exposure on the entity-level and quantified information on all relevant risk areas. The committee will function for mitigating the risks and understanding the origin of various risks faced by the company.

Penalty for Contravention

The company law has entrusted board committees and the directors with responsibilities and duties, some of which require public disclosures of policies as well as positive affirmation of the adequacy and effective working of systems and processes relating to internal financial controls, risk management, regulatory compliance, remuneration and corporate social responsibility. Contravention of these and other provisions attract both civil and criminal penalties.

The civil penalties for contravention of the provisions of Section 177 and 178 are:

- The penalty for companies is a fine between rupees 1 Lakh to rupees 5 Lakh.
- For every officer in default the penalties are imprisonment up to one year and / or a fine between rupees 25,000 to rupees 1 Lakh.

CONCLUSION

Board committees play an essential role in corporate governance of the companies as the Board can delegate specific functions to the committee, which can closely monitor those functions. These committees are promoted for their potential to mitigate the weaknesses of corporate governance. Several cases of business scandals in the past have been caused by fraud, poor accounting or failure of internal control. These cases highlight the need for adequate monitoring. A review of literature suggests that researchers have emphasized most on the functioning of the audit committees. Audit committees play an important monitoring role in companies' financial reporting process and improve the quality of financial reporting. Klein (2002) suggests that audit committee independence reflects governance quality. An effectively functioning audit committee strengthens the internal audit (Marsh and Powell, 1989; Turnbull,

1999). Audit Committees can strengthen management's ability to identify and assess both internal and external risks and thereby also identify potential opportunities and challenges facing the company in achieving it's operating, financial, and compliance goals. Another committee playing a vital role in good governance of the Indian companies is the CSR committee which helps ensure that the companies are fulfilling their social responsibility as mandated by the company law.

REFERENCES

Aggarwal, R., Erel, I., Ferreira, M., & Matos, P. (2011). Does governance travel around the world? Evidence from institutional investors. *Journal of Financial Economics*, *100*(1), 154–181. doi:10.1016/j.jfineco.2010.10.018

Anderson, R. C., & Bizjak, J. M. (2003). An empirical examination of the role of the CEO and the compensation committee in structuring executive pay. *Journal of Banking & Finance*, *27*(7), 1323–1348. doi:10.1016/S0378-4266(02)00259-5

Andrews, K. R. (1981). Corporate strategy as a vital function of the board. *Harvard Business Review*, *59*(6), 174–184.

Brick, I. E., & Chidambaran, N. K. (2008). Board monitoring, firm risk, and external regulation. *Journal of Regulatory Economics*, *33*(1), 87–116. doi:10.100711149-007-9045-9

Bryan, S., & Klein, A. (2004). *Non-management director options, board characteristics, and future firm investments and performance*. Academic Press.

Carcello, J. V., Hermanson, D. R., Neal, T. L., & Riley, R. A. Jr. (2002). Board characteristics and audit fees. *Contemporary Accounting Research*, *19*(3), 365–384. doi:10.1506/CHWK-GMQ0-MLKE-K03V

Chan, K. C., & Li, J. (2008). Audit committee and firm value: Evidence on outside top executives as expert-independent directors. *Corporate Governance*, *16*(1), 16–31. doi:10.1111/j.1467-8683.2008.00662.x

Fama, E. F., & Jensen, M. C. (1983). Separation of ownership and control. *The Journal of Law & Economics*, *26*(2), 301–325. doi:10.1086/467037

Finkelstein, S., & Hambrick, D. (1996). *Strategic leadership*. St. Paul, MN: West Educational Publishing.

Harrison, J. R. (1987). The strategic use of corporate board committees. *California Management Review*, *30*(1), 109–125. doi:10.2307/41165269

Hermalin, B. E., & Weisbach, M. S. (1988). The determinants of board composition. *The Rand Journal of Economics, 19*(4), 589–606. doi:10.2307/2555459

Jensen, M. C. (1993). The modern industrial revolution, exit, and the failure of internal control systems. *The Journal of Finance, 48*(3), 831-880.

Jensen, M. C., & Meckling, W. H. (1976). Theory of the firm: Managerial behavior, agency costs and ownership structure. *Journal of Financial Economics, 3*(4), 305–360. doi:10.1016/0304-405X(76)90026-X

John, K., & Senbet, L. W. (1998). Corporate governance and board effectiveness1. *Journal of Banking & Finance, 22*(4), 371–403. doi:10.1016/S0378-4266(98)00005-3

Klien, A. (2002). Economic determinants of audit committee. *The Accounting Review, 77*(2), 30–56.

Marsh, H. L., & Powell, T. E. (1989). The audit committee charter: Rx for fraud prevention. *Journal of Accountancy, 167*(2), 55.

Patton, A., & Baker, J. C. (1987). Why wont directors rock the boat. *Harvard Business Review, 65*(6), 10.

Pfeffer, J. (1972). Size and composition of corporate boards of directors: The organization and its environment. *Administrative Science Quarterly, 17*(2), 218–228. doi:10.2307/2393956

Pfeffer, J., & Salancik, G. R. (1978). *The external control of organizations: A resource dependence approach.* Harper and Row Publishers.

Rediker, K. J., & Seth, A. (1995). Boards of directors and substitution effects of alternative governance mechanisms. *Strategic Management Journal, 16*(2), 85–99. doi:10.1002mj.4250160202

Rosen, S. (1990). *Contracts and the Market for Executives (No. w3542).* National Bureau of Economic Research. doi:10.3386/w3542

Ruigrok, W., Peck, S. I., & Keller, H. (2006). Board characteristics and involvement in strategic decision making: Evidence from Swiss companies. *Journal of Management Studies, 43*(5), 1201–1226. doi:10.1111/j.1467-6486.2006.00634.x

Stiles, P., & Taylor, B. (2001). *Boards at work: How directors view their roles and responsibilities: How directors view their roles and responsibilities.* OUP Oxford.

Sun, J., & Cahan, S. F. (2012). The economic determinants of compensation committee quality. *Managerial Finance, 38*(2), 188–205. doi:10.1108/03074351211193721

Sun, J., Cahan, S. F., & Emanuel, D. (2009). Compensation committee governance quality, chief executive officer stock option grants, and future firm performance. *Journal of Banking & Finance*, *33*(8), 1507–1519. doi:10.1016/j.jbankfin.2009.02.015

Turley, S., & Zaman, M. (2004). The corporate governance effects of audit committees. *The Journal of Management and Governance*, *8*(3), 305–332. doi:10.100710997-004-1110-5

Vicknair, D., Hickman, K., & Carnes, K. C. (1993). A note on audit committee independence: Evidence from the NYSE on" grey" area directors. *Accounting Horizons*, *7*(1), 53.

Vig, S., & Datta, M. (2018). Corporate governance and value creation: A study of selected Indian companies. *International Journal of Indian Culture and Business Management*, *17*(3), 259–282. doi:10.1504/IJICBM.2018.094582

Zahra, S. A., & Pearce, J. A. II. (1989). Boards of directors and corporate financial performance: A review and integrative model. *Journal of Management*, *15*(2), 291–334. doi:10.1177/014920638901500208

Section 2

Governance and Financial Institutions

Chapter 4
Systemic Financial Institutions' Corporate Governance Features:
Comparative Insights

Iustina A Boitan
https://orcid.org/0000-0001-6510-5063
Bucharest University of Economic Studies (ASE), Romania

ABSTRACT

Several international and European regulatory and supervisory authorities, such as the Basel Committee for Banking Supervision, the European Banking Authority or the European Central Bank, are increasingly emphasizing that the structure of banks' managing bodies is a key driver of future financial stability and ask for reviews of existing skills, competencies, and expertise in order to cope with the newest economic, social, and technological challenges. The chapter subscribes to these views and aims at investigating two research directions: 1) whether there are resemblances in large, systemic banks' management board structure and 2) whether systemic banks' financial performance is determined by the management board's features (board size, number of women in the board, number of independent members). The empirical approach relies on several complementary methods (descriptive statistics, cluster analysis, panel regression) to reveal dominant board features in a sample of 29 European systemic banks, over a time frame of 11 years.

DOI: 10.4018/978-1-5225-9607-3.ch004

INTRODUCTION

Traditionally, the structure and composition of banks' management boards, their diverse range of professional qualifications, competencies, know-how, experience as well as personal reputation, age and gender balance are considered important features for the efficient conduct of a banking business. In establishing the composition of the board, large banks are increasingly more emphasizing the need for diversity in terms of banking and insurance expertise and experience, as well as awareness on societal and the most recent technological developments (such as digitalization or the heavily reliance on IT for providing banking products and services) which are compatible with the financial business.

Banks' managing boards are in charge with designing a proper business strategy, in defining the risk appetite framework and in developing and monitoring risk management capabilities in tight connection with the financial and non-financial risks they are going to undertake. These key issues have to be adapted, tailored to the size of the bank, the complexity of its financial operations, and the interconnection with other financial institutions on the interbank market.

Several international authorities such as the Basel Committee for Banking Supervision, the European Banking Authority or the European Central Bank (ECB), have taken the initiative and made important steps in elaborating guidelines and roadmaps focused on charting good bank governance.

The most comprehensive guideline is the one proposed by the Basel Committee on Banking Supervision (2015) which defines and explains a set of governance principles. It is highlighted the crucial intermediating role performed by banks within the economy, which makes corporate governance a critical issue in the safe and sound functioning of the banking sector. In the spotlight are large banks, playing a significant role in the financial system, whose governance weaknesses may trigger a spillover of their intrinsic, idiosyncratic vulnerabilities across the banking sector and the economy as a whole. The guideline explicitly mentions that the implementation of these principles should be adapted to the size, complexity, structure, economic significance, risk profile and business model of the bank or the financial group it belongs to. Systemically important banks need to implement corporate governance structure which is adequate with their potential impact on national and global financial stability.

At European Union level, the European Banking Authority has been mandated by the European Commission to develop guidelines in order to further harmonize financial institutions' internal governance mechanisms. The requirements within the 2017 EBA guidelines on internal governance entered into force in June 2018.

In order to comply with the principle of proportionality when tailoring the structure of the management board, it is proposed a comprehensive set of criteria to be taken into account, such as: institution's size in terms of the balance-sheet total; internal organization and nature of business activity; the complexity of its activities; the risk strategy, risk appetite and actual risk profile; whether the institution is listed on a stock exchange or not; the ownership and funding structure; the existing information technology (IT) systems; the geographical presence of the institution and the size of its operations in each jurisdiction. It is emphasized that large, significant financial institutions should have in place more sophisticated governance arrangements than smaller, less complex ones.

Lautenschläger (2018) outlines that management bodies' strategic decisions have to be always rooted in a sound analysis of risks, to guarantee bank's resilience. Although there will be always a trade-off between profit making and risk management, failures recorded by a bank in any of the two issues will trigger bank insolvency. The author emphasizes a board professional quality request, meaning that board members have to be experts on a particular area of activity, so that their collective knowledge is balanced and comprehensive.

Nouy (2018) stresses that good governance relies on good, sustainable decisions and brings into discussion a controversial issue, namely the appropriate, sufficient number of board members. Larger boards are prone to less fruitful, sensible debates and to the difficulty of reaching a consensus especially in times of crisis when there is little time to take sound decisions.

In complementing the above mentioned views made by the European Central Bank representatives, ECB has issued in mid-2017 a "Guide to fit and proper assessment" which mentions five key criteria to be used for assessing the appropriateness of banks' management body, from a supervisory authority perspective: (i) experience; (ii) reputation; (iii) conflicts of interest and independence of mind; (iv) time commitment; and (v) collective suitability.

The Financial Stability Fund in Greece has issued in early 2018 a guideline meant to improve Greek systemic banks' management board selection and nomination policies. The rationale for these guidelines reside in the belief that transparent, formal selection process will contribute to regaining stakeholders' trust in large banks' business and will improve boards' effectiveness. Before any appointment of new board members, the bank has to review its medium-term strategic objectives, its risk appetite, and the business environment new challenges so as to align the skills and competencies of the new board with these new developments in the banking business.

The analysis to be performed in this chapter gravitates around the specific features of the management boards which are leading the activity of Global Systemically Important Financial Institutions (GSIFIs) and is structured on two research questions:

i) is there a common, similar pattern regarding the composition of GSIFIs management boards? and ii) what is the impact of bank management board's composition (in terms of board size, number of women holding a position within the board, number of independent board members) on bank's financial performance?

A novel feature of this research resides in performing the empirical analysis on a sample of financial institutions comprising only representative European banks, which are included by the European Banking Authority into the GSIFIs category. These large scale banks, with complex, cross-jurisdictional financial activity are subject to enhanced prudential monitoring and systemic riskiness assessment. Therefore, their internal corporate governance model, with emphasis on the management board, gains an utmost importance and has to be strong and reliable. Banks' management board is ultimately responsible for the proper conduct of the banking business, in the benefit of shareholders, employees and public interest. Its specific responsibilities reside in defining and monitoring the implementation of the strategic vision and mission, in configuring bank's risk profile and its risk tolerance, in risk management and controlling, by complying with all prudential regulations issued by supervisory authorities as well as bank's internal rules.

Also, existing studies focusing on a European perspective of banks' corporate governance are still scarce, mainly country-level studies, and they do not address simultaneously issues related to board size, board independence and board gender diversity.

This research will involve quality information-gathering, by relying on financial data and corporate model features collected from 29 GSIFIs annual reports, and will employ a mix of statistical methods (Cluster Analysis, panel data regression). The remainder of the chapter is structured as follows: section 1 briefly synthesizes the findings of previous studies in the field, section 2 presents the methodology used for investigating the first research direction and the results obtained, section 3 explains the second research assumption, the specific methodology employed and the findings, while the last section concludes.

LITERATURE REVIEW

The impact of management board structure on banking profitability has been investigated by several authors. Stančić et al. (2014) performed a comprehensive study on 74 banks operating in South-Eastern European countries during 2005-2010 and found a negative relationship between board size and bank profitability. The share of independent members in total board members is too negatively-related to bank profitability, but it is not statistically significant. Bank size is also an important determinant of profitability. The same negative relationship between board size and performance, measured as return on equity, had been obtained by Conyon and Peck (1998) after empirically examining five European countries, and by Guest (2009). The latter found that this negative influence is stronger in the case of large institutions, which hold larger boards. The author attributes this result to the weak performance and effectiveness recorded by large boards, due to communication problems and lack of complementary competencies in the decision-making process.

Mamatzakis and Bermpei (2015) investigated 23 US investment banks and found a negative relationship between board size and various performance indicators (ROA, operating income, profit efficiency). This result holds too for US bank holdings (Pathan and Faff, 2013). In addition, the presence of independent members is in negative relation with ROA, ROE, and operating income while women involvement in the board generates a positive, although weak impact on performance indicators.

On the other hand, Andres and Vallelado (2008) explain that excessively independent boards might decrease the efficiency of bank governance, as they may lack the in-depth knowledge of the banking business and risks. Tanna et al. (2011) examined this topic for UK banks. Their findings outlined that larger boards' size and an increased share of independent members in total board's members exert a positive contribution towards improving banking efficiency.

Another similar study belongs to Agoraki et al. (2010) which have investigated a sample of 57 large European commercial banks over the period 2002-2006. As opposed to other empirical evidence, they uncovered a negative relationship between banks' efficiency and both board size and the number of independent, non-executive directors.

Belkhir (2009) tested the influence exerted by five governance characteristics (insider ownership, block holder ownership, the proportion of outside directors, board leadership structure and board size) on banking performance, for a sample of 260 banks and savings-and-loan holding companies. The findings indicated statistically significant relationships with banking performance, but also the presence of interdependencies between the board and bank ownership structures. Westman (2011) found a positive relationship between bank board and profitability for a sample of European banks.

These mixed, apparently conflicting results which gravitate around board size might be explained by relying on the findings of Andres and Vallelado (2008). They document the presence of a trade-off between the advantages and disadvantages of having a larger board size, claiming that the upper limit which ensures good governance, efficiency and returns is of around 19 directors.

A series of interesting conclusions has been provided by García-Olalla and Clifton (2018). The authors claim that larger board size is not always a feature of large banks and that banks holding large boards before the 2008 financial crisis didn't exhibit better performance during the crisis. Banks with complex activity need to design a large enough board, in order to ensure the proper combination of independent members and inside, executive members. Another finding points no statistical relationship between board size and profitability (ROE), either before or after the crisis.

Few other studies focused on the relationship between board members' knowledge and professional experience and banking development. For instance, Hau and Thum (2009) studied 29 largest German banks and uncovered that weak management and financial expertise exposes banks to higher losses. Berger et al. (2014) argues that the presence of board members with a PhD degree contributes to lowering the portfolio risk meanwhile increased presence of women and decreases of the average board age are significantly increasing the portfolio risk. In the same fashion, the educational level of the CEO positively influences bank return-on-assets performance for US large banks listed to the stock exchange (King et al. 2016). Bernile et al. (2018) noticed that greater board diversity is compatible with efficient innovation processes and broader investments in research and development of the business.

EXPLORING THE RESEMBLANCE PATTERNS OF BOARDS' COMPOSITION

The first research question aims at uncovering whether there are similarities in GSIFIs management board structure, or on the contrary, whether there is presence of heterogeneity. It will be considered three indicators of the intrinsic features exhibited by the board of directors' composition, namely: board size, the number of women holding a position within the board, and the number of independent board members. The list of the 29 GSIFs monitored by the European Banking Authority and included in the analysis is presented in Table 1 below.

A first insight into the statistical features of management boards' structure is provided by the analysis of basic descriptive statistics (see Table 2).

Standard deviation provides important information on the homogeneity pattern of the time series. The lower its values, the most homogenous are the time series. The number of board members and the number of independent members record the largest values of standard deviation, meaning that raw data is scattered around the mean and extreme values (larger or smaller) are more frequent. The number of women in management boards is less volatile. The maximum and minimum values provide a picture on the range of variation of these variables. All the three variables

Table 1. Global systemically important financial institutions

Country	GSIFIs Name
Austria	ERSTE Bank
Belgium	KBC
Denmark	Danske Bank
France	BNP Paribas, Credit Agricole, SocieteGenerale, BPCE
Germany	Bayern LB, Commerzbank, Deutsche Bank, LBBW
Italy	Intesa San Paolo, Unicredit
Netherlands	ABN AMRO, ING Bank, Rabobank
Norway	DNB
Spain	Santander, BBVA, La Caixa, Sabadell
Sweden	Nordea, SEB, Handelsbanken, Swedbank
UK	Barclays, HSBC, RBS, Standard Chartered

Source: http://www.eba.europa.eu/risk-analysis-and-data/global-systemically-important-institutions/2017

Table 2. Descriptive statistics of board's features

	Board Size (Number of Total Members)	Number of Women	Number of Independent Members
Mean	12.37	2.66	5.04
Median	13	2	6
Maximum	25	9	15
Minimum	4	0	0
Std. Dev.	4.77	2.16	4.88
Skewness	0.36	0.51	0.20
Kurtosis	2.58	2.46	1.51
Observations	312	312	312

Source: author, based on Eviews software package

are following a close to normal distribution function. This pattern is suggested by the closely-related values recorded by the mean and median statistics, as well as by the skewness and kurtosis. All the three-time series are platikurtic, being flatter than the normal distribution. In addition, there is also presence of positive asymmetry as indicated by skewness level. It means that the sample of observations is dominated by larger values of the three variables.

The most appropriate method for the purpose of the empirical research is the Hierarchical Cluster Analysis, a statistical technique designed to identify natural similarities within a larger dataset of indicators and create homogenous groupings (clusters) of banks, that otherwise aren't obvious.

The starting point of a hierarchical clustering is to define a clustering linkage method and a measure for calculating distance between two clusters, in order to allow resembling GSIFIs (from the standpoint of board features) to successively merge into the same group. The reasoning at the core of the clustering process is simple and intuitive: banks sharing similar board features should belong to the same group meanwhile those with different, apart features should be included in distinct clusters. Thus, this method benefits from increased flexibility in identifying resembling clusters. The computational peculiarities and algorithms make this method unsuitable for further extrapolations of results to the entire population, as is it the case for regression analyses. This is why Neri et al. (2017, p.81) claim that, due to specific evolutions over time, cluster analysis should be repeated over successive time frames in order to assess and compare the development path of every bank as well as the dynamics of this process.

The first distance metric, used to compute the resemblance between individual banks, is the Squared Euclidean distance. Its interpretation is straightforward and intuitive: the higher its level, the more pronounced the dissimilarities between banks, in terms of boards' structure, and hence increased heterogeneity among GSIFIs at European level. The proximity between two individual banks is computed with the formula:

$$\text{Squared Euclidean distance} = \sum_{i=1}^{n} \left(pi - qi\right)^2,$$

where p_i and q_i $(i = 1, \ldots n)$ are two points in the Euclidean n-space

The second distance metric, also called linkage rule is used in order to establish an inter-group resemblance pattern. The consequence is that resembling banks will be identified and merged together in the same group. The most emphasized distance metric is Ward method, due to its ANOVA-like features which allow the computation of variance by minimizing within-cluster contribution to the overall variance of a given variable, or the equivalent of maximizing between-cluster contribution (Irac and Lopez, 2015, p.6).

Ward method employs a computational algorithm that joins two clusters based on the size of an error sum-of-squares criterion. In other words, it minimizes the within-group sum-of-squared-errors, while maximizing between-group variance.

The sum of squares by combining clusters A and B = $\frac{nA \times nB}{nA + nB}\left(cA - cB\right)^2$

where

nA and *nB* represent the number of banks in clusters *A* and *B,* respectively
cA and *cB* are the centers of the two clusters

The final outcome of cluster analysis is synthesized in a graphical form, called dendrogram (known also as tree-like diagram or hierarchical tree). It summarizes all the clusters determined through the successive computation of Squared Euclidean and Ward distances and is used for interpreting the results. As a rule of thumb, the lately a bank joins the hierarchical tree, the more dissimilar it is from the previous ones. To account for the highest degree of resemblance between banks' board features, the focus is on the clusters formed in the lowest distance interval (0-5), as depicted in figure 1, figure 2 and figure 3.

The clustering algorithm has been run distinctly for each year of interest: 2008 - marking the financial crisis onset, 2012 – a post crisis period, witnessing the strengthening of European supervisory regulatory and institutional framework, and 2017 to account for the most recent available data. The findings indicate how the boards' structure has changed in each of the three years considered and how many GSIFIs exhibit a similar management board structure. The graphical clustering identified for the year 2008 is illustrated in Figure 1.

To increase the understandability of clusters' specific peculiarities, one has to rely on raw variables' values at end-2008. The 2008 clustering exhibits the following characteristics:

- GSIFIs included in the first cluster depict the lowest number of board members from the entire sample of banks, ranging between 5 and 9, while both the number of women and of independent members equals zero. These banks are the worst in terms of board diversity, the decision making in concentrated in the hands of few members, which also hold executive positions within the bank;
- the second cluster comprises those GSIFIs witnessing the second-largest values in the sample for all the three board features;
- the third one gathers GSIFIs recording a high number of board members, a good presence of women in the boards (maximum 5), but no independent members;

Figure 1. GSIFIs' clustering in 2008
Source: author, by using SPSS software

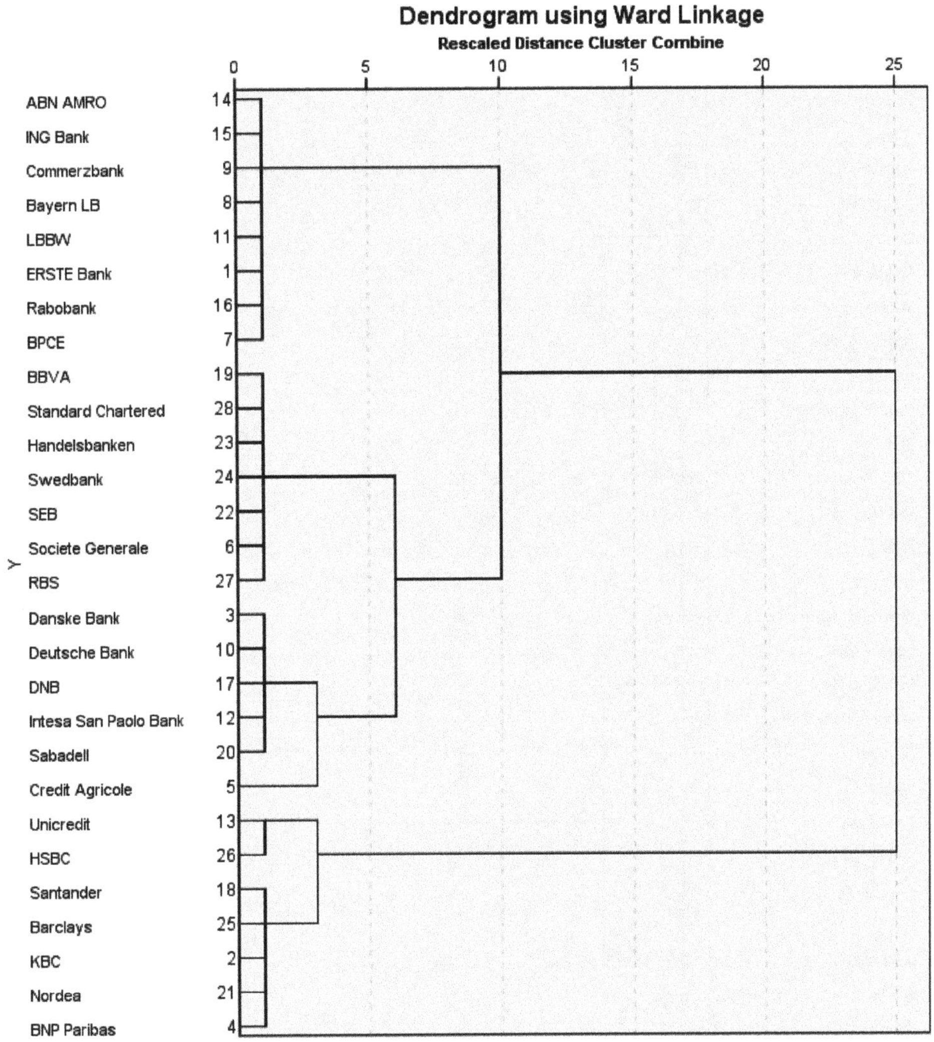

- the last cluster joins those banks exhibiting the highest number of board members, the same good involvement of women in the boards (maximum 5), and the highest number of independent members (between 9 and 15). GSIFIs in this group act as proponents of a diversity policy in terms of gender balance, and professional experience achieved both in-house and within other financial institutions.

Figure 2. GSIFIs' clustering in 2012
Source: author, by using SPSS software

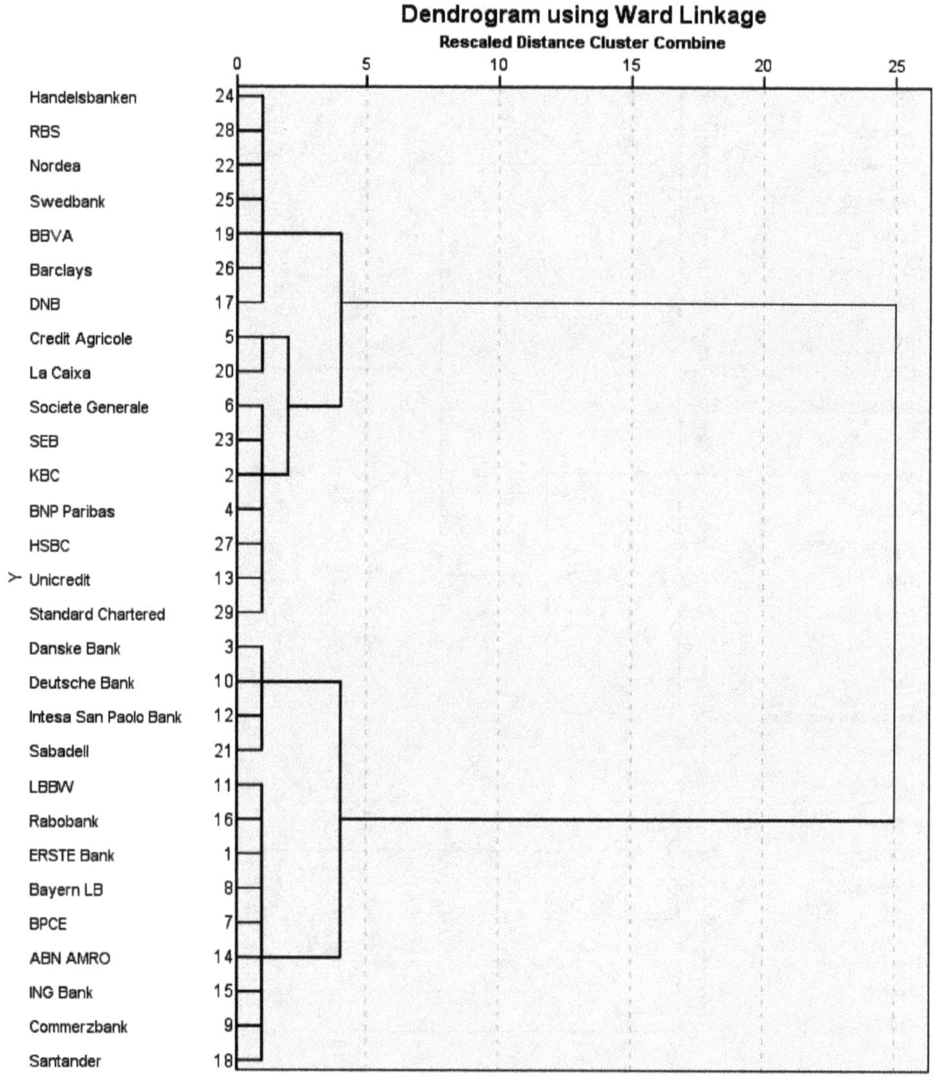

As regards the pattern of resemblance recorded by the management board indicators at end-2012, a first observation is related to the decrease of clusters' number to only 2 big ones. This finding suggests the presence of a convergence process towards more similar boards' composition. GSIFIs included in the first cluster depict the highest number of board members (between 11 and 24), the presence of most women (between 2 and 7) and of most independent members (between 6 and 13) in the board.

Figure 3. GSIFIs' clustering in 2017
Source: author, by using SPSS software

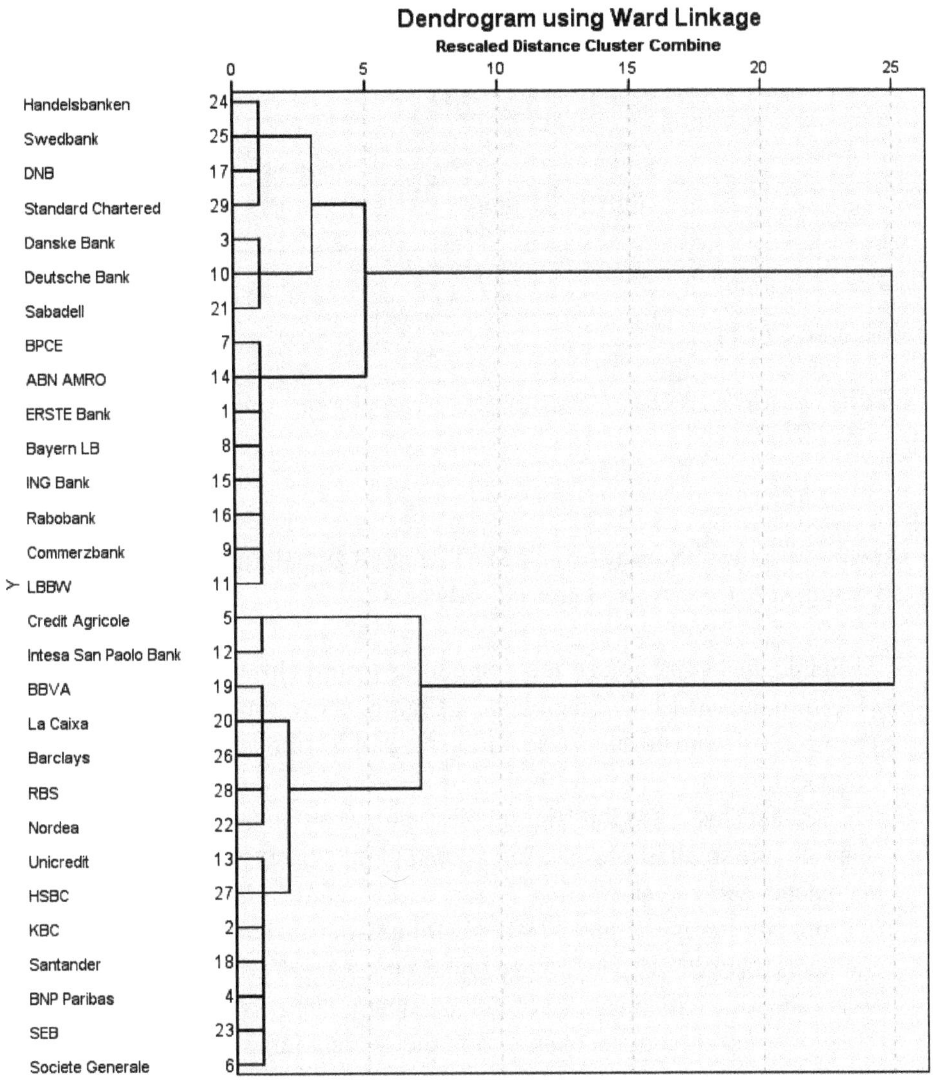

The second big cluster gathered those systemic banks recording the lowest values for all the three variables. There are still banks exhibiting no woman or independent member in their board.

Table 3. Estimation results

Independent Variables	Dependent Variables			
	ROE	**Net Interest Income**	**Net Fee Income**	**Net Trading Income**
	Model 1	**Model 2**	**Model 3**	**Model 4**
Board size	-0.026 (0.017)	0.007 (0.009)	0.014 (0.012)	0.007 (0.026)
Share of women	-0.017 (0.037)	-0.094 *** (0.02)	-0.057** (0.026)	0.124** (0.056)
Independent members	0.069*** (0.017)	0.054 *** (0.009)	0.060*** (0.012)	0.098 *** (0.025)
Bank size (log Total assets)	0.340*** (0.032)	1.498*** (0.017)	1.307*** (0.022)	0.987*** (0.046)

Notes: *** significant at 1 percent; ** significant at 5 percent; * significant at 10 percent; standard errors depicted in parentheses

Source: author, based on Eviews software package

At end-2017 the clustering revealed an increased granularity of systemic banks' board features, as there were identified 4 clusters:

- Systemic banks that joined the first cluster record close to sample's average (11.86) number of board members, a slightly above sample's average (3.62) presence of women and close to average (4.83) presence of independent members;
- The second cluster exhibits the smallest number of board members (between 4 and 8), the smallest presence of women in the board (between 0 and 2) and no independent member;
- The third cluster is composed by banks witnessing the largest number of board members (between 19 and 23), the highest presence of women (between 7 and 9) but the lowest involvement of independent members (between o and 2);
- The last cluster gathers banks with the second-largest number of board members (between 13 and 17), the second-largest number of women in the board and the highest number of independent members (between 8 and 13).

By summing up all the findings, it can be concluded that 10 years after a turmoil period generated by the 2008 financial crisis, systemic banks have returned to their specific governance features, which are closely resembling at end-2008 against end-

2017. Some of them have experienced changes (both increases and decreases) in the total number of board members, respectively women and independent members' involvement in the boards, as the end-2012 findings indicate. It means that they were open to changes, to experiencing a novel governance model, with a different board structure to counteract the detrimental effects of the financial crisis and better shape bank's financial conduct.

By comparing the clusters' features in 2008 against 2017, it is obvious that most systemic banks are practicing an almost unchanged composition of their board. For instance, the minimalist board structure has been maintained unchanged over time by eight systemic banks (3 from Netherlands, 3 from Germany, one from France and another one from Austria). Credit Agricole and Intesa San Paolo Bank are the only systemic banks which kept the largest number of board members and women involved in the board but have no independent members. However, more systemic banks seem to adhere to a diversity policy in defining their board, as the number of banks witnessing close to sample's average or large values for all the three indicators has increased in 2017, compared to 2008.

ASSESSMENT OF BOARD STRUCTURE IMPACT ON FINANCIAL PERFORMANCE INDICATORS

The second research direction aims at uncovering whether systemic banks' financial performance is determined by the management board's features (board size, number of women in the board, number of independent members). To investigate this impact, it will be employed the panel regression method, as it allows gathering both the cross-section and the time dimension to simultaneous analyze all systemic banks in the sample.

The dependent variables will be represented by a set of banking performance proxies, such as: ROE, the net interest income, the net fee income, and the net trading income. The explanatory variables will be represented by the number of board members (in natural logarithm), the share of women nominated in the board of directors in the total board members, the share of independent board members in the total board members and a control variable represented by the natural logarithm of GSIFIs total assets. The analysis will cover a comprehensive time frame of 11 years (2007 - 2017).

The panel data regression has the following general structure:

$$D_{i,t} = a0 + a1B_{i,t} + a2W_{i,t} + a3I_{i,t} + a4C_{i,t} + \delta_i + \theta_t + \varepsilon_{i,t}$$

where D is the dependent variable represented by a given banking performance indicator, B is the number of board members (in natural logarithm), W stands for the share of women nominated in the board of directors in the total board members, I represents the share of independent board members in the total board members and C is a control variable for systemic banks' size represented by the natural logarithm of GSIFIs total assets. The δ_i is the unobservable bank-specific (cross-section) effect and θ_t is the time-specific effect, with time periods $t = 2007 \ldots 2017$, and banks $i= 1,2,\ldots,29$ while $\varepsilon_{i,t}$ is the classical disturbance term.

We run 4 panel regressions, by changing each time only the dependent variable. Each regression had been tested for the presence of fixed effects in terms of both period effects and cross-section effects. All of them show no fixed effects, so the null hypothesis of a common intercept for all banks in the sample can be accepted and regressions have been estimated with the Pooled Least Squares method. In order to exert an influence on performance indicators, the estimated coefficients of the explanatory variables have to be highly statistically significant. The goodness-of-fit of the estimates has been validated by applying the White cross-section test. The previous model specifications have been re-estimated in order to check for the robustness of standard errors. The outcome of the regressions is summarized in Table 3.

Overall, results show that an increasing number of independent members in banks' boards, as well as expansions of banking activity (measured by means of total assets increases) are always highly statistically significant and exert a positive influence on each of the four financial performance indicators. This finding supports the view of involving a sufficient number of independent members in the decision-making process. The reasons are related to the fresh perspective they can bring, the power of challenging and influencing the decisions of non-independent board members. The increased diversity of opinions may counteract the risk of group thinking (Lautenschläger, 2018).

At the opposite is the total number of boards' members, whose effect is always non-significant from a statistical viewpoint. Hence, there is no direct, quantifiable effect on banking profitability coming from this variable. Moreover, the number of board members might be of importance from the standpoint of the quality and reliability of decisions taken for ensuring banking going concern and future development. The presence of women in large banks' boards determines a positive influence on the net trading income, and a negative impact on banks' regular, basic sources of revenues, namely net interest income and net fee and commission income. This result is in line with the findings of Berger et al. (2014) which claim that increases in board gender diversity are associated with increases of the portfolio risk arising from transactions with financial assets and liabilities.

CONCLUSION

Economic literature in the field as well as international and European organizations and financial professionals agree that there is no one-size-fits-all recipe for building a "perfect" board. Each bank has to design its own board management structure, in terms of appropriate size, diversity and composition (independent versus executive members, gender balance, and complementarily competencies) so as to increase its effectiveness and avoid the group thinking phenomenon. The recently developed guidelines by renowned and reputed institutions (Basel Committee on Banking Supervision, ECB, European Banking Authority) serve as a starting point in configuring the governance structures of the future.

The consensus arises when thinking of future bank board's features and challenges to be encountered. Both regulatory and supervisory authorities are aware and emphasize that the structure of banks' managing bodies is a key driver of future financial stability. The economic, social and technological environment is changing with a fast pace and the banking business has to adapt and even to implement these changes in its regular activity. Consequently, there is of utmost importance that bank managing bodies be prepared for this evolution, by holding appropriate, updated skills and expertise and revising them regularly.

The research conducted within this chapter adds to the existing literature in the field by providing answers at two research questions, by focusing exclusively on the managing board's features depicted by large, systemically important banks in EU. The findings indicated that an increased presence of women and of independent, non-executive members in GSIFIs managing board exhibits a significant impact on their performance indicators, while board size is not significant.

As regards the intrinsic characteristics of the managing board (board size, the number of women holding a position within the board, and the number of independent board members), there is presence of heterogeneity across systemic banks, which persisted over the timeframe considered. Some banks are proponents of a minimalist board size, with no or poor involvement of women and independent members, while others have in place a big board size, with increased presence of gender diversity and independent members.

REFERENCES

Agoraki, M.-E. K., Delis, M. D., & Staikouras, P. K. (2010). The effect of board size and composition on bank efficiency. *International Journal of Banking, Accounting and Finance*, *2*(4), 357–386. doi:10.1504/IJBAAF.2010.037155

Basel Committee on Banking Supervision. (2015). *Guidelines: Corporate governance principles for banks*. Author.

Belkhir, M. (2009). Board structure, ownership structure and firm performance: Evidence from banking. *Applied Financial Economics*, *19*(19), 1581–1593. doi:10.1080/09603100902967561

Berger, A. N., Kick, T., & Schaeck, K. (2014). Executive board composition and bank risk taking. *Journal of Corporate Finance*, *28*, 48–65. doi:10.1016/j.jcorpfin.2013.11.006

Bernile, G., Bhagwat, V., & Yonker, S. (2018). Board diversity, firm risk, and corporate policies. *Journal of Financial Economics*, *127*(3), 588–612. doi:10.1016/j.jfineco.2017.12.009

Conyon, M. J., & Peck, S. I. (1998). Board size and corporate performance: Evidence from European countries. *European Journal of Finance*, *4*(3), 291–304. doi:10.1080/135184798337317

de Andres, P., & Vallelado, E. (2008, December). Corporate governance in banking: The role of the board of directors. *Journal of Banking & Finance*, *32*(12), 2570–2580. doi:10.1016/j.jbankfin.2008.05.008

European Banking Authority. (2017). *Guidelines on internal governance under Directive 2013/36/EU*. Available at https://eba.europa.eu/documents/10180/1972987/Final+Guidelines+on+Internal+Governance+%28EBA-GL-2017-11%29.pdf

European Central Bank. (2017). *Guide to fit and proper assessment*. Author.

García-Olalla, M., & Clifton, J. (2018). *Contemporary Issues in Banking: Regulation, Governance and Performance*. Palgrave Macmillan Studies in Banking and Financial Institutions. doi:10.1007/978-3-319-90294-4

Guest, P. M. (2009). The impact of board size on firm performance: Evidence from the UK. *European Journal of Finance*, *15*(4), 385–404. doi:10.1080/13518470802466121

Hau, H., & Thum, M. (2009). *Subprime Crisis and Board (In-)Competence: Private vs. Public Banks in Germany*. CESifo Working Paper Series No. 2640; ECGI - Finance Working Paper No. 247/2009. Available at SSRN: https://ssrn.com/abstract=1360698

Hellenic Financial Stability Fund. (2018). *Guidelines on the Board of Directors' selection and appointment process in Greek Systemic Banks*. Author.

Irac, D., & Lopez, J. (2015). Euro area structural convergence? A multi-criterion cluster analysis. *International Economics*, *143*, 1–22. doi:10.1016/j.inteco.2015.01.005

King, T., Srivastav, A., & Williams, J. (2016). What's in an education? Implications of CEO education for bank performance. *Journal of Corporate Finance*, *37*, 287–308. doi:10.1016/j.jcorpfin.2016.01.003

Lautenschläger, S. (2018). *Good governance and the role of supervisory boards*. Member of the Executive Board of the ECB and Vice-Chair of the Supervisory Board of the ECB, Speech at the Luncheon of Chairs of Supervisory Boards of banks in Germany. Retrieved from https://www.ecb.europa.eu/press/key/date/2018/html/ecb.sp181106.en.html

Mamatzakis, E., & Bermpei, T. (2015). The effect of corporate governance on the performance of US investment banks. *Financial Markets, Institutions & Instruments*, *24*(2-3), 191-239.

Neri, L., D'Agostino, A., Regoli, A., Pulselli, F. M., & Coscieme, L. (2017). Evaluating dynamics of national economies through cluster analysis within the input-state-output sustainability framework. *Ecological Indicators*, *72*, 77–90. doi:10.1016/j.ecolind.2016.08.016

Nouy, D. (2018). *Good governance for good decisions*. Chair of the Supervisory Board of the ECB, Second banking supervision conference, "Governance expectations for banks in a changing financial environment", Frankfurt, Germany. Retrieved from https://www.bankingsupervision.europa.eu/press/speeches/date/2018/html/ssm.sp180322_1.en.html

Pathan, S., & Faff, R. (2013). Does board structure in banks really affect their performance? *Journal of Banking & Finance*, *37*(5), 1573–1589. doi:10.1016/j.jbankfin.2012.12.016

Stančić, P., Čupić, M., & Obradović, V. (2014). Influence of board and ownership structure on bank profitability: Evidence from South East Europe. *Economic Research-Ekonomska Istraživanja*, *27*(1), 573–589. doi:10.1080/1331677X.2014.970450

Tanna, S., Pasiouras, F., & Nnadi, M. (2011). The effect of board size and composition on the efficiency of UK banks. *International Journal of the Economics of Business, 18*(3), 441–462. doi:10.1080/13571516.2011.618617

Westman, H. (2011). The impact of management and board ownership on profitability in banks with different strategies. *Journal of Banking & Finance, 35*(12), 3300-3318. doi:10.1016/j.jbankfin.2011.05.013

KEY TERMS AND DEFINITIONS

Corporate Governance: A set of interdependent relationships established between bank's managing board, supervisory board, shareholders and stakeholders in order to meet bank's objectives.

Experience of Board Members: Comprises practical, professional experience gained in previous workplaces and theoretical experience (knowledge and skills) achieved through education and training.

Gender Diversity: The share held by women in the management board.

Independent Board Member: A non-executive member of the board who exerts no management responsibility within the bank.

Management Board: Responsible with establishing bank's strategy, objectives and risk appetite, and monitors the decision-making process throughout the business lines.

Risk Appetite: The aggregate level of all types of financial and non-financial risks a bank is willing to take on in order to achieve its strategic objectives and business plan.

Systemic Banks: Large-scale banks which have the potential to destabilize and disrupt the economy and financial system functioning, in case of failure.

Chapter 5
Effects of People's IPO on the Russian Financial Market and Corporate Governance Praxis

Dmitry Shevchenko
https://orcid.org/0000-0002-9758-4107
Southern Federal University, Russia

Parmenas Kimani Njoroge
Southern Federal University, Russia

ABSTRACT

People's IPO is a project that aims at distribution shares of state-owned entities to members of the public. Three Russian state-owned enterprises, VTB, SBERBANK, and ROSNEFT, conducted People's IPO between 2006 and 2007. The aim of these IPOs was to offer the general public an opportunity to own shares in state-owned enterprises. Such an investment opportunity would give ordinary citizens a stake in Russia's biggest state enterprises. Authors investigated the success or otherwise of these IPOs in distributing shares of government enterprises to ordinary citizens and gave recommendations on possible ways of improving public participation in People's IPOs. The aim of this chapter is to propose People's IPO as one of the ways of ensuring proper wealth distribution and eradicating injustice in the financial system. Authors recommend adoption of offer prices that friendly to small investors, creation of credit lines that would avail funds for investing in the IPOs. Companies going public should also adherer to the world's best to ensure growth in shareholders wealth.

DOI: 10.4018/978-1-5225-9607-3.ch005

INTRODUCTION

A state of fairness, justice and equity is most likely not obtainable in today's financial world as the main agents involved are egoistic and think only of their personal wellbeing. Proponents of fair markets may have to recheck their postulates to allow little intervention to reduce the rate at which hedge funds, payday lenders and offers of dubious financial products make astronomical and disproportionate profits from exploiting their clients. This chapter explores the effectiveness of these IPOs as a tool of wealth redistribution and recommends possible areas of improvement that would make such initiatives more beneficial to ordinary citizens. According to the Inclusive Development Index 2018 prepared by the World economic forum, Russia is ranked 19th among the emerging economies (World Economic Forum, 2018). Russians enjoy a decent standard of living compared to other emerging economies but the wealth inequality is high. Russia recorded a Gini index of 32, indicating that the wealth is concentrated in the hands of a few (World Bank, 2019). We are going to analyze the case of People's IPO in Russia to conclude proposed and real effects of this instrument on the Russian financial market as well as redistribution of wealth among the ordinary citizens. The authors will be taking a key interest on corporate governance since it creates investors' confidence thereby creating trust between shareholders and the management.

BACKGROUND

Initial public offering (IPO) is the sale of stock to the public for the first time. Before IPO, companies are either privately owned or owned by the state. Initial public offering is also referred to as Primary public offering (PPO). It is a way of raising capital for the company because money raised go directly to the company. If the company in the future decides to increase the number of outstanding shares by issuing more shares, this is called Secondary public offering SPO. PPO therefore refers to newly issued shares whereas SPO refers to an old issue. Both new and old issue can be offered at an IPO. At IPO both, new and old, meaning PPO+SPO, stocks can be included. IPO can offer a company an opportunity to raise additional funds for research and development, investment and growth as well as clearing debts. It is a good way of accessing foreign and domestic capital without paying interest. An IPO also creates brand awareness as investors get involved in the company's business and its future prospects. The company issuing shares is known as the issuer, it engages the services of an investment bank or an underwriter who acts as the intermediary between the company and the investors. He advises on the offer price, the number of shares to be offered the amount of money sought to be raised and the type of securities to be issued. Information about the company is compiled in a document known as the prospectus that details the company's growth prospects.

It is difficult to determine the offer price of IPO because shares start trading openly mostly only after IPO. Underwriters usually come up with an offer price that is lower than the market price of shares on the first day of trading. This is called underpricing. It allows traders to make a profit in the first days of trading. Many studies suggest that average IPO is underpriced (Aggarwal, Prabhala & Puri, 2002), (Loughran & Ritter, 2000).

The literature on underpricing IPO offers four basic theories of the determinants of underpricing. First, Allen and Faulhaber (1989), Grinblatt and Hwang (1989) and Welch (1989) argue that firms underprice their shares to signal their quality to the market. Later increase in price will give the firm a good name in the eyes of prospective investors. Raising prices due to previous underpricing allows the m to attract more capital in the future at more favorable rates. According to signaling theory, issuer companies, by the means of IPO with an undervalued stock, signal to investors about the financial health of their business. Informed investors are able to make a profit out of underpriced IPO because they can resell it at a higher price when the shares start trading.

Principal Agency theory of IPO underpricing also suggests that underwriters intentionally undervalue stock so that they can later get favors from informed investors.

According to litigation theory, underwriters intentionally underprice their shares to hedge against future liability. Many firms may underprice the shares to avoid future lawsuits which are likely to ruin its reputation. All material information is discussed in the prospectus to minimize the risk of future litigation and also minimize agency problem. The prospectus is a document that gives prospective buyers information such as business prospects of the company, biographies of officers and directors, any litigation affecting the company as well as any other material disclosure that may affect the future of the firm. Under many jurisdictions, it's mandatory to register the prospectus with security market authorities, to ensure it complies with laws governing disclosure. Laws governing disclosure depend on the jurisdiction in question. In the USA, The Securities Acts of 1933 and 1934 give investors the right to bring a lawsuit against an IPO firm for material untruths or omissions in the prospectus and provide guidelines for the calculation of associated damages. Ibbotson (1975) and Tinic (1988) hypothesize that underpricing represents a form of insurance against future litigation.

The information asymmetry theory assumes that the IPO pricing is a product of information disparities. Informed investors are able to distinguish stock that will make a profit from that which will not. Informed investors only invest in bids that are likely to make a profit whereas uninformed investors lack information to make this distinction. Underwriters therefore need to attract uninformed investors and one way of appealing to them is by undervaluing the IPO. Underpricing is lower when information about a stock is freely available and uninformed investors are not at a disadvantage.

While literature suggests that most companies are underpriced when undertaking IPO, any responsible corporate manager will ensure that the shares are well priced to avoid litigation afterward. good corporate governance will also ensure sound financial decisions that will ensure shareholders wealth is safeguarded. According to Williamson (1984), corporate governance is the institution that coordinates the interests of managers and shareholders. Good corporate governance protects shareholders investments and ensures the growth of shareholders wealth (Darani, 2012). A study by Black et al. (2006) found a correlation between corporate governance rating and market value of Russian companies. Good corporate governance would therefore ensure increase in share prices after the IPO. Although Russia has made significant strides towards better corporate governance to attract foreign capital, adherence to high code of ethics is till uneven among Russian companies including those involved in IPOs (Puffer & McCarthy, 2012).

Literature in many countries suggests that IPO can provide a golden opportunity for wealth creation to ordinary citizens (Kupor, 2013). For example, Microsoft went public in 1986 at roughly a $500 million market cap. In 2019, it has a market cap of $830.23 billion. The shares at IPO traded at $21 per share while in February 2019 the same shares traded at $108.22. Facebook went public in 2012 with a market capitalization of $104 billion. At the face value, IPO is a golden opportunity for citizens to invest in shares and create wealth. But is this always the case? The main buyers of shares in IPO are institutional investors as well as private individuals. Institutional investors include banks, hedge funds, pension funds, insurance companies, mutual funds etc. We investigate the IPO experience in Russia and its effectiveness as a tool of wealth distribution to ordinary Russians.

Economic Environment of Russian IPO Market

Most companies go public when equity demands cannot be satisfied by private investors. It gives an opportunity to raise additional funds for research and development, growth as well as servicing debts.

Russian financial market is now fully developed with over 100 companies trading daily on Moscow Stock Exchange. Its market capitalization makes it among the top 30 largest security exchange in the world. The first domestic IPO in Russia was conducted by RBC Information Systems in 2002. Development of Russian IPO market has been facilitated by numerous amendments in the legal and regulatory framework that has put Russian IPO regulations in line with the world best practice and made the process easy and straight forward.

People's IPO is a government program where shares of a state-owned corporation are sold to an unlimited number of persons. The main objectives of people's IPO are to give ordinary citizens an opportunity to buy shares in a state-owned enterprise, encourage investment culture among the general populace as well as creation and redistribution of wealth. People's IPO can also encourage savings and investment among the public and stir growth in developing economies. Russian financial market has experienced immense growth since 2004. In 2006 state oil company Rosneft made history when it raised 10.4 billion U.S. dollars in its IPO.

Russia has undergone numerous reforms since the dissolution of the Soviet Union. Before the 1990s, the average income of the top 1% not more than 4%-5% higher than that of an ordinary soviet citizen. Currently the ratio has changed to over 20% with Russia being one of the countries with the highest income disparities. The country adopted various economic reforms in 1990's shifting from a centrally planned economy to market economy. Most state-owned companies started to sell shares to private investors, the result was a rise in a class of new class of oligarchs under what was known as the loan for shares scheme, that transferred ownership of state companies to well politically connected oligarchs, at the detriment of the general population. Ordinary citizens continued to face economic problems such as unemployment and inflation. Russia's richness in natural resources endowment coupled with sound financial management has seen a significant rise in the standard of living of Russian citizens, and a recovering economy. In 2006, the government started privatization of state-owned companies aiming at transferring shares to the ordinary citizens. The problem of income inequality in Russia has also been accelerated by the flat taxation rate of 13% regardless of income levels. This means tax constitute a greater proportion of the poor's salary compared to their wealthy counterpart. A progressive tax system would take tax revenue from the rich and redistribute it to the poor through the provision of services. While this continues to be a heated debate among proponent and critics of both systems, it's clear that a flat tax system reduces disposable income for the poor. People's IPO can be considered as one of the tools for solving the problem of unequal income and wealth distribution in Russia.

Three Russian companies, Rosneft, Sberbank, and VTB Bank carried out people's IPO between 2006 and 2007. Of the three, only VTB made a share buyback at the backdrop of government directive. Several restrictions were put in place to ensure that only shares purchased at the IPO could be repurchased by the bank. the value of shares purchased could not exceed 500000 rubles per shareholder. Taking into consideration cultural factors, many ordinary Russians are likely to reflect on the relationship between the government and the firm when making a decision to invest. A good relationship would indicate a low risk of government intervention or risk associated with new regulations.

Floating of Rosneft Shares in London and Moscow

Rosneft is the leader of the Russian oil industry and one of the largest publicly traded oil and gas companies in the world. The main activities of Rosneft are the exploration and production of oil and gas, the production of petroleum products.

Rosneft went public on the 14th of July 2006 and started trading on London stock exchange as well as on RTS and MICEX. As part of the IPO, 1,411 million shares were placed for a total of $ 10.7 billion. The shares placed included 1,126,357,616 ordinary shares of Rosneftgaz and 253,874,997 newly issued Ordinary Shares in the form of Global Depositary Receipt. The GRDs were placed in the international market and were prohibited from circulation in the Russian Federation during the initial placement. Rosneft IPO was the largest in Russia and fifth largest globally by the time of its conclusion.

According to Rosneft, four investors bought 49.4% of all issued shares. Now, Rosneft has foreign firm among its major shareholders: British Petroleum that bought shares worth $ 1 billion, Malaysian Petronas ($ 1.5 billion) and Chinese CNPC ($ 0.5 billion). The identity of the fourth investor is unclear. The IPO was also marked with the participation of Russian billionaires. In July 2006, 'Financial Times' reported underparticipation of institutional investors in the IPO arguing that a company with such great potential should have fascinated more institutional investors than those who showed interest in Rosneft IPO. According to some investors, the shares were highly priced in comparison to other Russian companies in the oil and gas sector. The Price-to-Earnings Ratio (P/E Ratio) of Rosneft was 17 at the time of the IPO whereas that of Lukoil was 9 (Financial Times. 2006). According to its prospectus, Rosneft's total revenues increased from USD 3.64 billion in 2003 to USD 5.28 billion in 2004 and to USD 23.95 billion in 2005. Rosneft's total revenues increased from USD 4.36 billion in the first quarter of 2005 to USD 7.52 billion in the first quarter of 2006. The prospectus also outlined litigation risk. Government interference through taxes, regulations and political influence was also noted to be one of the risks that may interfere with Rosneft future activities because the government can use its influence to force Rosneft to engage in activities that do not maximize shareholders wealth.

Rosneft shares started trading on 14th July 2006 at an offer price of USD 7.55 per share (around 203.9 Rubles). The shares appreciated to 243 Rubles in December 2006 and fluctuated between 2007 and 2008, dropping to as low as 106.3 rubles in November 2008. According to Rosneft, only 115000 ordinary citizens bought these shares. Between 2007 and 2008 when the shares were dropping during the global financial crisis investors who were quick to trade off their shares incurred loss. Many securities fluctuate after IPO before stabilizing. Investors in IPO usually have two strategies, long term or short term. Short term investors seek to sell off the shares as soon as they start appreciating, to investors who may have missed in the initial offering. This may have been a bad strategy between 2006 and 2009 when the shares were fluctuating. The second strategy was to wait for shares to appreciate, and thereby increase the share your wealth. A trader, who bought 170 shares for 34000 rubles in 2006, owns shares worth around 68000 rubles in 2019 (Figure 1). The shares have literally doubled. A long-term investor who bought shares worth 1 million rubles can now sell the same shares for 2 million rubles. This IPO was the best for the common man because it allowed people to buy shares at an affordable

Figure 1. Price of Rosneft shares from 2007 to 2019
(Tradingview, 2019a)

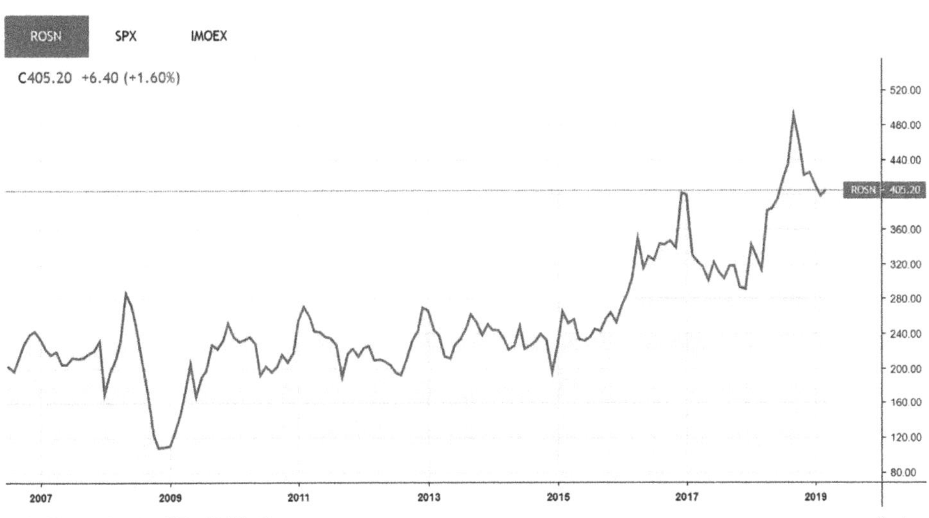

price, compared to Sberbank and other companies whose shares were too expensive at the initial public offer. In addition, the shareholder's wealth has appreciated by more than double.

The IPO raised $10.4bn which was an oversubscription, indicating investors' confidence in Rosneft's future prospect. However, according to Rosneft, 115000 ordinary Russian investors raised USD 750 million, in aggregate to become Rosneft shareholders. Although the share price has risen over the years above the offer price, many ordinary Russians are likely to have lost their investment if they sold their shares in the period between 2008 and 2009. In addition, the value of the ruble has depreciated by more than a half since 2014, making the market capitalization to be slightly less than it was during the IPO. Yahoo finance quotes the company to be worth $ 64.39919 billion in February 2014. Fall in global oil prices may have also contributed to this. Since only 115000 ordinary Russians purchased Rosneft shares and are likely to have sold them due to fluctuation of share during 2008 financial crisis, the impact of this IPO on wealth creation and redistribution is not significant. Despite this, Rosneft IPO was the good opportunities for ordinary citizens to create wealth if certain measures were put in place to increase their participation. Policies should be put in place to encourage citizen participation (buying and holding of shares). In addition, the Russian government stake at the company decreased from 100% to 75.5%. Rosneft's market capitalization at the IPO was USD 79.8 billion. About 50% of the issued stock was bought by four institutional investors as outlined above. This agrees with our hypothesis that IPO in Russia has not been an effective tool of wealth allocation and achieving financial inclusion. It therefore means that the government must come up with programs to ensure that such offers benefits ordinary Russians more than they do institutional investors.

The Initial Public Offering of Sberbank and the Aftermath

The main purpose of placing new shares was to increase equity capital in order to meet the capital adequacy standards set by the Central Bank of the Russian Federation. Due to growth and expansion, the bank needed to attract more equity so that the deposit equity ratio can be within set standard. The entrance of foreign banks in the Russian market increased competition prompting Sberbank to seek more capital for growth and investment. Sberbank held an IPO in February 2007. Initially, Sberbank planned to issue 3.5 million ordinary shares with a nominal value of 3 thousand rubles, which were to consist of 22.5 million ordinary shares and 50 million preferred shares. During the additional issue, the bank intended to attract 240 - 245 billion rubles. Shares were placed at a price of 89 thousand rubles per paper, 30,055 individuals and 188 legal entities became the new shareholders of the bank, the bank attracted 230 billion rubles. ($ 8.8 billion). In July 2007, the bank's shares were split up with a ratio of 1 to 1000; as a result, reducing the value of one share to 89 rubles. The minimum threshold to buy shares was too high and many ordinary Russian could not afford to participate in this exercise. The long application procedure also discouraged most foreigners from taking part in the IPO. This indicates that the Sberbank People's IPO couldn't be used as an effective tool for the distribution of wealth among the Russian population.

The bank ranked second in terms of placement among Russian issuers after Rosneft, which conducted an IPO in the summer of 2006. Shareholders bought 99.4% of their bids on preemptive rights, in conjunction with other investors, the proportion of bids realized was 95.6%

Sberbank shares have fluctuated over the years since the IPO. Today, the price of one share is about 94 rubles, which exceeds the cost of placement by only about 6%. At the same time, since the peak crisis value recorded in February 2009, Sberbank's share prices have increased more than six times - this is a record figure among Russian banks.

Since the announcement of IPO in October 2006, the price of Sberbank stock rose from 61.02 rubles in October 2006 to 96.31 rubles in 1st of February 2007. For the first time, the value of the bank's shares fell below the offering price on May 30, 2007, but then again exceeded 89 rubles, and on July 24, 2007, reached a maximum value of 113.05 rubles (27% higher than the initial price).

On the 8th of January 2008, the value of Sberbank's shares dropped below the offering price; following the results of the auction on 2nd of February 2009, it reached a minimum value of 13.5 rubles. (84% lower than the initial price). Many factors may have led to this, including the 2008 financial crisis. The decline of share price from 89 rubles in 2007 to around 13.5 rubles in 2009 indicates those who were not patient enough to wait for the appreciation of the shares incurred a huge loss. Strategic investors, as well as institutional investors who have access to the market information, are likely to have adopted a more informed strategy especially if they waited for the shares to appreciate before reselling them. The shares reached a peak of 274 rubles per share in February 2018. The shares have appreciated since the crisis, to a value of 208 Rubles as of 16th February 2019 (Figure 2).

Not only did Sberbank shares had a high minimum threshold for share purchase but also the share price largely fluctuated between 2007 and 2009 creating more possibilities for small scale investors to incur the loss. Given that only 30,055 individuals bought these shares, it's clear that this process left more resources and more control and voting rights in the hands of institutional investors. Sberbank's shares have considerably increased since the IPO and that qualifies it as a good opportunity for investors who buy and hold shares waiting for them to appreciate. Just like the Rosneft IPO, institutional investors made the largest investment. Value of 89000 rubles per share against very low average monthly salary among ordinary

Figure 2. Price of Sberbank shares from 2004 to 2019
(Tradingview, 2019b)

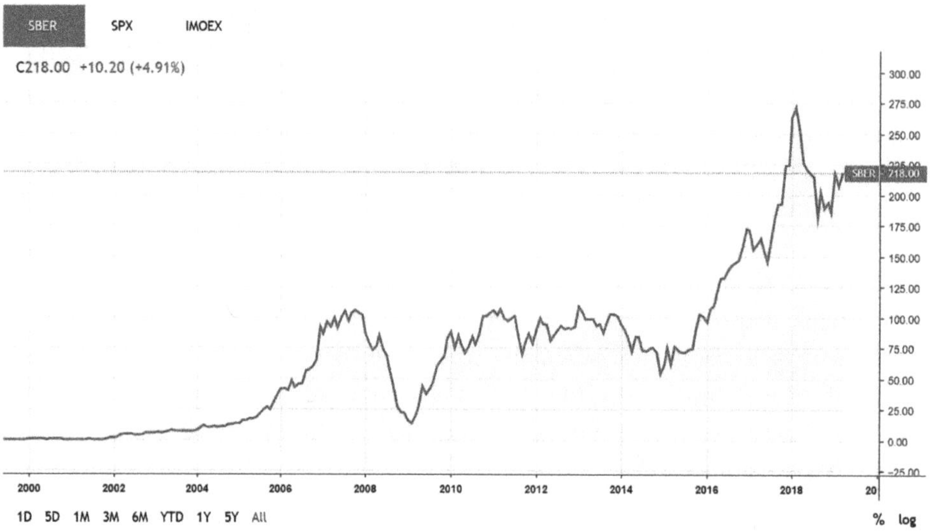

Russian might have contributed to the low participation of small investors. Lowering the minimum threshold for investment, making credit lines available for investment in stocks as well as campaigns to create public awareness can address this problem. The stock split was also wrongly timed because it happened in July 2007, after the IPO. This means both the employees of the bank and the ordinary citizens couldn't afford to buy these shares because the price was too high.

The Price Fluctuation of VTB Shares After IPO and Implication on Corporate Governance

VTB is the second largest bank in Russia in terms of assets and capital. In contrast to Sberbank, VTB mainly works with legal entities and actively meets the needs of its clients' foreign trade operations. The Bank has subsidiaries in Europe, the CIS countries, as well as in Asia and Africa.

Both Sberbank and VTB IPOs happened at a time when Russia was negotiating to enter into the world trade organization. Entry of foreign firms into the Russian market required local firms to increase their competitiveness. VTB undertook an IPO generate funds for growth and expansion, avail funds for lending in the real sector and also to open subsidiaries in the neighbouring CIS countries.

According to the head of VTB Andrei Kostin the bank was planning to invest the raised funds in the capital of subsidiary banks and the purchase of new banks. The funds were also used to expand operative operations in terms of lending to individuals and legal entities.

The IPO took place on the London Stock Exchange on May 17th 2007 at a price of 0.136 rubles ($ 0.00528) for one depositary receipt. VTB shares were admitted to the Moscow Exchange on May 28th. It should be noted that this figure is relatively low because shares of Sberbank, for example, were trading at 89 000 rubles a share when it went public and the share of Norilsk Nickel are priced at 14000 rubles in mid-March 2019. VTB sold 1.513 trillion new shares at a final price of 0.13 rubles for the Moscow listing and priced the global depositary receipts for its London quotation at $10.56, raising $8 billion (Reuters, 2007). VTB attracted sizeable participation from ordinary Russians. VTB reported that it sold $1.6 billion to 131,000 retail investors (Norton, 2007). Although this was the third People's IPO in Russia, it attracted more ordinary citizens than Sberbank and Rosneft. This is because of a massive advertisement campaign that was conducted to popularize the IPO. Placing of shares in both Moscow and London increased the number of investors. The duration for application was 4 weeks and the minimum threshold was only 30000 rubles. During the IPO, approximately 8.2 billion dollars were attracted, and VTB's capitalization with additional emission amounted to 36.7 billion dollars. 35% of the volume of placement of shares is placed in Russia, 65% in the form of GDRs abroad. Shortly after the IPO, the shares began to fall. In March 2009 (exactly two years after the VTB IPO), the American SP500 index sank by 50%, while the Russian RTS index by the end of 2008 has reduced its quotes by as much as four times. VTB shares fell nearly six times to 0.0233 rubles in the junction of 2008-2009. It has been over 17 years since VTB went public and the shares have never traded above the offer price. The price was below 0.04 rubles in February 2019 (Figure 3). And if, when calculating losses, we consider inflation, then the losses of minority shareholders significantly exceed half of the originally invested funds. Then there were several additional issues that were eroding the shares of shareholders. In the crisis year of 2009, when VTB suffered heavy losses, and stocks fell to historic lows to 0.02 rubles, the bank decided to issue more shares. The number of ordinary securities increased one and a half times, to 10,460 billion. Almost the entire issue was bought by the state, increasing its share to 85.5%. Shares of minority shareholders were naturally eroded. The transaction price was 0.0482 rubles per share, which at that time was higher than market quotes by about 12%.

VTB bank has struggled to increase the price of its shares above the IPO, prompting a presidential directive to undertake a share repurchase. In February 2012, the government ordered VTB to buy back the shares sold at the IPO, at the initial offer price of 0.136 rubles which above the market price.

Figure 3. Price of VTB shares from 2006 to 2019
(Tradingview, 2019c)

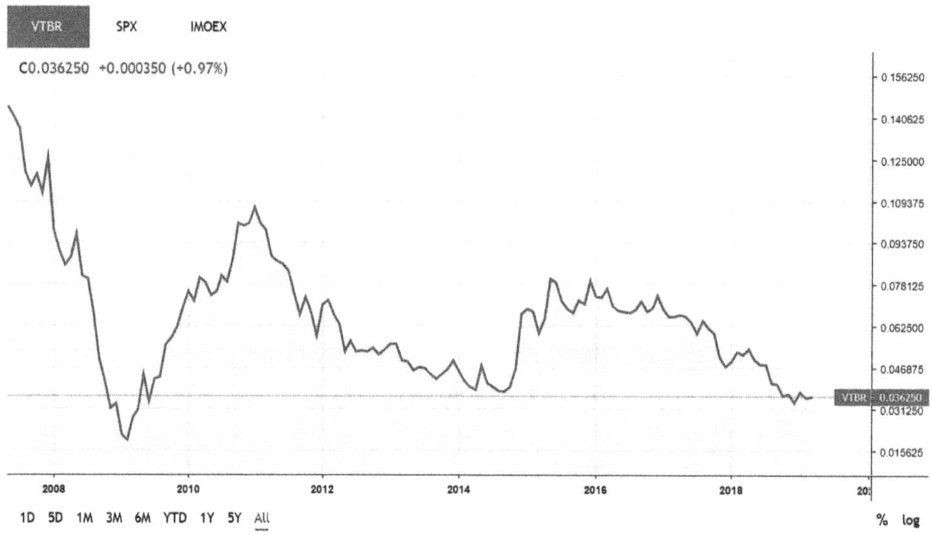

Ordinarily, a company buying back its own shares to reduce their circulation or to resell them in the future at a higher price. That is, firms buy shares when they are cheap, and buyback is a signal to the market that the company considers the market price of shares to be low. It is a signal to investors that the company considers the shares to be undervalued and are likely to be worth more in the future. Vermaelen (1981) documented positive abnormal returns upon an announcement of a buyback program. This is because investors believe that the company is sending a signal about the undervaluation of the shares and that the price is likely to increase in the future. The bank bought securities at a price substantially higher than the market. Given that this was a government directive, the buyback program is likely to caution investors of the existence of political interference risk that may hinder maximization of shareholder wealth. The shares traded at around 0.0361 rubles in March 2019 compared to the offer price of 0.13 rubles in 2007. Government interference in decision making of state-owned companies may caution investors that the investment is risky and that the firm may be forced to make economically illogical decisions in order to comply with directives of the state. Small scale investors may see shares in state-owned companies as risk-free because government intervention may mitigate possible fall in price in future.

Ordinarily, an investor takes to himself or herself all the risks of the company upon purchase of shares and therefore this intervention violates this market logic. This political interference in decision making processes poses another threat to corporate governance in Russia. The principles of "People's IPO" can be upheld if there is a regulatory framework to enforce its execution. If the ordinary man on the street is encouraged to partake in the financial sector, sustainable growth will be recorded for the benefit of all. The main objective of peoples IPO in many countries is to offer citizens a chance to own shares in big companies. It is also a saving and investment plan for ordinary citizens because these shares can be resold in future at a higher price. An IPO also helps companies to mobilize resources for future growth.

SOLUTIONS AND RECOMMENDATIONS

Considering the income disparity in Russia, it is prudent for the government to come up with ways of equitable wealth distribution to achieve social justice and correct previous injustices that have disadvantaged ordinary Russians. It is an unarguable fact that the wealth of nations is in the possession of just a few extremely privileged individuals and this poses serious economic and social problems to the wellbeing of these nations. The wealthy usually highly benefit from politically motivated decisions. A good example is the infamous loan for share scheme of the 1990s that saw the rise of a few wealthy Russians. Imbibing the tenets of 'People's IPO' into business practice can considerably help in solving the problem of wealth concentration and thus reduce social injustice.

Rosneft, Sberbank and VTB bank carried out people's IPO at initial share prices of 203.9, 93.0 and 0.136 rubles, respectively. In the beginning of January 2008, the shares dropped to 172.00, 87.80 and 0.0986, respectively. The prices fluctuated in 2008 and 2009 and started to appreciate in 2010. (Table 1). Only VTB bank carried out a share buyback among the three companies.

Table 1. Share prices of Rosneft, Sberbank and VTB after IPO investing (2019a), investing (2019a) investing (2019a)

Company	Initial share prices	Prices in January 2007	Prices in January 2008	Prices in January 2009	Prices in January 2010	Price in mid March 2019
Rosneft	203.9	234.70	172.00	111.18	236.25	401.25
Sberbank	93.0	86.5	87.80	16.4	88.41	203.55
VTB	0.136	n/a	0.0986	0.0220	0.0754	0.0374

From the information above it is clear that a great number of individuals purchased the right to vote and partake in the decision-making process of these big Russian companies. This not only gave the individuals the opportunity to make extra income from dividends but also enhanced their saving and investing capabilities, improved their psychological sense of belonging to a society and above all, helped the country build a strong and all-inclusive capital market.

This information shows that two of the three Russian companies which carried out "People's IPO" recorded a significant increase in stock price with time which is a win-win situation for both the stockholders and the companies.

On the other hand, VTB Bank lost value with time. It is noteworthy that the shareholders of VTB bank did not totally lose their investments because of a slight government intervention which made the management to buy back the shares at their initial value. This may have momentarily prevented loss of money by small investors but it sets a precedent that the government can intervene and force a buyback if shares fall drastically. The authors recommend minimal government intervention on the corporate affairs of firms. This can help to build investors' confidence and guarantee that only economically sound decisions will be undertaken. A clear policy should be adopted to set out penalties to be paid by management or the firm in case of drastic reduction its share prices after IPO. This clarity reduces risk, creates a good investment environment thereby reducing the cost of capital. In order to secure the interest of very small shareholders and hedge against the risk of a sudden fall in share price, regulations should be put in place to ensure that if the share price of a certain issuer falls too suddenly after a public offer, the management is obliged to buy them back at the initial price. This will make managements think fairly and avoid issuing overvalued shares. Management should also consider the timing of IPOs because bad timing can create a negative attitude among investors and make it impossible for the share prices to recover. VTB shares were issued in May 2007 and the global financial crisis picked up in 2008.

VTB attracted the highest number of small investors (131000) and raised the highest amount of money ($1.6 billion) (Table 2). This is as a result of vigorous advertisements and a low minimum threshold for VTB shares. However, in all the three IPOs, ordinary Russian contributed only a small percentage of total funds raised.

Although "People's IPO" is supposed to encourage individuals to cash in on the advantages of the stock market, big institutional investment houses unfortunately still control a major proportion of all stocks issued. Policies should be enacted by appropriate bodies to increase the proportion of stocks held by individuals. Policies should be put in place to encourage citizen participation (buying and holding of

Table 2. Ordinary citizens participation in IPO of Rosneft, Sberbank and VTB

Company	Number of Ordinary Russians Who Invested	Money Raised From Ordinary Russians	Total Raised
Rosneft	115000	$776 million	$10.4bn
Sberbank	30000	$ 540 million	$ 8.8 billion
VTB	131000	$ 1.6 billion	$8 billion

(Sergaev, 2019)

shares) in companies through programs such as "people's IPO" as it gives the citizenry a sense of belonging and help distribute the financial gains of companies among the general populace. Sberbank shares, for instance, were valued at 89000 rubles at the time of issue. This price can lock out a good number of ordinary Russians. The highest average monthly income historically was recorded in December 2018 at an average of 55150 RUB/Month. This implies that very few Russians had the means to participate in Sberbank IPO.

Authors also recommend that companies wishing to undertake people's IPO, should adopt the best corporate governance standards. From the IPO management team to the managers of the company, best management practices should be adopted to ensure rise in shareholders wealth. Management team should have depth of experience and expertise. Executive compensation should also be made so that managers and employees can have a stake at the company. This way, agency problem will be reduced, and managers will be more likely to make decisions that increase shareholders wealth.

Managers should also consider the type of shares being offered at the IPO, possibility of them being split up so that small investors can comfortably buy them. At the IPO, Sberbank shares were priced at 89000 rubles per share making it impossible even for employees of the company to take part in the IPO. The shares were later split into 1000 new shares per old share. This split would have been very useful at earlier time because many small-scale investors could afford this.

Researchers have documented a positive correlation between price of shares and dividend payouts (Khanal & Mishra, 2017). It is therefore imperative for companies to plan ahead of the IPO, so that they can comfortably pay dividends after the IPO.

Russia has made tremendous steps in streamlining IPO process and making it at par with the world's best practices. As a consequence, there has been a consistent growth in the Russian security market, with more and more foreign and domestic companies listing their shares on the Moscow Stock Exchange. However, there still remain some legislation that can assist in giving the general public a better chance in acquiring shares of government corporations or on privately owned companies. According to Joint Stock Companies Law (the JSC Law), all shareholders of a public joint-stock company have statutory pre-emptive rights to subscribe to the company's shares proposed to be issued to the ordinary citizens. This means that the shareholders have an upper hand in obtaining newly issued shares at the expense of the ordinary citizens.

CONCLUSION

This research concentrates on People's IPO by state-owned corporations and their effectiveness as a tool for addressing wealth inequality in Russia. Non-state-owned firms have also undertaken IPO and it would be prudent to investigate the effect of private companies IPOs on income distribution in Russia. While state companies are controlled by the government and sometimes face government/political interference, private companies are owned by individuals and influential families. Effect of ownership structure on corporate governance and its effect on share prices after IPO is also an interesting area of research. Authors also take note of an emerging trend whereby startups are getting opportunities to raise money from the stock market. Companies that started off as inventions of only a few groups of people become huge companies once they list their shares on the stock exchange and get access to capital. In the US, hedge funds and investment banks are competing with private investors as the preferred source of capital. It will be prudent to research on startup IPOs as a tool of wealth creation by the general populace.

The authors have noted that income inequality is a major challenge in Russia and it can be addressed by giving ordinary citizens an opportunity to take ownership in government-owned corporations through IPOs. The authors conclude that IPO should be priced fairly, to allow the ordinary citizens to take part. Policies should be put in place to ensure more public participation, including creating awareness and extending credit lines. IPO prospectus usually is many paged and contain a lot of technical terms that are not very clear to a layman. This should be summarized to few pages, with very simple language that can be understood by people without financial education. This will give investors opportunity to understand the nature of the business and future prospect. Corporate governance is an issue of big concern and companies going public should adhere to the best corporate governance practices before, during and after IPO to ensure shareholders wealth is protected. On the same note, a clear policy should be adopted to hedge against sudden fall in price. This will give all the players right on what to expect in case of a sudden fall in price. These policies can include buyback plans, in case of a sudden fall in price. Moreover, managers should take due diligence to ensure shares are not overpriced. Government interventions should be avoided in order to create investors confidence in the Russian financial market.

REFERENCES

Aggarwal, R., Prabhala, N. R., & Puri, M. (2002). Initial public offerings. *Journal of Management*, *40*, 1066–1089.

Allen, F., & Faulhaber, G. (1989). Signaling by underpricing in the IPO market. *Journal of Financial Economics*, *23*(2), 303–324. doi:10.1016/0304-405X(89)90060-3

Black, B. S., Love, I., & Rachinsky, A. (2006). Corporate Governance and Firms' Market Values: Time Series Evidence from Russia. *Emerging Markets Review*, *7*(4), 361–379. doi:10.1016/j.ememar.2006.09.004

Darani, E. H. (2012). Corporate Governance, IPO (Initial Public Offering) Long Term Return in Malaysia. *International Conference on Economics, Business and Marketing Management*, 29.

Financial Times. (2006). *Rosneft IPO fails to attract big players.* Retrieved February 10, 2019 from Financial times: https://www.ft.com/content/0781b0de-1366-11db-9d6e-0000779e2340

Grinblatt, M., & Hwang, C. Y. (1989). Signalling and the Pricing of New Issues. *The Journal of Finance*, *44*(2), 393–420. doi:10.1111/j.1540-6261.1989.tb05063.x

Ibbotson, R. (1975). Price performance of common stock new issues. *Journal of Financial Economics*, *2*(3), 235–272. doi:10.1016/0304-405X(75)90015-X

Investing. (2019a). *NK Rosneft PAO (ROSN).* Retrieved March 25, 2019 from https://www.investing.com/equities/rosneft_rts

Investing. (2019b). *Sberbank Rossii PAO (SBER).* Retrieved March 25, 2019 from https://www.investing.com/equities/sberbank_rts

Investing. (2019c). *VTB (VTBR).* Retrieved March 25, 2019 from https://www.investing.com/equities/vtb_rts

Khanal, A. R., & Mishra, A. K. (2017). Stock price reactions to stock dividend announcements: A case from a sluggish economic period. *The North American Journal of Economics and Finance*, *42*, 338–345. doi:10.1016/j.najef.2017.08.002

Kupor, S. (2013). *The US can battle wealth inequality by letting startups IPO earlier.* Retrieved February 10, 2019 from Quartz: https://qz.com/66371/us-can-battle-wealth-inequality-by-letting-startups-ipo-earlier/

Loughran, T., & Ritter, J. (2000). Uniformly least powerful tests of market efficiency. *Journal of Financial Economics*, *55*(3), 361–389. doi:10.1016/S0304-405X(99)00054-9

Norton, G. (2007). *Russia: VTB puts on a good show with $8 billion IPO.* Retrieved March 12, 2019 from Euromoney: https://www.euromoney.com/article/b13222cnkc8y08/russia-vtb-puts-on-a-good-show-with-$8-billion-ipo?copyrightInfo=true

Puffer, S. M., & McCarthy, D. J. (2012). Corporate governance and initial public offerings in Russia. In A. Zattoni & W. Q. Judge Jr., (Eds.), *Corporate Governance and Initial Public Offerings* (pp. 354–377). Cambridge, UK: Cambridge University Press. doi:10.1017/CBO9781139061513.016

Reuters. (2007). *Russia's VTB Raises $8 Billion in IPO, Shares Surge.* Retrieved March 13, 2019 from: https://www.cnbc.com/id/18607910

Sergaev, S. (2019). Placement of shares of banks: Sberbank and VTB. *Banking*, *6*, 40–43.

Tinic, S. (1988). Anatomy of initial public offerings of common stock. *The Journal of Finance*, *43*(4), 789–822. doi:10.1111/j.1540-6261.1988.tb02606.x

Tradingview. (2019a). *Rosneft Oil Co MOEX:ROSN.* Retrieved March 15, 2019 from https://www.tradingview.com/symbols/MOEX-ROSN/

Tradingview. (2019b). *Sberbank Co MOEX:SBER.* Retrieved March 15, 2019 from https://www.tradingview.com/symbols/MOEX-SBER/

Tradingview. (2019c). *VTB Co MOEX:VTB.* Retrieved March 15, 2019 from https://www.tradingview.com/symbols/MOEX-VTBR/

Vermaelen, T. (1981). Common stock repurchases and market signaling: An empirical study. *Journal of Financial Economics*, *9*(2), 139–183. doi:10.1016/0304-405X(81)90011-8

Welch, I. (1989). Seasoned offerings, imitation costs, and the underpricing of initial public offerings. *The Journal of Finance*, *44*(2), 421–450. doi:10.1111/j.1540-6261.1989.tb05064.x

Williamson, O. E. (1984). Corporate Governance. *The Yale Law Journal*, *93*(7), 1197–1230. https://digitalcommons.law.yale.edu/fss_papers/4392. doi:10.2307/796256

World Bank. (2019). *GINI index (World Bank estimate)*. Retrieved March 17, 2019 from World Bank: https://data.worldbank.org/indicator/SI.POV.GINI?locations=RU

World Economic Forum. (2018). *The Inclusive Development Index 2018*. Retrieved February 10, 2019 from World Economic Forum: http://www3.weforum.org/docs/WEF_Forum_IncGrwth_2018.pdf

KEY TERMS AND DEFINITIONS

Buy Back: This is the re-acquisition by a company of its own stock Normally it is seen as a signal to investors that the company considers the shares to be underpriced.

CIS Countries: A free trade area of independent countries that were formerly in the Soviet Union.

Global Depositary Receipt: A bank certificate issued in multiple countries for foreign stock.

Price Earning Ratio: This is the amount an investor is paying for one unit of investors profit (current share price relative to its per-share earnings).

Primary Listing: The first issue of the company's securities, conducted simultaneously with the change of its legal form in the process of reorganization: transformation, merger, accession, separation.

Prospectus: A legal document issued by companies that are offering securities, describing the assets, liabilities. Risks and other material information about a company.

Secondary Listing: Any subsequent offer of purchase of shares that after the primary listing.

Share Split: This is when a company divides its existing shares to multiple shares to improve liquidity. For example, Sberbank split 1 share worth 89000 ruble to 1000 new shares worth 89 rubles each.

Underpricing: Placing shares in the IPO at a price that is lower than the market price.

Chapter 6
Financial Distress Overview, Determinants, and Sustainable Remedial Measures:
Financial Distress

Fredrick Ikpesu
Pan-Atlantic University, Lagos, Nigeria

Olusegun Vincent
School of Management and Social Sciences, Pan-Atlantic University, Lagos, Nigeria

Olamitunji Dakare
School of Management Sciences, Pan-Atlantic University, Lagos, Nigeria

ABSTRACT

The failure of top firms in the world who once represented the icon of their industries has renewed the interest of research scholars, practitioners, policymakers, and academics on the subject matter of financial distress. A firm is financially distressed when the operating cash flow is not sufficient for meeting the current obligation of the firm. It also involves a situation where the firm constantly experiences loss, breach loan contract, and find it difficult in honouring organisational commitment. This chapter is set out to synthesize the recent development in the topics of financial distress and corporate recovery. This chapter primarily focuses on financial distress, its determinants, and the way forward on how firms can recover from financial distress. The chapter also discussed the financial distress theories as well as sustainable remedial measures of financial distress. Finally, the chapter provides the concluding remarks and policy implications.

DOI: 10.4018/978-1-5225-9607-3.ch006

INTRODUCTION: AN OVERVIEW OF FINANCIAL DISTRESS

In recent times, the world at large, has witnessed numerous cases of firms going into financial distress (Bender, 2013). As pointed out by Ikpesu and Eboiyehi (2018) many top firms who once represent the icon of their industries have become financial distress. For Taffler (1983) during an economic downturn and financial crises, the possibilities of firms going into distress increased greatly. For instance, the Asian financial crisis in 1997 and global financial crisis between 2007and 2008 saw many big firms becoming financially distressed as cash flow and profit declined causing the firms to default on their financial obligation (Thim et al., 2011).

A firm is financially distressed when there is a constant loss, breach of loan contract and difficulty in honouring organisational commitment. Chow *et al.* (2011) also maintained that a firm is financially distressed when the operating cash flows of the organisation is inadequate in meeting the current obligation of the firm, thus necessitating the actions such as mergers and acquisition, issuing additional capital, restructuring and renegotiation of loan agreement. Thakor (2014) opined that, financial distress of firms can be classified into four categories, these include, decline in performance, failure, insolvency, and default. However, while insolvency and default are rooted in its liquidity, a decline in performance and failure affects firm profitability.

Meanwhile, numerous studies have also accounted for symptoms and cause of financial distress among firms that are either caused by internal and external factors (Slatter & Lovett, 1999; Muigai, 2016; Eboiyehi & Ikpesu, 2017). These factors, however, include poor management, over trading, poor working capital management, changes in market demand, leverage, competition, adverse movement in commodity prices, and loss of confidence by investors, creditors, and suppliers, weak corporate governance among others.

It is against this backdrop that this chapter is utmost significance for financial managers, the board of directors as well as the government. The rest of the chapter will be divided into the following sections. First, the financial distress theories will be examined. The determinants of financial distress which include internal and external factors will be considered next. The sustainable remedial measures of financial distress which will focus on steps firms can take to corporate recovery will be discussed thereafter in this chapter. Finally, the chapter will provide the concluding remarks and policy implications for business owners, managers, and policymakers.

FINANCIAL DISTRESS THEORIES

There are several theories that have been used to explain financial distress in finance management literature. For instance, the cash management theory postulates that the continuing imbalance between the cash outflow and cash inflow would result in financial distress in an organisation (Aziz & Dar, 2006). The imbalance in the cash flows arises due to cash management failure. The theory is of the opinion that for firms to avoid distress situation, there is a need for effective and efficient utilisation of fund. Improper cash management leads to an imbalance between the cash inflows and cash outflow and this often leads to financial distress in firm.

The theory of credit risk is another theory that is used to explain why financial distress occurs in firms. This theory states that when firms do not properly manage their credit risk, it might lead to the firm becoming financial distress. Credit risk refers to the potential that a counterparty will not honour its obligation as agreed. Credit risk directly threatens the continued survival of an organisation and if not properly managed leads to distress situation in firms. An organisation needs to have a sound credit risk management framework to be able to identify, assessed and control credit risk in an organisation. Developing a sound credit risk management framework also involve having a good credit risk policy. One of the early signs of financial distress is when an organisation has a high credit risk.

The Pecking order theory has also been used to explain financial distress. The pecking order theory was first introduced by Donaldson in 1961 although it was Myers and Majluf (1984) that popularised and modified the concept. According to the theory, firm prefer to use their internal source of finance, before deploying the external source of fund in a bid to preserve the stability of the firm and also the value of the firm. The frequent deployment of external source of fund (debt) in financing the firm operation might expose the firm to the likelihood of financial distress especially when it becomes difficulty for the firm in meeting recurring obligation (Wesa & Otinga, 2018). In a bid to increase the value of the firm and preserve the financial stability of the firm, the pecking order theory suggests the need for the organisation to balance the different source of finance available to them (Muigai, 2016)

Other financial distress theories include the trade-off theory postulated by Modigliani and Miller (1963) formulated. This theory maintains that the use of debt is beneficial to the firm since it raises the value of the firm, however, there is a limit to the use of debt finance because, at a certain point, the continuous uses of debt reduces the value of the firm and expose the firm to the probability of financial distress. Furthermore, this theory advocates for optimal capital structure which can be attained through the trade-off of the cost of using debt against the benefit in the use of debt.

Figure 1. Determinants of financial distress

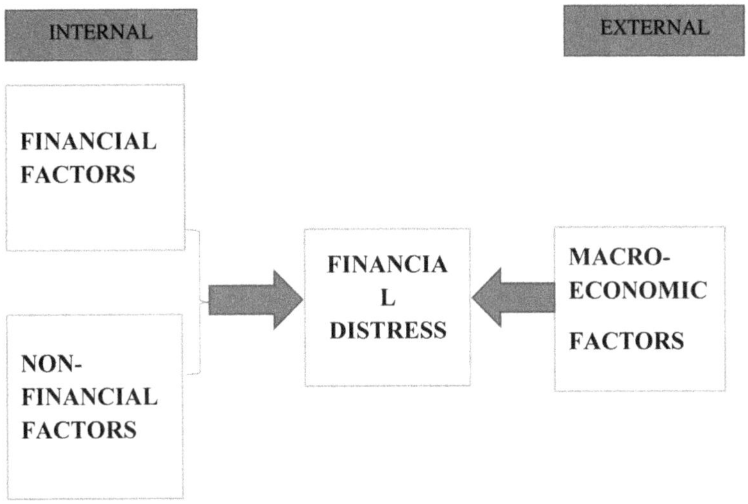

DETERMINANTS OF FINANCIAL DISTRESS

The determinants of financial distress of a firm have been classified into two groups according to financial Management literature. These are internal factors and external factors. The internal factor is further divided into financial factors and the non-financial factors while the external factors are the macroeconomic factors. These factors all have effects on the firm operations and therefore, they can threaten the continued survival of the organisation leading to liquidation of the enterprise if not properly managed.

DETERMINANTS OF FINANCIAL DISTRESS: FINANCIAL FACTORS

In the literature and practice there is a general consensus that financial factors has been one of the key determinants of financial distress(Turetsky & McEwen, 2001; Le clere, 2005; Nahar, 2006; Chancharat, 2008;Honjo, 2010; Parker et al., 2011; Thim et al., 2011; Tesfamariam, 2014; Kristanti et al., 2016; Devji & Suprabha, 2016; Idrees & Qayyum, 2018; Ikpesu & Eboiyehi, 2018; Wesa & Otinga, 2018). Failure by firms in managing the financial factor usually result in firms not meeting their obligation as at when due. A situation when a firm cannot honour obligation at the right time is an early warning signal of financial distress. The financial factors include liquidity, leverage, profitability, firm size, share price, and revenue growth.

Notables studies such as (Elloumi & Gueyee, 2001; Turetsky & McEwen, 2001; Nahar, 2006; Thim et al., 2011; Wesa & Otinga, 2018) have reinforced that firms that have low level of liquidity are more likely to experience financial distress due to their inability of such firms to meet their recurring obligations as at when due. These studies have revealed that liquidity is one of the financial factors that determine financial distress in firm. A firm experience liquidity problem when her current assets are insufficient to cover its current liability. This situation can lead to the inability of meeting and honouring organisational commitment. Failure in meeting organisational commitment increases the likelihood of financial distress.

Leverage is also a key financial factor of what causes financial distress in a firm (Pranowo et al., 2010; Chancharat, 2008; Kristanti et al., 2016; Gathecha, 2016). As pointed out by Tesfamariam (2014), leverage reduces the ability of a firm to survive when the firm experience negative shock in its cash flows. For instance, the more leverage a firm has, the more the risk of indebtedness the firm is exposed to. Consequently, an increase in firm leverage may lead to financial distress in a firm, if the borrowed fund is not properly utilized and when the firm operating condition deteriorates leading to difficulty in meeting her obligations.

From the myriad of financial management literature, profitability has also been identified as one of the financial factors that could lead to financial distress (Thim et al., 2011; Baimwera & Murinki, 2014; Campbell et al., 2015; Ikpesu & Eboiyehi, 2018). For example, a firm that has low profitability level may experience a low-level liquidity and in turn, may affect the firm in meeting her obligations and as such the firm is exposed to distress condition.

Another factor is the size of a firm. Notable studies has also documented that firm size also determines financial distress in firm (Turetsky et al., 2001; Le clere, 2005; Chancharat, 2008;Honjo, 2010; Parker et al., 2011; Thim et al., 2011; Tesfamariam, 2014; Kristanti et al., 2016). The size of the firm represents the total assets of the firm which reflects how big or small a firm is. Meanwhile, small firms are said to easily face distress conditions more especially when there is a negative shock of firm cash flows. Also, most small firms do not have the resources to employ an expert to manage the firm resources effectively and efficiently. In addition, inadequate financial and non-financial resources have usually been the problem of small firms. Consequently, the afore-mentioned reasons explain why most of the small firms undergo financial distress. In the case of large firms, they have the capacity to raise more debt finance in the capital market; this could expose the firms to financial distress more especially when the firms find it difficult to repay the borrowed fund with interest payment.

The growth of the firm is another financial factor that determines financial distress in a firm (Thim et al., 2011; Ikpesu & Eboiyehi, 2018). The growth of the firm is mostly measured by revenue growth. A decline in revenue growth is an early warning signal of financial distress. Firms that continue to experience low revenue growth usually find it difficult to meet creditors' repayment period and other obligations. Firms in such condition find it difficult to embark on profitable ventures.

Finally, the share price is another financial factor that determines financial distress (Devji & Suprabha, 2016; Idrees & Qayyum, 2018). Many studies have maintained that share price has an inverse link with financial distress. For instance, a decline in firm share price might increase the probability of such firm under-going distress. Meanwhile, a persistent fall in the share price of an organisation is an early warning signal of financial distress. When a firm share price continues to decline in the capital market, it might discourage the existing shareholders which in turn cause existing shareholders pull out their investment from such firm. The consequence of such action may affect the stability and viability of the firm and therefore, exposes the firm to financial distress.

Other notable financial factors that determine financial distress in firms include; high operating expenses, excessive non-current assets, embezzlement by employee/ management, irregular disposal of non-current assets, and over expansion.

DETERMINANTS OF FINANCIAL DISTRESS: NON- FINANCIAL FACTORS

According to Dun and Bradstreet (1986) on business failure report, the non-financial factors could also be responsible for financial distress among firms. The non-financial factor as highlighted in the report includes customer cause, experience cause, sales cause, and the disaster cause. Meanwhile, the customer cause arises when a firm has receivables difficulties and few customers' patronage. The experience cause arises as due to incompetence management team, non-participation of the board of directors, and poor leadership skills. For experience cause, this occurs when there is unbalanced experience and lack of managerial experience in an organisation. The sales cause arises when a firm is located in a poor location, experience low sales, has inventory difficulties, and its product faced stiff competition that may lead to poor demand of the firm's products. Finally, the disasters cause arises as an act of God, burglary, strikes, fire and sudden death of the owner.

DETERMINANTS OF FINANCIAL DISTRESS: MACROECONOMIC FACTORS

The external factors also known as macroeconomic factors also affect the operations and performance of firms and in turn, could lead to financial distress if firms fail to strategically identify and manage these factors. The macroeconomic factors include; inflation, exchange rate, interest rate, political unrest and instability in government policy. The inflation rate in a country, for example, can affect firm operation. Most firms likely to outperform when the country inflation rate is stable and low. The rising of inflation rates creates uncertainties within the business environment and consequently, discourages investment. Also, inflation could make the export of firms to be less competitive in the global market and raise the cost of production of firms. This, therefore, leads to a decline in firm profitability and persistence decline in firm profitability could lead to financial distress.

The exchange rate can also affect a firm's operations and performance. For example, the instability of exchange rate can adversely affect firms who rely on imported raw materials/technology in order to carry out or perform their operations. The depreciation of currency makes import expensive and in turn, increases the cost of production. In a situation when a firm cannot break-even due to high cost of production, makes the firm to experience low liquidity, loss as well as preventing the firm to fulfill her contractual obligations as at when due.

Furthermore, an increase in the interest rate on borrowed funds has the implication of discouraging firm from borrowing, hence, difficulties in resuscitating a distressed firm. Consequently, an increase in interest rate often serves as a disincentive to investment because discerning investors are discouraged by high borrowing cost which negatively impacts on the business margin. In addition, the rise in the interest rate is a huge impediment to the ability of investors to make good their borrowing obligation, in the area of principal and interest repayments. This dilemma to repay the debt owes by the firm as at when due may expose the firm to financial distress.

Another macroeconomic factor is political unrest and instability of government policies. The political unrest for example, in a country, may halt the operations of firms and this could have an adverse effect on the organisation such as threatens its continual survival. More so, the frequent change in government policies may also affect the activities of the firm and this may likely affect the viability of the firm and cause financial distress for the firm. Again, the frequent change in government policies could also affect the sales, distribution, the supply chain of the organisation, its reputation in the global market, its vision of expansion and decision- making process. Consequently, the ability of firms to overcome political unrest and instability of government policy may expose the firm to financial distress.

SUSTAINABLE REMEDIAL MEASURES

In this chapter, we have examined internal factors and external factors that result in financial distress of a firm. Most definitely, there is no gainsaying the fact that, in today's globalised economy and markets, strategic actions are required for a distressed firm to bounce back in order to compete effectively within its competitive landscape. Stuart *et al.* (2011) however, identified the following as some of the sustainable remedial measures to curb financial distress in a firm, these are; crisis stabilisation, organisational change, change in leadership, technology upgrading, business process improvement, financial restructuring, and strategic focus.

Crisis stabilisation means to restore and build stakeholder confidence that the top management is in control of the situation. It also involves ensuring effective and efficient cash management, asset reduction, cost reduction, and short term financing while providing the firm ample opportunity to develop a restructuring and turnaround plan that will improve the firm from its current state.

Organisational change involves a change in strategy. The organisation needs to carry out a holistic analysis of the operations in the firm so as to determine the root cause of the financial distress and adopt the appropriate strategy to solve the identified problems as well as to prevent reoccurrence. Changing the firm structure include structural change, bringing in the people for change, building capabilities and commitment, ensuring enhanced communication across the firm, and setting-up new terms and conditions of contract of employment.

Jim (2011) however, pointed out lack of competence of the CEO and management team as a major reason many firms go into financial distress. Therefore, replacing the CEO and management team will send a strong signal to the business communities that the firm is ready to improve from its current state. It should be noted that changing the leaders would be ineffective if the cause of the financial distress is caused by an external factor.

Technology is another sustainable remedial measure that a firm faced with financial distress needs to put up. For example, upgrading an obsolete technology of a firm can strengthen the firm operations and makes it offers a competitive product in the market than its competitors. The improvement of business processes would the help the firm to reduce costs, improved marketing skills and sales, quality improvement and time improvement.

Also, there is a need for financial restructuring of the firm, which primary aim is to restore the financial distressed faced by the firm. Financial restructuring involves raising additional fund and/or replacing the existing capital structure of the firm through capital restructuring. Finally, financial distressed firm needs to develop a strategic focus in order to become solvent. A strategic focus involves re-defining the core of the business, product market refocusing, asset reduction and divestment, and downsizing, outsourcing and investment.

CONCLUSION AND POLICY IMPLICATIONS

This chapter has provided an overview of financial distress in a firm. It has also examined various factors that could affect an organisation operations and performance which in turn would lead to financial distress. These factors include the internal and external factors. A firm therefore, needs to pay crucial to the internal factors (financial and non-financial factors) and the external factor (macroeconomic factors) that may cause financial distress. The chapter also highlights the sustainable remedial measures to curb financial distress in a firm.

The chapter provides some significant policy directions. First, the board of director and financial manager needs to set-up internal control and risk management measures to detect early warning signals of distress conditions and takes preventive measures to avert the looming danger. Second, the board of director and the financial manager needs to pay crucial attention not only to the internal factors (financial and non-financial factors) but also the external factor (macroeconomic variables) that may occasion financial distress in a firm. The macroeconomic policies of the government have a direct impact on the operations of the firm. Board of directors and financial managers needs to find out how government policy and new legislation can affect their operations and performance since firms must be law abiding. Third, the government must also factor in the business communities when designing their policies. That is, government policies must be business friendly so as not to retard the growth of firms but rather promote and enhance firm growth. Finally, the government should also provide infrastructural facilities and a conducive atmosphere for business to thrive.

REFERENCES

Aziz, M. A., & Dar, H. A. (2006). Predicting corporate financial Distress: Where we stand? Corporate governance. *The International Journal of Business in Society*, *6*(1), 18–33.

Baimwera, B., & Muriuki, A. M. (2014). Analysis of corporate financial distress determinants: A survey of non-financial firms listed in the NSE. *International Journal of Current Business and Social Sciences*, *1*(2), 58–80.

Bender, R. (2013). *Corporate financial strategy*. Routledge. doi:10.4324/9780203082768

Campbell, J. Y., Hilscher, J. D., & Szilagyi, J. (2011). Predicting financial distress and the performance of distressed stocks. *Journal of Investment Management*, *9*(2), 14–34.

Chancharat, N. (2008). *An empirical analysis of financially distressed Australian companies: the application of survival analysis*. A thesis submitted to University of Wollongong.

Choy, S. L. W., Munusamy, J., Chelliah, S., & Mandari, A. (2011). Effects of financial distress condition on the company performance: A Malaysian perspective. *Review of Economics & Finance*, *1*(4), 85–99.

Devji, S., & Suprabha, K. R. (2016). Corporate financial distress and stock return: Evidence from Indian stock market. *Nitte Management Review*, *10*(1), 34–44. doi:10.17493/nmr/2016/105514

Dun, & Bradstreet, Inc. Business Economics Division. (1986). *The Business Failure Record*. Business Economics Division, Dun and Bradstreet.

Eboiyehi, O. C., & Ikpesu, F. (2017). An empirical investigation of capital structure and tax shield on business distress in Nigeria: An Application of Panel Corrected Standard Error (PCSE) Approach. *Journal of Global Economics. Management and Business Research*, *8*(2), 67–75.

Elloumi, F., & Gueyie, J. P. (2001). Financial distress and corporate governance: An empirical analysis. c*orporate governance. The International Journal of Business in Society*, *1*(1), 15–23.

Gathecha, J. W. (2016). *Effect of firm characteristics on financial distress of non-financial listed firms at Nairobi Securities Exchange* (Doctoral dissertation). Kenyatta University.

Honjo, Y. (2000). Business failure of new firms: An empirical analysis using a multiplicative hazards model. *International Journal of Industrial Organization*, *18*(4), 557–574. doi:10.1016/S0167-7187(98)00035-6

Idrees, S., & Qayyum, A. (2018). *The impact of financial distress risk on equity returns: A case study of non-financial firms of Pakistan stock exchange*. Retrieved from https://mpra.ub.uni-muenchen.de/85346/1/MPRA_paper_85346.pdf

Ikpesu, F., & Eboiyehi, O. C. (2018). Capital structure and corporate financial distress of manufacturing firms in Nigeria. *Journal of Accounting and Taxation, 10*(7), 78–84. doi:10.5897/JAT2018.0309

Jim, C. (2011). Leadership the Triumph Of Humility and Fierce Resolve. *Harvard Business Review*.

Kristanti, F. T., Rahayu, S., & Huda, A. N. (2016). The determinant of financial distress on Indonesian family firm. *Procedia: Social and Behavioral Sciences, 219*, 440–447.

LeClere, M. J. (2005). Time-dependent and time-invariant covariates within a proportional hazards model: A financial distress application. *Review of Accounting and Finance, 4*(4), 91–109. doi:10.1108/eb043439

Modigliani, F., & Miller, M. H. (1963). Corporate income taxes and the cost of capital: A correction. *The American Economic Review, 53*(3), 433–443.

Muigai, R. G. (2016). *Effect of capital structure on financial distress of non-financial companies listed in Nairobi securities exchange* (Doctoral dissertation). COHRED, Finance, JKUAT.

Myers, S. C., & Majluf, N. S. (1984). Corporate financing and investment decisions when firms have information that investors do not have. *Journal of Financial Economics, 13*(2), 187–221. doi:10.1016/0304-405X(84)90023-0

Nahar Abdullah, S. (2006). Directors' remuneration, firm's performance and corporate governance in Malaysia among distressed companies. *corporate governance: The International. Journal of Business and Society, 6*(2), 162–174.

Parker, S., Peters, G. F., & Turetsky, H. F. (2002). Corporate governance and corporate failure: a survival analysis. *Corporate Governance: The International Journal of Business in Society, 2*(2), 4-12.

Pranowo, K., Achsani, N. A., Manurung, A. H., & Nuryartono, N. (2010). Determinant of corporate financial distress in an emerging market economy: Empirical evidence from the Indonesian stock exchange 2004-2008. *International Research Journal of Finance and Economics, 52*(1), 81–90.

Ray, S. (2011). Assessing corporate financial distress in automobile industry of India: An application of Altman's model. *Research Journal of Finance and Accounting, 2*(3), 155-168.

Slatter, S. (2011). *Leading corporate turnaround: How leaders fix troubled companies*. John Wiley & Sons.

Slatter, S., & Lovett, D. (1999). *Corporate turnaround*. Penguin, UK.

Taffler, R. J. (1983). The assessment of company solvency and performance using a statistical model. *Accounting and Business Research*, *13*(52), 295–308. doi:10.1080/00014788.1983.9729767

Tesfamariam, Y. (2014). *The determinants of financial distress in the case of manufacturing share companies in Addis Ababa-Ethiopia*. A Thesis in the Department of Accounting and Finance Addis Ababa University.

Thakor, A. V. (2014). Bank capital and financial stability: An economic trade-off or a Faustian bargain? *Annual Review of Financial Economics*, *6*(1), 185–223. doi:10.1146/annurev-financial-110613-034531

Thim, C. K., Choong, Y. V., & Nee, C. S. (2011). Factors affecting financial distress: The case of Malaysian public listed firms. *Corporate Ownership and Control*, *8*(4), 345–351. doi:10.22495/cocv8i4c3art3

Turetsky, H. F., & McEwen, R. A. (2001). An empirical investigation of firm longevity: A model of the ex ante predictors of financial distress. *Review of Quantitative Finance and Accounting*, *16*(4), 323–343. doi:10.1023/A:1011291425075

Wesa, E. W., & Otinga, H. N. (2018). Determinants of financial distress among listed firms at the Nairobi securities exchange. *The Strategic Journal of Business & Change Management*, *5*(4), 1057–1073.

Chapter 7
Equilibrium in Corporate Governance:
Effects in Developing Countries

Sonia Marcos
University of Burgos, Spain

Luis A. Castrillo
University of Burgos, Spain

ABSTRACT

Corporate governance systems around the world are shaped by legal traditions, but the most important determinant of their effectiveness is law enforcement. Developing countries tend to have weak institutional structures and contracting environments. In this context, markets are inefficient and ownership concentration becomes the main corporate governance mechanism in order to protect property rights. How can developing countries design an optimal corporate governance system in their poor business environments? Corporate governance mechanisms are interdependent, and each country needs to search for a set of mechanisms in equilibrium—that is, an optimal combination of control and incentives—that solves its own agency problems. But another problem in developing countries is the lack of public enforcement. Just as internal mechanisms may substitute for ineffective external mechanisms, private initiatives may reinforce weak public enforcement.

DOI: 10.4018/978-1-5225-9607-3.ch007

INTRODUCTION

Firms' stakeholders can choose among different internal corporate governance mechanisms that aim to control agency problems. This choice is conditioned by the availability and efficiency of external corporate governance mechanisms, which in turn depend on the institutional framework in which the firm operates. Legal and political systems and stakeholders' pressure are the starting point of corporate governance design in each country. Each country's legislation determines the protection of investors in their relations with firms, thus influencing the predominant external control by markets. This relationship between legislation and market control also gives rise to various conflicts and agency problems, specific to each institutional environment, which have to be resolved through different combinations and arrangements of corporate governance mechanisms (La Porta, Lopez-de-Silanes, Shleifer, & Vishny, 1997, 1998, 2000). Each firm shapes its own corporate governance structure according to external controls and incentives, leading to an equilibrium.

This chapter provides a theoretical framework to elucidate the complexity of corporate governance taken as a whole and explain how corporate governance models are built. The institutional framework, corporate governance mechanisms, and performance are not independent variables. Rather, they interact to generate an equilibrium solution, which is the corporate governance model shared by most of the firms in the same country. Developing countries have very heterogeneous institutional frameworks, and each environment provides a starting point for corporate governance to thrive. A lack of external control from markets and government could be compensated by strong insider mechanisms, such as concentrated ownership or family control. Developing countries' weak capital markets, poor investor protection, and lack of board independence elicit an insider approach to corporate governance that compensates for these weaknesses (Agyemang, Kyeraa, Ansong, & Frimpong, 2017; Humayun & Adelepo, 2012; Isukul & Chizea, 2016). The result expected will be an equilibrium corporate governance structure.

The main goal of this chapter is to present a dynamic corporate governance model in balance that shows how, in developing countries, the relationship between internal corporate governance and firm performance is conditioned by legal and colonial origins, investor protection and confidence, capital market development and efficiency, among other factors.

This chapter is organized as follows. First, it explains agency conflicts and corporate governance through agency theory. The next section explains how institutional frameworks and law enforcement determine corporate governance models around the world. The two next sections discuss how corporate governance is in developing countries and how corporate governance mechanisms interact as either alternatives or complements. The chapter also explains the equilibrium phenomenon, and its implications in empirical studies. Finally, the chapter discusses how it can affect corporate governance in developing countries, the future research directions, and conclusion.

BACKGROUND

Over the last two decades, extensive research has focused on how to design corporate governance mechanisms that will control manager-shareholder agency problems and improve performance (e.g., Agrawal & Knoeber, 1996; Bhagat & Black, 2002; Hermalin & Weisbach, 1991, 2003; Mehran, 1995; Yermarck, 1996; Zingales, 1998). All governance mechanisms provide benefits and impose costs that differ across firms depending on their unique agency problems (Demsetz & Lehn, 1985). Firms can choose to use different organizational monitoring mechanisms and incentives to oversee the activities of the CEO and top managers. Corporate governance mechanisms are aimed at reducing the possibility of opportunistic behavior. These mechanisms will discourage activities or behaviors aimed at altering the outcome of ex-post bargaining and therefore will balance that bargaining among the stakeholders. Therefore, the development of effective corporate governance structures, in equilibrium, makes more likely the balanced distribution of firm value and the satisfaction of every stakeholder's claims.

Corporate finance studies have mostly focused on a single internal governance mechanism. However, individual corporate governance mechanisms are not independent of each other, as has been assumed in much of the previous empirical literature (Coles, McWilliams, & Sen, 2001; Rediker & Seth, 1995). Firms can select a mix of governance mechanisms in order to compensate for the lack of external market control (Williamson, 1983) and to substitute for each other, and the choice of one mechanism will depend on the choice of another.

In agency theory, the company is seen as a contractual miscellany (Hill & Jones, 1992; Jensen & Meckling, 1976) of co-specialized resource holders (Rajan & Zingales, 2000), maintained in a continual tug-of-war between co-operation among its stakeholders to create value (Alchian & Demsetz, 1972; Freeman, 1984; Rappaport, 1998) and competition to distribute it (Freeman & Evan, 1990; Hill & Jones, 1992; Jensen & Meckling, 1976). Greater firm value lessens conflict over value distribution, but the sustainability of the firm depends not only on the creation of enough value but also on a balanced distribution of this value that fulfills every stakeholder's claims.

However, in this contractual miscellany, uncertainty and bounded rationality make complete contracts that address every contingency impossible. Most contracts are incompletely worded, and as they become complete in practice, in the effective development of the relation, some stakeholders may spend resources in inefficient activities whose main purpose is to alter the outcome of the ex-post bargaining in their favor (Zingales, 1998). For example, a manager may specialize the firm in activities he/she is best at running because this increases his/her contribution and thus his/her share of ex-post rents (Shleifer & Vishny, 1986). Interestingly, this problem is not limited to the top of the hierarchy: subordinates who do not have much decision power may waste resources trying to capture the benevolence of a powerful superior (Milgrom, 1988), or suppliers may give presents to managers to increase their ex-post bargaining (Delgado, Quevedo, & Fuente, 2010). Corporate governance, defined as the complex set of constraints that shapes the distribution among its stakeholders of the value generated by a firm (Aguilera & Jackson, 2003; Aoki, 2000; Zingales, 1998), is aimed at reducing discretion for opportunism.

THE INSTITUTIONAL FRAMEWORK AND LAW ENFORCEMENT

Understanding legal approaches to corporate governance is the first step in designing corporate governance models around the world. The origin of the legal system determines the content of the law and markets development. Legal tradition is one the main causes of corporate governance differences among countries (La Porta et al., 1997, 1998, 2000). David and Brierley (1985) identify four Western legal traditions: English, French, German, and Scandinavian. These systems spread to other countries and their colonies. Each one gives a different investor protection level. In a pioneering paper, La Porta et al. (1998) examine the legal protection of shareholders and the enforcement of these rules in 49 countries.

In developed countries, legal traditions have given rise to two main corporate governance models. Common-law countries have stronger investor protection laws and market-based financial systems (La Porta et al., 1997, 1998). In these countries, large quoted firms are owned by a large number of small shareholders and institutional investors. Developed capital markets and widespread ownership create potential agency problems between owners and managers (the "separation between ownership and control")—problems that require monitoring by markets and independent board members. In contrast, civil law countries have poor investor protection and bank-based financial systems. Majority ownership is usually held by a single family, corporation, or bank (Franks & Mayer, 1997), and this concentrated ownership compensates for a poor market for corporate control and the lack of investor protection. In this context, the agency problems appear between large shareholders and small investors (Johnson, La Porta, Lopez-de-Silanes, & Shleifer, 2000). Each country's legislation determines investor rights, the legal protection of other stakeholders, and the prevailing corporate governance model.

Developing countries' legal systems are the outcome of conquest and colonization processes. In the nineteenth century, Western legal traditions spread throughout the world. Many countries in southeast Asia and Africa share the common law system. Spanish, French, Belgian, and Dutch colonies followed the civil law tradition (La Porta et al., 2000). La Porta et al. (1998) identify Kenya, Malaysia, Nigeria, Pakistan, Zimbabwe, and South Africa as having English legal origins, while Argentina, Chile, Colombia, Ecuador, Egypt, Indonesia, Peru, and the Philippines have French legal origins. However, developing countries are very heterogeneous, with each country having developed different institutions, not necessarily in organic response to companies' and social needs. Some separation of executive, legislative, and judicial power is desirable for a good business environment. Government integrity, property rights, regulatory efficiency, and market openness are related to the liberty of individuals and firms to trade and invest. Also, the institutional framework and business environment are related to other factors such as poverty, life expectancy, education opportunities, literacy, health care, and the standard of living (Miller, Kim, & Roberts, 2018). But many developing countries are characterized by informational opaqueness, political instability and corruption, institutional weaknesses, and government interference in the private sector, as well as monopoly, squatter settlements, crime, ethnic violence, and war. Many of these problems are consequences of colonial transplantation (Djankov, Glaeser, La Porta, Lopez-de-Silanes, & Shleifer, 2003).

Middle Eastern and North African countries are distinguished by high concentrations of wealth and poverty. Structural and institutional problems reflect a lack of economic dynamism and economic opportunities. Citizens demand more freedom, but unrest, violence, and war are not a good environment for markets and business development. Among these economies, Israel, the United Arab Emirates, and Qatar have strong protection of property rights, strong trade, and some significant improvements in government integrity (Miller et al., 2018). Tunisia and Egypt have experienced an improvement in their institutional structures since the Arab Spring. But Yemen, Iraq, Iran, Libya, Syria, and Algeria can be categorized as unstable.

Several countries in sub-Saharan Africa are experiencing an uptick of economic growth, but the region needs to boost institutional reforms to guarantee long-term economic development. These countries commonly show a lack of progress toward regulatory efficiency and open markets, inadequate protection of property rights, corruption, or low government integrity (Miller et al., 2018). Consequently, stocks markets in most African countries are not well-developed and are characterized by serious deficiencies (Agyemang, Gatsi, & Ansong, 2018; Ngare, Nyamongo, & Misati, 2014).

Asia's developing countries have achieved a quiet economic growth over the past years, driven by trade-oriented economies like China and India. China has lived for decades under socialist economic policies. Nowadays, China is a global economy. However, there are many bureaucratic hurdles to investment and imports, state-owned firms still dominate the main economic sectors, property rights are not well protected, and economic freedom is low. India is looking to become an open-market economy. Privatization of state-owned firms, liberalization of the economy, and deregulation are boosting economic growth. But India still has much poverty and many underdeveloped regions.

Djankov and colleagues (2003) argue that legal tradition is not the main difference between developed and developing countries; what matters is institutions' effectiveness. Differences in the strength of institutional structures explain the divergence in investor protection across countries (La Porta et al., 2000); in turn, enforcement of laws and the degree to which property rights are respected explain the development of countries (Acemoglu, Johnson, & Robinson, 2001; Berglöf & Claessens, 2006; Francis, Khurana, & Pereira, 2001). In developing countries, corporate governance differences originate in the effectiveness of law. An effective institution in the origin country may not remain efficient in a colony, and institutions exert a significant influence on economic development and corporate governance (Djankov et al., 2003).

OWNERSHIP CONCENTRATION: A CHARACTERISTIC OF CORPORATE GOVERNANCE IN DEVELOPING COUNTRIES

Legal system origin and law enforcement determine investor protection across countries. Common law countries have stronger laws and enforcement than civil law countries (La Porta et al., 2000). Protection of minority shareholders' interest fosters investments and capital market development (Hart, 1995; La Porta et al., 2000). On the other hand, strong investor protection typically separates ownership and management and thus causes agency problems described by Berle and Means (1932) and Jensen and Meckling (1976). In developed market economies, which have smaller differences in law enforcement than developing economies, legal system origin and investor protection constitute the starting point in corporate governance model design.

In developing countries, independently of the legal tradition prevailing in each country, weak contracting environments and less protected property rights lead to concentrated ownership of firms (Shleifer & Vishny, 1997). There are arguments for and against ownership concentration. Large shareholders help monitor management and align incentives, but also undermine the effectiveness of other mechanisms of corporate governance, such as capital markets. Ownership concentration reduces liquidity in capital markets (Demsetz, 1968), access to external financing (Berglöf & Claessens, 2006), and the effect of markets for corporate control (John & Kedia, 2006; John & Senbet, 1998).

Concentrated ownership is a robust characteristic of many developing economies—among others, India (Khanna & Palepu, 2005), in spite of its having been a British colony; South Africa, where the Johannesburg Stock Exchange is dominated by a small group of pyramid holding companies (Barr, Gerson, & Kantor, 1997) and dispersed and concentrated ownership operate "side by side" in a mixed system (Mongalo, 2004); Ghana, where listed and unlisted companies have controlling shareholders (Agyemang & Castellini, 2015); China, the world's second largest economy, where most companies are state owned or controlled by the state through holding companies (Jiang & Kim, 2015); Chile, where there is a pyramidal ownership structure with many firms owned by the same shareholder (Jara & López, 2007); and Russia, where ownership is highly concentrated in the hands of the state and anonymous private owners (Chernykh, 2008).

Concentrated ownership is a substitute for capital market monitoring. In developing countries with weak institutional structures, poor investor protection, and undeveloped capital markets, companies tend to have large shareholders in order to protect property rights and be more attractive to investors (Agyemang et al., 2017).

Large shareholders can be inclined to abuse minority shareholders (Johnson et al., 2000). Although ownership concentration exposes minority shareholders to wealth expropriation, it also prevents the exercise of managerial discretion and induces managers to create value for all shareholders (Berglöf & Claessens, 2006). This means that other corporate governance mechanisms must be found to protect minority investors.

EQUILIBRIUM IN CORPORATE GOVERNANCE: COMPLEMENTARITY, SUBSTITUTION, AND INTERACTION EFFECTS

Agency problems can arise among different groups of firm stakeholders, such as managers and shareholders or large and minority shareholders. Several corporate governance mechanisms can reduce these agency problems (Agrawal & Knoeber, 1996).

There is interdependence among corporate governance mechanisms and among them and the institutional framework. The choice of one of them will depend on previous decisions both inside and outside the company, and their monitoring functions can overlap and substitute for each other or complement the effect of other external or internal mechanisms. Thus it is possible to design effective corporate governance structures, in equilibrium, with mechanisms to satisfy every stakeholder. Table 1 lists some academic papers that have proposed interrelationships among various governance mechanisms.

Alternative mechanisms can also be used to improve firm performance. However, in measuring such effects we have to recognize and control for unobserved heterogeneity, simultaneity, and dynamic endogeneity (Wintoki et al., 2012). Performance and corporate governance are jointly determined by unobservable firm-specific factors, they are simultaneously determined in each period, and current corporate governance depends on past performance. Empirical studies of corporate governance often neglect to monitor these endogeneity problems and thus obtain biased and inconsistent results that are hard to interpret (Roberts & Whited, 2013). If firm-specific characteristics are controlled, there should be no statistically significant relationship between governance mechanisms and firm performance. This doesn't mean that the mechanisms are ineffective, but that the mix of governance mechanisms is chosen as a whole optimally, in equilibrium (Agrawal & Knoeber, 1996; Marcos & Castrillo, 2018; Schultz et al., 2010; Wintoki et al., 2012).

SEARCHING FOR BETTER CORPORATE GOVERNANCE IN DEVELOPING COUNTRIES

John and Senbet (1998) ask how countries that diverge in their institutional frameworks can design an optimal corporate governance system. This is a good question for developing countries. While it is true that legal tradition determines corporate governance, there are multiple ways to create a good business environment.

In developing countries capital markets are not very active, so takeover bids aren't likely. Capital and finance markets can't provide enough protection to investors and creditors, and external finance is expensive. Agency problems between managers and shareholders and between controlling and minority shareholders need to be solved by corporate governance to guarantee creditors' and investors' confidence and encourage markets development.

The main corporate governance mechanism used in developing countries to reduce agency problems is ownership concentration. Blockholding and state ownership are a natural consequence of weak institutional frameworks (Berglöf & Claessens, 2006; Claessens, 2006), in spite of other problems like tunneling or free-riding.

Table 1. Analyses of complementarity, substitution, and interaction effects among corporate governance mechanisms

Paper	Corporate Governance Mechanisms	Effect
La Porta et al., 2000	Capital market and ownership structure.	Substitution
Bertrand & Mullainathan, 1998	Capital market and executive compensation.	Substitution
John & Senbet, 1998 Hirshleifer & Thakor, 1994 Kini, Kracaw, & Mian, 1995 Williamson, 1983	Takeovers and board independence.	Substitution
Mínguez & Martín, 2003	Market liquidity and ownership structure.	Substitution
Aggarwal & Samwick, 1999	Product market competition and executive compensation.	Substitution
Coles et al., 2001	Board independence and incentives.	Complementarity
Berger, Ofek, & Yermack, 1997	Board size and debt.	Complementarity
Mehran, 1995	Executive ownership and incentives.	Complementarity
Hallock, 1997	Board composition and CEO salary.	Complementarity
Agrawal & Knoeber, 1996	Insider shareholding, institutional shareholding, ownership concentration, board outsiders, CEO human capital, leverage, CEO tenure, CEO founder, number of insiders, capital market control, and firm performance.	Interaction
John & Kedia, 2006	Insider ownership, bank debt, and takeovers.	Interaction
Schultz, Tan, & Walsh, 2010	Board composition, CEO duality, executive chairperson, board size, executive director compensation, non-executive director compensation, insider shareholding, ownership structure, leverage, and firm performance.	Interaction
Wintoki, Linck, & Netter, 2012	Board size, board independence, CEO duality, leverage, and firm performance.	Interaction
Marcos & Castrillo, 2018	Board size, board independence, board efficiency, ownership concentration, nature of ownership, insider shareholding, leverage, and firm performance.	Interaction

But what then happens to minority shareholders? In developed countries, the independence of the board of directors is a crucial mechanism to protect stakeholders' interests. Board independence increases with the number of outside directors, and isn't likely under concentrated ownership. The degree of board independence is usually a measure imposed by government institutions in developed countries through good corporate governance initiatives and codes, but is quite unfamiliar in developing countries (Rashid, 2018).

Ownership concentration also undermines the effectiveness of executive compensation, since many of the executives may be related to owners, especially in family firms.

Bank debt and auditing can substitute for capital market monitoring when ownership is concentrated and contract enforcement is weak. But the development of the banking and auditing sectors also depends on a good business environment, an effective regulatory framework, and public enforcement (Berglöf & Claessens, 2006).

What happens when developing countries make corporate governance effectiveness conditional on large shareholders' power? When public enforcement can't guarantee firm compliance with good corporate governance practices, private ordering and private enforcement can help to improve enforcement.

Nowadays, following the reform path in developed countries during the nineties and the beginning of the twenty-first century, there is an extensive list of corporate governance codes in developing countries. But recommendations and written laws are not enough; they need to be enforced.

There are different ways to enforce laws: private ordering, private enforcement, public enforcement, and state control (Berglöf & Claessens, 2006; Djankov et al., 2003). All of them are alternative forms of control of business. Private ordering refers to the sharing of regulatory authority with private actors (Schwardz, 2002). It's a legal concept in which individual parties agree on how to manage an activity, instead of relying on public legislation (Levin, 2015). Private ordering transactions protect property rights in the absence of law by unilateral, bilateral, or multilateral enforcement among parties. Private enforcement occurs "when private agents avail themselves of the framework defined by law or regulations to punish violations from contracts, using the courts to adjudicate and the state to enforce the final judgment" (Berglöf & Claessens, 2006, p. 125). Public enforcement is the enforcement of the law by government institutions. Finally, in some situations, only state control can eliminate disorder and state ownership is the only one solution (Djankov et al., 2003).

In the absence of appropriate public enforcement by the government, unilateral firm initiatives can be very important and may be rewarded by investors and markets. Good corporate governance initiatives voluntarily adopted by firms, like improving transparency and disclosure or board independence, can send positive signals to the market, improve reputation, and attract foreign and domestic investors. Bilateral and multilateral arrangements among firms also can substitute for public enforcement in weak contracting environments. Alliances between companies can provide incentives for best management and good corporate governance practices in both of them in order to ensure compliance with contracts.

Associations of stakeholders, such as customers, professional associations, financial sector associations, auditors, and academics, can adopt their own good corporate governance practices and codes of conduct (Berglöf & Claessens, 2006). Self-regulation is a very important means of law enforcement in developing countries, but not all groups of stakeholders have incentives to take part in private enforcement. Stakeholder groups act in their own interest, but knowing they depend on each other. Identifying the main stakeholder groups and their incentives is the first step toward promoting multilateral mechanisms among them in order to improve law enforcement. For example, self-regulation by professional associations of accountants and auditors can improve disclosure by firms. Stock exchanges may set minimum requirements for being listed and control capital market activities to boost market development.

This is not just about codification, but also about improving legal enforcement. Private and public good corporate governance initiatives may reinforce corporate governance mechanisms.

The optimal corporate governance system balances control and incentives. In developing countries, other insider corporate mechanisms should complement ownership concentration to avoid abuse by controlling shareholders as board independence or bank debt. These insider corporate governance mechanisms should substitute for control by the capital market. Most of the time, good corporate governance practices will come from private entities. Private enforcement initiatives should substitute for weak public institutional structures in order to improve the business environment.

FUTURE RESEARCH DIRECTIONS

Empirical studies of corporate governance in developing countries are needed to elucidate the effectiveness of legal enforcement and corporate governance, taken as a whole. Corporate finance studies in these countries have mostly focused on a single internal governance mechanism. But institutional framework, capital market development, ownership structure, board of directors, debt, firm performance, and firm characteristics are interrelated variables. Since each economy has different legal traditions and institutional structures, it would be very useful to study how corporate governance mechanisms interact among themselves and with institutional framework variables in order to design an optimal corporate governance model in each country. Which are the best private initiatives in corporate governance in weak contracting environments? What are the incentives for private enforcement? Can private enforcement replace public enforcement in a weak business environment? Can ownership concentration solve all kinds of agency conflicts in developing market economies?

Studies that address endogeneity problems, and comparative corporate governance studies, are usually focused on developed countries (Delgado et al., 2010; Marcos & Castrillo, 2018; Schultz et al., 2010; Wintoki et al., 2012). Given an institutional framework that allows researchers to identify the degree of law enforcement, a dynamic estimation of corporate governance relationships could shed light on the equilibrium of optimal corporate governance in developing countries.

CONCLUSION

Corporate governance mechanisms have endogenous relationships and therefore can interact to solve firm agency problems. External and internal mechanisms can be combined in different ways to balance controls and incentives. More or less widespread use of a particular mechanism can reduce conflict or improve firm performance for a short period of time, but this effect is of no relevance. For example, high ownership concentration can substitute for market control in weak contracting environments, but also may create other conflicts between large and minority shareholders. What matters is whether corporate governance is efficient as a whole and contributes to sustainable value creation for all stakeholder groups.

Corporate governance practices and recommendations take place in a specific institutional framework with specific regulations and enforcement. Legal tradition and enforcement impose the initial choice of corporate governance mechanisms. In developing countries, weak law enforcement and the lack of external market control over firm decisions lead large shareholders to control management actions, but also undermine the protection of other stakeholders like individual minority investors.

Law enforcement is key to corporate governance. The balance among private ordering, private law enforcement, and public law enforcement determines the success of corporate governance. Private initiatives—unilateral corporate governance reforms by firms, efforts to improve company reputation, private shareholders' agreements, bylaw amendments, bilateral alliances between companies, corporate governance codes adopted by trade associations, self-regulation, and private arbitration, among many others (Berglöf & Claessens, 2006)—need public law to be effective. In developing countries the private sector may need to be active to improve the business environment and to promote good corporate governance practices. In turn, private initiatives must be strengthened and verified by public enforcement of the law to avoid wealth expropriation from other stakeholder groups.

REFERENCES

Acemoglu, D., Johnson, S., & Robinson, J. A. (2001). The colonial origins of comparative development: An empirical investigation. *The American Economic Review*, *91*(5), 1369–1401. doi:10.1257/aer.91.5.1369

Aggarwal, R. K., & Samwick, A. A. (1999). Executive compensation, strategic competition, and relative performance evaluation. *The Journal of Finance*, *54*(6), 1999–2043. doi:10.1111/0022-1082.00180

Agrawal, A., & Knoeber, C. R. (1996). Firm performance and mechanisms to control agency problems between managers and shareholders. *Journal of Financial and Quantitative Analysis*, *31*(3), 377–397. doi:10.2307/2331397

Aguilera, R. V., & Jackson, G. (2003). The cross-national diversity of corporate governance: Dimensions and determinants. *Academy of Management Review*, *28*(3), 447–465. doi:10.5465/amr.2003.10196772

Agyemang, O. S., & Castellini, M. (2015). Corporate governance in an emergent economy: A case of Ghana. *Corporate Governance*, *15*(1), 52–84. doi:10.1108/CG-04-2013-0051

Agyemang, O. S., Gatsi, J. G., Ansong, A., & McMillan, D. (2018). Institutions structures and financial market development in Africa. *Cogent Economics & Finance*, *6*(1), 1–15. doi:10.1080/23322039.2018.1488342

Agyemang, O. S., Kyeraa, M., Ansong, A., & Frimpong, S. (2017). Institutional structures and the strength of investor confidence in Africa. *International Journal of Law and Management*, *59*(6), 899–915. doi:10.1108/IJLMA-03-2016-0033

Alchian, A. A., & Demsetz, H. (1972). Production, information cost, and economic organization. *The American Economic Review*, *62*(5), 777–795.

Aoki, M. (2000). *Information, corporate governance, and institutional diversity: Consequences in Japan, the USA, and the transnational economies*. Oxford, UK: Oxford University Press.

Barr, G., Gerson, J., & Kantor, B. (1997). Shareholders as agents and principals: The case for South Africa's corporate governance system. In D. H. Chew (Ed.), *Studies in international corporate finance and governance systems. A comparison of the U.S., Japan, & Europe* (pp. 297–310). Oxford, UK: Oxford University Press.

Berger, P. G., Ofek, E., & Yermack, D. (1997). Managerial entrenchment and capital structure decisions. *The Journal of Finance*, *52*(4), 1411–1438. doi:10.1111/j.1540-6261.1997.tb01115.x

Berglöf, E., & Claessens, S. (2006). Enforcement and good corporate governance in developing countries and transition economies. *The World Bank Research Observer*, *21*(1), 123–150. doi:10.1093/wbro/lkj005

Berle, A. A., & Means, G. C. (1932). *The modern corporation and private property*. New York: Commerce Clearing House.

Bertrand, M., & Mullainathan, S. (1998). *Executive compensation and incentives: The impact of takeover legislation* (NBER Working Paper 6830).

Bhagat, S., & Black, B. S. (2002). The non-correlation between board independence and long-term firm performance. *The Journal of Corporation Law*, *27*, 231–273.

Chernykh, L. (2008). Ultimate ownership and control in Russia. *Journal of Financial Economics*, *88*(1), 169–192. doi:10.1016/j.jfineco.2007.05.005

Claessens, S. (2006). Corporate governance and development. *The World Bank Research Observer*, *21*(1), 91–122. doi:10.1093/wbro/lkj004

Coles, J. W., McWilliams, V. B., & Sen, N. (2001). An examination of the relationship of governance mechanisms to performance. *Journal of Management*, *27*(1), 23–50. doi:10.1177/014920630102700102

David, R., & Brierley, J. E. (1985). *Major legal systems in the world today. An introduction to the comparative study of law* (3rd ed.). London: Stevens & Sons.

Delgado, J. B., Quevedo, E., & Fuente, J. M. (2010). The impact of ownership structure on corporate reputation: Evidence from Spain. *Corporate Governance*, *18*(6), 540–556. doi:10.1111/j.1467-8683.2010.00818.x

Demsetz, H. (1968). The cost of transacting. *The Quarterly Journal of Economics*, *82*(1), 33–53. doi:10.2307/1882244

Demsetz, H., & Lenh, K. (1985). The structure of corporate ownership: Causes and consequences. *Journal of Political Economy*, *93*(6), 1155–1177. doi:10.1086/261354

Djankov, S., Glaeser, E., La Porta, R., Lopez-de-Silanes, F., & Shleifer, A. (2003). The new comparative economics. *Journal of Comparative Economics*, *31*(4), 595–619. doi:10.1016/j.jce.2003.08.005

Francis, J., Khurana, I., & Pereira, R. (2001). *Investor protection laws, accounting and auditing around the world.* SSRN Electronic Library, Working Paper Series.

Franks, J. R., & Mayer, C. (1997). Corporate ownership and control in the U.K., Germany and France. In D. Chew (Ed.), *Studies in international corporate finance and governance systems. A comparison of the U.S., Japan, & Europe* (pp. 281–296). Oxford, UK: Oxford University Press. doi:10.1111/j.1745-6622.1997.tb00622.x

Freeman, R. E. (1984). *Strategic management: A stakeholder approach*. Boston: Pitman.

Freeman, R. E., & Evan, W. M. (1990). Corporate governance: A stakeholder interpretation. *The Journal of Behavioral Economics*, *19*(4), 337–359. doi:10.1016/0090-5720(90)90022-Y

Hallock, K. (1997). Reciprocally interlocking boards of directors and executive compensation. *Journal of Financial and Quantitative Analysis*, *32*(3), 331–344. doi:10.2307/2331203

Hart, O. D. (1995). *Firms, contracts, and financial structure*. London: Oxford University Press. doi:10.1093/0198288816.001.0001

Hermalin, B. E., & Weisbach, M. S. (1991). The effects of board composition and direct incentives on firm performance. *Financial Management*, *20*(4), 101–112. doi:10.2307/3665716

Hermalin, B. E., & Weisbach, M. S. (2003). Boards of directors as an endogenously determined institution: A survey of the economic literature. *Economic Policy Review*, *9*, 7–26.

Hill, C. W. L., & Jones, M. T. (1992). Stakeholder-agency theory. *Journal of Management Studies*, *29*(2), 131–154. doi:10.1111/j.1467-6486.1992.tb00657.x

Hirshleifer, D., & Thakor, A. V. (1994). Managerial performance, boards of directors and takeover bidding. *Journal of Corporate Finance*, *1*(1), 63–90. doi:10.1016/0929-1199(94)90010-8

Humayun, K., & Adelepo, I. (2012). Corporate governance disclosure practices by Swaziland public enterprises. *African Journal of Business Management*, *6*(24), 7136–7148.

Isukul, A. C., & Chizea, J. J. (2016). A comparative analysis of corporate governance disclosure in Nigerian and South African banks. *Asian Journal of Economics. Business and Accounting*, *1*(3), 1–15.

Jara, B. M., & López, F. J. (2007). Earnings management and internal control mechanisms: Evidence from Chilean firms. In L. W. Cornwall (Ed.), *New developments in banking and finance* (pp. 159–178). Hauppauge, NJ: Nova Science Publishers.

Jensen, M. C., & Meckling, W. (1976). Theory of the firm: Managerial behaviour, agency cost and ownership structure. *Journal of Financial Economics*, *3*(4), 305–360. doi:10.1016/0304-405X(76)90026-X

Jiang, F., & Kim, K. A. (2015). Corporate governance in China: A modern perspective. *Journal of Corporate Finance*, *32*, 190–216. doi:10.1016/j.jcorpfin.2014.10.010

John, K., & Kedia, S. (2006). *Design of corporate governance: Role of ownership structure, takeovers, and bank debt* (NYU Working Paper FIN-00-048). New York: Stern School of Business.

John, K., & Senbet, L. W. (1998). Corporate governance and board effectiveness. *Journal of Banking & Finance*, *22*(4), 371–403. doi:10.1016/S0378-4266(98)00005-3

Johnson, S., La Porta, R., López-de-Silanes, F., & Shleifer, A. (2000). Tunneling. *The American Economic Review*, *90*(2), 22–27. doi:10.1257/aer.90.2.22 PMID:11031284

Khanna, T., & Palepu, K. (2005). The evolution of concentrated ownership in India: Broad patterns and a history of the Indian software industry. In R. Mork (Ed.), *A history of corporate governance around the world: Family business groups to professional managers* (pp. 283–324). Chicago: National Bureau of Economic Research, The University of Chicago Press.

Kini, O., Kracaw, W., & Mian, S. (1995). Corporate takeovers, firm performance, and board composition. *Journal of Corporate Finance*, *1*(3-4), 383–412. doi:10.1016/0929-1199(94)00011-I

La Porta, R., López-de-Silanes, F., Shleifer, A., & Vishny, R. (1997). Legal determinants of external finance. *The Journal of Finance*, *52*(3), 1131–1150. doi:10.1111/j.1540-6261.1997.tb02727.x

La Porta, R., López-de-Silanes, F., Shleifer, A., & Vishny, R. (1998). Law and finance. *Journal of Political Economy*, *106*(6), 1113–1155. doi:10.1086/250042

La Porta, R., López-de-Silanes, F., Shleifer, A., & Vishny, R. (2000). Investor protection and corporate governance. *Journal of Financial Economics*, *58*(1-2), 3–27. doi:10.1016/S0304-405X(00)00065-9

Levin, M. R. (2015). *What is private ordering?* Retrieved from http://www.theactivistinvestor.com/The_Activist_Investor/Blog/Entries/2015/9/29_What_is_Private_Ordering.html

Marcos, S., & Castrillo, L. A. (2018, June). *Equilibrium in corporate governance.* Paper presented at the XXVIII meeting of the Asociación Científica de Economía y Dirección de la Empresa, Valladolid, Spain.

Mchran, H. (1995). Executive compensation structure, ownership, and firm performance. *Journal of Financial Economics*, *38*(2), 163–184. doi:10.1016/0304-405X(94)00809-F

Milgrom, P. (1988). Employment contracts, influence activities, and efficient organization design. *Journal of Political Economy*, *42*(1), 42–61. doi:10.1086/261523

Miller, T., Kim, A. B., & Roberts, J. M. (2018). *Index of economic freedom*. Washington, DC: The Heritage Foundation.

Mínguez, A., & Martín, J. F. (2003). *El consejo de administración como mecanismo de control: Evidencia para el mercado español* (Working Paper). Instituto Valenciano de Investigaciones Económicas. (WP-EC 2003-02)

Mongalo, T. (2004). South Africanizing company law for a modern, competitive global economy. *South African Law Journal*, *121*(1), 93–116.

Ngare, E., Nyamongo, E. M., & Misati, R. N. (2014). Stock market development and economic growth in Africa. *Journal of Economics and Business*, *74*, 24–39. doi:10.1016/j.jeconbus.2014.03.002

Rajan, R. G., & Zingales, L. (2000). The governance of the new enterprise. In X. Vives (Ed.), *Corporate governance* (pp. 201–232). Cambridge, UK: Cambridge University Press. doi:10.1017/CBO9781139175333.007

Rappaport, A. (1998). *Creating shareholder value*. New York: Free Press.

Rashid, A. (2018). Board independence and firm performance: Evidence from Bangladesh. *Future Business Journal*, *4*(1), 34–49. doi:10.1016/j.fbj.2017.11.003

Rediker, K. J., & Seth, A. (1995). Boards of directors and substitution effects of alternative governance mechanisms. *Strategic Management Journal*, *16*(2), 85–99. doi:10.1002mj.4250160202

Roberts, M. R., & Whited, T. M. (2013). Endogeneity in empirical corporate finance. In G. M. Constantinides, M. Harris, & R. M. Stulz (Eds.), Handbook of the economics of finance (vol. 2, Part A, pp. 493-572). Amsterdam: North Holland.

Schultz, E. L., Tan, D. T., & Walsh, K. D. (2010). Endogeneity and the corporate governance-performance relation. *Australian Journal of Management*, *35*(2), 145–163. doi:10.1177/0312896210370079

Schwarcz, S. T. (2002). Private ordering. *Northwestern University Law Review*, *97*(1), 319–350.

Shleifer, A., & Vishny, R. (1986). Large shareholders and corporate control. *Journal of Political Economy, 94*(3), 461–488. doi:10.1086/261385

Shleifer, A., & Vishny, R. (1997). A survey of corporate governance. *The Journal of Finance, 52*(2), 737–783. doi:10.1111/j.1540-6261.1997.tb04820.x

Williamson, O. E. (1983). Organizational form, residual claimants, and corporate control. *The Journal of Law & Economics, 26*(2), 351–366. doi:10.1086/467039

Wintoki, M. B., Linck, J. S., & Netter, J. M. (2012). Endogeneity and the dynamics of internal corporate governance. *Journal of Financial Economics, 105*(3), 581–606. doi:10.1016/j.jfineco.2012.03.005

Yermack, D. (1996). Higher valuation of companies with a small board of directors. *Journal of Financial Economics, 40*(2), 185–212. doi:10.1016/0304-405X(95)00844-5

Zingales, L. (1998). Corporate governance. In P. Newman (Ed.), *The New Palgrave Dictionary of Economics and the Law*. London: Palgrave Macmillan.

ADDITIONAL READING

Aggarwal, R., Schloetzer, J. D., & Williamson, R. (2015). *The impact of governance mandates on the evolution of firm value and governance culture*. Georgetown McDonough School of Business Research Paper. Retrieved from https://ssrn.com/abstract=2605825

Chhaochharia, V., & Laeven, L. (2007). *The invisible hand in corporate governance* (CEPR Discussion Paper N° DP6256). Retrieved from http://ssrn.com/abstract=1135494

Coles, J. L., Lemmon, M. L., & Meschke, J. F. (2012). Structural models and endogeneity in corporate finance: The link between managerial ownership and corporate performance. *Journal of Financial Economics, 103*(1), 149–168. doi:10.1016/j.jfineco.2011.04.002

Djankov, S., La Porta, R., López-De-Silanes, F., & Shleifer, A. (2008). The law and economics of self-dealing. *Journal of Financial Economics, 88*(3), 430–465. doi:10.1016/j.jfineco.2007.02.007

Easterbrook, F. H. (1997). International corporate differences: Markets or law? *Journal of Applied Corporate Finance, 9*(4), 23–30. doi:10.1111/j.1745-6622.1997.tb00621.x

Fama, E. F., & Jensen, M. C. (1983). Agency problems and residual claims. *The Journal of Law & Economics*, *26*(2), 327–349. doi:10.1086/467038

Hofstede, G. (1980). *Culture's consequences. International differences in work-related values*. Beverly Hills: Sage Publications.

Roe, M. J. (2003). *Political determinants of corporate governance: Political context, corporate impact* (Discussion Paper N° 451). Harvard Law School.

Watts, R., & Zimmerman, J. (1986). *Positive accounting theory*. Englewood Cliffs, NJ: Prentice-Hall.

Wymeersch, W. (2005). *Enforcement of corporate governance codes* (Law Working Paper N°46/2005). European Corporate Governance Institute.

KEY TERMS AND DEFINITIONS

Agency Problem: Conflict between parties in a contract from an agent-principal perspective in agency theory.

Corporate Governance Model: Characteristic combination of external and internal corporate governance mechanisms in an institutional framework or country, for example the Anglo-Saxon, Continental, and Japanese corporate governance models.

Institutional Framework: Set of several legal, economic, cultural, and social variables that constitute a key feature of a geographic area and determine the actions of institutions, companies, and people in this location.

Law Enforcement: Effectiveness of and compliance with regulations and laws through private or public initiatives.

Legal Tradition: Origin of a legal framework. The two main legal traditions are civil law and common law.

Optimal Corporate Government System: Interaction of external and internal corporate governance mechanisms, institutional framework variables, and firm characteristics in order to reach an equilibrium that allows value creation for all stakeholders.

Weak Contracting Environment: Institutional framework characterized by lack of compliance with contractual commitments and insufficient protection of property rights from wealth expropriation by other parties.

Chapter 8
Cash Holdings and Corporate Governance:
Evidence From Turkey

Elif Akben-Selcuk
Kadir Has University, Turkey

Pinar Sener
OCRE Lab, EDC Paris Business School, France

ABSTRACT

This chapter investigates the empirical factors affecting corporate cash holdings with special emphasis on corporate governance variables for a sample of Turkish-listed nonfinancial firms over the period 2006 to 2010. The findings reveal a significant non-linear relation between family ownership and cash holdings. In addition, while board structure does not significantly affect the level of cash holdings, tunneling increases cash reserves of firms. Furthermore, the results indicate that cash flow, leverage, other liquid assets that can be used as cash substitutes, the degree of tangibility of assets, and firm size are important in determining cash holdings among Turkish companies.

DOI: 10.4018/978-1-5225-9607-3.ch008

INTRODUCTION

One of the most important financial policies of a firm is the cash policy. Holding sufficient cash serves to maintain daily operations, finance profitable investment projects, decrease the likelihood of financial distress, minimize the costs of raising external funds and so on (Ferreira and Vilela, 2004; Uyar and Kuzey, 2014). That is why, cash represents a considerable asset for firms. For instance, cash forms 9% of the total assets in UK (Al-Najjar and Belghitar, 2011) and firms hold 18.5% of assets in cash in Japan (Pinkowitz et al., 2003).

Three commonly used theoretical models by previous studies to investigate cash holding of firms include the trade off theory, the pecking order theory and the free cash flow theory. While trade-off model states that the optimal level of cash holdings depends on the trade-off between the marginal benefits and the marginal costs of holding cash (Al-Najjar & Belghitar, 2011; Ferreira & Vilela, 2004), the pecking order argues that firms do not have target cash levels (Myers and Majluf, 1984). Finally, the free cash flow theory suggests that agency conflicts between managers and shareholders affect cash holding policy (Jensen, 1986).

Based on free cash flow theory the objective of this study is to examine the relationship between corporate governance characteristics and cash holdings in Turkish firms. Specifically, the influence of family involvement and excess control rights on cash policy will be explored. The chapter attempts to fill the following gaps in the literature.

First, the empirical literature regarding the determinants of corporate cash holdings has mainly focused on developed countries, such as United States (Opler et al., 1999; Dittmar and Mahrt-Smith, 2007; D'Mello et al., 2008), UK (Ozkan and Ozkan, 2004; Al-Najjar & Belghitar, 2011), and EU countries (Ferreira and Vilela, 2004). The decision of holding cash is still considered under-researched in emerging countries (Al-Najjar, 2013; Uyar and Kuzey, 2014). By providing empirical evidence from an emerging market, Turkey, the study attempts to contribute to the general literature on cash holding determinants.

Second, limited attention has been devoted to the question of whether agency conflicts between controlling and minority shareholders impact cash holding policy of firms, especially in family firms (Liu et al., 2015; Kuan et al., 2011). Indeed, Al-Najjar (2013) indicates the necessity of further discussion about the impact of internal corporate governance factors on corporate cash holdings in developing countries. Uyar and Kuzey (2014) also call a new research which incorporates corporate governance variables into the model that explains the determinants of cash holdings in Turkey. Therefore, the study attempts to contribute to the corporate governance literature by exploring the role of corporate governance factors in explaining cash holding policies of Turkish firms.

Third the cash holding policy of firms under family control remains unexplored in the literature except a few studies (e.g. Ozkan and Ozkan, 2004; Kuan et al. 2011; Liu et al., 2015). Despite that, the contribution of family firms to national economies is significant in many countries, and Turkey is no exception. Previous studies have revealed that family firms are complex, because, in addition to considering financial objectives, they have nonfinancial motivations such as the preservation of family dynasty and values, altruism toward family members (Lubatkin, Schulze, Ling, & Dino, 2005; Gomez-Mejia et al., 2011). Nonfinancial objectives shape their decisions and they have strong incentives to pursue activities that fit their personal interest but come at the expense of minority shareholders, especially in countries with poor investor protection (Claessens et al., 2002; Villalonga & Amit, 2006). Accordingly the final contribution of this study will on family firm literature.

The results reveal a non-linear relationhip between family ownership and cash holdings. Board structure does not significantly affect the level of cash holdings but tunneling increases cash reserves of firms. In addition, the results indicate that cash flow, leverage, other liquid assets that can be used as cash substitutes, the degree of tangibility of assets and firm size are important in determining cash holdings of Turkish companies.

The remainder of the chapter is organized as follows. The next section contains a review of literature. The methodology is elaborated in the following section. Then, results of empirical analyses are discussed. The chapter concludes with a summary of main findings and implications.

THEORY AND EMPIRICAL HYPOTHESES

Country Specific Characteristics

Business groups emerged as the most common type of organization in Turkey in response to the dominant role of the state in creating the business environment (Oba, Tigrel, & Sener, 2014). These business groups are mostly owned and managed by families (Goksen and Usdiken 2001) and are characterised by high ownership concentration and low free-float ratios to preserve family control (OECD 2013). High ownership concentration is also considered an outcome of weak legal environment in Turkey (La Porta et al., 1998; Goksen & Usdiken, 2001). Turkey is a French origin civil law country and offers a weak level of investor protection (La Porta et al., 1998). Shareholders are poorly protected against self-dealing and do not have preemptive rights, cumulative voting and share blocking (Oba et al. 2014). In addition, the enforcement of law is considered poor in Turkey.

Corporate governance standards are set and enforced by Capital Markets Board (CMB). Principles operate on comply or explain basis and mainly address publicly held joint stock companies (Ugur & Ararat, 2006). Since 2005, the CMB follows the compliance of listed firms with principles and applies sanctions for non-implementation. While private enforcement practices are not commonly used in Turkey, the corporate governance framework relies on public supervision and enforcement (OECD, 2013). Turkey has recently experienced new legislative reforms, such as the adoption of the new Turkish Commercial Code (TCC) as of 2012 and the revision of Capital Market Law, which affect corporate governance standards (OECD, 2013).

In Turkey, joint stock companies have a one-tier board by law (Ararat & Orbay, 2006). A simple majority is adequate to select board members at the general shareholders' meeting. Therefore, if a controlling block of shareholders exists, all board members may be selected by the majority shareholders (Okutan-Nilsson, 2007). TCC does not impose any requirements for board independence and board composition. However, governance principles published by the CMB requires listed companies at least one third of board directors to be independent and classify their board members as executive, non-executive and independent non-executive members (Ugur & Ararat, 2006).

Although major economic reforms have been observed in financial markets in the post-2001 period, financial sector still remains small and shadow in Turkey compared to other developing countries (TBB, 2009). For instance, the size of financial markets as percentage of GDP, which was 460 percent for Malaysia, 260 percent for Thailand, 295.8 percent for Brazil and 341.4 percent for South Korea, was 164.1 percent for Turkey at the end of 2009. However, Turkish economy has shown a substantial growth (an average annual real GDP growth of 5% between the period of 2002 and 2012) and experienced declining inflation and interest rates (Uyar & Kuzey, 2014). Therefore, the expansion potential of financial sector is considered high (WB, 2011). Turkey's stock market, which has experienced a 600 percent increase in market capitalization between 2002 and 2010 is still smaller than other countries that have similar per capita income. Corporations consider banks the main source of finance (Uyar & Kuzey, 2014). Only 12% of the largest Turkish companies are listed and the average free-float ratio of largest 20 companies (in terms of market capitalization) was 28% (WB, 2011).

Cash Holding Theories

The trade-off theory by Miller and Orr (1966) argues that the trade-off between the marginal costs and marginal benefits of holding cash determines the optimal level of cash held by firms. There are two motives of cash holdings: minimizing the transaction costs and precautionary motives (Opler et al., 1999). According to this theory, the cost of raising funds from external sources is higher than using internal funds (Ozkan & Ozkan, 2004), especially transaction costs for firms with limited access to capital markets are higher (Opler et al., 1999). The second motive believes that firms with an access to capital markets might still prefer holding cash to use in case of emergency (Al-Najjar, 2013). In spite of these two benefits, the main cost of holding cash is its lower return compared to other assets.

According to the pecking order theory there is no optimal level of cash holdings for the company (Myers, 1984; Myers & Majluf, 1984). The theory suggests that in presence of information asymmetry, firms, in order to minimize the costs related to the asymmetric information, choose to finance their new investments projects first with internal sources of cash, then debt and lastly with equity (Myers & Majluf, 1984). In this theory, cash is considered a low cost source of financing for the companies.

Finally, the free cash flow theory of Jensen (1986) suggests that the incentive of accumulating cash for managers is to have more assets under their control and not loose power over the firms' decisions. This results in an agency problem because excess cash allows managers to invest in projects that serve their own interests rather than those of company shareholders. The free cash flows hypothesis considers cash holdings an instrument of managerial discretion. On the other hand, when firms are controlled by large shareholders, those shareholders have also incentives to hold greater cash holdings to invest in projects that benefit them personally but may come at the expense of outside investors. This leads to another type of agency problem (Pinkowitz et al. 2003). Hence, high information asymmetries and a low quality of corporate governance would lead cash holdings to build up under this theory (Dittmar et al., 2003).

Empirical Evidences

The amount and determinants of cash holdings is highly discussed in the literature especially after 1990s. For instance, Opler et al. (1999), based on the US listed firms' data between 1971-1994, reveal that firms with higher growth opportunities, higher business risk and smaller size have higher level of cash holdings than other firms.

Bates et al. (2009) argue that the U.S firms average cash ratio doubled from 1980 to 2006. According to Ozkan and Ozkan (2004) firms' growth opportunities, cash flows, liquid assets, leverage and bank debt affect corporate cash holdings in UK firms. Al-Najjar and Belghitar (2011) by using the United Kingdom data conclude that dividends, leverage, growth, size, risk, profitability, and working capital ratio are significant determinants of cash holdings. Garcia-Teruel and Martinez-Solano (2008) use Spanish SMEs data and conclude that firms have a target cash level which is increased by strong growth opportunities and large cash flows and decreased by bank loans and substitutes for cash.

In addition to those determinants, other researchers have investigated the corporate governance impact on cash holdings. For example, Dittmar et al. (2003) by using an international sample of 45 countries reveal that firms in countries where shareholder protection is poor hold more cash than firms in countries with good shareholder protection. Guney et al. (2007) show that firms with strong shareholder protection hold lower levels of cash in Japan, France, Germany, and the US. Regarding the impact of internal corporate governance mechanism on cash holdings, Ozkan and Ozkan (2004) find the existence of a non-monotonic relationship between managerial ownership and cash holdings and reveal that board composition and the presence of ultimate are not significantly related to cash holdings. Liu et al. (2015) conclude that family firms hold high levels of cash holdings for tunneling in China.

Hypotheses

Based on the specific features of the Turkish institutional context, the three theories and empirical evidences discussed above, we anticipate that the following two groups of variables are relevant to firms' cash holding decisions: corporate governance variables and the other control variables.

Corporate Governance Variables

Board Structure

Scholars regard board of directors as an instrument of control which decreases agency costs (Baysinger and Butler, 1985; Jensen and Meckling, 1976). On the one hand, it is a tool to align interests between shareholders and managers (Klein 2002). On the other hand, it is used to reduce the opportunistic behavior of any controlling shareholder that may lead to expropriation of minority shareholders (Anderson & Reeb, 2004; Boubaker et al. 2015). More specifically, outside directors, who have no financial interests in the firm, have incentives to objectively monitor the actions of management and majority shareholders (Yermack, 2004; Anderson & Reeb, 2004).

Board independence also depends on the leadership structure. While CEO duality strengthens the discretionary power of CEOs, separating the board chairperson and CEO positions increases board's ability to properly perform its monitoring role (Muth & Donaldson, 1998). Dual leadership structure is more likely to restrict managerial discretion over resources and reduce wealth expropriation by controlling shareholders. Board size is another attribute that affects monitoring activities of boards by facilitating the communication and cooperation in the boardroom (Boubaker et al. 2015). Scholars consider smaller boards more beneficial in supervising top management (Brennan, 2006; Muth and Donaldson, 1998) than larger boards which suffer from loss of productivity (Steiner, 1972). Firms with small boards are more effective in ousting their CEOs and appointing outsiders instead of them (Faleye, 2004).

To the extent that boards with greater outside director representation, dual leadership and small size perform effectively monitoring activities, reduce the tension between managers and shareholders and prevent controlling shareholders from pursuing their own objectives at the expense of minority shareholders, the cost of external financing is more likely to be low for firms with these board characteristics (Ozkan and Ozkan, 2004; Boubaker et al. 2015). Therefore, these firms are expected to hold lower levels of cash.

Family Involvement

It is argued that while the unification of ownership and control eliminates agency conflicts between managers and shareholders in family firms (Fama & Jensen, 1983; Villalonga & Amit, 2006), they suffer from agency conflicts between controlling and non-controlling shareholders (Claessens et al., 2002; Villalonga & Amit, 2006). If family shareholders gain nearly full control of the firm, they may prefer to pursue their own interest and generate private benefits of control at the expense of minority shareholders (Claessens et al., 2002). When family firms want to raise capital in the market, this agency problem leads to higher financing costs. Therefore, they hold more cash than nonfamily firms (Kuan et al. 2011).

While empirical evidence is scarce, Ozkan and Ozkan (2004) find that when families are controllers of firms, they increase the amount of cash holdings under their control to preserve their privileged position. In order to extend their analysis, we focus on family ownership and family management separately and investigate the non-linearity of family ownership-cash holdings relationship. Based on the argument that the family shareholder's level of control should be high enough to have an impact on decision-making and the agency conflict between controlling and noncontrolling shareholders is amplified at high level of control (Kuan et al. 2011), we expect a negative relationship between low level of family control and cash holdings since the cost of external financing is low at that level. However, we expect a positive relationship between high level of family control and cash holdings.

When family members occupy CEO and other top management positions, family's interests and firm's interests can be easily aligned (Anderson & Reeb, 2003). Family CEOs and managers who consider the firm an extension of themselves are more likely to invest in long-term projects (Le Breton-Miller & Miller, 2006). Therefore, they may want to accumulate more cash to avoid underinvestment and higher external financing costs which may harm both the health of firm and the wealth of family. We propose a positive relationship between family CEO and cash holdings.

Separation of Control and Cash Flow Rights

Large shareholders are more likely to expropriate wealth from minority shareholders as their ownership goes beyond a certain level (Shleifer and Vishny, 1997). They, in general, use control-enhancing mechanisms which lead to the separation of ownership and control to gain dominant control and extract private benefits from the firm (La Porta et al. 1999; Villalonga and Amit 2006). The use of control enhancing mechanisms by violating one share-one vote rule reinforces wealth expropriation from minority shareholders (Villalonga and Amit 2006). As the wedge between voting and control rights increases, firms are more likely to make inefficient choices which increase agency costs (Bebchuk et al. 1999). Controlling shareholders holding voting rights in excess of their cash-flow rights become entrenched (Kuan et al. 2011) and tend to engage in non-value-maximizing activities (Morck and al. 1988).

Recent studies have showed that the use of control-enhancing mechanisms, especially in family firms, harms firm value especially in countries with weak investor protection (Peng & Jiang, 2010). Liu et al. (2015) find that controlling family holding excess control rights have high cash holdings in China. Belkhir et al. (2014) also show that the value of cash holdings is negatively related to the separation of control and cash-flow rights in France. On the other hand, Ozkan and Ozkan (2004) reveal that the divergence between control and cash flow rights negatively affects cash holdings in UK, supporting that the shared benefits of control dominate the private benefits accruing to controllers. Considering that the country-level shareholder protection is weak in Turkey, we expect a positive relationship between excess control rights in family firms and cash holdings.

Tunneling

The reallocation of funds by controlling shareholders from firms in which they hold a small share to firms in which they have a large share is called tunneling (Johnson et al., 2000; Gonenc and Hermes, 2008). Tunneling activities come at the expense of minority shareholders since assets and profits are transferred out of companies for the benefit of controlling shareholders. The protection of investor rights at country and firm level impacts the occurrence of those activities (Johnson et al., 2000; Jiang et al., 2010; Peng et al., 2011; Liu et al. 2015). For instance, bright line rules of civil law are more likely to encourage tunneling. Liu et al. (2015) also show that excess control rights hold by family shareholders and direct family involvement in firm trigger tunneling activities. Considering the weak investor protection in Turkey, we propose a positive relationship between tunneling and cash holdings. We expect that resources transferred from group firms are appropriated by the largest shareholder and to avoid the shortage of cash, firms hold high level of cash holdings.

Control Variables

Firm Size

Larger firms hold less cash compared to smaller firms due to the economies of scale (Miller & Orr, 1966), better access to capital markets (Fazzari & Petersen, 1993; Kim et al., 1998; Ozkan & Ozkan; 2004) and the diversification benefits (Rajan & Zingales, 1995; Titman & Wessels, 1988). These theoretical findings were also empirically demonstrated in several studies (D'Mello, Krishnaswami, & Larkin, 2008; Fazzari & Petersen, 1993; Ferreira & Vilela, 2004; Kim, Mauer, & Sherman, 1998; Opler et al., 1999, Ozkan & Ozkan, 2004; Rajan & Zingales, 1995). Hence, we expect a negative relationship between firm size and cash levels.

Liquid Asset Substitutes

According to trade-off theory, a negative relationship between cash holdings and liquid assets is expected since firms can liquidate these in times of cash shortage. Empirical findings also suggest that as the availability of non-cash liquid assets increases, firms are less likely to hold cash (Ferreira & Vilela, 2004; Hardin et al., 2009; Ozkan & Ozkan, 2004). Accordingly, we propose a negative relationship between non-cash liquid assets held by firms and their cash levels.

Dividend Policy

The trade-off theory argues that firms can raise funds by decreasing their dividend payments. Empirically, the majority of existing studies found a negative or insignificant relationship between dividend policy and corporate cash holdings (e.g., Bates et al., 2009; Al-Najjar & Belghitar, 2011; Ferreira & Vilela, 2004; Ozkan & Ozkan, 2004). Based on the above arguments, we expect a negative relation between dividend payments and cash holdings.

Leverage

According to the pecking order theory, there is a negative association between leverage and cash holdings. When investment levels are greater than retained earnings, debt levels tend to increase and cash levels tend to decrease. The trade-off theory predicts an ambiguous relationship between debt and cash levels. On the one hand, firms with higher debt levels prefer to have more cash to decrease the probability of financial distress. On the other hand, highly leveraged firms might hold less cash since current leverage is a proxy for the probability to borrow in the future. Finally, the trade-off theory suggests that highly levered firms hold less cash because they are more closely monitored, leaving less room for managerial discretion. Based on the above theoretical discussion, and the majority of existing empirical (Bates et al., 2009; D'Mello et al., 2008; Hardin, Highfield, Hill, & Kelly, 2009; Kim et al., 1998; Opler et al., 1999; Ozkan & Ozkan, 2004), we hypothesize a negative relation between leverage and cash holdings.

Growth Opportunities

The precautionary motive concept in trade-off theory (Bates et al., 2009; Hardin et al., 2009; Ozkan & Ozkan; 2004) suggests that firms with a larger growth opportunity set hold more cash due to potential losses which may arise from foregoing valuable positive NPV investments. Moreover, the pecking order theory suggests that more investment opportunities lead to higher need for cash, thus predicting a positive relationship between investment opportunities and corporate cash holdings (Ferreira and Vilela, 2004). Most previous studies empirically find this positive relationship between investment opportunities and cash holdings (Bates et al., 2009; Ferreira & Vilela, 2004; Hardin et al., 2009; Kim et al., 1998; Opler et al., 1999; Ozkan & Ozkan, 2004). Based on those studies and theoretical background, we expect a positive relationship between investment opportunities and cash holding.

Cash Flow Volatility

According to trade-off theory, firms with more volatile cash flows are faced with a higher likelihood of experiencing cash shortage, causing them to give up valuable investments and holding more cash (Ferreira & Vileila, 2004). The empirical findings, however, are inconsistent. Some studies report a negative relation between the two variables (Ferreira and Vilela, 2004; Paskelian et al., 2010), some report a positive relation (Guney et al., 2007; Al-Najjar and Belghitar, 2011; Bigelli and Sánchez-Vidal, 2012), and some insignificant (Uyar & Kuzey, 2014). Hence we do not make an a priori assessment of the relationship between cash flow volatility and cash holdings.

Capital Expenditures

The pecking order theory suggests that firms simply hold less cash when they invest (i.e. when capital expenditure level is higher). Accordingly, we propose a negative relationship between capital expenditures and corporate cash holdings. However, empirical studies reveal contradictory findings about the capital expenditure's effect on the cash holdings. For instance, according to Bates et al. (2009) capital expenditures are negatively associated with cash holdings, while Opler et al. (1999) and Riddick and Whited (2009) find a positive relationship between them.

Bank Debt

Since bank debt is a substitute for cash, companies with higher amounts of financial debt in their capital structure should hold less cash (Uyar & Kuzey, 2014). In addition, it is easier for firms with more financial debt to have access to external capital markets (Ozkan and Ozkan, 2004). This relationship has also been shown empirically (Ferreira and Vilela, 2004; Ozkan and Ozkan, 2004; Uyar and Kuzey, 2014). Accordingly, we expect a negative relationship between corporate cash holdings and financial debt.

Tangibility

Companies with higher amounts of tangible assets can sell them when they need cash or can use these as a collateral when borrowing externally (Drobetz and Grüninger, 2007). Therefore, firms with more tangible assets are less likely to hold cash as empircally demonstrated (Drobetz and Grüninger, 2007; Uyar & Kuzey, 2014). Based on that, we suggest a negative relationship between asset tangibility and corporate cash holdings.

Cash Flow

The trade-off theory suggests that firms generating more cash flow from their operations are less likely to amass cash reserves. However, the pecking order theory predicts that firm generating higher amounts of cash flows are likely to keep some of these as cash reserves as a precaution. Despite these two contradictory theoretical predictions, the majority of the empirical studies provided support for the pecking order theory (Opler et al., 1999; Ozkan & Ozkan, 2004; Uyar & Kuzey, 2014). Accordingly, we expect a positive relationship between a firm's cash flows and its cash holdings.

R&D Intensity

Since R&D projects are uncertain in nature and can arise at times of cash shortage, firms heavily involved in R&D activities should hold more cash (Sanchez & Yurdagul, 2013). The same logic was also emprically confirmed (Opler et al., 1999; Pinkowitz et al., 2012). Based on the preceding argument, we expect a positive relationship between a firm's R&D expenditures and its cash holdings.

Profitability

There are two conflicting view points related to the impact of profits on cash holdings. On the one hand, firms generating more profits could be using these to accumulate more cash, leading to a positive relationship between cash holdings and profitability. On the other hand, more profitable firms can use their profits as cash substitutes to provide a source of liquidity in case of cash shortage, suggesting a negative relationship between the two variables. Empirically, Ogunpide et al. (2012) demonstrated that firms with higher return on assets had more cash holdings. Accordingly, we also expect a positive relationship between profitability, measured by return on assets, and cash holdings.

METHODOLOGY

Sample and Data

The sample used in this paper consists of companies listed on Borsa Istanbul from 2006 to 2010. The initial sample was the set of all firms for which data were available. In order to construct the final panel data set, we excluded financial firms because of their unique accounting standards (Liu et al., 2015). Thus, the final sample is left with 190 firms and consists of an unbalanced panel of about 950 firm-years observations.

Data on family ownership and management and board characteristics of firms were manually collected from the articles of associations, compliance and annual reports of firms published on the website of Public Disclosure Platform. Data on other firm-specific variables (such as ROA, Leverage) were obtained from a database developed by FINNET[1]. To minimize the effect of outliers, we winsorized variables at the 5th and 95th percent for their distributions (Campbell et al., 2008). Dummies for 6 industries and another dummy variable for observations belonging to years 2008 and 2009 to control the effect of the crisis were also included.

Variables

Cash Holdings

Following prior studies in the literature (Uyar & Kuzey, 2014; Kuan et al., 2011; Liu et al., 2015) the dependent variable, cash holdings, is measured by dividing cash and cash equivalents to total assets.

Governance Variables

In order to investigate the effect of board structure on cash holdings, this study uses three variables: Board independence, CEO duality and Board size. We divided the number of independent directors by board size to calculate board independence (Anderson & Reeb, 2003). CEO duality is a dummy that equals 1 if the CEO also serves as board chair and 0 otherwise. Board size is defined as the natural logarithm of the number of board members.

In this study, we chose to employ the definition proposed by Villalonga and Amit (2006, p.390) to identify family firms. Accordingly, family firm is recognized as a firm whose founder or a member of the family by either blood or marriage is an officer, a director, or the owner of at least five percent of the firm's equity, individually or as a group. Family ownership is defined as the percentage of ultimate voting rights held by family. We followed the method introduced by La Porta, Lopez-de-Silanes and Shleifer (1999) to find voting rights of firms. We used a dummy variable, Family CEO, which takes the value of 1 in the presence of a family CEO and 0 otherwise to measure the effect of family management on cash holdings. Wedge refers to the difference between the family shareholder's control rights and cash-flow rights. In this study, we also utilised Orecta to measure inter-corporate loans to controlling shareholders and proxy tunneling. It is defined as other receivables scaled by total assets (Jiang et al. 2010; Liu et al. 2015).

Control Variables

The leverage ratio is calculated as the ratio of total debt to total assets. Profitability is computed by the return on assets, the ratio of net income to total assets. Growth opportunities are captured by market-to-book ratio which is measured as the market value of equity plus the book value of debt, divided by the book value of assets. The level of investments is proxied by capital expenditures defined as the change in fixed assets plus depreciation divided by total assets. The fifth variable which is included into the analysis is firm size measured by the natural logarithm of total assets.

Bank debt is defined as the ratio of financial debt to total debt. The availability of cash substitutes is captured by non-cash assets calculated as the ratio of net working capital less cash to total assets. Tangibility is defined as the ratio of tangible fixed assets to total assets. We also include the ratio of research and development expenditures to net sales. Cash flow ratio is the ratio of operating income or loss to total assets. Volatility is the standard deviation of operating cash flow divided by total assets. Dividend payout ratio is calculated by dividing a firm's cash dividends by its net profit.

Estimation

Previous studies in the literature have documented that cash holdings are not exogenous and jointly determined by other firm-specific variables (Liu et al., 2015). Therefore, we employed a dynamic GMM model to control for endogeneity and to account for the impact of previous periods' cash levels on the cash holdings in a given period. For our dynamic panel data, difference GMM (Arellano & Bond, 1991) and system GMM (Arellano & Bover, 1995; Blundell & Bond, 1998) estimators were employed. In the difference GMM, all regressors were transformed by first differencing. In the system GMM, the assumption that the first difference in instrumenting variables are not correlated with the fixed effects was added to improve efficiency (Uyar & Kuzey, 2014). Industry clustered standard errors are reported in both cases.

We estimated the following dynamic panel data model:

$$CASH_{it} = \beta_0 + \beta_1 CASH_{it-1} + \beta_2 G_{it} + \beta_3 X_{it} + \varepsilon_{it} \quad (1)$$

where: $CASH_{it}$ denotes the cash holdings of firm *i* in year *t*, G_{it} is a vector of governance variables for firm i in year *t*, X_{it} is a vector of control variables for firm *i* in year *t*, $B_{0,}$ $\beta_{1,}$ $\beta_{2,}$ and β_3 are vectors of parameters to be estimated, and ε_{it} is the error term.

RESULTS

Descriptive Statistics

The descriptive statistics related to our variables are presented in Table 1. The mean cash ratio is 8.7%. The average voting rights held by families is 39%. The mean value for the difference between voting and cash flow right is 6%. The number of firm-years in our sample that belongs to firm managed by family CEOs is 97. On the other hand, the average percentage of directors in the boards of the companies in the sample is 5%. The average number of directors on the board registers a mean value of 6. Finally, 60 of the firm-year observations in the sample belong to firms where CEO also serves as board chair.

Table 1. Summary statistics of variables for the full sample

Variable	N	Mean	Std. Dev.	Min	Max
Cash holdings$_{(t-1)}$	950	8.70	10.81	0.002	84.96
Board size	919	1.80	0.31	1.10	2.83
CEO Duality	856	0.07	0.26	0	1
Board independence	919	0.05	0.11	0	0.60
Family CEO	882	0.11	0.31	0	1
Family Ownership	882	0.39	0.30	0	1.00
Wedge	882	0.06	0.12	-0.001	0.68
Orecta	950	3.12	8.03	0	33.09
Capital expenditures	950	3.44	6.71	-6.73	20.87
Market-to-book ratio	912	1.62	1.19	0.38	4.99
Leverage	950	45.90	23.85	9.14	92.36
Return on assets	950	2.77	9.82	-18.26	22.66
Bank debt	950	19.22	18.31	0	58.43
Non-cash assets	950	7.71	20.30	-39.10	42.89
Tangibility	950	35.92	19.67	2.13	72.35
R&D/sales	945	0.15	0.36	0	1.35
Dividend payout ratio	948	19.62	30.36	0	89.48
Firm size	950	19.12	1.53	14.871	23.44
Cash flow ratio	950	0.50	0.78	0.003	2.94
Volatility	950	0.81	2.41	0.000	26.86

Table 2 presents the correlation matrix for dependent and explanatory variables. As can be seen, all correlations are below 0.7 hence multicollinearity is not a concern (Lehman et al., 1988). The correlation table indicates that cash holdings variable has significant positive association with board size and wedge and significant negative association with family ownership. Cash holdings has no significant relationship with other governance variables including CEO duality, board independence and Orecta.

Regression Results

According to the results of the first specification which only includes board characteristics and control variables, board size, CEO duality and board independence do not have a significant impact on Turkish firms' cash holdings. Regarding control variables, results showed that firms which use higher leverage in their capital structure tend to hold less cash. As expected, the availability of other current assets which can be used as cash substitutes by the firm is negatively related to the level of cash holdings. The negative and significant coefficient of the tangibility variable suggests that firms which have higher levels of tangible assets tend to hold less cash. Finally, there is a positive relationship between cash flow and cash holding.

In the second specification, we also include variables related to family involvement. According to these results, the relationship between voting rights held in families and cash holdings is convex, meaning that as the concentration of voting rights held by families increases, the level of cash holdings augments at an increasing rate. The existence of a family CEO or the difference between voting and cash flow rights do not significantly affect cash holding. The results regarding board characteristics and control variables are consistent with the first specification except that a significantly negative relationship between firm size and cash holding is found in this second model.

In the third and final specification, Orecta is included to investigate the impact of controlling shareholders' tunneling on cash holdings. The positive and statistically significant sign of this variable suggests that as funds appropriation by controlling shareholder increases, the level of cash holdings increases. The signs and significance of other variables are the same as the second specification. It should also be noted that the use of system GMM and dynamic GMM does not affect the results in any of the specifications.

This table presents the estimates of a system GMM estimation. All variables are truncated at the 1% and 99% levels. The dependent variable, Cash Holdings, is calculated by dividing cash & equivalents by total assets. All explanatory variables are explained in the text. ***, ** and * indicate significance at the 1%, 5%, and 10% level, respectively. The t-statistics are reported in parantheses.

Table 2. Correlation matrix

	1	2	3	4	5	6	7	8	9	10	11	12	13	14	15	16	17	18	19	20
1) Cash holdings	1																			
2) Board size	0.2001*	1																		
3) Duality	0,0372	-0.1696*	1																	
4) Board independence	0,0157	0.1451*	-0,0389	1																
5) Family CEO	-0,0125	-0.167*	0.3678*	0,0273	1															
6) Ownership concentration	-0.1212*	-0,0239	-0.1019*	0,0468	0.1584*	1														
7) Wedge	0.0745*	0.0966*	-0.1122*	0,0385	-0,0178	0.4468*	1													
8) Related party loans	-0,0144	-0.1634*	0,0303	0,032	0,0337	-0,0479	-0,0513	1												
9) Capital expenditures	-0,0418	0.0847*	-0,0097	0,0489	0,0135	-0,0039	-0.0175	-0.0701*	1											
10) Market-to-book ratio	0,0343	0,0372	0,0286	-0,0264	-0,0325	-0.171*	-0.0926*	0,0462	0.0743*	1										
11) Leverage	-0.3526*	-0.2035*	-0,0533	0,0524	0,036	0,0622	-0.0876*	0,0587	0,048	0.1986*	1									
12) Return on assets	0.315*	0.2738*	-0,0231	-0,0224	-0,0053	-0,0543	0.0304	-0.1328*	0.0801*	0.0899*	-0.4377*	1								
13) Bank debt	-0.2088*	-0.1347*	-0,0475	0.1356*	0,0275	0.126*	0,0438	0,0321	-0.0969*	-0,0488	0.2772*	-0.1959*	1							
14) Non-cash assets	0.0737*	0.1219*	0,0465	-0,0281	0,0043	-0,0274	0,059	0,0048	-0.1139*	-0.2532*	-0.5768*	0.3496*	-0.1655*	1						
15) Tangibility	-0.2307*	-0,0138	-0,0072	-0,0229	-0,0283	0,0401	-0.0795*	-0,0311	0.2616*	0,0316	-0,019	-0.1884*	0,0047	-0.3377*	1					
16) R&D/sales	0,027	0,0165	0,0018	0,0524	0.0948*	0,0211	0,0491	-0,0002	-0,0584	-0.1138*	-0,0009	-0.0766*	0.1046*	0,0618	-0,057	1				
17) Dividend payout ratio	0.2747*	0.319*	-0.0902*	-0,0347	-0.1224*	-0.0908*	0.0872*	-0.1338*	0.0914*	0.1228*	-0.2951*	0.4944*	-0.0988*	0.1457*	-0,04	-0,024	1			
18) Firm size	0.1059*	0.5148*	-0.1904*	0.1693*	-0.1369*	-0,0214	0,043	-0.2491*	0.1799*	-0.0687*	0,027	0.3257*	0,0338	-0.1082*	0,0524	0,0528	0.2975*	1		
19) Cash flow ratio	0.7611*	0.1909*	0,0429	-0.0682*	-0,0235	-0.1469*	-0,005	-0,0037	-0,0493	0,0207	-0.5737*	0.3359*	-0.3207*	0.2095*	-0.109*	-0,007	0.248*	-0,01	1	
20) Volatility	0,0129	0,0272	-0,0256	-0,0005	-0,0134	0,0007	-0,0209	-0,0089	0,0364	-0,0189	-0,0199	-0,0312	0,0081	0,0025	0,0326	-0,009	-0,0167	0,031	0	1

[1]FINNET Elektronik Yayincilik Data Iletisim San. Tic. Ltd. Sti.

Table 3. Dynamic panel data estimation results (System GMM)

	Model 1	Model 2	Model 3
Cash Holdings$_{(t-1)}$	-0.01 (-0.13)	-0.01 (-0.05)	0.01 (0.20)
Board Size	3.74 (1.52)	3.58 (1.47)	3.51 (1.44)
CEO Duality	0.47 (0.28)	0.84 (0.50)	0.83 (0.50)
Board Independence	-3.46 (-0.68)	-1.15 (-0.21)	-0.81 (-0.15)
Family CEO		1.92 (0.84)	1.80 (0.79)
Family Ownership		-18.62** (-2.01)	-17.15* (-1.84)
Family Ownership^2		19.07* (1.88)	17.68* (1.73)
Wedge		9.90 (0.83)	8.55 (0.72)
Orecta			0.07* (1.78)
Capital expenditures	-0.05 (-1.22)	-0.03 (-0.81)	-0.03 (-0.91)
Market-to-book ratio	-0.36 (-1.12)	0.07 (0.20)	0.02 (0.05)
Leverage	-0.15*** (-4.13)	-0.14*** (-3.97)	-0.14*** (-4.01)
Return on assets	-0.01 (-0.38)	-0.02 (-0.50)	-0.02 (-0.47)
Bank debt	-0.03* (-1.69)	-0.01 (-0.47)	-0.01 (-0.45)
Non-cash assets	-0.33*** (-11.42)	-0.28*** (-9.62)	-0.28*** (-9.68)
Tangibility	-0.22*** (-6.12)	-0.18*** (-5.02)	-0.18*** (-5.03)
R&D/sales	-0.31 (-0.40)	-0.58 (-0.75)	-0.39 (-0.50)
Dividend payout ratio	0.01 (1.32)	0.01 (0.88)	0.01 (0.79)
Firm size	-1.35 (-1.25)	-2.18** (-2.04)	-2.21** (-2.06)
Cash flow	10.40*** (19.95)	10.75*** (20.85)	10.72*** (20.74)
Volatility	-0.08 (-1.14)	-0.12 (-1.62)	-0.10 (-1.41)
CONSTANT	25.53 (1.18)	33.15 (1.56)	34.96 (1.64)
Wald $\chi 2$ (p-value)	<.01	<.01	<.01
Sargan test (p-value)	0.22	0.28	0.22
AR(2) test (p-value)	0.39	0.35	0.33
N	649	614	614

Table 4. Dynamic panel data estimation results (Difference GMM)

	Model 1	Model 2	Model 3
Cash Holdings(t-1)	-0.01 (-0.13)	0.00 (-0.05)	0.01 (0.20)
Board Size	3.74 (1.52)	3.58 (1.47)	3.51 (1.44)
CEO Duality	0.47 (0.28)	0.84 (0.50)	0.83 (0.50)
Board Independence	-3.46 (-0.68)	-1.15 (-0.21)	-0.81 (-0.15)
Family CEO		1.92 (0.84)	1.80 (0.79)
Family Ownership		-18.62** (-2.01)	-17.15* (-1.84)
Family Ownership^2		19.07* (1.88)	17.68* (1.73)
Wedge		9.90 (0.83)	8.55 (0.72)
Orecta			0.07* (1.78)
Capital expenditures	-0.05 (-1.22)	-0.03 (-0.81)	-0.03 (-0.91)
Market-to-book ratio	-0.36 (-1.12)	0.07 (0.20)	0.02 (0.05)
Leverage	-0.15*** (-4.13)	-0.14*** (-3.97)	-0.14*** (-4.01)
Return on assets	-0.01 (-0.38)	-0.02 (-0.50)	-0.02 (-0.47)
Bank debt	-0.03* (-1.69)	-0.01 (-0.47)	-0.01 (-0.45)
Non-cash assets	-0.33*** (-11.42)	-0.28*** (-9.62)	-0.28*** (-9.68)
Tangibility	-0.22*** (-6.12)	-0.18*** (-5.02)	-0.18*** (-5.03)
R&D/sales	-0.31 (-0.40)	-0.58 (-0.75)	-0.39 (-0.50)
Dividend payout ratio	0.01 (1.32)	0.01 (0.88)	0.01 (0.79)
Firm size	-1.35 (-1.25)	-2.18** (-2.04)	-2.21** (-2.06)
Cash flow	10.40*** (19.95)	10.75*** (20.85)	10.72*** (20.74)
Volatility	-0.08 (-1.14)	-0.12 (-1.62)	-0.10 (-1.41)
CONSTANT	42.28** (2.05)	56.76** (2.74)	57.17** (2.75)
Wald $\chi2$ (p-value)	<.01	<.01	<.01
Sargan test (p-value)	0.21	0.27	0.21
AR(2) test (p-value)	0.36	0.34	0.32
N	470	435	435

This table presents the estimates of a difference GMM estimation. All variables are truncated at the 1% and 99% levels. The dependent variable, Cash Holdings, is calculated by dividing cash & equivalents by total assets. All explanatory variables are explained in the text. ***, ** and * indicate significance at the 1%, 5%, and 10% level, respectively. The t-statistics are reported in parantheses.

CONCLUSION

The objective this chapter was to investigate the factors affecting cash holdings among Turkish firms with special emphasis on corporate governance variables such as board structure, family ownership and tunneling. The sample consisted of 190 companies listed on Borsa Istanbul from 2006 to 2010. Dynamic panel data methodology with system GMM and difference GMM approaches were employed and both estimations provided the same results regarding our variables in terms of significance and direction.

Regarding corporate governance variables, none of the factors related to board structure including board size, CEO duality and board independence turned out to be significant predictors of cash holdings among Turkish firms. These findings suggest that the effectiveness of board structure is questionable for in Turkey. In fact, Turkish firms meet only minimum regulative and legal requirements in designing and structuring boards and disregard requirements that would directly hamper large shareholders' control and private benefits (Oba et al., 2014). Moreover, independent directors are not independent enough to effectively perform their role in Turkey (Ararat et al., 2010). Considering the fact that board structure can reduce the tension between managers and shareholders or prevent controlling shareholders from expropriation of minority shareholders, Turkish firms should work on improving the effectiveness of their boards to mitigate agency problems like excessive cash holdings.

The existence of a family CEO or the magnitude of excess voting rights above cash flow rights did not have a significant impact on the level of cash holdings either. However, a convex relationship between family ownership and cash holdings has been found. This suggests that as family voting rights increase, family shareholders who gain nearly full control of the firm generate private benefits of control at the expense of minority shareholders by keeping more cash. This result extends the findings of previous studies which investigated the impact of family involvement in firm on the firm cash policy by a family dummy variable (e.g. Ozkan and Ozkan, 2004; Kuan et al., 2011) and implies that investors should be careful when investing in family firms due to potential agency problems like idle cash.

Another important finding which emerged from the analysis is that the existence of tunneling leads to higher levels of cash being held within the company rather than being invested or distributed to owners as dividends (Liu et al., 2015). This finding indicates that funds transferred from group firms are not considered substitute of cash and firms still accumulate cash reserves. This result reinforces the tendency of controlling shareholders to generate private benefits of control and implies that group firms should be carefully monitored for excessive cash holdings.

Overall, the results of this study imply that not all corporate governance characteristics are important in explaining the level of cash holdings among Turkish companies. Considering the fact that higher levels of cash could lead to agency problems, which is especially important for emerging markets like Turkey, it is relevant to know that this problem is higher among firms with higher family voting rights and group firms which use tunneling. In addition, the findings related to control variables suggest that both the trade-off and pecking order theories play a significant role in explaining the cash holdings for firms in Turkey. These results are also important for other emerging markets which are subject to agency problems due to concentrated ownership structures, strong presence of family firms and weak shareholder protection.

ACKNOWLEDGMENT

This research received no specific grant from any funding agency in the public, commercial, or not-for-profit sectors.

REFERENCES

Al-Najjar, B. (2013). The financial determinants of corporate cash holdings: Evidence from some emerging markets. *International Business Review*, *22*(1), 77–88. doi:10.1016/j.ibusrev.2012.02.004

Al-Najjar, B., & Belghitar, Y. (2011). Corporate cash holdings and dividend payments: Evidence from simultaneous analysis. *Managerial and Decision Economics*, *32*(4), 231–241. doi:10.1002/mde.1529

Anderson, R. C., & Reeb, D. M. (2003). Founding-family ownership and firm performance: Evidence from the S&P 500. *The Journal of Finance*, *58*(3), 1301–1328. doi:10.1111/1540-6261.00567

Anderson, R. C., & Reeb, D. M. (2004). Board composition: Balancing family influence in S&P 500 firms. *Administrative Science Quarterly*, *49*, 209–237.

Ararat, M., Aksu, M. H., & Tansel Cetin, A. (2010). *The impact of board diversity on boards' monitoring intensity and firm performance: evidence from the Istanbul Stock Exchange*. Available at SSRN 1572283.

Ararat, M., & Orbay, H. (2006). Corporate governance in Turkey, implications for growth and investments. In *World Bank Investment Climate Assessment Report Survey for Turkey*. Washington, DC: World Bank Publications. doi:10.2139srn.2375767

Arellano, M., & Bond, S. (1991). Some tests of specification for panel data: Monte Carlo evidence and an application to employment equations. *The Review of Economic Studies*, *58*(2), 277–297. doi:10.2307/2297968

Arellano, M., & Bover, O. (1995). Another look at the instrumental variable estimation of error-components models. *Journal of Econometrics*, *68*(1), 29–51. doi:10.1016/0304-4076(94)01642-D

Bates, T. W., Khale, K. M., & Stulz, R. M. (2009). Why do US firms hold so much more cash than they used to? *The Journal of Finance*, *64*(5), 1985–2021. doi:10.1111/j.1540-6261.2009.01492.x

Baysinger, B. D., & Butler, H. N. (1985). Corporate governance and the board of directors: Performance effects of changes in board composition. *Journal of Law Economics and Organization*, *1*(1), 101–124.

Bebchuk, L. A., Kraakman, R. H., & Triantis, G. G. (1999). *Stock pyramids, cross-ownership, and the dual class equity: the creation and agency costs of separating control from cash flow rights*. NBER Working Paper. No. W6951.

Belkhir, M., Boubaker, S., & Derouiche, I. (2014). Control–ownership wedge, board of directors, and the value of excess cash. *Economic Modelling*, *39*, 110–122. doi:10.1016/j.econmod.2014.02.026

Bigelli, M., & Sánchez-Vidal, J. (2012). Cash holdings in private firms. *Journal of Banking & Finance*, *36*(1), 26–35. doi:10.1016/j.jbankfin.2011.06.004

Blundell, R., & Bond, S. (1998). Initial conditions and moment restrictions in dynamic panel data models. *Journal of Econometrics*, *87*(1), 115–143. doi:10.1016/S0304-4076(98)00009-8

Boubaker, S., Derouiche, I., & Hassen, M. (2015). Family Control And The Value Of Cash Holdings. *Journal of Applied Business Research*, *31*(2), 647. doi:10.19030/jabr.v31i2.9159

Boubaker, S., Derouiche, I., & Nguyen, D. K. (2015). Does the board of directors affect cash holdings? A study of French listed firms. *The Journal of Management and Governance*, *19*(2), 341–370. doi:10.100710997-013-9261-x

Brennan, N. (2006). Boards of directors and firm performance: Is there an expectations gap? *Corporate Governance*, *4*(6), 577–593. doi:10.1111/j.1467-8683.2006.00534.x

Campbell, J. Y., Hilscher, J., & Szilagyi, J. (2008). In search of distress risk. *The Journal of Finance*, *63*(6), 2899–2939. doi:10.1111/j.1540-6261.2008.01416.x

Cheung, Y., Rau, P. R., & Stouraitis, A. (2006). Tunneling, propping, and expropriation: Evidence from connected party transactions in Honk Kong. *Journal of Financial Economics*, *82*(2), 343–386. doi:10.1016/j.jfineco.2004.08.012

Claessens, S., Djankov, S., Fan, J. P. H., & Lang, L. H. P. (2002). Disentangling the incentive and entrenchment effects of large shareholdings. *The Journal of Finance*, *57*(6), 2741–2471. doi:10.1111/1540-6261.00511

D'Mello, R., Krishnaswami, S., & Larkin, P. J. (2008). Determinants of corporate cash holdings: Evidence fromspin-offs. *Journal of Banking & Finance*, *32*(7), 1209–1220. doi:10.1016/j.jbankfin.2007.10.005

Dittmar, A., & Mahrt-Smith, J. (2007). Corporate governance and the value of cash holdings. *Journal of Financial Economics*, *83*(3), 599–634. doi:10.1016/j.jfineco.2005.12.006

Dittmar, A., Mahrt-Smith, J., & Servaes, H. (2003). International corporate governance and corporate cash holdings. *Journal of Financial and Quantitative Analysis*, *38*(01), 111–133. doi:10.2307/4126766

Drobetz, W., & Grüninger, M. C. (2007). Corporate cash holdings: Evidence from Switzerland. *Financial Markets and Portfolio Management*, *21*(3), 293–324. doi:10.100711408-007-0052-8

Faleye, O. (2004). *Are large boards poor monitors? Evidence from CEO turnover*. EFMA Basel Meetings Paper.

Fama, E. F., & Jensen, M. C. (1983). Separation of ownership and control. *The Journal of Law & Economics*, *26*(2), 301–326. doi:10.1086/467037

Fazzari, S. M., & Petersen, B. (1993). Working capital and fixed investment: New evidence on financing constraints. *The Rand Journal of Economics*, *24*(3), 328–342. doi:10.2307/2555961

Ferreira, M. A., & Vilela, A. S. (2004). Why do firms hold cash? Evidence from EMU countries. *European Financial Management*, *10*(2), 295–319. doi:10.1111/j.1354-7798.2004.00251.x

García-Teruel, P., & Martínez-Solano, P. (2008). On the determinants of SME cash holdings: Evidence from Spain. *Journal of Business Finance & Accounting*, *35*(1-2), 127–149. doi:10.1111/j.1468-5957.2007.02022.x

Goksen, N. S., & Usdiken, B. (2001). Uniformity and diversity in Turkish business groups: Effects of scale and time of founding. *British Journal of Management*, *12*(4), 325–340. doi:10.1111/1467-8551.00213

Gomez-Mejia, L. R., Cruz, C., Berrone, P., & De Castro, J. (2011). The bind that ties: Socioemotional wealth preservation in family firms. *The Academy of Management Annals*, *5*(1), 653–707. doi:10.1080/19416520.2011.593320

Gonenc, H., & Hermes, N. (2008). Propping: Evidence from new share issues of Turkish business group firms. *Journal of Multinational Financial Management*, *18*(3), 261–275. doi:10.1016/j.mulfin.2007.11.002

Guney, Y., Ozkan, A., & Ozkan, N. (2007). International evidence on the non-linear impact of leverage on corporate cash holdings. *Journal of Multinational Financial Management*, *17*(1), 45–60. doi:10.1016/j.mulfin.2006.03.003

Hardin, W. G., Highfield, M. J., Hill, M. D., & Kelly, W. (2009). The determinants of REIT cash holdings. *The Journal of Real Estate Finance and Economics*, *39*(1), 39–57. doi:10.100711146-007-9103-1

Jensen, M. C. (1986). Agency cost of free cash flow, corporate finance, and takeovers. *Corporate Finance, and Takeovers. The American Economic Review*, *76*(2).

Jensen, M. C., & Meckling, W. H. (1976). Theory of the firm: Managerial behaviour, agency costs, and ownership structure. *Journal of Financial Economics*, *3*(4), 305–306. doi:10.1016/0304-405X(76)90026-X

Jiang, G., Lee, C. M., & Yue, H. (2010). Tunneling through intercorporate loans: The China experience. *Journal of Financial Economics*, *98*(1), 1–20. doi:10.1016/j.jfineco.2010.05.002

Johnson, S., La Porta, R., Lopez-de-Silanes, F., & Shleifer, A. (2000). Tunneling. *The American Economic Review*, *90*(2), 22–27. doi:10.1257/aer.90.2.22 PMID:11031284

Kim, C. S., Mauer, D. C., & Sherman, A. E. (1998). The determinants of corporate liquidity: Theory and evidence. *Journal of Financial and Quantitative Analysis*, *33*(3), 305–334. doi:10.2307/2331099

Klein, A. (2002). Audit committee, board of director characteristics, and earnings management. *Journal of Accounting and Economics*, *33*(3), 375–400. doi:10.1016/S0165-4101(02)00059-9

Kuan, H. T., Li, C. S., & Chu, S. H. (2011). Cash Holdings and Corporate Governance in Family-Controlled Firms. *Journal of Business Research*, *64*(7), 757–764. doi:10.1016/j.jbusres.2010.07.004

La Porta, R., Lopez-de-Silanes, F., & Shleifer, A. (1999). Corporate ownership around the world. *The Journal of Finance*, *52*(2), 471–517. doi:10.1111/0022-1082.00115

La Porta, R., Lopez-de-Silanes, F., Shleifer, A., & Vishny, R. W. (1998). Law and finance. *Journal of Political Economy*, *106*(6), 1113–1155. doi:10.1086/250042

Le Breton-Miller, I., & Miller, D. (2006). Why do some family businesses outcompete? Governance, long-term orientations and sustainable capability. *Entrepreneurship Theory and Practice*, *30*(6), 731–746. doi:10.1111/j.1540-6520.2006.00147.x

Lehmann, D. R., Gupta, S., & Steckel, J. (1988). *Marketing research.* Reading, MA: Addison-Wesley.

Liu, Q., Luo, T. & Tian, G. (2015). Family control and corporate cash holdings: evidence from China. *Journal of Corporate Finance, 31*, 220-245.

Lubatkin, M., Schulze, W., Ling, Y., & Dino, R. (2005). The effects of parental altruism on the governance of family-managed firms. *Journal of Organizational Behavior*, *26*(3), 313–330. doi:10.1002/job.307

Miller, M., & Orr, D. (1966). A model of the demand for money by firms. *The Quarterly Journal of Economics*, *80*(3), 413–435. doi:10.2307/1880728

Morck, R., Shleifer, A., & Vishny, R. (1988). Management ownership and market valuation: An empirical analysis. *Journal of Financial Economics*, *20*, 293–315. doi:10.1016/0304-405X(88)90048-7

Muth, M. M., & Donaldson, L. (1998). Stewardship theory and board structure: A contingency Approach. *Corporate Governance*, *6*(1), 5–28. doi:10.1111/1467-8683.00076

Myers, S. C. (1984). The capital structure puzzle. *The Journal of Finance*, *39*(3), 575–592. doi:10.2307/2327916

Myers, S. C., & Majluf, N. (1984). Corporate financing and investment decisions when firms have information that investors do not have. *Journal of Financial Economics*, *13*(2), 187–221. doi:10.1016/0304-405X(84)90023-0

Oba, B., Tigrel, E., & Sener, P. (2014). Board structure in listed firms: Evidence from an emerging economy. *Corporate Governance: The International Journal of Business in Society*, *14*(3), 382–394. doi:10.1108/CG-05-2012-0044

OECD. (2013). *Supervision and enforcement in corporate governance. Corporate Governance*. OECD Publishing. doi:10.1787/9789264203334-

Ogundipe, L. O., Ogundipe, S. E., & Ajao, S. K. (2012). Cash holding and firm characteristics: Evidence from Nigerian emerging market. *Journal of Business Economics and Finance*, *1*(2), 45–58.

Okutan-Nilsson, G. (2007). Corporate governance in Turkey. *European Business Organization Law Review*, *8*(2), 196–236.

Opler, T., Pinkowitz, L., & Stulz, R. (1999). The determinants and implications of corporate cash holdings. *Journal of Financial Economics*, *52*(1), 3–46. doi:10.1016/S0304-405X(99)00003-3

Ozkan, A., & Ozkan, N. (2004). Corporate cash holdings: An empirical investigation of UK companies. *Journal of Banking & Finance*, *28*(9), 2103–2134. doi:10.1016/j.jbankfin.2003.08.003

Paskelian, O. G., Bell, S., & Nguyen, C. V. (2010). Corporate governance and cash holdings: A comparative analysis of Chinese and Indian Firms. *The International Journal of Business and Finance Research*, *4*, 59–73.

Peng, K. C., Wei, Z., & Yang, Z. (2011). Yang, (2011). Tunneling or propping: Evidence from connected transactions in China. *Journal of Corporate Finance*, *17*(2), 306–325. doi:10.1016/j.jcorpfin.2010.08.002

Peng, M. W., & Jiang, Y. (2010). Institutions behind family ownership and control in large firms. *Journal of Management Studies*, *47*(2), 253–273. doi:10.1111/j.1467-6486.2009.00890.x

Pinkowitz, L., Stulz, R. M., & Williamson, R. (2003). *Do firms in countries with poor protection of investor rights hold more cash? (No. w10188)*. National Bureau of Economic Research. doi:10.3386/w10188

Pinkowitz, L., Stulz, R. S., & Williamson, R. (2012). *Multinationals and the high cash holdings puzzle*. National Bureau of Economic Research (NBER) Working Paper No. 18120.

Rajan, R. G., & Zingales, L. (1995). What do we know about capital structure? Some evidence from international data. *The Journal of Finance*, *50*(5), 1421–1460. doi:10.1111/j.1540-6261.1995.tb05184.x

Riddick, L. A., & Whited, T. M. (2009). The corporate propensity to save. *The Journal of Finance*, *64*(4), 1729–1766. doi:10.1111/j.1540-6261.2009.01478.x

Sánchez, J. M., & Yurdagul, E. (2013). Why are corporations holding so much cash? *The Regional Economist*, *21*(1), 4–8.

Shleifer, A., & Vishny, R. (1997). A survey of corporate governance. *The Journal of Finance*, *52*(2), 737–783. doi:10.1111/j.1540-6261.1997.tb04820.x

Steiner, I. D. (1972). *Group processes and group productivity*. New York: Academic.

TBB. (2009). *The financial system and banking sector in Turkey*. Retrieved from http://www.tbb.org.tr/Dosyalar/Arastirma_ve_Raporlar/The_Financial_System_and_Bankin g_Sector_in_Turkey.pdf

The World Bank. (2011). *Sustaining high growth: The role of domestic savings: Turkey country economic memorandum* (World Bank Report No. 66301-TR). Retrieved from http://wwwwds.20121128233319/Rendered/PDF/NonAsciiFileName0.pdf

Titman, S., & Wessels, R. (1988). The determinants of capital structure choice. *The Journal of Finance*, *43*(1), 1–19. doi:10.1111/j.1540-6261.1988.tb02585.x

Ugur, M., & Ararat, M. (2006). Does macroeconomic performance affect corporate governance: Evidence from Turkey. *Corporate Governance*, *14*(4), 325–348. doi:10.1111/j.1467-8683.2006.00510.x

Uyar, K., & Kuzey, C. (2014). Determinants of corporate cash holdings: Evidence from the emerging market of Turkey. *Applied Economics*, *46*(9), 1035–1048. doi: 10.1080/00036846.2013.866203

Villalonga, B., & Amit, R. (2006). How do family ownership, control and management affect firm value? *Journal of Financial Economics*, *80*(2), 385–417. doi:10.1016/j.jfineco.2004.12.005

Yermack, D. (2004). Remuneration, retention, and reputation incentives for outside directors. *The Journal of Finance*, *59*(5), 2281–2308. doi:10.1111/j.1540-6261.2004.00699.x

ADDITIONAL READING

Bugra, A. (1994). *State and business in modern Turkey: A comparative study*. Albany, NY: State University of New York Press.

Cameron, A. C., & Trivedi, P. K. (2010). *Microeconometrics using Stata* (revised edition). College Station, TX: Stata Press.

Chrisman, J. J., Chua, J. H., & Litz, R. A. (2004). Comparing the agency cost of family and nonfamily firms: Conceptual issues and exploratory evidence. *Entrepreneurship Theory and Practice*, *28*(4), 335–354. doi:10.1111/j.1540-6520.2004.00049.x

Claessens, S., Djankov, S., & Lang, L. H. P. (2000). The separation of ownership and control in East Asian corporations. *Journal of Financial Economics*, *58*(1-2), 81–112. doi:10.1016/S0304-405X(00)00067-2

Demsetz, H., & Lehn, K. (1985). The structure of corporate ownership: Causes and consequences. *Journal of Political Economy*, *93*(6), 1155–1177. doi:10.1086/261354

Demsetz, H., & Villalonga, B. (2001). Ownership structure and corporate performance. *Journal of Corporate Finance*, *7*(3), 209–233. doi:10.1016/S0929-1199(01)00020-7

Faccio, M., & Lang, L. (2002). The ultimate ownership of Western European corporations. *Journal of Financial Economics*, *65*(3), 365–395. doi:10.1016/S0304-405X(02)00146-0

La Porta, R., Lopez-de-Silanes, F., Shleifer, A., & Vishny, R. (2002). Investor protection and corporate valuation. *The Journal of Finance*, *57*(3), 1147–1170. doi:10.1111/1540-6261.00457

KEY TERMS AND DEFINITIONS

Agency Costs: The costs arising from conflicts of interest between managers and shareholders (type 1 agency problem) or controlling shareholders and minority shareholders (type 2 agency problem).

Controlling Shareholder: A shareholder who owns most of the outstanding shares in a corporation and has the power of influencing corporate decisions.

Corporate Governance: The set of rules and regulations used to operate and control corporations and define their stakeholders' rights.

Expropriation: The extraction of private benefits by the controlling shareholders at the expense of minority shareholders, mostly in the form of tunneling.

Minority Shareholder: A shareholder whose proportion of shares is not adequate to exert control over the corporate decisions and who may be subject to expropriation.

One Share One Vote Principle: A principle of corporate governance which gives one voting right to each person who owns one share of the corporation.

Pyramidal Ownership Structure: A chain of ownership relations which separates cash flow rights from voting rights for the ultimate owner.

Chapter 9
Corporate Governance and Performance

Şaban Çelik
https://orcid.org/0000-0002-4918-4598
Independent Researcher, Turkey

Tuna Can Güleç
https://orcid.org/0000-0003-2551-6460
Manisa Celal Bayar University, Turkey

ABSTRACT

The purpose of the present study is to evaluate the current state of the linkage between corporate governance and performance. Corporate governance is by far the most important subject that should be studied due to its role and significance. Accordingly, there is intensive literature on corporate governance and its possible impact on performance. By conducting a systematic literature review, the authors provide the results of frequently used variables that supposed to reflect the character of corporate governance on firm performance. The study covers the findings of empirical papers that analyze the impact of "board size," "percentage of independent directors," "CEO duality," "ownership concentration," "audit committee and auditor reputation," "board meetings," and "firm size." The examination of the reviewed studies indicates that there is a need to explain the competing findings observed among firms, markets, and countries by developing a theoretical explanation.

DOI: 10.4018/978-1-5225-9607-3.ch009

INTRODUCTION

The delegation of one's powers to their subordinates is considered a problematic process in any social structure. In a corporate structure, this delegation of power process is most significant between shareholders and managers who are being paid to represent the interests of shareholders. The conflict of interest between shareholders and managers has been an influential topic in the literature ever since the foundation of the first share company. Even in the 18th century, this conflict of interest was considered one of the main issues concerning joint-stock companies. In his masterpiece book named "Wealth of Nations" (Smith, 1776), Adam Smith states this issue to be one of the most important elements in the field of business management. One thing that is certain is that humans strive to maximize their utility. Highly debated behavior "Homo-Economicus", shows a deviation from a fixed behavioral algorithm due to the difference between the utility functions of individuals.

Another early argument in the field of corporate governance is the difference between theory and the reality of the business and environment. In the start of 20th century, it was often argued that economics as of theorized back in the day, were influenced by mechanisms that are either untraceable or that mechanism that exist only in the theory but not in the real world. Factors that are considered to measure the effectiveness of corporate governance has been discussed in length. A widely recognized and cited study in this regard has been added to the literature by Coase (1937). In this scope, Properties such as measurability and relevance to corporate governance element has been taken to account when determining the factors to use in this study as representatives and indicators of the success of corporate governance.

One of the most comprehensive attempts to create a standard measurement basis for the success of corporate governance was published by Brown & Caylor (2004). Using dataset provided by Institutional Shareholder Services, a composite measure consisting of 51 subfactors under 8 categories was presented. Main categories are listed as audit, the board of directors, charter by-laws, education, executive compensation, ownership, progression, and level of incorporation. Measurement from the end results of these factors is named "Gov-Score". The study then uses its measurement system for determining the relationship between operating performance, valuation and shareholder payout in a dataset consisting of 2327 firms. According to the findings of the analysis, companies that have a higher Gov-Score value are relatively more profitable, has higher shareholder value, and pay out more dividends. Overall higher "Gov-Score"s are associated with higher firm performance. In addition to this, the study also reports interesting and meaningful facts, such as the relationship between consulting fees and audit fees paid to auditors. Firms that pay their auditors more than what they pay to their consultants have generally worse performance than those that do the reverse.

Following this, another study that is formulated with the intention of measuring the effectiveness of corporate governance practices was conducted by Brown and Caylor (2006). Brown & Caylor have combined some of the most significant previous attempts to create a corporate governance measurement system into a single study and added some elements to it creating one of the most comprehensive corporate governance measurement methods to date. The first study they laid the foundation on, was conducted in 2003 (Gompers, Ishii, & Metrick, 2003), which was a summary measure of corporate governance using 24 firm-specific provisions. The main finding of the study was that more democratic firms perform better on a corporate level. 24 firm-specific provision, which was also named G-Index, are further studied in another study (Bebchuk & Cohen, 2005) in which the authors created the entrenchment indexes on six provisions of G-Index. Combining these studies, Brown & Caylor, concludes that out of 51 governance provisions, five are relevant to accounting and public policy and four of them are also audit-related but none of them are related with firm value. The most striking finding of the study is that, out of 7 provisions that are related to firm value, only one is regulated by the Sarbanes Oxley Act. In the perspective of defining corporate governance, the study is significant in using a broader scope than previous studies in defining the context of corporate governance and also reflects the changes to corporate governance as a result of Sarbanes Oxley Act.

The effects of the 2008 financial crisis turned the gaze of international banks back to factors that are related to corporate governance strategies. One such study focuses on the risk management-related corporate governance mechanisms as well as whether the CRO reports to the CEO or directly to the board of directors. These two factor's effects on bank performance across several banks are analyzed in order to clarify the risk management and relevant corporate governance mechanisms. Results indicate that during the peak period of the crisis, the firms that had their CRO (Chief Risk Officer) in the board of directors, had better performance. The banks that have their CFOs report to CEO had lower performance. The study measures corporate performance by share return on a buy and holds basis. Corporate governance factor is assessed by using CEO duality, board size, and board independence factors. Study finds no evidence between corporate governance factors and firms performance except for the reporting hierarchy of CRO (Aebi, Sabato, & Schmid, 2012).

With the purpose of examining the suitability of measurement techniques used in evaluating the success of corporate governance, Dedman and Filatotchev (2008) have reviewed several relevant studies. Their conclusion was that the most of the studies conducted so far have ignored the importance and significance of environmental disturbances, therefore, the results prior studies are thought to be irrelevant as long as the environment in which they are conducted in are different.

In this study, our aim is to gather a conceptual framework on the topic of corporate governance and to evaluate the various topics which are thought to be the factors affecting the corporate performance. With this purpose, we divide corporate governance into eight categories "Board Size", "Percentage of Independent Directors", "CEO Duality", "Ownership Concentration", "Audit Committee and Auditor Reputation", "Board Meetings", and "Firm Size". Each topic is evaluated and discussed extensively using relevant sources from literature to reach a conclusion on the effect of corporate governance on the firm performance.

CORPORATE GOVERNANCE AND PERFORMANCE

Defining what "Corporate Governance" is has been the biggest issue by itself in the literature. It is hard to find studies that agree upon a common ground on the content and the extent of corporate governance. A recent study on the topic has been published in 2012 (Aguilera & Desender, 2012) with the purpose of determining the key methodological and research design problems to take into account for the comparative corporate governance topic in the future. The study fails to address methodological issues in the measurement of comparative corporate governance. However, the study points out to three significant issues that prevent this standardization of measurement from happening. The first problem is determining whether if an effect is a direct or indirect result of firm performance. The second problem is named as the causality problem, corporate governance decisions are made upon firm performance, however, the firm performance is also a result of corporate governance practices, hence the causality seems to be bidirectional. The third problem is explained as measuring the firm performance. A firm's profits may have risen in a period at the cost of increased leverage and higher employee turnover rate and reduced R&D expenditures. How will the performance of this firm be calculated? How much weight should be allocated to R&D or Firm profits? Answering these questions on a baseline that every researcher agrees on is, therefore, is presented as the third problem. While this study didn't reach a conclusion on what should be done about these issues, it helps the literature by pointing out and categorizing the problems that need to be addressed.

A study that focused on procedures of corporate governance explored the relationship between corporate governance and sustainability using FTSE100 companies as the dataset (Aras & Crowther, 2008). Using corporate performance reports, the study gathered basic corporate governance principles of each firm. According to the findings, some aspects of corporate governance have significant effects on a firm's sustainability while others statistically insignificant.

Role of cultural factors in corporate governance has been another topic of interest. The influence of Japanese corporate governance values has been compared with traditional corporate governance values with the aim of determining the importance of cultural factors in corporate governance. Study of Eberhart (2012), used panel data from Tokyo stock exchange listed companies. Corporations have been grouped separately depending on their choice of legal systems. Using Tobin's q as an independent variable, the study finds a statistically significant difference in firm valuation in favor of companies that do not use traditional Anglo-American type committee systems. However, the study also finds that the companies that use Anglo-American committee systems are safer in terms of signal sending and transparency.

Bhatt and Bhatt (2017) focuses on the effect of the Malaysian Code on Corporate Governance on the performance of the companies listed in Malaysia. The study uses 113 companies that are publicly listed to determine the relationship between corporate governance, firm performance and leverage. The success of corporate governance is based upon Malaysian Corporate Governance Index (MCGI) rankings. Findings in the study indicate that there is a strong and statistically significant relationship between Corporate Governance Index rankings and corporate performance. Additionally, the study suggests that the existence of a corporate governance ranking system such as MCGI promotes the success of corporate governance based upon evidence between years 2007 to 2012.

Another recent study that investigates the effects of firm-level corporate governance applications is published (Chauhan, Lakshmi, & Dey, 2016). The study focuses on the ownership concentration of founder in firms. Results of the study indicate that there is a positive relationship between corporate governance performance and firm performance.in firms where owner concentration is high, the importance of proper corporate governance practices becomes more important. Additionally, the study finds that effective corporate governance practices also prevent self-trading of the firm, hence improving the lifetime value of the firm.

The effectiveness of corporate governance and its relationship with firm performance is measured in Chinese cross-listed companies (S. Chen, Lin, Wang, & Wu, 2008). The first study evaluates the effects of cross-listing and finds that companies that are cross-listed have on average more effective corporate governance performances. Consequently, the study finds that more effective corporate governance results in more efficient operating performance. Results of the study are in line with the bonding hypothesis. Due to the relationship between corporate performance and corporate governance practices, the study finds that companies that are cross-listed have higher corporate performances.

Study of Chong (2004), discusses the importance of executive remuneration, corporate leadership and their effect on the value of the company. The study examines the board of directors and corporate strategy in the risk management context.

Additionally, the study evaluates the effects of Basel II banking regulations and International Accounting Standards and arrives at the conclusion that new regulations are going to increase the effectiveness of corporate governance in the long run and that this in return will increase the profitability of the firms.

A few studies in the literature suggest that there is no significant relationship between corporate governance performance and firm performance. One such study is published in 2018 (Funchal & Pinto, 2018). Agency theory suggests that lower corporate performance is associated with the success of corporate governance. In order to test this hypothesis, Funchal and Pinto have analyzed firms from the Brazilian Stock Market. Results of the study indicate that there is no significant difference between the corporate performance of firms that are categorized successfully governed and firms categorized as unsuccessfully governed. In a similar paper, corporate governance practices in Indian and South Korean companies were studied (Gupta & Sharma, 2014). Independence of the Board and its sub-elements like board structure were discussed in depth. According to the findings of the study, the relationship between corporate governance and firm performance is statistically significant but its effect is very limited due to a weak magnitude of coefficients.

Board Size

Board size, as one of the proxy variables, is used frequently in related literature of corporate governance and performance researches. The primary reason behind using board size as a variable is attributed to its controlling and monitoring roles on the executives. Due to these roles, it is expected that conflict of interest between principles (shareholders) and agents (executives) should be reduced (Fama & Jensen, 1983). In the context of agency theory, it is proposed that managing and controlling the firm should be separated. On the one side, the board of directors has responsibilities to set the strategies, supervise and monitor the executives and report the performance to the shareholders. On the side, executives have responsibilities to apply the strategies determined by the board of directors. This separation property lay the ground for both sides to do their sole responsibility. As a result, efficiency and effectiveness are supposed to increase. However, there is no consensus on the number of board of directors. There are mix results coming from an empirical investigation all over the World. Although there is no theoretical ground for the exact size for the board, there are some suggestions regarding the board size. In addition, there are two contradictive views whether board size should smaller or larger. For the lessor, the argument is that a smaller board may act and decide more promptly and produce effective monitoring. For the latter, the argument is that a larger board may bring more insight into the decision-making process.

Beside the theoretical justification for the role of board size on firm performance, there might be a regulatory directive in a specific sector. The Basel Committee on Banking Supervision has a recent call for the need to study, understand and improve the corporate governance of financial entities. This call is specifically about the corporate structure of the board of directors and executives. The theme of this call is about the conviction that good corporate governance increases monitoring efficiency(De Andres & Vallelado, 2008).

While there are numerous findings to various hypotheses studies regarding board size, literature is separated into 3 categories as to how board size affects the firm performance. While there are enough studies to support any one of these hypotheses, an overview of the literature signals the same significant characteristics. First of all, studies that find a positive relationship between board size and firm performance are almost unmistakably conducted in developed countries with comparatively efficient markets. Additionally, studies that have found a positive correlation or neutral relationship in the context of board size are more up-to-date than studies that have found negative relationships.

Reviewed literature according to their respective findings is summarized in Table 1.

Among compiled studies, the articles that report positive relationships start with the article of Goodstein (1994). The study examines the potential conflict between the institutional, governance, and strategic goals of the boards. The study not only considers board size as a number but also the composition of the board size as a subcategory of board size. Therefore, the diversity of the board is also added to the equation as well. While diversity in board composition is generally considered a value adding feature in the context of corporate governance, in some cases it may prove to be a disadvantage. Board diversity, theoretically allows the board to handle matters with multilateral perspectives, but at the same time slows down the decision-making process. In line with this theory, study finds that while board size is positively correlated with firm performance when paired with board diversity, it negatively affects the corporate performance due to significant constraints it puts to strategic change. In line with these findings, Kiel & Nicholson (2003) studies 348 Australian firms board demographics and sizes. After controlling for factors such as firm size, they find a significant positive correlation between board size and corporate performance. Results of the study are comparative more robust than rest of the similar studies. In terms of board demographics, however, a positive relationship between the proportion of inside directors and the market-based measure of firm performance. Which supports the former studies in literature by pointing out that, as a percentage of inside board members increases so does the performance of the firm. Using a dataset consisting of 34 years of banking firm data, Adams and Mehran

Table 1. The impact of board size on performance

Author (Date)	Country	Positive Relationship	Negative Relationship	Neutral Relationship
(Pearce & Zahra, 1992)	USA	X		
(Goodstein, Gautam, & Boeker, 1994)	USA	X		
(Kiel & Nicholson, 2003)	Australia	X		
(Adams & Mehran, 2012)	USA	X		
(Jaafar & El-Shawa, 2009)	Jordan	X		
(Aktan, Turen, Tvaronavičienė, Celik, & Alsadeh, 2018)	Bahrain	X		
(Yermack, 2015)	USA		X	
(Eisenberg, Sundgren, & Wells, 1998)	Finland		X	
(Vafeas, 1999)	USA		X	
(Ahmed, Hossain, & Adams, 2006)	New Zealand		X	
(Coles, Daniel, & Naveen, 2008)	USA		X	
(Dahya, Dimitrov, & McConnell, 2008a)	22 countries		X	
(Afrifa & Tauringana, 2015)	UK		X	
(Beiner, Drobetz, Schmid, & Zimmermann, 2004)	Switzerland			X
(Bin & Yi, 2015)	Malaysia			X
(Zabri, Ahmad, & Wah, 2016)	Malaysia			X
(Agyemang, Aboagye, Antwi, & Frimpong, 2014)	Ghana			X
(Darko, Aribi, & Uzonwanne, 2016)	Ghana			X

(2012) have analyzed the effects of board size and board independence of corporate performance. Results of their study indicated that board independence and corporate performance are not related. However, board size is found to be positively correlated with the performance. Additionally, findings of the study suggest that the addition of directors with subsidiary directorships contributes to the firm value as the level of corporate governance increases. Study of Aktan et al. (2018) also supports these findings, in their study which uses a database consisting of annual data of all listed financial firms on the Bahrain Bourse over the period of 2011-2016. According to the findings of the study, Board size has a significant positive relationship with corporate performance in terms of Return on Assets (ROA). The study also supports the side findings of previous studies in this context by reporting that the percentage of independent board members is negatively correlated with firm performance in terms of Return on Equity (ROE). In a similar vein, there are some studies that have found similar results in this context (Al Daoud, Ismail, & Lode, 2015; Bin & Yi, 2015; Pearce & Zahra, 1992).

One of the most comprehensive studies that report a negative relationship between board size and firm performance is studied by Dahya, Dimitrov, and McConnell (2008a). Using a dataset consisting of 799 companies across 22 different countries, researchers sought to determine the relationship between the percentage of independent board members and firm performance. A significant detail in this study, however, is that all of the companies taken into the study had at least one dominant shareholder. Results of the study indicate a strong positive relationship between firm performance and the percentage of independent board members. Another interesting finding is that, in markets that are underdeveloped, this relationship gets even stronger. While not being the main target of the study, it is also reported that after a certain number of members, increasing the size of the board negatively effects the firm performance. A localized but more up-to-date study was conducted by Afrifa and Tauringana (2015). Using a 10-year data gathered from 234 SMEs from the UK market, the study reports that there is a significant negative relationship between board size and firm performance. The article however also points that, in SMEs however these results may be misleading due to the company size and board expenditure ratios. Similarly, there are more studies that support the negative relationship between corporate performance and board size (Ahmed et al., 2006; Coles et al., 2008; Eisenberg et al., 1998; Vafeas, 1999; Yermack, 2015).

Percentage of Independent Directors

The number of independent directors in the board has been used as a variable in related literature of corporate governance for the purpose of examining its impact on firm performance. Structure of the board consists of inside and outside of directors. It is assumed that independent directors are in a better position to monitor and control managers (Dunn, 1987). These independent directors may bring a wider scope of experience and act more freely to evaluate the executives (Cornett, Marcus, Saunders, & Tehranian, 2007). There is another important argument that shed light on the importance of independent directors. It is assumed that outsiders may play a vital role in monitoring the honesty of the firm's financial reporting. This monitoring activity may involve prevention of financial frauds (Beasley, 1996). The last but not least, it is assumed that firms with more independent directors are more likely to issue earnings forecast more accurately and more frequently (Ajinkya, Bhojraj, & Sengupta, 2005).

Literature regarding independence of shareholders can be categorized under three outcomes. However, the number of studies that find a positive relationship between the percentage of independent directors and firm performance is overwhelmingly high. Studies that find a negative relationship between the percentage of independent directors and firm size are however are generally conducted on emerging country markets or markets with less regulation in sense of shareholder rights. Additionally, literature regarding independence of directors overlaps with the literature of board size. In other words, studies that questioned the effect of board size have also questioned the effects of independent directors.

Reviewed literature according to their respective findings is summarized in Table 2.

Table 2. The impact of independent directors on performance

Author (Date)	Country	Positive Relationship	Negative Relationship	Neutral Relationship	Mix Relationship
(Rosenstein & Wyatt, 1990)	USA	X			
(Shivdasani & Yermack, 1999)	USA	X			
(Cornett et al., 2007)	USA	X			
(De Andres & Vallelado, 2008)	6 OECD Countries	X			
(Dahya et al., 2008a)	22 countries	X			
(Aggarwal, Bhagat, & Rangan, 2009)	The USA and Multiple Countries	X			
(Liang, Xu, & Jiraporn, 2013)	China	X			
(Liu, Miletkov, Wei, & Yang, 2015)	China	X			
(Agyemang et al., 2014)	Ghana	X			
(Brown & Caylor, 2006)	USA		X		
(Alias, Yaacob, & Jaffar, 2017)	Malasia		X		
(Aktan et al., 2018)	Bahrain		X		
(Fogel & Geier, 2007)	USA			X	
(Mersland & Strøm, 2009)	60 countries			X	
(Kent Baker & Powell, 2009)	USA			X	
(Salim, Arjomandi, & Seufert, 2016)	Australia			X	

While most of the studies in the literature are consistent with the hypothesis that outside directors are chosen in the interest of shareholders, their context varies. Earliest reviewed study in this context belongs to Rosenstein and Wyatt (1990). With the aim of questioning the effects of outside director appointments, they have closely inspected and analyzed several companies listed in the USA. Their findings indicate that existence of independent directors in strongly related to firm performance in a positive way. In addition to that, increasing the percentage of independent directors in the firm has a positive effect of firm performance as well. One of the most comprehensive studies in this regard belongs to De Andres and Vallelado (2008). Using 6 countries within OECD, they perform a set of analyses on companies that are operating in the banking sector. Results of their analyses indicate that increasing the number of independent directors severely increases the firm performance. Considering the fact that there are no small or medium-sized banks or family company banks in OECD countries, the results are perfectly in line with previous studies and financial theories. Additionally, the study shows that bank board composition and size are related to directors' ability to monitor and advise management. However, the study stresses that there is an optimum point in the number of independent directors and board size. Supporting this claim with the results that indicate that overcrowded boards or overpopulated directors negatively impact firm performance. Study of Dahya, Dimitrov, & McConnell (2008), as previously discussed also has very robust results in line with this study as well. In the line with this view, there are few studies (Agyemang et al., 2014; Cornett et al., 2007; Liu et al., 2015; Shivdasani & Yermack, 1999).

Studies that find a negative relationship between the percentage of independent directors and firm value are rather rare in the literature. As previously discussed under firm size, the study of Aktan et al. (2018)supports the view that inclusion of higher percentage on independent directors negatively affects firm performances. While these results seem to conflict with the general theory of finance, there is a niche explanation in the context of these studies. As a general property, studies that find a genitive correlation between the percentage of independent directors are either focuses on Small on medium-sized enterprises of developed country markets, or any company within emerging markets. Study of Aktan et.al. is conducted in the Bahrain market which included a very high percentage of family shareholder dominant corporations. The same situation is also seen in the study of Brown and Caylor (2006). Therefore, it may be speculated that under lightly regulated market conditions, independent directors cannot function efficiently.

CEO Duality

Another key variable in related literature that reflects corporate governance characteristic is known as CEO Duality condition. CEO duality or board duality refers to the condition where the board chairman and CEO are the same people. The results of this situation have been studied and produced two contradicting conclusions. On the one side, it is assumed that CEO duality is a constraint on the monitoring and controlling activities of the board on executives. As suggested, CEO duality may damage monitoring and controlling activities and thereby increase agency cost (Fama & Jensen, 1983). Consequently, there might be an adverse effect of this situation on firm performance due to ineffective monitoring and controlling. On the other side, supporters of CEO duality claim that firm performance can be improved if executives take the full responsibility and authority over the firm. It is claimed that there would be less conflict of interest if there is a CEO duality situation (Davis, Schoorman, & Donaldson, 1997). It should be noted that there is no universally accepted leadership structure for the corporation. Therefore, there are costs and benefits of both types of leadership. This situation is highly related to the cultural aspect of the community in which firms are operating.

In the context of CEO duality, literature is heavily in dispute. When the CEO also occupies the position of the chairman of the board, the intended separation of power within the corporate environment suffers in theory. In practice, however, lessened bureaucracy and more focused and organized operational efficiency contribute to the firm by providing stability.

Reviewed literature according to their respective findings is summarized in Table 3.

Mixed results reported in the literature is clearly caused by the difference between used datasets. The main difference is caused by firm size and structure and the secondary difference is caused by the development of the country in which the dataset is taken from. Overview of the literature suggests that first of all, large and institutionalized corporations within developed economies rarely benefit from CEO duality in the short run and never benefit in the long run (Bhagat & Bolton, 2008; Gill et al., 2011; Mollah & Zaman, 2015). In developing country markets, however, the duality of CEO is found to be comparatively positively related in large corporations and definitely positively related with Small and medium-sized companies.

As an exception to above generalization, measuring the success of corporate governance and firm performance was aimed by the study of Bhagat and Bolton (2008). While considering the existence of endogeneity, the study intends to answer three questions on the topic. According to the findings of the study, there is a

Table 3. The impact of CEO duality on performance

Author (Date)	Country	Positive Relationship	Negative Relationship	Neutral Relationship	Mix Relationship
(Peng, Bartholomae, Fox, & Cravener, 2007)	China	X			
(Bhagat & Bolton, 2008)	USA	X			
(Gill, Biger, & Mathur, 2011)	Canada	X			
(Judge, Naoumova, & Koutzevol, 2003)	Russia		X		
(Dogan, Elitas, Agca, & Ögel, 2013)	Turkey		X		
(Ujunwa, Salami, & Umar, 2013)	Nigeria		X		
(Mollah & Zaman, 2015)	25 Countries		X		
(Alix Valenti, Luce, & Mayfield, 2011)	USA			X	
(Agyemang et al., 2014)	Ghana			X	
(Aktan et al., 2018)	Bahrain			X	
(Z. Chen, Cheung, Stouraitis, & Wong, 2005)	Hong Kong				X

significant positive relationship between CEO-Duality and corporate performance. Contradicting with the results of former studies in this regard, the study finds no relationship between corporate governance and stock futures. Additionally, the study finds that, under the circumstances in which corporate performance is low, there is a positive relationship between board independence and disciplinary management run over. Which can be translated as, if the board of directors is independent, managers are more likely to be punished for poor performance.

Ownership Concentration

Ownership concentration is widely studied phenomena in the context of corporate governance researches and assumed to be an important characteristic of corporate governance (Shleifer & Vishny, 1986). Corporate governance practices are assumed to reduce conflict of interest between shareholders and managers. In this perspective, ownership concentration has been an interesting issue to analyze its impact on firm performance. On the theoretical ground, there are two competing views on ownership concentration whether ownership should be concentrated or dispersed. On the side of view that ownership should be concentrated, it is claimed that ownership concentration increases the monitoring and controlling mechanism of large shareholders in a way to lead executives to be aligned with the objective of increasing shareholders wealth (Demsetz, 1983; Shleifer & Vishny, 1986). Under the situation of high ownership concentration, there might be less conflict of interest between shareholders and executives whereas there is another issue has to be solved which is known as principle-principle conflict (Young, Peng, Ahlstrom, Bruton, & Jiang, 2008). In this case, there might be a conflict of interest between large shareholders and minority shareholders. Therefore, empirical evidence coming from researches that examine the possible relationship between ownership concentration and firm performance produce mixed results.

In the literature, the impact of ownership concentration is almost indisputably in favor of a positive relationship. Studies that did not come up with a positive relationship between ownership structure and firm performance are either niche or a by-product of another studies that did not focus on ownership concentration specifically(Alimehmeti & Paletta, 2012a; Demsetz & Lehn, 1985; Leech & Leahy, 1991; Lichtenberg & Pushner, 1994; Shleifer & Vishny, 1988; Vintilă & Gherghina, 2014).

Reviewed literature according to their respective findings is summarized in Table 4.

Reviewed studies that question the effects of owner concentration on firm size goes as far back as 1983. As a 50-year-old issue, study first focuses on the separation of ownership from controlling power and then moves on to the importance of minority rights. The study argues that delegation of power from owners to managers in a democratic environment is of the utmost importance. Furthermore, in the study, the relationship between ownership concentration and firm performance is analyzed. According to the findings of the study, there is a positive relationship between ownership concentration and firm performance (Demsetz, 1983). Another study that finds a significant relationship between ownership concentration and firm performance was conducted in (2014) by Vintilă and Gherghina. Using a multivariate regression model study analyses Romanian firm' performances. According to the results of the analyses, ownership concentration is positively related with the firm performance for up to first three major stockholders. The study also points out that the benefit of ownership concentration gradually declines to start from first until the third. Then adding major stockholders to the firm negatively effects the firm performance.

Most recent of the rare studies that reported a negative relationship between ownership concentration and firm performance is done by Abdullah and Ismail (2017). They conduct their research in Gulf Cooperation Council Countries' firms. According to the findings of their study, the governance quality across GCC

Table 4. The impact of ownership concentration on performance

Author (Date)	Country	Positive Relationship	Negative Relationship	Neutral Relationship	Mix Relationship
(Demsetz, 1983)	USA	X			
(Leech & Leahy, 1991)	UK	X			
(Lichtenberg & Pushner, 1994)	Japan	X			
(Alimehmeti & Paletta, 2012b)	Italy	X			
(Vintilă & Gherghina, 2014)	Romania	X			
(Aktan et al., 2018)	Bahrain	X			
(Abdallah & Ismail, 2017)	Gulf Cooperating Council (GCC) Countries		X		
(Omran, Bolbol, & Fatheldin, 2008)	Egypt, Jordan, Oman and Tunisia			X	
(Demsetz & Lehn, 1985)	USA			X	
(Shleifer & Vishny, 1988)	USA				X
(Önder, DELIKTAS, & Lenger, 2003)	Turkey				X

country firms vary greatly. The relationship between corporate governance and firm performance increases in firms with dispersed ownership structures. However, most of these companies in this market have an almost absolute concentration on boards, therefore the companies that have dispersed board of directors are generally foreign direct investments within the region. Therefore, results might be misleading. Overall, ownership concentration seems to be a performance enhancing factor as long as minority right are also rightfully cared for and as long as ownership is not too concentrated.

Audit Committee and Auditors Reputation

One of the important aspects of corporate governance is the auditing mechanism that ensures transparency, reliability, and validity. These duties are supposed to be carried out by the board of directors whereas there are sub-committees devoted to investigating these roles such as audit and remuneration committees. Ensuring high-quality financial reporting has become an important concern for a long time due to the increasing number of financial fraud and misleading reporting. In this context, audit committee and its characteristics play a vital role in establishing and monitoring the internal financial and accounting reporting process to provide relevant and credible information to all stakeholders (Beasley, 1996). It is assumed that the audit committee has a direct influence on the number of frauds and a positive relationship with firm performance(McMullen, 1996). The conceptual argument here is that the audit committee ensure high quality of reporting and controlling that improve firm performance (Klein, 2002). There are many empirical studies examining the characteristics of the audit committee on firm performance including the presence of audit committee, size of the audit committee, number of independent directors in audit committee and meeting frequency of audit committee. The empirical studies reviewed here are those that investigated the size of the audit committee which is a contradictory issue. There are mixed results coming from the empirical evidence on the relationship between audit committee size and firm performance.

There is another aspect of auditing mechanism that attracted researchers to study which is the auditor reputation. Independent auditing which is widely known as external accounting auditing has been a Worldwide consulting business. There are relatively big companies which are labeled as big 4, big 6 or big 8 depending upon the location. Therefore, it is assumed that having an independent auditing service from these companies increase and ensure the quality of financial reporting standards which leads to better firm performance (Reed, 2002). The conceptual argument behind this assumption is that these relatively big auditing firms are more independent and face greater liability for making an error so that they ensure transparency and eliminate mistakes in financial reporting (Michaely & Shaw, 1995). Some researchers have examined the linkage between firm performance and having an independent auditing service from these relatively big companies.

Reviewed literature according to their respective findings is summarized in Table 5.

Impact of auditor reputation on firm performance is one of the few topics that corporate governance literature commonly agrees on. Auditors not only control

Table 5. The impact of auditor reputation on performance

Author (Date)	Country	Positive Relationship	Negative Relationship	Neutral Relationship	Mix Relationship
(Mitton, 2002)	Five Countries	X			
(Wahab, Zain, & James, 2011)	Malasia	X			
(Zagorchev & Gao, 2015)	USA	X			
(Aktan et al., 2018)	Bahrain	X			

the firm but also structure it is such a way that it is able to perform successfully regardless of whom the manager is. Additionally, in modern markets auditors that are trusted carry a brand value to the firm they control. This brand value, reduces the perceived risk factor in investing in a company, therefore increasing its value in the financial sense. All of the studies that are reviewed have a common ground of this matter(Aktan et al., 2018; Mitton, 2002; Wahab et al., 2011; Zagorchev & Gao, 2015). With no dispute in this context, next question on auditing is the relationship between firm performance and the Audit Committee.

Reviewed literature according to their respective findings is summarized in Table 6.

In the context of the audit committee, studies that have found both positive and negative relationship can actually be categorized under the same category as the studies that confirm the meaningful relationship between the impact of the audit committee on firm performance. The existence of an audit committee is not optional in publicly traded corporations in any developed or developing countries included in studies that are reviewed. One of the early studies reviewed in this context belongs to Bozec (2005). In his study on Canadian firms, Bozec has found a statistically significant relationship between audit committee performance and firm performance. The coefficient of this relationship is found to be positive in the firms that are operating in an uncompetitive environment while the coefficient is negative for the firms that are operating in a competitive environment. Another study

Table 6. The impact of audit committee on performance

Author (Date)	Country	Positive Relationship	Negative Relationship	Neutral Relationship
(Anderson, Mansi, & Reeb, 2004)	USA	X		
(Bauer, Pitschel, & Studinger, 2010)	USA	X		
(Reddy, Locke, & Scrimgeour, 2010)	New Zealand	X		
(de Oliveira Gondrige, Clemente, & Espejo, 2012)	Brazil	X		
(Bozec, 2005)	Canada		X	
(Mollah & Talukdar, 2007)	Bangladesh		X	
(Al-Matari, Al-Swidi, Fadzil, & Al-Matari, 2012)	Kuwait		X	
(Ghabayen, 2012)	Saudi Arabia			X
(Agyemang et al., 2014)	Ghana			X
(Ojeka, Iyoha, & Obigbemi, 2014)	Nigeria			X
(Darko, Aribi, & Uzonwanne, 2016)	Ghana			X

in this context is conducted for New Zealand companies (Reddy et al., 2010). New Zealand firms have been analyzed in the study for years 1999 to 2007. Findings of the study indicate that there is a significant positive relationship between audit committee member counts and firm performance. Additionally, the study suggests that the ideal size for the committee is 7 members. Generally, there are many studies that argue that the effects of the audit committee are positively or negatively related to firm performance. However, common ground is found on the significant effect of the existence of auditor committees.

Board Meetings

The frequency of board meetings is considered as potential input for sustaining corporate governance. The grounding argument here is that fulfilling duties require sufficient time in order to enhance the board's effectiveness (Lipton & Lorsch, 1992). Therefore, it is assumed that a higher frequency of board meetings could result in more effective and efficient monitoring and controlling activities. However, there is a contradictory argument implying that board meeting might not necessarily be effective due to the shortage in time for outsiders to exchange valuable ideas (Jensen, 1993). The literature on the impact of board meetings focused on the field in the context of the number of board meetings.

Reviewed literature according to their respective findings is summarized in Table 7.

Rather than suggesting that the number of board meetings increase or decrease the firm performance indefinitely, it is suggested that there is an optimal number of meetings until which the firm performance increases. After reaching this optimal line, additional meetings have either no effect or affect the firm performance negatively. The first reviewed study in this regard belongs to Andreou (2016). Andreou investigates whether ownership structure, accounting opacity, board structure & processes, and managerial incentives attributes relate to future stock price crash risk in his study.

Table 7. The impact of board meetings on performance

Author (Date)	Country	Positive Relationship	Negative Relationship	Neutral Relationship	Mix Relationship
(Andreou, Antoniou, Horton, & Louca, 2016)	USA	X			
(Salim et al., 2016)	Australia	X			
(Chauhan et al., 2016)	India	X			
(Agyemang et al., 2014)	Ghana	X			
(Aktan et al., 2018)	Bahrain		X		

Among his findings regarding corporate governance, he finds a positive relationship between the number of board meetings and firm performance. Another study (Salim et al., 2016) investigates Australian banks for a period of 14 years from 1999 to 2013. Study finds that the board size and committee meetings have significant positive effects on banking efficiency in Australia. Another significant study (Chauhan et al., 2016) investigates the effects of firm-level corporate governance practices on firm performance for publicly traded Indian firms where founder ownership is concentrated. As a by-product of research, it is also reported that firm performance has a positive relationship with board meetings. Lastly, the study of Aktan (2018), reports that for companies located in Bahrain board meeting counts and firm performance has a negative relationship. Rather than categorizing this finding as contradictory, it can be argued that firms within that specific market are conducting an optimal or above optimal amount of board meetings already.

Firm Size

Researchers have used several control variables in related literature of corporate governance in order to eliminate the potential impact of firm, industry, and country-specific characteristics. Firm size, sales growth, firm age, leverage, the origin of country, financial market structure, among others are few of them. Firm size as a control variable is one of the most frequently used variables. Although there is no clear-cut theoretical ground for the usage of firm size in performance researches, it is assumed that a firm requires to reach to a certain size for implementation of the corporate governance standards. Evanoff and Israilevich (1991) point out that larger bank size might be a prerequisite to gain scale and scope-related economics in order to achieve higher performance. Hence, these banks may possess higher skilled executives to improve performance. A vast majority of the literature in this subject lean towards the neutrality. In other words, there is no significant relationship between firm size and firm performance (Ahmed et al., 2006; Aktan et al., 2018; Dahya et al., 2008a; Eisenberg et al., 1998; Jaafar & El-Shawa, 2009).

Reviewed literature according to their respective findings is summarized in Table 8.

Studies that find a positive relationship between firm size and firm performance is conducted first by Afrifa and Tauringana (2015). In their study evaluating companies in the United Kingdom in the context of corporate governance, they also report finding a significant relationship between firm size and firm performance. However, the study used small, medium and large size companies all together in the same regression. Therefore, results might be misleading, as a small and medium-size enterprise, in general, is sure to have less operational efficiency than a large corporation. Another study that reports similar results with same dataset trap belongs to Darko, Aribi, & Uzonwanne (2016). A contradictory study belongs to De Andres (2008). In his

Table 8. The impact of firm size on performance

Author (Date)	Country	Positive Relationship	Negative Relationship	Neutral Relationship	Mix Relationship
(Afrifa & Tauringana, 2015)	UK	X			
(Darko, Aribi, & Uzonwanne, 2016)	Ghana	X			
(De Andres & Vallelado, 2008)	6 OECD Countries		X		
(Eisenberg et al., 1998)	Finland			X	
(Beiner et al., 2004)	Switzerland			X	
(Ahmed et al., 2006)	New Zealand			X	
(Dahya et al., 2008b)	22 countries			X	
(Jaafar & El-Shawa, 2009)	Jordan			X	
(Aktan et al., 2018)	Bahrain			X	

study specifically targeting banks, Andres analyses the firms of 6 OECD countries. According to the results of the study, as bank size get smaller firm performance gets higher. It can be interpreted from here that, small banks might be more profitable or efficient than larger ones in terms of corporate governance.

CONCLUDING REMARKS AND RECOMMENDATIONS

In this study, the linkage between corporate governance and firm performance was explored based on the empirical and theoretical paper in related literature. Since corporate governance has a multi-facet characteristic, there are different results for these facets. However, there is a strong tendency of accepting the fact that corporate governance practices are positively correlated with firm performance. The debate is mainly about how this correlation exists and/or what the direction of causality between corporate governance and firm performance.

The following remarks are derived from this review:

- The direction of causality between corporate governance and firm performance is not well studied. Although it was not intended to review the econometrical aspects of the reviewed papers here, it is safe to state that there is a need to examine the causality condition within well-structured research design taking endogeneity and simultaneity problems into account.

- In the cross-country analyses, market infrastructure should be analyzed under the framework of corporate governance. Researchers have used several control variables for fixing the impact of market infrastructure without referring to its dynamics whereas there are more variables that might be omitted in their econometrical models.
- Theoretical justifications are needed to explain the differences in empirical results. Why there are competing results for the same aspect of corporate governance? These differences should be properly explained within the theory of the firm.
- Agency theory, stewardship theory, resource dependency theory, property right cost and transaction cost among others are assumed to be a grounding framework for empirical investigation whereas there is no tendency to justify these theories with respect to empirical findings which do not favour the theory. In other words, there are no attempts to criticize the theoretical ground and give a solid argument for developing and/or improving the theory. One exception is the study carried out by (Young et al., 2008) who introduce the conflict between larger and minority shareholders.

Empirical papers depict that corporate governance practices could not be the same for all firms implying that there is no optimal system. This should be considered by policymakers who have responsibilities in regulatory bodies. If corporate governance practices vary from market to market (manufacturing vs banking) and country to country (developing vs developed), then it is wise to take the structural and institutional differences into account in the process of implementing these practices.

REFERENCES

Abdallah, A. A.-N., & Ismail, A. K. (2017). Corporate governance practices, ownership structure, and corporate performance in the GCC countries. *Journal of International Financial Markets, Institutions and Money*, *46*, 98–115. doi:10.1016/j.intfin.2016.08.004

Adams, R. B., & Mehran, H. (2012). Bank board structure and performance: Evidence for large bank holding companies. *Journal of Financial Intermediation*, *21*(2), 243–267. doi:10.1016/j.jfi.2011.09.002

Aebi, V., Sabato, G., & Schmid, M. (2012). Risk management, corporate governance, and bank performance in the financial crisis. *Journal of Banking & Finance*, *36*(12), 3213–3226. doi:10.1016/j.jbankfin.2011.10.020

Afrifa, G. A., & Tauringana, V. (2015). Corporate governance and performance of UK listed small and medium enterprises. *Corporate Governance*, *15*(5), 719–733. doi:10.1108/CG-03-2015-0029

Aggarwal, R., Bhagat, S., & Rangan, S. (2009). The impact of fundamentals on IPO valuation. *Financial Management*, *38*(2), 253–284. doi:10.1111/j.1755-053X.2009.01035.x

Aguilera, R. V., & Desender, K. A. (2012). Challenges in the measuring of comparative corporate governance: a review of the main indices. In West Meets East: Building Theoretical Bridges (pp. 289–322). Emerald Group Publishing Limited. doi:10.1108/S1479-8387(2012)0000008014

Agyemang, O. S., Aboagye, E., Antwi, S., & Frimpong, J. (2014). Board of Directors and Firm Performance of Banking Institutions: A Ghanaian Experience. *European Journal of Economics, Finance and Administrative Sciences,* (67), 16.

Ahmed, K., Hossain, M., & Adams, M. B. (2006). The effects of board composition and board size on the informativeness of annual accounting earnings. *Corporate Governance*, *14*(5), 418–431. doi:10.1111/j.1467-8683.2006.00515.x

Ajinkya, B., Bhojraj, S., & Sengupta, P. (2005). The association between outside directors, institutional investors and the properties of management earnings forecasts. *Journal of Accounting Research*, *43*(3), 343–376. doi:10.1111/j.1475-679x.2005.00174.x

Aktan, B., Turen, S., Tvaronavičienė, M., Celik, S., & Alsadeh, H. (2018). Corporate governance and performance of the financial firms in Bahrain. *Polish Journal of Management Studies, 17*.

Al Daoud, K. A., Ismail, K. N. I. K., & Lode, N. A. (2015). The impact of internal corporate governance on the timeliness of financial reports of Jordanian firms: Evidence using audit and management report lags. *Mediterranean Journal of Social Sciences*, *6*(1), 430.

Al-Matari, Y. A., Al-Swidi, A. K., Fadzil, F. H. B. F. H., & Al-Matari, E. M. (2012). Board of directors, audit committee characteristics and the performance of Saudi Arabia listed companies. *International Review of Management and Marketing*, *2*(4), 241–251.

Alias, N., Yaacob, M., & Jaffar, N. (2017). Governance structure, corporate restructuring and performance. *Polish Journal of Management Studies, 15.*

Alimehmeti, G., & Paletta, A. (2012). Ownership concentration and effects over firm performance: Evidences from Italy. *European Scientific Journal, 8*(22).

Alix Valenti, M., Luce, R., & Mayfield, C. (2011). The effects of firm performance on corporate governance. *Management Research Review, 34*(3), 266–283. doi:10.1108/01409171111116295

Anderson, R. C., Mansi, S. A., & Reeb, D. M. (2004). Board characteristics, accounting report integrity, and the cost of debt. *Journal of Accounting and Economics, 37*(3), 315–342. doi:10.1016/j.jacceco.2004.01.004

Andreou, P. C., Antoniou, C., Horton, J., & Louca, C. (2016). Corporate governance and firm-specific stock price crashes. *European Financial Management, 22*(5), 916–956. doi:10.1111/eufm.12084

Aras, G., & Crowther, D. (2008). Governance and sustainability: An investigation into the relationship between corporate governance and corporate sustainability. *Management Decision, 46*(3), 433–448. doi:10.1108/00251740810863870

Bauer, M. W., Pitschel, D., & Studinger, P. (2010). *Governance Preferences of Subnational Administrative Elites in the European Union: An Empirical Analysis.* Academic Public Administration Studies Archive-APAS.

Beasley, M. S. (1996). An empirical analysis of the relation between the board of director composition and financial statement fraud. *The Accounting Review*, 443–465.

Bebchuk, L. A., & Cohen, A. (2005). The costs of entrenched boards. *Journal of Financial Economics, 78*(2), 409–433. doi:10.1016/j.jfineco.2004.12.006

Beiner, S., Drobetz, W., Schmid, F., & Zimmermann, H. (2004). Is board size an independent corporate governance mechanism? *Kyklos, 57*(3), 327–356. doi:10.1111/j.0023-5962.2004.00257.x

Bhagat, S., & Bolton, B. (2008). Corporate governance and firm performance. *Journal of Corporate Finance, 14*(3), 257–273. doi:10.1016/j.jcorpfin.2008.03.006

Bhatt, P. R., & Bhatt, R. R. (2017). Corporate governance and firm performance in Malaysia. *Corporate Governance: The International Journal of Business in Society, 17*(5), 896–912. doi:10.1108/CG-03-2016-0054

Bin, R. L. L., & Yi, L. S. (2015). Board mechanisms and performance of government-linked companies on Bursa Malaysia. *Procedia Economics and Finance*, *31*, 399–417. doi:10.1016/S2212-5671(15)01215-0

Bozec, R. (2005). Boards of directors, market discipline and firm performance. *Journal of Business Finance & Accounting*, *32*(9-10), 1921–1960. doi:10.1111/j.0306-686X.2005.00652.x

Brown, L. D., & Caylor, M. L. (2004). *Corporate governance and firm performance*. Academic Press.

Brown, L. D., & Caylor, M. L. (2006). Corporate governance and firm valuation. *Journal of Accounting and Public Policy*, *25*(4), 409–434. doi:10.1016/j.jaccpubpol.2006.05.005

Chauhan, Y., Lakshmi, K. R., & Dey, D. K. (2016). Corporate governance practices, self-dealings, and firm performance: Evidence from India. *Journal of Contemporary Accounting & Economics*, *12*(3), 274–289. doi:10.1016/j.jcae.2016.10.002

Chen, S., Lin, B.-X., Wang, Y., & Wu, L. (2008). Cross-listing, corporate governance and operating performance–evidence from The Chinese market. In *Advances in Business and Management Forecasting* (pp. 19–46). Emerald Group Publishing Limited.

Chen, Z., Cheung, Y.-L., Stouraitis, A., & Wong, A. W. (2005). Ownership concentration, firm performance, and dividend policy in Hong Kong. *Pacific-Basin Finance Journal*, *13*(4), 431–449. doi:10.1016/j.pacfin.2004.12.001

Chong, Y. Y. (2004). Corporate governance: Risk management starts at the top. *Balance Sheet*, *12*(5), 42–47. doi:10.1108/09657960410563586

Coase, R. H. (1937). The nature of the firm. *Economica*, *4*(16), 386–405. doi:10.1111/j.1468-0335.1937.tb00002.x

Coles, J. L., Daniel, N. D., & Naveen, L. (2008). Boards: Does one size fit all? *Journal of Financial Economics*, *87*(2), 329–356. doi:10.1016/j.jfineco.2006.08.008

Cornett, M. M., Marcus, A. J., Saunders, A., & Tehranian, H. (2007). The impact of institutional ownership on corporate operating performance. *Journal of Banking & Finance*, *31*(6), 1771–1794. doi:10.1016/j.jbankfin.2006.08.006

Dahya, J., Dimitrov, O., & McConnell, J. J. (2008a). Dominant shareholders, corporate boards, and corporate value: A cross-country analysis. *Journal of Financial Economics*, *87*(1), 73–100. doi:10.1016/j.jfineco.2006.10.005

Dahya, J., Dimitrov, O., & McConnell, J. J. (2008b). Dominant shareholders, corporate boards, and corporate value: A cross-country analysis. *Journal of Financial Economics*, *87*(1), 73–100. doi:10.1016/j.jfineco.2006.10.005

Darko, J., Aribi, Z. A., & Uzonwanne, G. C. (2016). Corporate governance: The impact of director and board structure, ownership structure and corporate control on the performance of listed companies on the Ghana stock exchange. *Corporate Governance*, *16*(2), 259–277. doi:10.1108/CG-11-2014-0133

Davis, J. H., Schoorman, F. D., & Donaldson, L. (1997). Toward a stewardship theory of management. *Academy of Management Review*, *22*(1), 20–47. doi:10.5465/amr.1997.9707180258

De Andres, P., & Vallelado, E. (2008). Corporate governance in banking: The role of the board of directors. *Journal of Banking & Finance*, *32*(12), 2570–2580. doi:10.1016/j.jbankfin.2008.05.008

de Oliveira Gondrige, E., Clemente, A., & Espejo, M. M. dos S. B. (2012). Composition of the board and firm value of brazilian public companies. *Brazilian Business Review (English Edition)*, *9*(3).

Dedman, E., & Filatotchev, I. (2008). Corporate governance research: A contingency framework. *International Journal of Managerial Finance*, *4*(4), 248–258. doi:10.1108/17439130810902778

Demsetz, H. (1983). The structure of ownership and the theory of the firm. *The Journal of Law & Economics*, *26*(2), 375–390. doi:10.1086/467041

Demsetz, H., & Lehn, K. (1985). The structure of corporate ownership: Causes and consequences. *Journal of Political Economy*, *93*(6), 1155–1177. doi:10.1086/261354

Dogan, M., Elitas, B. L., Agca, V., & Ögel, S. (2013). The impact of CEO duality on firm performance: Evidence from turkey. *International Journal of Business and Social Science*, *4*(2).

Dunn, D. J. (1987). *Directors Arent Doing Their Jobs*. Academic Press.

Eberhart, R. (2012). Corporate governance systems and firm value: Empirical evidence from Japan's natural experiment. *Journal of Asia Business Studies*, *6*(2), 176–196. doi:10.1108/15587891211254399

Eisenberg, T., Sundgren, S., & Wells, M. T. (1998). Larger board size and decreasing firm value in small firms1. *Journal of Financial Economics*, *48*(1), 35–54. doi:10.1016/S0304-405X(98)00003-8

Evanoff, D. D., & Israilevich, P. R. (1991). Productive efficiency in banking. *Economic Perspectives*, *15*(4), 11–32.

Fama, E. F., & Jensen, M. C. (1983). Separation of ownership and control. *The Journal of Law & Economics*, *26*(2), 301–325. doi:10.1086/467037

Fogel, E. M., & Geier, A. M. (2007). Strangers in the house: Rethinking Sarbanes-Oxley and the independent board of directors. *Del. J. CorP. L.*, *32*, 33.

Funchal, B., & Pinto, J. P. (2018). Corporate events' performance and corporate governance: The Brazilian evidence. *Corporate Governance: The International Journal of Business in Society*, *18*(1), 14–34. doi:10.1108/CG-11-2016-0219

Ghabayen, M. A. (2012). Board characteristics and firm performance: Case of Saudi Arabia. *International Journal of Accounting and Financial Reporting*, *2*(2), 168–200. doi:10.5296/ijafr.v2i2.2145

Gill, A., Biger, N., & Mathur, N. (2011). The effect of capital structure on profitability: Evidence from the United States. *International Journal of Management*, *28*(4), 3.

Gompers, P., Ishii, J., & Metrick, A. (2003). Corporate governance and equity prices. *The Quarterly Journal of Economics*, *118*(1), 107–156. doi:10.1162/00335530360535162

Goodstein, J., Gautam, K., & Boeker, W. (1994). The effects of board size and diversity on strategic change. *Strategic Management Journal*, *15*(3), 241–250. doi:10.1002mj.4250150305

Gupta, P., & Sharma, A. M. (2014). A study of the impact of corporate governance practices on firm performance in Indian and South Korean companies. *Procedia: Social and Behavioral Sciences*, *133*, 4–11. doi:10.1016/j.sbspro.2014.04.163

Jaafar, A., & El-Shawa, M. (2009). Ownership concentration, board characteristics and performance: evidence from Jordan. In *Accounting in Emerging Economies* (pp. 73–95). Emerald Group Publishing Limited. doi:10.1108/S1479-3563(2009)0000009005

Jensen, M. C. (1993). The modern industrial revolution, exit, and the failure of internal control systems. *The Journal of Finance*, *48*(3), 831–880. doi:10.1111/j.1540-6261.1993.tb04022.x

Judge, W. Q., Naoumova, I., & Koutzevol, N. (2003). Corporate governance and firm performance in Russia: An empirical study. *Journal of World Business*, *38*(4), 385–396. doi:10.1016/j.jwb.2003.08.023

Kent Baker, H., & Powell, G. E. (2009). Management views on corporate governance and firm performance. In *Corporate Governance and Firm Performance* (pp. 83–118). Emerald Group Publishing Limited. doi:10.1108/S1569-3732(2009)0000013006

Kiel, G. C., & Nicholson, G. J. (2003). Board composition and corporate performance: How the Australian experience informs contrasting theories of corporate governance. *Corporate Governance*, *11*(3), 189–205. doi:10.1111/1467-8683.00318

Klein, A. (2002). Audit committee, board of director characteristics, and earnings management. *Journal of Accounting and Economics*, *33*(3), 375–400. doi:10.1016/S0165-4101(02)00059-9

Leech, D., & Leahy, J. (1991). Ownership structure, control type classifications and the performance of large British companies. *Economic Journal (London)*, *101*(409), 1418–1437. doi:10.2307/2234893

Liang, Q., Xu, P., & Jiraporn, P. (2013). Board characteristics and Chinese bank performance. *Journal of Banking & Finance*, *37*(8), 2953–2968. doi:10.1016/j.jbankfin.2013.04.018

Lichtenberg, F. R., & Pushner, G. M. (1994). Ownership structure and corporate performance in Japan. *Japan and the World Economy*, *6*(3), 239–261. doi:10.1016/0922-1425(94)90014-0

Lipton, M., & Lorsch, J. W. (1992). A modest proposal for improved corporate governance. *Business Lawyer*, 59–77.

Liu, Y., Miletkov, M. K., Wei, Z., & Yang, T. (2015). Board independence and firm performance in China. *Journal of Corporate Finance*, *30*, 223–244. doi:10.1016/j.jcorpfin.2014.12.004

McMullen, D. A. (1996). Audit committee performance: An investigation of the consequences associated with audit committees. *Auditing*, *15*(1), 87.

Mersland, R., & Strøm, R. Ø. (2009). Performance and governance in microfinance institutions. *Journal of Banking & Finance*, *33*(4), 662–669. doi:10.1016/j.jbankfin.2008.11.009

Michaely, R., & Shaw, W. H. (1995). Does the choice of auditor convey quality in an initial public offering? *Financial Management*, *24*(4), 15–30. doi:10.2307/3665948

Mitton, T. (2002). A cross-firm analysis of the impact of corporate governance on the East Asian financial crisis. *Journal of Financial Economics*, *64*(2), 215–241. doi:10.1016/S0304-405X(02)00076-4

Mollah, S., & Talukdar, B. (2007). *Ownership Structure, Corporate Governance, and Firm's Performance in Emerging Markets: Evidence from Bangaldesh*. Academic Press.

Mollah, S., & Zaman, M. (2015). Shari'ah supervision, corporate governance and performance: Conventional vs. Islamic banks. *Journal of Banking & Finance*, *58*, 418–435. doi:10.1016/j.jbankfin.2015.04.030

Ojeka, S., Iyoha, F., & Obigbemi, I. F. (2014). effectiveness of audit committee and firm financial performance in Nigeria: an empirical analysis. *Journal of Accounting and Auditing: Research & Practice*.

Omran, M. M., Bolbol, A., & Fatheldin, A. (2008). Corporate governance and firm performance in Arab equity markets: Does ownership concentration matter? *International Review of Law and Economics*, *28*(1), 32–45. doi:10.1016/j.irle.2007.12.001

Önder, A. Ö., Deliktas, E. R., & Lenger, A. (2003). Efficiency in the manufacturing industry of selected provinces in Turkey: A stochastic frontier analysis. *Emerging Markets Finance & Trade*, *39*(2), 98–113. doi:10.1080/1540496X.2003.11052537

Pearce, J. A., & Zahra, S. A. (1992). Board composition from a strategic contingency perspective. *Journal of Management Studies*, *29*(4), 411–438. doi:10.1111/j.1467-6486.1992.tb00672.x

Peng, T.-C. M., Bartholomae, S., Fox, J. J., & Cravener, G. (2007). The impact of personal finance education delivered in high school and college courses. *Journal of Family and Economic Issues*, *28*(2), 265–284. doi:10.100710834-007-9058-7

Reddy, K., Locke, S., & Scrimgeour, F. (2010). The efficacy of principle-based corporate governance practices and firm financial performance: An empirical investigation. *International Journal of Managerial Finance*, *6*(3), 190–219. doi:10.1108/17439131011056224

Reed, M. I. (2002). New managerialism, professional power and organisational governance in UK universities: A review and assessment. In *Governing higher education: National perspectives on institutional governance* (pp. 163–185). Springer. doi:10.1007/978-94-015-9946-7_9

Rosenstein, S., & Wyatt, J. G. (1990). Outside directors, board independence, and shareholder wealth. *Journal of Financial Economics*, *26*(2), 175–191. doi:10.1016/0304-405X(90)90002-H

Salim, R., Arjomandi, A., & Seufert, J. H. (2016). Does corporate governance affect Australian banks' performance? *Journal of International Financial Markets, Institutions and Money*, *43*, 113–125. doi:10.1016/j.intfin.2016.04.006

Shivdasani, A., & Yermack, D. (1999). CEO involvement in the selection of new board members: An empirical analysis. *The Journal of Finance*, *54*(5), 1829–1853. doi:10.1111/0022-1082.00168

Shleifer, A., & Vishny, R. W. (1986). Large shareholders and corporate control. *Journal of Political Economy*, *94*(3, Part 1), 461–488. doi:10.1086/261385

Shleifer, A., & Vishny, R. W. (1988). Value maximization and the acquisition process. *The Journal of Economic Perspectives*, *2*(1), 7–20. doi:10.1257/jep.2.1.7

Smith, A. (1776). *An inquiry into the nature and causes of the wealth of nations* (vol. 1). London: Printed for W. Strahan; and T. Cadell, 1776.

Ujunwa, A., Salami, P., & Umar, A. (2013). CEO duality and firm performance: An integration of institutional perceptive with agency theory. *International Journal of Social, Behavioral, Educational, Economic. Business and Industrial Engineering*, *7*(1), 180–186.

Vafeas, N. (1999). Board meeting frequency and firm performance. *Journal of Financial Economics*, *53*(1), 113–142. doi:10.1016/S0304-405X(99)00018-5

Vintilă, G., & Gherghina, Ş. C. (2014). The impact of ownership concentration on firm value. Empirical study of the Bucharest stock exchange listed companies. *Procedia Economics and Finance*, *15*, 271–279. doi:10.1016/S2212-5671(14)00500-0

Wahab, E. A. A., Zain, M. M., & James, K. (2011). Political connections, corporate governance and audit fees in Malaysia. *Managerial Auditing Journal*, *26*(5), 393–418. doi:10.1108/02686901111129562

Yermack, D. (2015). Is Bitcoin a real currency? An economic appraisal. In *Handbook of digital currency* (pp. 31–43). Elsevier. doi:10.1016/B978-0-12-802117-0.00002-3

Young, M. N., Peng, M. W., Ahlstrom, D., Bruton, G. D., & Jiang, Y. (2008). Corporate governance in emerging economies: A review of the principal–principal perspective. *Journal of Management Studies*, *45*(1), 196–220. doi:10.1111/j.1467-6486.2007.00752.x

Zabri, S. M., Ahmad, K., & Wah, K. K. (2016). Corporate governance practices and firm performance: Evidence from top 100 public listed companies in Malaysia. *Procedia Economics and Finance*, *35*, 287–296. doi:10.1016/S2212-5671(16)00036-8

Zagorchev, A., & Gao, L. (2015). Corporate governance and performance of financial institutions. *Journal of Economics and Business*, *82*, 17–41. doi:10.1016/j.jeconbus.2015.04.004

Chapter 10
The Promotion of Partnership Value Through Employee Share Ownership and Customer Share Ownership

Sara Elouadi
https://orcid.org/0000-0001-5412-2714
Hassan II University, Casablanca, Morocco

ABSTRACT

This chapter proposes an enriched analysis of value creation seeking to integrate all the stakeholders. To this end, they suggest two practices that counterbalance the power of shareholders and managers by allowing other stakeholders to exercise political and financial power. They are interested in employee share ownership and customer shareholding. In fact, the property grants customers and employees the superior status of the shareholder in order to enjoy a higher power likely to limit the attempts of managerial entrenchment and shareholder supremacy.

DOI: 10.4018/978-1-5225-9607-3.ch010

INTRODUCTION

All areas of management are pinpointed for breach of ethics and morality which produces a crisis of values and undermines public confidence in companies and leaders.

Companies are guilty of numerous scandals, such as tax evasion, massive corruption, slippage of marketing practices and cases of mistreatment of human resources. Companies view the customer as a target of their business practices and not as an individual in their own right to understand, reassure and retain. And his claims only raise the interest when it comes to structured movements like boycotts or trials.

The current responsible consumer seeks participation and inclusion in the decision-making arena and is ready to use his power against companies that do not adhere to his beliefs and who show contempt for the citizen.

The latest cases of boycotts and protests recorded at the international level perfectly illustrate this phenomenon. Indeed, faced with rising prices and the refusal of any communication. the citizens do not skimp on the means to amplify the collective mobilization, between messages, caricatures, parodies and videos, the web is the theater of a boundless creativity.

For example, we can mention the movement of yellow vests in France, which expresses widespread anger towards politicians and their unfair decisions that favor the wealthy classes at the expense of the middle and poor classes. The activists demand equal sharing of wealth and the reinstatement of the Wealth Tax 'ISF' is one of the flagship claims of "yellow vests".

This state of discontent with current practices is generating a growing awareness of the importance of good governance that is respectful of people and the environment. Good governance must inevitably allow the recognition and integration of stakeholders, in order to humanize and moralize the process of creation and sharing of value.

The measure we propose for this purpose is hybridization to provide employees and customers with more power. Indeed, and in accordance with pluralistic partnership governance, the company must integrate all its stakeholders in the process of creating value and break with the dictatorship shareholder who gives full importance to the shareholders of the company and financial results.

This work begins with the criticism of the shareholder value system and proposes the partnership vision based on the integration of all stakeholders. Then, we analyze the theoretical aspects of partnership governance by using the arguments and definitions proposed by stakeholder theory which recognizes from the outset the existence of several actors affected by the company. Finally, we conclude our study with the proposal of two partnership hybridization frameworks and their virtues, namely employee ownership and customer share ownership.

FROM SHAREHOLDER VALUE TO PARTNERSHIP VALUE: A PARADIGM SHIFT

Governance is concerned with the architecture and the exercise of power within companies, two great opposing visions coexist. The first, provides a monistic description of power called shareholder value, the second presents a pluralistic vision allowing the integration of all stakeholders in the process of value creation called, then, the partnership value.

Our work proposes a new reading grid of partnership creation of value by focusing on employee share ownership and customer share ownership.

Ownership, provided by these two managerial practices, provides additional power to the two targeted stakeholders in order to limit the managerial entrenchment and the dictatorship of external shareholders.

The preponderance of shareholder value emerged under the Anglo-Saxon influence which gives a decisive role to the financial markets.

In addition to this institutional reason, shareholder value finds another justification in traditional financial theory; this theory considers shareholders as the only residual creditors of the company (Charreaux & Desbrières 1997).

Thus, the configurations of corporate governance systems that exist are those that maximize the wealth of shareholders. The only concern of the executives is then maximizing dividends to pay the shareholders more and better. This situation undermines the interests of other stakeholders who are confined to serving the shareholder vision. Employees and shareholders are sacrificed for the creation of wealth distributed to shareholders.

Lorino (1998) describes this vision as a "dictatorship of the shareholder". Indeed, the creation of value is not only the result of the contribution of capital, but the combination of the efforts of all stakeholders of the company.

Charreaux and Desbrières (1997: 5-6) present the following arguments that justify the transition to a pluralistic view of the firm:

1. The analysis of the process of value creation, through the decisions of the leaders, shows that it is not only constrained by the shareholders and the financial markets. Aoki (1994) argues that the Japanese system represents a set of complementary mechanisms and the functioning of the different markets are linked, namely the financial market, the labor market and the goods and services market.
2. By referring to the theory of property rights, the authors assert that there are several societal configurations, and the definition of property as an exercise of the right of control and the appropriation of gains leads to include a larger number stakeholders.

3. The creation of value cannot be reduced to the only enrichment of the shareholders, because it leads to ignore, as emphasize the two authors, the other forms of creation of value as the wellbeing, the satisfaction and the sharing of the power.

This restrictive and purely financial view of value is supported by the preponderance of financial performance indicators.

According to Ben Larbi and Lacroux (2011), the measurement indicators of shareholder value present three sets of criticisms.

The first is related to the manipulability of accounting information. The second criticism refers to the short-term horizon of EVA and its "abusive" use as an indicator of performance. The third critique focuses on the "reductive" and "quantitative" nature of shareholder value.

In this respect, Charreaux (1997) emphasizes the importance of taking all stakeholders into account in the assessment of performance by establishing "new performance indicators", according to him by the association of all stakeholders in the activities of creation and distribution of rents.

The partnership value then passes through the recognition of the contribution of all stakeholders to the process of value creation. Indeed, the integration of the concept of partnership value is a continuation of the positive theory of the agency, by broadening the traditional agency relationship between managers and capital contributors to all contractual relationships. within the company.

According to Chatelin and Trebucq (2003: 12), the enterprise is seen as a set of contracts, and governance mechanisms that safeguard the interests of each stakeholder, align them and mitigate their loss, respective utility.

The consideration of all stakeholders in the process of creation and distribution of value presents, according to Charreaux and Desbrières (1998: 84) a theoretical interest, for two main reasons. The first is justified by its foundation on the analysis of the rent created. The second reason is linked to the pluralistic and enriched vision of value creation that goes beyond the monistic and restrictive view of shareholder value.

Charreaux and Desbrières add that the partnership value offers a modification of traditional reading grids. This new vision would make it possible to resituate the shareholders' power because the reinforcement of the latter, to the detriment of other stakeholders, goes against the Similarly.

Bughin's (2004) study finds a positive relationship between the level of stakeholder satisfaction and the profitability indicators used.

Similarly, the survey conducted by Tiras, Ruf and Brown (1998), reveals that companies that enjoy good relations with stakeholders are those who perform better stock market performance.

Ben Larbi and Lacroux (2011) explain that both shareholder and partnership approaches are not antagonistic, they complement each other to the extent that maximization of the value of shareholders passes by the satisfaction of other stakeholders. The authors state that this is a relationship of "cause to cyclical effect ".

STAKEHOLDER THEORY, HYBRIDITY, AND PARTNERSHIP GOVERNANCE

Berle and Means (1932) are the first to explore the concept of stakeholders, without explicitly using the term stakeholder .Indeed, the two authors note, in their work, the social pressure exerted on the leaders to recognize their responsibilities to the different groups, affected by the decisions of the firm. This is accompanied by a questioning of the supremacy of the shareholders and the property they represent (Mercier 2006, 11).

The term stakeholder was then generalized by the literature on strategic management by Freeman (1984). He provides the most widely used definition in the literature, according to him, the stakeholders represent "any group or individual who can affect or who can be affected by the achievement of the objectives of the company. Freeman (1984: 46).

There were later different meanings of the stakeholder concept, reflecting the lack of consensus on the rights attributed to them (Phillips et al., 2003).

For Mitroff (1983, p.4), stakeholders are any group or actor that influences decisions and is equally affected by those decisions. As such, Caroll (1989) highlights the classic distinction between primary and secondary stakeholders:

The "primary" stakeholders concern the actors, in direct and contractually determined relation with the company, still qualified as "contractual" stakeholders. The "secondary" stakeholders are the actors around the company, who are affected by the actions of the company, without being bound by contractual links. We then speak of "diffuse" links.

Clarkson (1995) develops a new definition that includes the impact of risk. According to him, the stakeholders are the parties who incur a risk in relation to the products of the company's activities, due to the incompleteness of the contracts, which confronts the stakeholders with the possibility of the expropriation of their rents.

Mitchell, Agle and Wood (1997) provide the following typology for ranking stakeholders: dormant (1), discretionary (2), latent (3), dominant (4), dangerous (5), dependent (6) stakeholders and "definitive" stakeholders (7). They retain the following relevance criteria: power, legitimacy and urgency.

For their part, Charreaux and Desbrières (1998: 58) define stakeholders as agents whose utility is affected by the decisions of the firm.

Kochan and Rubinstein (2000: 373) provide a new definition, which focuses on the value of resources contributed by stakeholders and their contribution to performance. A broader definition has been proposed by Post, Preston and Sachs (2002, p.8) which include in their meaning the contribution to value creation and the risk incurred.

Governance most often refers to a plural definition of the exercise of power, based on greater openness of the decision-making process, its decentralization, the simultaneous presence of several statutes of stakeholders.

Also, stakeholder theory recognizes the permeability between different groups of stakeholders and asserts the existence of a plurality of identities and statuses within the same groups. As such, Martinet (1984) discerns the internal stakeholders of external stakeholders while recognizing the existence of a third category called "ubiquitous" stakeholders to describe parties with plural status.

Similarly, Gibson (2000) evokes the possibility for the same stakeholder to belong to several groups. Also, Cazal (2011) specifies that the boundaries between the different groups are now highly porous and these groups are partially superimposable or even substitutable.

The enterprise must be considered as a collective dynamic, that is to say an action that an isolated individual can not carry out by the exercise of his own abilities whatever his hierarchical level. The achievement of the company's objectives must therefore involve the mobilization of several stakeholders. This pluralistic governance improves the decision-making process and enriches the development of the company by a cognitive flow generated by the wealth of statutes and the multiplicity of stakeholders.

According to Bréchet and al (2015), This new qualification of the firm induces a different conception of the governance of the company. The cognitive stream, stricto sensu, of governance abandons the question of appropriability, to place at the center of its concerns the link between the system of governance and the creation or preservation of a competitive advantage based on knowledge. The governance system is no longer a disciplinary matrix but a cognitive matrix simultaneously enabling and binding

This new qualification of the firm induces a different conception of the governance of the company. The cognitive stream, stricto sensu, of governance abandons the question of appropriability, to place at the center of its concerns the link between the system of governance and the creation or preservation of a competitive advantage based on knowledge. The governance system is no longer a disciplinary matrix but a cognitive matrix simultaneously enabling and binding

THE INCREASE OF PARTNERSHIP VALUE THROUGH OWNERSHIP

Our research proposes an enriched analysis of the creation of value to integrate all stakeholders. For this purpose, we suggest two practices that can counterbalance the power of shareholders by allowing other stakeholders the exercise of power. We are interested in employee shareholding and customer shareholding, the property allows to grant customers and employees the superior status of the shareholder in order to enjoy a higher power likely to limit the attempts of managerial entrenchment and shareholders supremacy.

The partnership value is multidimensional and offers a plural vision from to firm. This new measure is based on the approach of the chain sectoral value of Porter (1986), which allows a better representation of the actors in the creation of value (Charreaux 2006).

These two authors introduce the two concepts of "willingness to pay" and "opportunity costs" and place their reflection within the framework of the theory of cooperative games. The firm then buys resources such as raw materials, labor and capital and transform into products and services. The created value is equal to the difference between the willingness to pay and the opportunity cost.

This created value represents the organizational rent generated by the firm with the help of its various partners. Charreaux and Desbrières call this global organizational rent "partnership value", as opposed to the rent that belongs to the shareholders alone and constitutes the shareholder value (Charreaux 2006).

Charreaux and Desbrières (1998) propose to extend the measure of partnership value by including other contributors resources, like the employees, managers and shareholders.

The value created is then calculated by the difference between the sales evaluated at the willingness to pay and the sum of the opportunity costs for the different providers of resources (Figure 1).

Charreaux and Desbrières (1998: 62) propose expanding the partnership value measure by including other resource providers such as employees, managers and shareholders. The value created is then calculated by the difference between the sales evaluated at the willingness to pay and the sum of the opportunity costs for the different contributors of resources.

According to the partnership value creation scheme, the increase in value can be obtained by acting either on the opportunity prices, the willingness to pay or simultaneously on the two dimensions of this construct.

By focusing on the process of creating value, we decided to restrict our scope of analysis to consumer shareholders and employee shareholders.

Figure 1.

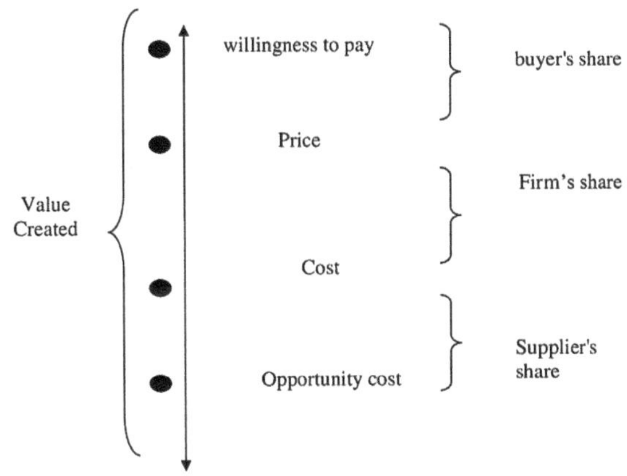

Determining the opportunity costs of employee shareholders and consumer shareholders is not easy in practice. In theory, this cost can be perceived as the cost of renouncing an employee shareholder to bring both his work (as an employee) and his financial and cognitive resources (as a shareholder). And for the consumer customer is the cost of renouncing the products of the competition as well as the financial risk related to the investment of its capital.

Measuring the partnership value has a definite theoretical interest, for two main reasons, the first is justified by its foundation on the analysis of the rent created. The second reason is related to the pluralistic and enriched vision value creation that goes beyond the monistic view of shareholder value.

We present below the analysis of the promotion of partnership value through employee share ownership and customer shareholding.

How to Increase Value Creation Through Employee Ownership ?

The majority of studies that favor the virtues of employee share ownership are based on its behavioral effects and attitudinal and neglect the question of the creation of partnership value. To our knowledge, very few studies have invested the relation between employee ownership and the concept of partnership value, we cite the works of Poulain-Rehm (2006), Garfatta (2010) and Elouadi (2014).

In order to determine the role of employee shareholding in the partnership value, Poulain-Rehm (2006) used two methods, first and traditionally, a value indicator added, more precisely the author used the stock market value relative added in 2001. The second method adopted is based on the calculation of sharing added value.

The author justifies the imperfection of his measures which do not use the costs and opportunity prices by the major difficulty that poses the operationalization of the measure of partnership value.

Following a similar path, Garfatta (2010) retains the added value in the accounting sense of the term as a measure of the partnership value. The author justifies his choice by the difficulty of the operationalization of partnership value. He defines then, two indicators of partnership value: “value added” and “the share of added value allocated to employees “.

The study by Garfatta (2010) proves that Shareholder value creation is positive for low levels of employee share ownership, however, when staff hold more than 3% of the voting rights, the value creation becomes negative.

The author explains his results by the existence of an incentive effect and alignment of interests for low levels of employee share ownership, and he adds that the negative performance is the consequence of the instrumentalisation of employee share ownership by the managerial entrenchment purposes.

Elouadi’s thesis (2014) and according to the scheme of the creation of partnership value, shows that the increase in the value partnership can be obtained, acting either on the opportunity costs, either on the willingness to pay or simultaneously on the two dimensions of this construct.

The author has analyzed the effects of employee share ownership on the opportunity costs of resource providers. The aim is to study the influence of financial participation on the willingnes to pay of employee shareholders and lenders of funds, in order to appreciate the overall effect induced on the creation of value.

The author has used organizational trust as a proxy for reducing opportunity costs in order to circumvent the obstacles related to the operationalization of the terms of the partnership value. The results of the study carried out in the context of SBF 250 index companies prove that shareholding influences positively the trust of employee shareholders and lenders of funds which has a positive impact on the creation of partnership value.

According to Elouadi (2014), it is, also, possible to envisage an effect on the willingness to pay for customers by granting employees more than their opportunity costs (considering dividends and shares as an additional remuneration, employees demonstrate greater commitment, creativity and productivity and thus contribute to improving competitiveness of the company. This will result in increased dependence of customers on the company’s products which will increase the partnership value by increasing the willingness to pay of customers.

How to Increase Value Creation Through Customer Shareholding?

Customer shareholding is a device that allows the customer to integrate the capital in order to take advantage of the synergies associated with this grouping. The customer has a hybrid status, he is both a customer and a shareholder of the same company.

This status has many similarities with the cooperative model, indeed, the two statutes are characterized by the consumption of products and services of companies in which the two actors hold shares of capital. In addition, this superior ownership status provides benefits such as access to information, political participation and the collection of interest and dividends. In addition, both profiles benefit from privileged treatment by receiving commercial benefits and discounted services.

On the other hand, we believe that the main difference between customer shareholding and the membership lies in the asymmetry of status. In fact, the member is first and foremost a client who has made the choice of the condominium. On the other hand, the relationship of the customer shareholding is reached according to two different configurations. The first model is that of the loyal customer who has chosen to cross the cape of the property to become a customer shareholder. The second configuration is that of the individual shareholder who chose to consume the products of the same company (Figure 2).

According to the proponents of the customer shareholding approach, it is assumed that the customer shareholder has a long-term commitment, consumes more, has less tendency to choose competitors - even when their products are more competitive - and unveils to be a true ambassador for the company, both in equity investment and in consumer spending(Duran 2012).

The customer, acquiring the status of individual shareholder strengthens his sense of belonging to the company; this leads to more loyalty, thus generating more volume and margin for the company.

As for the individual shareholder, by becoming a current customer, he intensifies his relationship with the company and develops his loyalty on two levels, as a provider of funds and as a consumer; thus generating better performance for the company.

The study conducted by Duran (2012) confirms the presence of the customer shareholding in France and shows its positive impact on loyalty and the involvement of the consumer shareholder. The study also states that customer share ownership is formed from an individual shareholder, initiated in the financial markets.

In France, apart from cooperative banks, there are several cases of fundraising with clients. We cite the case of Carrefour which encourages its customers to buy shares by using a speech that highlights the values of solidarity and the creation of partnership value.

Figure 2.

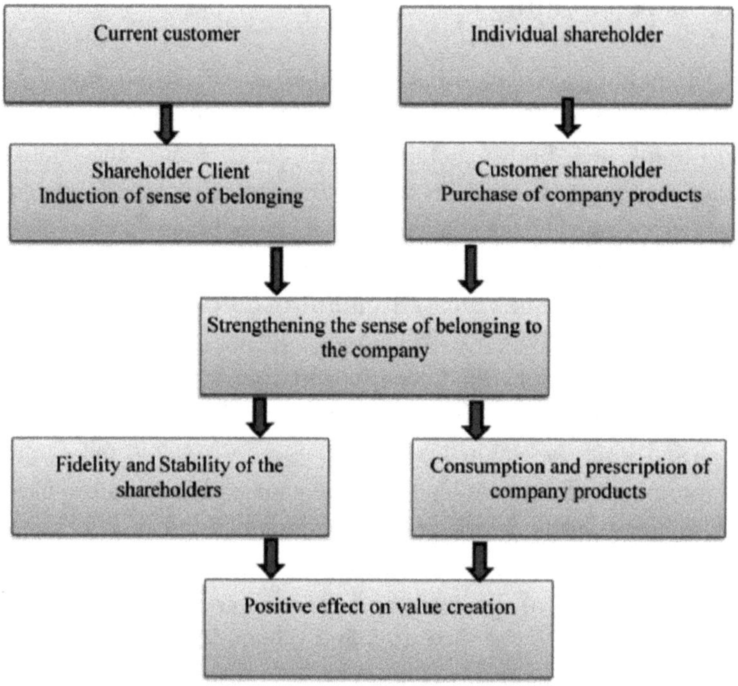

Similarly, special attention is reserved for shareholders who are clients of certain French companies. In this respect, we mention LVMH, which offers exclusive design and home delivery of high-end products to shareholders. As such, the company Total, double the loyalty points of the customer shareholders following each fuel consumption and offers, in addition, significant discounts on several hotels, travel sites and car rental sites.

And during the last communication of November 2, 2017, sent by the company Seb to its shareholders, an explicit presentation of Seb products is offered at preferential prices. This shows the awareness of the effect on the value of converting shareholders into loyal consumers.

The integration of the customer shareholder into the process of value creation begins with the recognition of its existence and, secondly, the adoption of a targeted financial communication. These efforts can be realized through interactions with investors through the creation of communication support including websites (Elouadi & Elotmani 2018).

CONCLUSION

In this work, we attempt to make an operationalization to the abstract concept of partnership governance by proposing two managerial practices that could increase the value of the company.

Indeed, property is the keystone of our research, the ownership of shares by employees and customers, who are the most influential stakeholders

for the survival of the company, is likely to increase their commitment and their implication and thus induce a strong creation of value.

Our research is clearly inspired by the current of cognitive governance which emphasizes the role of plurality, learning and mutual enrichment in value creation by using the argument of facilitation of coordination and the capacity of stakeholders to propose new and more creative managerial solutions Charreaux (2011).

The financial participation of employees and customers induces attachment and loyalty to the company, which allows for better value creation. For this purpose, the empirical studies carried out, in particular, concerning the employee shareholding confirm the positive link between ownership and value creation.

With regard to customer share ownership, and despite the scarcity of empirical work, the studies consulted highlight the positive impact of customer share ownership on the value of the company.

REFERENCES

Aoki, M. (1984). *The cooperative game theory of the firm*. Oxford, UK: Oxford University press.

Ben Larbi, S., & Lacroux, A. (2011). RSE et performance sociétale des entreprises: vers un renouvellement du paradigme de la valeur. In l'Alter Management. Paris: Hermès.

Brandenburger, A. M., & Stuart, H. W. Jr. (1996). Value based business strategy. *Journal of Economics & Management Strategy*, *5*(1), 5–24. doi:10.1111/j.1430-9134.1996.00005.x

Bréchet, J. P., Charreaux, G., Desreumaux, A., & de Montmorillon, B. (2015). L'entreprise, son projet, sa gouvernance: Éléments d'une vision partenariale. *Économies et sociétés*, (23): 33–65.

Bughin, C. (2004). La gouvernance par la valeur partenariale est-elle performante? *La Revue des Sciences de Gestion: Direction et Gestion*, *39*(210), 89–104. doi:10.1051/larsg:2004041

Charreaux, G. (1997). *Le gouvernement des entreprises – Corporate Governance –Théories et Faits*. Paris: Economica.

Charreaux, G. (2006). Théorie financière et stratégie financière. *Revue française de gestion*, (1), 109-137.

Charreaux, G. (2011). *Quelle théorie pour la gouvernance? De la gouvernance actionnariale à la gouvernance cognitive et comportementale.* Université de Bourgogne-CREGO EA7317 Centre de recherches en gestion des organisations.

Charreaux, G., & Desbrières, P. (1998). Gouvernance des entreprises: Valeur partenariale contre valeur actionnariale. *Finance Contrôle Stratégie*, *1*(2), 57–88.

Chatelin, C., & Trébucq, S. (2003). *Stabilité et évolution du cadre conceptuel en gouvernance d'entreprise: un essai de synthèse*. Communication pour les neuvièmes journées d'histoire de la comptabilité et du management, Jeudi, 20.

Duran, N. (2012). *L'actionnaire individuel client: étude du cas français*. Toulon: Université de Toulon.

Elouadi, S. (2014). *Analyse des effets induits par l'actionnariat salarié sur la création de valeur partenariale des entreprises du SBF 250*. Thèse de doctorat. IAE de Toulon, Université du Sud.

Elouadi, S., & Elotmani, R. (2018). Customer Shareholding as a Radical Approach to a Sustainable and Profitable Relationship. In *Marketing Techniques for Financial Inclusion and Development* (pp. 35–47). IGI Global. doi:10.4018/978-1-5225-4035-9.ch003

Garfatta, R. (2010). *Actionnariat salarié et création de valeur dans le cadre d'une gouvernance actionnariale et partenariale: application au contexte français*. Doctorat en sciences de gestion, Bourgogne: Université de Bourgogne.

Lorino, P. (1998). Valeur pour l'actionnaire: Une mode à risques. *Alternatives Economiques*, *162*, 55.

Poulain-Rehm, T. (2006). *L'actionnariat salarié en France, un facteur de création de valeur? Woking paper*. Université Montesquieu-Bordeaux IV.

Tiras, S., Ruf, B., & Brown, R. (1998). The Relation Between Stakeholders. *Implicit Claims and Firm Value', National American Accounting Association Meeting*.

Chapter 11
Ethics and CSR Practices for Enduring Corporate Governance Culture

Olusegun Vincent
School of Management Sciences, Pan-Atlantic University, Lagos, Nigeria

Fredrick Ikpesu
Pan-Atlantic University, Lagos, Nigeria

Olamitunji Dakare
School of Management Sciences, Pan-Atlantic University, Lagos, Nigeria

ABSTRACT

The studies in corporate governance have explained different motives responsible for adoption of corporate governance. This chapter provides answers to why business should be morally responsible and practice CSR. The authors shed light on crucial areas of corporate responsibilities of business and various theoretical justification advanced in previous studies in CSR. They look at the relationship between CSR and corporate governance – their crucial points of divergence and convergence. They also look at ethics and responsibilities for unethical behaviours and ethical theories with their limitations. Finally, they evaluate CSR and ethics from African perspective – how CSR in Africa is framed from by sociocultural influences, like communalism, ethnic-religious beliefs, and charitable tradition (ubuntu philosophy).

DOI: 10.4018/978-1-5225-9607-3.ch011

INTRODUCTION

CSR is an issue that has captured the attention of national and international, political and business leaders across the globe and the developed world. The creation of wealth has led to various social and environmental impacts such as depletion of non-renewable resources, global warming, diminution of land resources, acidification, reduction of water resources and potential threats to health and safety of employees (Singh et al., 2007). The issue of board room failures, insider abuses, moral hazard and environmental abuses and degradation has led various sectors, governments and NGOs to engage with corporate governance and CSR debates and initiate strategies for responding to the challenges of sustainable development.

A broad range of corporate stakeholders have regarded CSR and corporate governance as important, these include consumers, shareholders, potential investors, creditors, regulators, employees and the general public (Duckitt et al., 2010; Marshall et al., 2009; Lopez et al., 2007; Cottrell, 2003; Bringer & Benforado, 1994; Makower, 1993). From an investment standpoint, shareholder value suffers when companies pay millions of dollars in fines, cleanup fees, and court costs to keep corporate officers out of jail (Coleman, 2011; Minow & Deal, 1991). From a consumer perspective, growing numbers of customers are showing preference for greener companies and products. For example, approximately a third of all adults in the UK pay premium of 15-50% for organically-sourced foods (Oliff & Vandermerwe, 1990). From an employment perspective, it is becoming more difficult to attract top executives and other key employees to positions in industries without corporate governance framework (Clark, 1990). From the general public's standpoint, surveys conducted in the aftermath of the Exxon Valdez spill reported that approximately 60% of Americans named pollution as a very serious threat to their health and the environment, and approximately 75% believe that business should be responsible for the cleanup (Smith, 1990). The BP Plc (April 2010) deep water rig explosion in the Gulf of Mexico resulted in loss of employee lives and biodiversity (all living things) in the ocean, further, the collapse of goldmine fields in both Chile and Ecuador in August and October 2010 respectively led to the loss of employees and permanent impairment to the landscape, which have been greeted with public outcry and expressions of dismay.

Businesses for many decades have ignored the impact of their activities on the natural and social environment in which they operated, unless it had direct repercussions on the profit and loss account. Friedman (1970) famously supported this classical view of business objectives by stating that the sole reason for a firm's existence is to maximise the wealth of the shareholders, and that any act of philanthropy equates to stealing from the shareholders' wealth. Failure of a business to meet this fiduciary obligation was not only reprehensible but would result in sanctions such as a drop-in share price or an enforced change of management (Friedman, 1970).

However, the neglect by business of the negative externalities arising from the pursuit of economic objectives along with various environmental abuses by companies (e.g. Royal Dutch/Shell Brent Spar dumping and Ogoni crises in 1995 and BP's Gulf of Mexico rig explosion in 2010) have created less than positive attitudes amongst stakeholders towards business. Rodriguez and Cruz (2007) argued that customers are gradually altering their purchasing attitudes towards behaviours that are more sensitive to the natural and social environment. This then risks a tarnished image for those firms not taking CSR issues seriously. The politico-legal system has also undergone drastic transformation, directed at limiting the abuses caused by business activities.

This chapter x-ray both ethics and CSR and provide a good understanding of the subject along with the various theoretical justifications for practice of CSR. The ethical lenses used by individual agents (managers) are magnified for proper understanding of how individual's action or inaction could shape the company's fortune or misfortune. Also, various ethical theories underpinning agents' actions are also reviewed. The developing economies perspective of CSR is equally explained.

Ethics as Precursor for Corporate Governance

The numerous unethical behaviours in organisations can be attributed to individuals and not corporate entities (Barraquier, 2011). The corporate irresponsible behaviours may be traced to an organisation and the company may be fined for such, but the act was perpetrated by the managers responsible for the day-to-day affairs of the company. The endless business and environmental scandals such as those at AIG, WorldCom, Enron and BP have raised many concerns about the increasing level of unethical and irresponsible behaviours in organisations. The seemingly unending occurrence of the instances of irresponsible behaviours has activated the need to unpick and evaluate such actions from the view point of ethical theory.

The focus of this book (corporate governance) inevitably draws our attention to ethics as a key set of frameworks for sustainable governance structure. The need to make the right decisions at management level necessitates the espousal of ethical philosophy: does one see 'right' in terms of maximising outcomes, fundamental universal principle, notions of justice and fairness, or question over the action constitutive of a 'good' company? The literatures in ethics posited that business life is a fruitful source of ethical dilemmas because its fundamental purpose is that of material gain through the making of profit which requires a constant search for potential advantage over others and puts managers under pressure to do whatever yields such advantage. The outcome of such decisions may be perceived as ethical or unethical, depending on which ethical lens is used.

Contrary to the ideas of Friedman (1962), most people nowadays recognise that business organisations must participate in society in an ethically symbiotic way (Kaptein, 2003; Hooghiemstra and Van Manen, 2002; Joyner and Payne, 2002). Organisations trying to attain this goal have to assure that individual employees behave according to 'ethical' values and norms (Pater and Gils, 2003). The barrage of recent business scandals has made clear that employees sometimes tend to make unethical decisions. The ethical theories discussed in this chapter endeavour to explain the causes of this type of behaviour. Different strands of views hold on unethical behaviour: while some studies hold individual characteristics responsible for the unethical behaviour (e.g. Kohlberg, 1969; Trevino and Youngblood, 1990), others highlight the importance of organisational factors (e.g. Victor and Cullen, 1988; Schwartz, 2001). Ethical theory helps to unpick the components at work in such perspectives.

WHAT IS ETHICS?

Ethics is the study of values, rules, and justifications (Solomon and Greene, 1999). It is the study of what the appropriate actions are for an individual or a group in a moral dilemma. The ethical considerations can be right versus wrong action (i.e. means) (Kant, 1785), good versus bad results (i.e. ends) (d'Inverno, et al, 2004), virtuous versus vicious character (leading to right action or good results) (Paul, et al, 1901), fairness (Rawls, 1971) among many others. In practice, such perspectives are drawn on to develop a decision support system for ethical problem solving and guide the conducts of managers in sustaining the environment. These perspectives maybe further assembled according to normative, descriptive and contemporary theories of ethical behaviour. Cremer et al. (2011) argue that the standard approach to the study of ethics in business and management has been a normative or descriptive approach, which focuses on what managers, employees and people in general 'should' do to act as morally responsible actors. However, such approaches also integrate the everyday practical issues that may impact economic actors' abilities to reach an 'ethical' decision.

Normative Ethical Theories

There are four important categories of normative ethical problem-solving techniques: character-based, duties-based, utility-based, and consequences-based. While these theories are normative, their rationales for determining moral essence are often what are referred to when solving ethical problems. Normative theories strive at systematic, rational, and widely understandable arguments so that they can be adequately defended, justified, and explained to relevant stakeholders (Simon, 1991, Gert, 1988; Rawls, 1971).

Virtue (or Character-Based) Ethics

Virtues comprise a set of acquired traits of character that enable a person to lead a good life. Different types of virtues can be differentiated into intellectual virtues - 'wisdom' being the most prominent one, and moral virtues, which comprise a long list of possible characteristics such as honesty, courage, friendship, mercy, loyalty, modesty, patience, etc (Crane and Matten, 2010). These virtues are manifested in actions that are a habitual pattern of behaviour of the virtuous person rather than just one-off decisions. These traits are not ours by birth; we acquire them by learning the behaviour of virtuous individuals, and most notably, in business, by being in relationships with others in a community of practice (Maclntyre 1984).

Virtue ethics is an approach to ethics that emphasises the character of the moral agent, rather than rules or consequences, as the key element of ethical thinking (Rodger and Michael, 1997). This contrasts with consequentialism, which holds that the consequences of a particular act form the basis for any valid moral judgment about that action, and deontology, which derives rightness or wrongness from the character of the act itself rather than the outcomes. Faunce and Jeffery (2007) are of the view that the difference between these three approaches to morality tends to lie more in the way moral dilemmas are approached than in the moral conclusions reached. For instance, a consequentialist may argue that lying is wrong because of the negative consequences produced by lying - though a consequentialist may allow that certain foreseeable consequences might make lying acceptable. A deontologist might argue that lying is always wrong, regardless of any potential "good" that might come from lying. A virtue ethicist, however, would focus less on lying in any particular instance and instead consider what a decision to tell a lie or not tell a lie said about one's character and moral behaviour (Faunce and Jeffery, 2007)

Crane and Matten (2004) argue that what is central to an ethics of virtue is the notion of a 'good life'. For Aristotle, one of the original proponents of virtue ethics, this consists of happiness, not in a limited hedonistic, pleasure-oriented sense, but in a broader sense. This most notably includes virtuous behaviour as an integral part of the good life: a happy business person would not only be one who finally makes the most money, but one who does so by at the same time savouring the pleasures of a virtuous manner of achieving their success. In a business context, the 'good life' means far more than being a profitable company. Virtue ethics takes a much more holistic view by also looking at the way this profit is achieved, and, most notably, by claiming that economic success is just one part of the good business life-with satisfaction of employees, good relations among all members of the company, and harmonious relations with all stakeholders being equally important (Collier, 1995).

The notable flaw of virtue ethics is its conflict with company law. Globally, the position of laws regulating companies is that a company is a separate legal entity with its own separate legal duties and rights separated from the principals (i.e. shareholders) and the agents (i.e. the management). In law, corporate abuses are blamed on the companies involved and not the managers. A corporation involved in environmental pollution pays huge fines and incur clean-up cost with no financial strain on the managers responsible for day-to-day management of the company. For example, Tony Hayward, the BP former CEO was given a soft landing by posting him as a non-executive director to another BP subsidiary after the monumental April 2010 Gulf of Mexico oil spill, that occasioned payment of billions of dollars as compensation and clean-up fees. Another flaw of virtue ethics is that virtuous traits are acquired by learning the behaviour of a virtuous individual; suggesting the need for a role model. In cases where there is no role model, learning the virtuous ethical characteristics becomes difficult. Equally, where the role model has changed from a virtuous to a bad person, the probability of a moral agent learning a bad life style is high.

It may be clever to say a company is an artificial being but human beings represent the 'hands' and 'limbs' needed to function. The ethical conduct of a company may not go beyond the character, moral and ethical standard of the managers responsible for the direction of the company.

Deontological (or Duty-Based) Ethics

Deontological ethics (Crisp, 1995) prescribes the ethical solution to be the one that contains acts that have intrinsic moral worth, and does not contain acts with no intrinsic moral worth. Certain acts are, at their very core, right or wrong. The deontological view is that society is best served by everyone following certain rules, and obeying them no matter what the results are; what can and cannot be done exists as rules.

The rules essentially define duties one person has to another, often to protect each person's inherent rights. The popular theorist in this school of thought is Immanuel Kant (Kant, 1785), who suggested that all of deontological ethics can be condensed to one rule, the *categorical imperative.*

Teleological or Consequentialist Ethics

Teleological or Consequentialist Ethics, a third type of normative theories, do not focus on the character of the problem solver, nor the moral worth or universality of acts within the ethical problem, but instead focus on the potential positive or negative consequences that may happen under alternative scenarios (Griffin, 1995). Acts are judged to be right or wrong based on their possible consequences. Consequentialist methods are based on estimating what the likely outcomes of a given course of action will be, and then choosing the method that has the most positive consequences and the fewest negative consequences. According to consequentialist approaches, those actions to be chosen are those that lead to more positive and fewer negative outcomes, and those actions should be rejected which lead to more negative and fewer positive ends (Kerns, 2011).

Utilitarianism Theory

This theory suggests that the ethical solution to be the solution that provides the most good for the most number of people (Bentham in Harrison, 1945). This approach can be summed up in the "greatest good" principle – "greatest happiness" of the "greatest number". This means that when deciding on a course of action we should choose the one that is likely to result in the greatest good for the greatest number of people. Utilitarian ethical theory is founded on the ability to predict the consequences of an action. To a utilitarian, the choice that yields the greatest benefit to the most people is the choice that is ethically correct. One benefit of this ethical theory is that the utilitarian can compare similar predicted solutions and use a point system to determine which choice is more beneficial for more people. This point system provides a logical and rationale argument for each decision and allows a person to use it on a case-by-case context (Ridley, 1988).

Descriptive Ethical Theories

Descriptive ethics is the study of people's beliefs about morality. It contrasts with prescriptive or normative ethics, which is the study of ethical theories that prescribe how people ought to act. Descriptive ethics aim to uncover people's beliefs about such things as values, which actions are right and wrong, and which characteristics of moral agents are virtuous. Research into descriptive ethics may also investigate people's ethical ideals or what actions societies condemn or punish in law or politics. Two descriptive theories that are important to include in any integrative model of ethical problem solving are the Theory of Moral Development (Kohlberg, 1969) and taxonomy of ethical ideologies (Forsyth, 1980). Theories of personal values are also important and are also discussed.

The Theory of Moral Development (Kohlberg, 1969) postulates that individuals can move sequentially through six stages of development stage that is classified into three levels, thus, pre-conventional, conventional and post-conventional.

Pre-conventional level, the decision individuals make on ethical matters will have nothing to do with the ethical issues involved, but instead will depend on the personal advantage or disadvantage to the individual. In stage one: the individual will see ethical decisions in terms of the reward and punishment that will result from the decisions. While in stage two, individuals will see ethical decisions in the more complex terms of acting in their own best interests. They will see the decisions in terms of the deals they can make and whether these deals are fair for them. For example, a manager might view CSR and environmental compliance from instrumental economic motive for winning more customers and enhancing corporate profitability. Without the promises of increased profitability, he/she might not voluntarily be socially or environmentally responsible.

Conventional level, this comprises stages three and four. Stage three can be defined as individuals learning to live up to what is expected of them by their immediate circle (stakeholders) and accepting the value of compliance. This can work both ways in a business context; an individual manager might feel pressured into complying with the code of corporate governance or ISO 14001 (Environmental Management Systems) because every other company complies. In stage four, individuals are seen as operating on a higher stage within the conventional level, if they operate in line with social or cultural accord rather than just the opinion of those around them. This certainly means complying with the law as it codifies social accord. For instance, an accountant may be operating at this level, he/she genuinely comply with financial reporting and corporate governance requirements.

Post conventional, this is the most advanced level which relates to individual development towards making their own ethical decisions in terms of what they themselves believe to be right, not just acquiescing. Stage five, which is the lower stage at this level is of the view that what individuals believe to be right is in terms of the basic values of their society, including ideas of mutual self-interest and the welfare of others. On the higher stage (stage six), individuals base their decisions on wider universal ethical principle such as justice, equity, rights, or Kant's framework. It also means respecting the demands of individuals' consciences. Business decisions made on these grounds could be disclosure on grounds of right-to-know that is not compelled by law, or stopping purchasing from suppliers who test products on animals, on the grounds that animal rights to be free from suffering should be respected. It must be stressed, however, that using stage six reasoning may involve personal cost, since it may mean failing to comply with existing social norms and regulations as they are seen as unethical.

Most adults stop at about stage 5, where individuals act so as to fulfil duties and obligations to which they have agreed. "These individuals aim to uphold laws except in extreme cases where they conflict with fixed social duties..." (Kohlberg, p. 67). The Theory of Moral Development does have critics. For example, Gilligan indicates that a bias exists (especially at the highest stages) within the Theory of Moral Development (because of its justice orientation) in favour of individuals that often hold a justice-oriented view, typically men (Gilligan, 1977).

Other Contemporary Ethical Theories

In recent times, some contemporary ethical perspectives have been developed. We have explained three major contemporary ethical theories, which include feminist ethics, discourse ethics and environmental ethics.

Feminist Ethics

Crane and Matten, (2004) defined feminist ethics as an approach that prioritises empathy, harmonious and healthy social relationships, care for one another, and avoidance of harm above abstract principles. Care-focused feminism is a branch of feminist thought, informed primarily by ethic of care as developed by Gilligan (1982). The care-focused feminists regard women's capacity for care as a human strength which can and should be taught to and expected of men as well as women.

Noddings (2005) proposes that ethical caring has the potential to be a more concrete evaluative model of moral dilemmas, than an ethic of justice. The feminist approach to business ethics starts from the assumption that men and women have fairly different attitudes towards organising social life, with a significant impact on the way ethical conflicts are handled (Gilligan 1982). In addressing ethical problems, traditional ethical theory has looked for rules and principles to be applied in a fair, objective, and consistent way (Gilligan, 1982; Kohlberg, 1969)

According to Maier (1997) feminist ethics has a different approach that sees the individual deeply embedded in a network of interpersonal relations. Consequently, responsibility for the members of this network and maintenance of connectedness, rather than allegiance to abstract moral principles is the predominant concern of feminist ethics. This approach, often therefore called an 'ethic of care', consequently results in significant differences in the view of ethical issues (Maier 1997; Rabouin 1997). Moral problems are conflicts of responsibilities in relationships rather than conflicts of rights between individuals. They therefore can only be solved by personal, subjective reasoning which particularly stresses the importance of intuition and feeling.

Discourse Ethics

Discourse ethics refers to a process of un-coerced and undistorted communicative interaction between individuals in open discourse (Apel, 1973; Habermas, 1983; Wellmer, 1986). Discourse ethics aims to solve ethical conflicts by providing a process of norm generation through rational reflection on the real-life experience of all relevant participants (Crane and Matten, 2004). There are many examples of discursive processes suggestive of discourse ethics which include, conflict resolution, dispute mediation, and communicative settlements of various kinds. Many have been successful at generating consensus among participants at least on part of their agenda. Discourse ethics presupposes no norms other than the acceptance of a reasoned, reflective, and practical potential for discourse: that is, the mutual recognition and acceptance of others as responsible subjects (Habermas, 1983). This mutual recognition and acceptance constitute ethical quality.

The philosophical underpinning of this theoretical approach is the argument that norms ultimately cannot be justified by rational arguments, but that they have to be generated and applied to solve ethical conflicts on a day-to-day basis (Preuss 1999). Steinmann and Lohr (1994), as the main proponents of a discourse approach to business ethics, argue that ethical reflection has to start from real-life experiences (rather than belief systems, which could be too diverse). They contend that the ultimate goal of ethical issues in business should be the peaceful settlement of conflicts. With this goal in mind, different parties in a conflict should sit together and engage in a discourse about the settlement of the conflict, and ultimately provide a solution that is acceptable to all. This 'ideal discourse', as it is usually called, is more than an occasional chat or business meeting; it has to answer certain philosophical criteria such as impartiality, non-persuasiveness, non-coercion, and expertise of the participants (Habermas 1983). The approach to ethics is based on rationality and requires a dialogue in which people are able and willing to exchange arguments and follow the 'non-coercive coercion of the best argumentation' (Habermas, 1983). Equally there are certain practical limits to this approach, especially the considerable amount of time it involves, and the fairly optimistic assumptions about rational human behaviour in discourses. Nevertheless, discourse ethics has been the underlying concept for the settlement of numerous disputes about environmental impacts of corporate decisions, in which various stakeholders with completely divergent value systems had to come to a common decision on certain controversial projects (Renn et al. 1995). Discourse ethics has gained much wider application to stakeholder management in extractive sector projects, even, to the extent of requests for stakeholder understanding and terms of engagement by project financiers as one of the prerequisites for project financing. For example, it is an out of court plea bargain strategy in conflicts between host communities, oil companies and government. Shell Petroleum used discourse ethics approach to pacify Ogoni Community in Nigeria's Niger Delta in 2009 by an out- of- court settlement of $15.5Million to resolve the alleged involvement of the company in the execution of the Ogoni nine environmental activists, among them Ken Saro-Wiwa, playwright and environmental rights activist (Pilkington, 2009).

Environmental Ethics

Environmental ethics is a systematic and comprehensive account of the moral relationships between human beings and their natural environment (Des Jardins, 2001). It is the discipline that studies the moral relationship between human beings and nature, and also the value and moral status of the environment.

The notion of value is important in understanding the application of environmental ethics in for-profit contexts. Value theory as applied to environmental ethics distinguishes between instrumental and intrinsic values for individual organisms and populations, species, biomes, ecosystems, and even cataleptic landscapes. Instrumental means useful for humans to obtain something of value. In environmental terms, clean water is valued because of the benefits it brings to human safety and health. The environment has intrinsic value when it is valued for itself and not for what benefit it brings to people. For example, the bald eagle has symbolic value for Americans well beyond its instrumental value as a bird of prey (Des Jardins, 2001). Callicot (1984) stated that all values are human-created (anthropogenic), but need not be human centered (anthropocentric). Rolston (2003) argued that environmental values are objective; pre-existing humans, continuing in all species and ecosystems, and would continue without man.

A commitment to environmental ethics requires a belief that non-human beings and natural states (biodiversity) have intrinsic value. Rolston (cited in Light and Rolston, 2003) makes the point and counterpoint that valuing always occurs from the viewpoint of the value. That, "viewing constitutes an object's value, which is not present independent of human valuing. Value thus requires subjectivity to coagulate it in the world" (p. 143). Value does exist without a valuer. "Perhaps there can be no science without a scientist, no religion without a believer. But there can be law without a law giver, history without a historian; there is biology without biologists, physics without physicists…and value without valuers" (p. 152). As humans, we discover value in nature, we do not create it.

The second important characteristic of environmental ethics is the moral status of nature. The primary concern of environmental ethics is how we understand the value of nature and how we organise human endeavours, including business and evaluation accordingly. The question is whether nature is directly morally considerable, "rather than morally considerable because it is appreciated or needed by humans" (Light and Rolston, 2003, p. 2). If it is a resource for human use, nature, including animals, plants, ecosystems and biotic communities has only instrumental value. This belief dictates how we treat the ecosystem and nature.

Conversely, if we appreciate nature for its intrinsic value, "the determinations have to be made regarding how these values are carried by natural things and how they are to be traded against other human values and the demands of industry and business for economic growth" (Buchholz, 1993, p. 63). Can moral extensionism include non-sentient landscape, or should we extend ethics to only living beings with 'interests', or cognitive equipment as some philosophers suggest? Rather than pose arguments on either side of this debate, it seems reasonable to suggest an alternative albeit anthropocentric ethic that poses the supposition that no human welfare, liberty, prosperity, or future exists apart from that ecological matrix in which life must exist (Nash, 1989).

This holistic environmental ethic denies that species are equal, and that humans are superior because we realize a greater range of values and are able to create ethical values systems that impart value on other life-forms (Rolston, 2003). The values differentiation offered by this ethic provides a foundation for value theory in evaluation by suggesting that human values can extend beyond the instrumental value of a social program or evaluation of a training program. This includes biotic communities and ecosystems as valuable "reference groups… and evaluators thinking of themselves as embedded within communities" (Mathison, 1999, p. 34). It offers a restrained approach to ethics that does not require evaluators to step outside an anthropocentric worldview or their role as protectors that attach values to non-human entities. It also supports the Guiding Principles for Evaluators (American Evaluation Association) statement concerning stakeholders: "…evaluators should consider important perspectives and interests of the full range of stakeholders", and the Joint Committee on Standards for Educational Evaluation (1994) standard that calls for identification of "people involved in or affected by the evaluation" (p. 25).

Ethical Behaviour Determinants

The foregoing theories are meant to shape moral agent's (i.e. manager) ethical behaviour, strengthen corporate governance and ethical decision making. The ethical behaviour determinants identified by Barraquier (2011) have their roots in ethical relativism and pragmatism. They are based on dynamic factors which include instrumental determinants, environmental determinants and experiental determinants.

Instrumental Determinants

Organisations use ethics to reach their economic objectives. Numerous studies have examined the firm's capacity to reduce social costs (Jones, T., 1995), the positive link between social-environmental responsibility and financial performance (Coleman, 2011; Marshall, et al., 2010; Rodrigue & Cruz, 2007), the positive effect of ethical behaviours on the firm's reputation (Fomrun et al., 2000; Fombrun &Shanley, 1990) and the firm's capability to attract and retain talent (Turban & Greening, 1996). Conversely unethical behaviours do not seem to pay (Baucus & Baucus, 1997; Rao, 1997).

Environmental Determinants

External pressures force the managers to adopt different ethical approaches. The model of stakeholder salience (Mitchell, Agle & Wood, 1997) examines managerial responses to stakeholder pressures. It concludes that managers respond to stakeholders only when they hold either power and legitimacy or power and urgent claims. Sethi and Sama (1998) argue that industry characteristics explain the propensity of firms to adopt an environmentally responsible attitude. In their model, socially responsive organisations' competitive environments and industry structures can be classified under four typologies: ethically hostile, high growth economic activity, regulated or highly stable and mature, and intensely competitive and entrepreneurial. In line with their results, other research work suggests that firms moving in industries with higher levels of competitive rivalry also respond better to stakeholders' expectations (Jones, M., 1999; Van de Ven & Jeurissen, 2005). The intensity level of competition determines the degree of firms' responsibility. Therefore, in a fierce competition context, legal compliance can be considered as extremely responsible behaviour.

Experiential Determinants

Experiential determinants refer to either shared (cultural) or personal experiences of individuals. Experiences lead to the formation of values, beliefs, norms, codes, standards, judgments, meanings, mental models, rituals or assumptions (Barraquier, 2011). The cultural, personal and organisational factors are experience gained from multiple sources (Hunt & Vitell, 2006). The ideology and philosophy, as well as all moral assumptions stemming from religious teachings and spiritual guidance, are spiritual experiences which play a role in shaping ethical behaviour (Barraquier, 2011). Schein (2004) argues that the accumulated shared learning of a group becomes its culture. In organisations, leaders are considered as powerful agents of organisational behaviour (Gini. 2005), because the role of leadership is to create and change cultures (Schein, 2004). Individuals are more likely to make ethical choices if the organisation has a value-based orientation and is committed to the reinforcement of ethics (Ramus & Oppegaard, 2006; Trevino et al, 1999). For instance, codes of ethics have been identified as positive determinants of ethics in organisations (O'Fallon & Butterfield, 2005).

CSR AND CORPORATE GOVERNANCE

Corporate Governance is ensuring that an organization is run in a responsible manner by ensuring accountability, transparency and compliance with due regard to its key stakeholders. It is the whole set of legal, cultural, and institutional arrangements that determine what publicly traded corporations can do, who controls them, how that control is exercised, and how the risks and returns from the activities they undertake are allocated (Margaret Blair, 1995)

Corporate Social Responsibility (CSR) is corporate form of self-regulation integrated into the business model to create a positive impact on the stakeholders and the environment. CSR is a concept whereby companies integrate social and environmental concerns in their business operations and in their interactions with their stakeholders on a voluntary basis (European Commission, 2001). Carroll and Buchholtz (2000) provided a detailed definition of CSR as encompasses the economic, legal, ethical and philanthropically expectations placed on organisations by the society at a given point in time.

In a contemporary view, CSR is one of the strategies deploy to achieve the CG objectives. Both CSR and CG deliberately move away from single constituency (shareholder view) of business to multiple business constituencies (stakeholder view). However, a traditional view suggested a contradiction between CSR and Corporate Governance. Corporate Governance was related to profit maximization and provided protection to shareholders who have provided capital to firm, while CSR apparently was against profit maximization because it suggested a set of actions beneficial for external stakeholders that may not be good for a shareholder. But not anymore. Corporate Governance is an umbrella term and CSR is gradually getting fused into the company's corporate governance practices. Their relationship can be interpreted by abandoning the standard view of the firm as a shareholder value maximizer and embracing the view of a firm as a stakeholder value maximizer. This convergence paves the way for Corporate Governance to be driven by ethical norms and the need for accountability, and it enables CSR to adapt prevailing business practices. Today both Corporate Governance and CSR focus on ethical practices in business and the responsiveness of an organization to its stakeholders and the environment in which it operates

Drivers of CSR

The studies on factors influencing CSR have considered a wide range of potential determinants including the following: (1) role of competitive dynamics (Hoffman, 2001), (2) organizational culture (Sharma, 2000), (3) history and capability (Hart, 1995), (4) perceptions of risk and organizational learning (Okereke & Kung, 2013), (5) leadership values (Egri & Herman, 2000), (6) regulation (Delmas & Toffel, 2004), and (7) pressure from non-governmental organizations (Aragón-Correa, 1998).

A popular and very useful framework for organising the drivers of CSR puts these factors into three main categories: economic, institutional and ethical motives (Carroll, 1971; 1991, 1999; Garriga & Mele, 2004; Wood, 1991; Jamali & Karam, 2016). This is based, on over four decades of work derived essentially from refining Friedman's (1970) original proposition that the primary motive of business was to make profits and enhance shareholders' wealth, and Carroll's (1979; 1991) critique of that work which proposed a four-part definition of CSR drivers that comprised economic, institutional, ethical and discretionary responsibilities (philanthropy).

Economic Drivers

Economic drivers comprise all incentives that are centrally concerned with profit making and increasing the market competitiveness of companies. Economic drivers are widely known as the most critical factors determining CSR of companies in developed countries (Vincent, 2012; Coleman, 2011). The primacy of economic factors is rooted in the theory of the firm (Friedman 1970; McWilliams & Siegel, 2001), and casts managers as *homo economicus,* which make decisions primarily by materialist-instrumental reasoning (Porter & Kramer, 2002). As Windsor (2001:226) puts it, 'a leitmotiv of wealth creation progressively dominates the managerial conception of responsibility'. Garriga & Mele (2004:54), affirms that profit maximisation is the 'supreme criterion to evaluate particular corporate social and environmental activity' in the West. The business case for responsibility is that firms *do well* (financially) by *doing good* (acting responsibly).

Institutional Pressure

Institutional drivers are incentives that stem from the broad socio-political context in which companies are embedded. Prominent among these are regulation, peer-pressure resulting from membership of industry associations, and wider public pressure mostly from civil society organisations (Dimaggio & Powell, 1983; 1991). Studies focused on developed countries suggest that state regulation, NGO activism, and pressures from customers are the three most important institutional factors driving CSER (Campbell, 2007; Hoffman, 2001). In contrast, CSER research on developing countries suggests that these factors exert little influence (Idemudia, 2011; Jamali & Mirshark, 2007; Darko-Mensah & Okereke, 2013). The main reasons cited are a lax regulatory environment, weak institutions, lack of environmental awareness by the public and a very low or near-absent number of so-called environmental consumers. The broad consensus is that institutional factors encouraging CSER in companies are much stronger in the West than in developing countries (Ozen & Kusku, 2009). More recent research suggests, however, a steadily growing institutional pressure on businesses operating in developing countries (Azmat & Ha, 2013; Jamali & Karam, 2016; Nwagbara, 2013; Nyuur et al., 2016).

Ethical Pressure

Ethical drivers significantly overlap with philanthropy (discretional activities) and cover all non-coercive and non-instrumental motives. In general, ethical approaches to business are united in the 'idea that business must contribute to a good society and in this respect do the right thing' (He & Chen, 2009:329). Here, CSR is largely based on the innate desire to do right. Note that this definition oversimplifies since ethics is a very loaded term. For example, there is such a notion of instrumental ethics where action is based not simply on what is deemed right but also what is beneficial to one in the long run. Here, we are using ethics as shorthand for virtue ethics where action is based not on consequences, or duty, but purely on moral virtue and the common good. The common good approach places emphasis on the personhood of business and corporations. A company is likened to a citizen and, 'as with any other group or individual in society, has to contribute to the common good because it is part of society' (Garriga & Mele, 2004:62). This approach bears very close resemblance to the *Ubuntu* philosophy, which according to some scholar represent the CSR driver in Africa.

It is important to stress that following seminal contributions from Wood (1991), many scholars (e.g. Jamali & Mirshak, 2007; Okpara & Wynn, 2012) have recognised that the CSR choices of firms are ultimately shaped by the intricate interactions between these three domains of responsibilities, and crucially by individual managers' perceptions, values, preferences and inclinations. A company is, after all, an artificial entity managed by moral agents who are responsible for its day-to-day operations (Hancock, 2005). Hence, the nature, influence and implications of firm-level forces are constantly mediated and filtered through managers' perceptions and their interpretation of organisational contexts (Sharma, 2000; Okereke & Kung, 2013). In the end, it is the perceptions, orientations and actions of these moral agents that determine the company's morals, values and ethical views (Barraquier, 2011).

THEORETICAL PERSPECTIVES IN CSR

Levitt (1958) could be credited with setting the agenda for the debate about the social responsibility of business in his *Harvard Business Review* article 'The Dangers of Social Responsibility', in which he cautions that 'government's job is not business, and business's job is not government' (1958, p. 47). Friedman (1970) expressed similar sentiment and added that the mere existence of CSR was a signal of an agency problem within the firm. An agency theory perspective implies that CSR is a misuse of corporate resources by business agents (i.e. appointed executive management); that would be better spent on valued-added internal projects or returned to shareholders. It also suggests that CSR is an executive perk, in the sense that managers use CSR to advance their careers or other personal agendas.

Freeman (1984), building on Chester Barnard's (1938) 'inducement-contribution' framework, presented a more positive view of managers' support of CSR. Freeman's stakeholder theory declares that managers must satisfy a variety of constituents (e.g. workers, customers, suppliers, local community organizations) who can influence firm results. According to this view, it is not sufficient for managers to focus exclusively on the needs of shareholders, or the owners of the corporation. Stakeholder theory implies that it can be beneficial for the firm to engage in certain CSR activities that non-financial stakeholders perceive to be important, because, absent this, these groups might withdraw their support for the firm. Stakeholder theory was expanded by Donaldson and Preston (1995) who stressed the moral and ethical dimensions of CSR, this however, might have contributed to the introduction of ethical theory in studies of social-environmental responsibility. It was later expanded (Donaldson and Davis, 1991) and based on the idea that there is a moral imperative for managers to 'do the right thing', without regard to how such decisions affect firm financial performance.

Institutional theory has also been applied to CSR in a paper by Jones (1995). The author concludes that companies involved in repeated transactions with stakeholders on the basis of trust and cooperation are motivated to be honest, trustworthy, and ethical because the returns to such behaviour are high. Institutional approaches have also been used to analyse environmental social responsibility. More specifically, Jennings and Zandbergen (1995) analyse the role of institutions in shaping the consensus within a firm regarding the establishment of an 'ecologically sustainable' organisation. Institutional theory emphasises the role of social and cultural pressures imposed on organisations that influence organisational practices and structure (Scott, 1992)

The first theoretical paper to apply the resource-based-view-of-the-firm (RBV) framework to corporate environmental responsibility was Hart (1995), who focused exclusively on environmental social responsibility. Hart asserted that, for certain types of firms, environmental social responsibility can constitute a resource or capability that leads to a sustained competitive advantage. Russo and Fouts (1997) tested this theory empirically using firm-level data on environmental and accounting profitability and found that firms with higher levels of environmental performance had superior financial performance, which they interpreted to be consistent with the RBV theory.

Using the RBV framework, a more formal theory-of-the-firm model of 'profit maximizing' CSR was posited in McWilliams and Siegel (2001). These authors outlined a simple model in which two companies produce identical products, except that one firm adds an additional 'social' attribute or feature to the product, which is valued by some consumers or, potentially, by other stakeholders. In this model, managers conduct a cost/benefit analysis to determine the level of resources to devote to CSR activities/attributes. That is, they assess the demand for CSR and also evaluate the cost of satisfying this demand.

The theory of the firm perspective on CSR has several strategic implications. The first is that CSR can be an integral element of a firm's business and corporate-level differentiation strategies. Therefore, it should be considered as a form of strategic investment. Even when it is not directly tied to a product feature or production process, SER can be viewed as a form of reputation building or maintenance.

Elkington (2004) propounded triple bottom line reporting for organisations. It is expected that every organisation gives a stewardship account beyond economic activities but must concurrently report on the social and environmental aspect of the business. Cheney (2004) argues that it is a method for the organisation to show its engagement in legitimate environmentally and socially responsible events.

Table 1. Summary of previous studies' theoretical perspectives

Author	Nature of Theoretical Perspective	Key Argument
Friedman (1970)	Agency theory	CSR is indicative of self-serving behaviour on the part of managers, and thus, reduces shareholder wealth.
Freeman (1984)	Stakeholder theory	Managers should tailor their policies to satisfy numerous constituents, not just shareholders. These stakeholders include workers, customers, suppliers, and community organisations.
Donaldson and Davis (1991)	Ethical theory	There is a moral imperative for managers to 'do the right thing', without regard to how such decisions affect firm performance.
Donaldson and Preston (1995)	Moral and ethics	Stressed the moral and ethical dimensions of stakeholder theory, as well as the business case for engaging in CSR.
Jones (1995)	Stakeholder theory	Firms involved in repeated transactions with stakeholders on the basis of trust and cooperation have an incentive to be honest and ethical, since such behaviour is beneficial to the firm.
Hart (1995)	Resource-based view of the firm	For certain companies, environmental social responsibility can constitute a resource or capability that leads to a sustained firm competitive advantage.
Jennings and Zandbergen (1995)	Institutional theory	Institutions play an important role in shaping the consensus within a firm regarding the establishment of an 'ecologically sustainable' organisation
Baron (2001)	Theory of the firm	The use of CSR to attract socially responsible consumers is referred to as strategic CSR, in the sense that firms provide a public good in conjunction with their marketing/business strategy.
McWilliams and Siegel (2001)	Theory of the firm	Presents a supply/demand perspective on CSR, which implies that the firm's ideal level of CSR can be determined by cost-benefit analysis.
Elkington (2004)	Triple bottom line	Need for social and environmental reporting along with the economic activities reporting.
Waldman et al. (2004)	Strategic leadership theory/Theory of the firm	Certain aspects of CEO leadership can affect the propensity of firms to engage in CSR. Companies run by intellectually stimulating CEOs do more strategic CSR than comparable firms.
Marshall et al. (2010)	Theory of reasoned action	Subjective norms and internal stakeholder pressure are drivers of adoption of good environmental practices.
Figure: Theoretical perspectives in CSR evolution		

Waldman et al. (2004) applies strategic leadership theory to CSR. These authors conjecture that certain aspects of transformational leadership will be positively correlated with the propensity of firms to engage in CSR and that these leaders will employ CSR activities strategically. Similarly, Marshall et al., (2010) applies theory of reasoned action (TRA) and stakeholder theory to study of environmental practice in the wind industry and the authors concluded that subjective norms and internal stakeholder pressure are drivers of adoption of good environmental practices.

CSR AND DEVELOPING ECONOMIES

Amaeshi et al (2006) found that indigenous firms perceive and practise CSR as corporate philanthropy aimed at addressing socio-economic development challenges in Nigeria. According to them, CSR is a localised and socially embedded construct which provides responses to socio-economic problems. Subsequently, Okereke et al (2018) countered the mainstream literature and posited that CSR is strongly influenced by economic motives in the form of profit maximisation, cost reduction and competitive advantage. Institutional and ethical pressures are found not very influential enough in determining CSR of Nigerian MNCs.

The emerging practices severely undercuts mainstream literature on CSR literature in Africa, which suggests the dominance of culturally-based, altruistic African *Ubuntu* philosophy. The recent trend speaks to the homogenising propensity of economic globalisation and global capitalism on managers' attitudes towards CSR. However, understanding exactly how the profit-maximising impetus meshes with the native Ubuntu philosophy to shape African managers' CSR responses remains a subject of theoretical and policy priority. African countries transit from an era of peripheral influence towards a period of significant contribution to global wealth creation; managers from these countries are coming under the same type of economic pressure that shape CSR decision-making frameworks in industrialised nations. This view is broadly consistent with the global hegemony of capitalism thesis (Robinson 2005; Sklair, 2001) which proposes that developing country managers are increasingly being integrated into the growing cadre of what Sklair (2001) calls the *transnational capitalist class* (TCC) found in virtually all nations of the world (cf. Carroll et al., 2010). The values and orientation of African managers are now far more subject to transnational social norms consistent with capitalism (competition, survival, profit, etc.) than culturally inspired philosophies such as *Ubuntu*. The focus of CSR activity may well be different (efficient packing of cheap meat by supermarkets *versus* drilling boreholes for oil-bearing communities) in the global North and South. However, as far as the decision-making frame or fundamental reasons for CSR are concerned, Western and developing country managers are far more alike than previously thought.

It is notable that a number of other research in other developing regions of the world including Küskü (2009) (Turkey), Mitra (2007) (India); Haslam (2004) (Latin America and the Caribbean), more or less confirm this asertion. In a direct comparison of attitudes of the United States and South African managers to CSR, Orpen (1987) finds that the United States managers have, in fact, a more positive attitude than their South African counterparts. The main difference, he finds, lies in the fact that the 'United States managers felt that their society expected more corporate involvement in social responsibility than the South African managers felt was expected from their society' (Orpen, 1987:89). So, while managers from both countries are essentially motivated by the economic logic of profit maximization, attitudes and behaviour are tempered by regulations and wider societal expectations.

In fact, the notion that Ubuntu inspires African managers's CSR may be a product of a romantic view of Africa rather than a 21st century, Africa. Many African managers receive their CSR training in Western countries and through Western consultants. Moreover, many of these managers are faced with similar profit maximisation and internal promotion related pressures that confront their Western counterparts. These all provide powerful means for the socialisation of African managers within any given MNC (Feldman, 1981). Organizational scholars have long understood the role of acculturation as an important part of cross-cultural psychology although the concentration of studies has been in the context of mergers and acquisitions (Lee, 1987; Romero, 2004) with little application surprisingly made in the context of CRS research. With the rapid spread and intensification of global capitalism, it is not baffling that norms inherent in capitalism, such as competition, survival, profit and competitive dynamics, are becoming embedded in different societies around the world and leading to the acculturation of developing country managers. A similar observation has been made by scholars working from institutional theory perspective who aptly notes the role of globalisation and managerial values in diffusing global management practices and standards (e.g. Thauer, 2014; Prakash, & Potoski, 2007). Ananthram & Nankervis (2014) have discovered that the quest for a 'global mind-set' is pushing more Indian managers to try to become more like their North American Western counterparts, while Huang and Staples (2017) found that Chinese MNCs are keen to export their governance practices as they internationalise. However, such a conceptualization of institutionalism continues to receive less attention from mainstream CSR scholars who seem drawn to stressing cultural based variations and marginal contingencies (Matten and Moon 2008; Jamali & Karam, 2016).

All this, it should be carefully noted, is not to suggest that developing economies managers in MNC do not have *any* communitarian and religious propensity. It may well be that *Ubuntu* has a moderating effect on profit-maximisation instincts of African managers or that the urge to 'do good' by these managers is mitigated by wider structural forces at play in the company hierarchy (cf. Altman, 2005). For example, Kunda and Hinson (2012) suggest there is a difference between CSR perception of foreign and local managers in Ghana with the latter tending to give more weight to ethical considerations. It may also be that African managers find it easier to express their duty of care through marginal social, economic activities than through the more consequential internal environmental business activities. Research by Rondinelli and Berry (2000) provide some evidence to suggest that this might indeed be the case. They find that when CSR is defined narrowly in terms of an external relationship with stakeholders to address social problems, the picture that most likely emerges is that of a flurry of activities that tend to cast corporations in a positive light. The picture becomes less positive, however, when the focus changes to 'substantive internal environment management activities' like the adoption of pollution-preventing and clean manufacturing practices, waste treatment, life-cycle assessment, redesign of products and material reduction.

It is instructive that most CSR research that highlights the altruistic propensity of African managers has focused on social themes and especially on the external socio-economic activities of companies, i.e. what companies are doing for their host communities. In contrast, the few pieces of research that have focused on the environmental aspects of CSR in Africa tend to come to more critical conclusions than those that focus on social schemes (cf. Kolk & Lenfant, 2009). For example, many of the studies on the environmental behaviour of international oil companies in Nigeria have highlighted the role of the economic incentives and profit maximization frame in decision-making and how this trumps environmental sustainability concerns (Dashwood, 2012; Idemudia, 2008; Ite, 2004; Okpara and Wynn, 2012; Wheeler *et al.*, 2002; Kuada & Hinson 2012). In sum, then, it seems *Ubuntu* may be a key factor when the focus of CSR research is on explaining the external philanthropic actions of the corporate actor. It has, however, little bearing in elucidating the motive for internal CSR practices and how companies take care of the environmental implications of their operations.

There are little grounds to hope that the several voluntary-based global initiatives designed to encourage improved business environmental performance in Africa and other developing countries, such as the UN Global Compact, the Extractive Industry Transparency Initiative (EITI), the Global Reporting Initiative and the UN Business and Human Rights initiative, will succeed. It is apparent that most such international corporate environmental initiatives are crafted on ideas based on the business–society relationship dominant in the West, particularly the assumption that increased voluntary reporting and disclosure by companies will enhance public awareness and pressure to promote higher environmental standards. This assumption, however, is fundamentally flawed in most developing country contexts, where illiteracy, low levels of societal expectations, weak institutions, poverty and corporate power are all-pervasive.

CONCLUSION

Contrary to popular assumptions and claims that CSR activities of companies in Africa are firmly rooted in ethical and philanthropic motives that stem from religious and cultural beliefs associated with *Ubuntu*, certain studies demonstrated that economic instrumentalism is the most significant predictor of CSR among companies in the developing economies. The decision-making frame of most companies is firmly shaped by the material calculus that reigns supreme in Western capitalist societies. Hence, the philanthropic activities of the emerging economies, to the extent that it is ethical, can only be seen as an outcome of utilitarian ethic rather than as duty or value driven. Multinational companies operating in developing world are still driven mostly by profit-making motives in their operation, and any development consequences of business activities are still largely incidental. The mode is, therefore, very much mercenary as opposed to missionary. It is believed that the dynamic and expansionary nature of world capitalism now certainly warrants us to speak of an emerging transnational capitalist class, the activities and CSR gestures are dictated far more by prevailing norms and values within their MNC and global capitalist class than by indigenous values. In the quest to get MNCs take better care of the environment and contribute to sustainable development in Africa, emphasis should not be on promoting voluntarism (because developing economies are yet to attain such maturity) but rather on strengthening institutions to regulate MNC activities and pressure businesses to show greater CSR.

REFERENCES

Altman, M. (2005). The ethical economy and competitive markets: Reconciling altruistic, moralistic, and ethical behaviour with the rational economic agent and competitive markets. *Journal of Economic Psychology*, *26*(5), 732–757. doi:10.1016/j.joep.2005.06.004

Amaeshi, K., Adi, B. C., Ogechie, C., & Amao, O. O. (2006). Corporate Social Responsibility in Nigeria: Indigenous practices or Western influences. *Journal of Corporate Citizenship*, *24*, 83–99. doi:10.9774/GLEAF.4700.2006.wi.00009

Ananthram, S., & Nankervis, A. R. (2014). Outcomes and Benefits of a Managerial Global Mind-set: An Exploratory Study with Senior Executives in North America and India. *Thunderbird International Business Review*, *56*(2), 193–209. doi:10.1002/tie.21611

Aragón-Correa, J. A. (1998). Strategic Proactivity and Firm Approach to the Natural Environment. *Academy of Management Journal, 41*, 556–567.

Azmat, F., & Ha, H. (2013). Corporate social responsibility, customer trust, and Loyalty—Perspectives from a developing country. *Thunderbird International Business Review, 55*(3), 253–270. doi:10.1002/tie.21542

Barraquier, A. (2011). Ethical Behaviour in Practice: Decision Outcomes and Strategic Implications. *British Journal of Management, 22*, 28–46. doi:10.1111/j.1467-8551.2010.00726.x

Baucus, M., & Baucus, D. (1997). Paying the piper: An empirical examination of longer term financial consequences for illegal corporate behaviour. *Academy of Management Journal, 40*, 129–151.

Bentham, J., & Harrison, W. (1945). *(edn). Introduction to the Principles of Morals and Legislation*. Oxford, UK: Hafner Press.

Buchanan, D. A., & Bryman, A. (2011). *Organisational Research Methods*. London: SAGE Publications Limited.

Campbell, J. L. (2007). Why would corporations behave in socially responsible ways? An institutional theory of corporate social responsibility. *Academy of Management Review, 32*(3), 946–967. doi:10.5465/amr.2007.25275684

Carroll, A. (1991). The Pyramid of Corporate Social Responsibility: Towards the Moral Management of Organisational Stakeholder. *Business Horizons, 34*(4), 39–49. doi:10.1016/0007-6813(91)90005-G

Carroll, A. (1991). The Pyramid of Corporate Social Responsibility: Towards the Moral Management of Organisational Stakeholder. *Business Horizons, 34*(4), 39–49. doi:10.1016/0007-6813(91)90005-G

Carroll, A. B. (1999). Corporate Social Responsibility Evolution of a Definitional Construct. *Business & Society, 38*(3), 268–295. doi:10.1177/000765039903800303

Carroll, A. B. (2008). A history of corporate social responsibility: concept and practices. In A. Crane, A. McWilliams, D. Matten, J. Moon, & D. S. Siegel (Eds.), *The Oxford Handbook of Corporate Social Responsibility*. Oxford, UK: Oxford University Press.

Carroll, A. B., & Shabana, K. M. (2010). The business case for corporate social responsibility: A review of concepts, research and practice. *International Journal of Management Reviews, 12*(1), 85–105. doi:10.1111/j.1468-2370.2009.00275.x

Carroll, W. K., Carson, C., Fennema, M., Heemskerk, E., & Sapinski, J. P. (2010). *The making of a transnational capitalist class: Corporate power in the twenty-first century*. Zed books.

Cheney, G. (2004). The Corporate Conscience and the Triple Bottom Line. *Accounting Today*.

Clark, S. E. (1990). How to survive in the environmental jungle. *The Institutional Investor*, *24*(16), 89–91.

Coleman, L. (2011). Losses from Failure of Stakeholder Sensitive Processes: Financial Consequences for Large US Companies from Breakdowns in Product, Environmental, and Accounting Standards. *Journal of Business Ethics*, *98*(2), 247–258. doi:10.100710551-010-0544-8

Cottrell, S. P. (2003). Influence of sociodemographics and environmental attitude on general responsible environmental behaviour among recreational boaters. *Environment and Behavior*, *33*(3), 347–375. doi:10.1177/0013916503035003003

Crane, A., & Matten, D. (2010). *Business Ethics* (3rd ed.). Oxford, UK: Oxford University Press.

Cremer, D. D., Dick, R., Tenbrunsel, A. E., Pillutla, M., & Murnighan, J. K. (2011). Understanding Ethical Behaviour and Decision Making in Management: A Behavioural Business Ethics Approach'. *British Journal of Management*, *22*, S1–S4. doi:10.1111/j.1467-8551.2010.00733.x

Cresswell, J. W. (1994). *Research design: quantitative and qualitative approaches*. London: SAGE Publications Limited.

d'Inverno, M., Luck, M., Georgeff, M., Kinny, D., & Wooldridge, M. (2004). The dMARS Architecture: A specification of the distributed multi-agent reasoning system. *Autonomous Agents and Multi-Agent Systems*, *9*(1/2), 5–53. doi:10.1023/B:AGNT.0000019688.11109.19

Darko-Mensah, A. B., & Okereke, C. (2013). 'Can environmental performance rating programmes succeed in Africa? An evaluation of Ghana's AKOBEN project'. *Management of Environmental Quality*, *24*(5), 599–618. doi:10.1108/MEQ-01-2012-0003

Dashwood, H. S. (2012). *The Rise of Global Corporate Social Responsibility: Mining and the Spread of Global Norms*. Cambridge University Press. doi:10.1017/CBO9781139058933

Des Jardins, J. R. (2001). Environmental ethics: an introduction to environmental philosophy (3rd ed.). Belmont, CA: Wadsworth/Thomson Learning.

DiMaggio, P. J., & Powell, W. W. (1983). The Iron Cage Revisited: Institutional Isomorphism and Collective Rationality in Organizational Fields. *American Sociological Review*, *48*(2), 147–160. doi:10.2307/2095101

Dimaggio, P. J., & Powell, W. W. (1991). *The New Institutionalism in Organisational Analysis*. Chicago: University of Chicago Press.

Donaldson, T., & Preston, L. E. (1995). The stakeholder theory of the corporation: Concepts, evidence, and implications. *Academy of Management Review*, *20*(1), 65–91. doi:10.5465/amr.1995.9503271992

Elkington, J. (2004). Enter the Triple Bottom Line. In A. Henriques & J. Richardson (Eds.), *The Triple Bottom Line: does it all add up*. London: EarthScan.

European Commission. (2000). *Communication from the commission on promoting sustainable development in the EU non-energy extractive industry*. Brussels: The European Commission.

Forsyth, D. R. (1980). A taxonomy of ethical ideologies. *Journal of Personality and Social Psychology*, *39*(1), 175–184. doi:10.1037/0022-3514.39.1.175

Freeman, R. E. (1984). *Strategic Management: A Stakeholder Approach*. Boston: Pitman.

Friedman, M. (1962). *Capitalism and Freedom*. Chicago: University of Chicago Press.

Friedman, M. (1970). The Social Responsibility of Business is to Increase Its Profits. *The New York Times Magazine, 13*, 32–33.

Garriga, E., & Mele, D. (2004). Corporate Social Responsibility Theories: Mapping the Territory. *Journal of Business Ethics*, *53*(1/2), 51–71. doi:10.1023/B:BUSI.0000039399.90587.34

Gilligan, C. (1993). Concepts of the Self and of Morality. Harvard Educational Review, 481–517.

Griffin, J. P. (1995). Consequentialism. In T. Honderich (Ed.), *The Oxford Companion to Philosophy* (pp. 154–156). New York: Oxford University Press.

Hancock, J. (2005). Introduction: Why this subject? Why this book? In *Investing in corporate social responsibility: A guide to best practice, business planning and the UK's leading companies*. London: Kogan Page.

Hart, S. L. (1995). A Natural-Resource-Based View of the Firm. *Academy of Management Review*, *20*(4), 986–1012. doi:10.5465/amr.1995.9512280033

Haslam, P. A. (2004). *The Corporate social responsibility system in Latin American and the Caribbean*. Ottawa: FOCAL.

He, M., & Chen, J. (2009). Sustainable development and corporate environmental responsibility: Evidence from Chinese corporations. *Journal of Agricultural & Environmental Ethics*, *22*(4), 323–339. doi:10.100710806-009-9147-8

Hoffman, A. (1993). The importance of fit between individual values and organizational culture in the greening of industry. *Business Strategy and the Environment*, *2*(4), 10–18. doi:10.1002/bse.3280020402

Hoffman, A. J. (2001). *Competitive environmental strategy*. Washington, DC: Island Press.

Hooghiemstra, R., & Van Manen, J. (2002). Supervisory directors and ethical dilemmas: Exit or voice. *European Management Journal*, *20*(1), 1–9. doi:10.1016/S0263-2373(01)00104-9

Huang, X., & Staples, W. (2017). Do Chinese corporations take their governance practices abroad? Evidence from Chinese mining subsidiaries in Australia. *Thunderbird International Business Review*.

Idemudia, U. (2008). Conceptualising the CSR – Development Debate: Bridging Existing Analytical Gaps. *Journal of Corporate Citizenship*, *29*(29), 91–110. doi:10.9774/GLEAF.4700.2008.sp.00011

Idemudia, U. (2011). Corporate social responsibility and developing countries moving the critical CSR research agenda in Africa forward. *Progress in Development Studies*, *11*(1), 1–18. doi:10.1177/146499341001100101

Ite, U. E. (2004). Multinationals and Corporate Social Responsibility in DevelopingCountries: A Case Study of Shell in Nigeria. *Corporate Social Responsibility and Environmental Management*, *11*, 1–11. doi:10.1002/csr.49

Ite, U. E. (2005). Poverty reduction in resource-rich developing countries: What have multinational corporations got to do with it? *Journal of International Development*, *17*(7), 913–929. doi:10.1002/jid.1177

Jamali, D., & Karam, C. (2016). CSR in developing countries as an emerging field of Study. *International Journal of Management Reviews*, 1–30. doi:10.1111/ijmr.12112

Jamali, D., & Mirshak, R. (2007). Corporate Social Responsibility (CSR): Theory and Practice in a Developing Country Context. *Journal of Business Ethics*, *72*(3), 243–262. doi:10.100710551-006-9168-4

Jones, T. (1991). Ethical decision making by individuals in organizations: An issue contingent model. *Academy of Management Review*, *16*(2), 366–395. doi:10.5465/amr.1991.4278958

Joyner, B. E., & Payne, D. (2002). Evolution and implementation: A study of values, business ethics and corporate social responsibility. *Journal of Business Ethics*, *41*(4), 297–311. doi:10.1023/A:1021237420663

Kant, I. (1981). *Grounding of the Metaphysics of Morals* (J. W. Ellington, Trans.). Indianapolis: Hackett Publishing Company. (Original work published 1785)

Kaptein, M. (2003). The diamond of managerial integrity. *European Management Journal*, *21*(1), 99–108. doi:10.1016/S0263-2373(02)00157-3

Kohlberg, L. (1969). Stage and sequence: the cognitive-developmental approach to socialization. In *Handbook of Socialization Theory and Research* (pp. 347–480). D.A. Goslin.

Kolk, A. (2016). The social responsibility of international business: From ethics and the environment to CSR and sustainable development. *Journal of World Business*, *51*(1), 23–34. doi:10.1016/j.jwb.2015.08.010

Kolk, A., & Lenfant, F. (2009). MNCS reporting on CSR and conflict in CentralAfrica. *Journal of Business Ethics*, *93*(S2), 241–255. doi:10.100710551-009-0271-1

Kuada, J., & Hinson, R. E. (2012). Corporate social responsibility (CSR) practices offoreign and local companies in Ghana. *Thunderbird International Business Review*, *54*(4), 521–536. doi:10.1002/tie.21481

Küskü, F. (2007). From Necessity to Responsibility: Evidence for Corporate Environmental Citizenship Activities from a Developing Country Perspective. *Corporate Social Responsibility and Environmental Management*, *14*(2), 74–87. doi:10.1002/csr.119

Makower, J. (1993). *The E factor: The Bottomline Approach to Environmentally Responsible Business*. New York: Random House.

Marshall, R. S., Akoore, M. E. M., Hamann, R., & Sinha, P. (2009). Environmental Practices in the wine industry: An empirical application of the theory of reasoned action and stakeholder theory in the United States and New Zealand. *Journal of World Business*, *45*(4), 405–414. doi:10.1016/j.jwb.2009.08.009

Matten, D., & Moon, J. (2008). "Implicit" and "Explicit" CSR: A Conceptual Framework for a Comparative Understanding of Corporate Social Responsibility. *Academy of Management Review*, *33*(2), 404–424. doi:10.5465/amr.2008.31193458

McWilliams, A., & Siegel, D. S. (2000). 'Corporate Social Responsibility and Financial Performance: Correlation or Misspecification'? *Strategic Management Journal*, *21*(4), 603–609. doi:10.1002/(SICI)1097-0266(200005)21:5<603::AID-SMJ101>3.0.CO;2-3

McWilliams, A., & Siegel, D. S. (2001). A Theory of the Firm Perspective. *Academy of Management Review*, *26*(1), 117–127. doi:10.5465/amr.2001.4011987

McWilliams, A., Siegel, D. S., & Wright, P. M. (2000). Corporate Social Responsibility: Strategic Implications. *Journal of Management Studies, 43*(1).

Milfont, T. L., & Duckitt, J. (2010). The environmental attitudes inventory: A valid and reliable measure to assess the structure of environmental attitudes. *Journal of Environmental Psychology*, *30*(1), 80–94. doi:10.1016/j.jenvp.2009.09.001

Mitchell, R. K., Agle, B. R., & Wood, D. J. (1997). Toward a theory of stakeholder identification and salience: Defining the principle of who and what really counts. *Academy of Management Review*, *22*(4), 853–886. doi:10.5465/amr.1997.9711022105

Nwagbara, U. (2013). The effects of social media on environmental sustainability activities of oil and gas multinationals in Nigeria. *Thunderbird International Business Review*, *55*(6), 689–697. doi:10.1002/tie.21584

Okereke, C., & Küng, K. (2013). Climate policy and business climate strategies: EUcement companies' response to climate change and barriers against action. *Management of Environmental Quality*, *24*(3), 286–310. doi:10.1108/14777831311322622

Okereke,, C., & Vincent,, O. (2018). Determinants of Nigerian managers' environmental attitude: Africa's Ubuntu ethics versus global capitalism. *Thunderbird International Business Review*, *2018*, 1–14.

Okpara, J. O., & Wynn, P. M. (2012). Stakeholders' perceptions about corporate social responsibility: Implications for poverty alleviation. *Thunderbird International Business Review*, *54*(1), 91–103. doi:10.1002/tie.21441

Oliff, M. D., & Vandermerwe, S. (1990). Customers drive corporations green. *Long Range Planning*, *23*(6), 10–17. doi:10.1016/0024-6301(90)90096-M

Orpen, C. (1987). The Attitudes of United States and South African Managers to Corporate Social Responsibility. *Journal of Business Ethics*, *6*(2), 89–96. doi:10.1007/BF00382022

Ozen, S., & Kusku, F. (2009). Corporate Environmental Citizenship Variation inDeveloping Countries: An Institutional Framework. *Journal of Business Ethics*, *89*(2), 297–313. doi:10.100710551-008-0001-0

Pilkington, E. (2009). Shell pays out $15.5 million over Saro-Wiwa Killing. *The Guardian*. Available at: http://www.guardian.co.uk/world/2009/jun/08/nigeria-usa

Prakash, A., & Potoski, M. (2007). Investing Up: FDI and the Cross-Country Diffusion of Iso 14001 Management Systems. *International Studies Quarterly*, *51*(3), 723–744. doi:10.1111/j.1468-2478.2007.00471.x

Rawls, J. (1971). *A Theory of Justice*. Cambridge, MA: Harvard University Press.

Ridley, A. (1998). *Beginning Bioethics*. New York: St. Martin's Press.

Robinson, W. I. (2005). Gramsci and Globalization: From Nation-State to Transnational Hegemony. *Critical Review of International Social and Political Philosophy*, *8*(4), 1–16. doi:10.1080/13698230500205243

Rodriguez, F. J. G., & Cruz, Y. M. A. (2007). Relationship between social-environmental responsibility and performance in hotel firms. *Hospital Management*, *26*(4), 824–839. doi:10.1016/j.ijhm.2006.08.003

Romero, E. J. (2004). Hispanic identity and acculturation: Implications formanagement. *Cross Cultural Management*, *11*(1), 62–71. doi:10.1108/13527600410797756

Rondinelli, D. A., & Berry, M. A. (2000). Environmental citizenship in multinational corporations: Social responsibility and sustainable development. *European Management Journal*, *18*(1), 70–84. doi:10.1016/S0263-2373(99)00070-5

Russo, M. V., & Fouts, P. A. (1997). A resource-based perspective on corporate environmental performance and profitability. *Academy of Management Journal*, *40*(3), 534–559.

Scott, W. R. (1992). *Organisational: Rational, Natural, and Open Systems*. Englewood Cliffs, NJ: Prentice-Hall.

Sharma, S. (2000). Managerial interpretations and organizational context as predictors of corporate choice of environmental strategy. *Academy of Management Journal*, *43*, 681–697.

Simon, J. (1997). *Endangered Mexico*. San Francisco, CA: Sierra Club Books.

Singh, R. K., Murty, H. R., Gupta, S. K., & Dikshit, A. K. (2007). Development of composite sustainability performance index for steel industry. *Ecological Indicators*, *7*(3), 565–588. doi:10.1016/j.ecolind.2006.06.004

Sklair, L. (2001). *The Transnational Capitalist Class*. Oxford, UK: Blackwell.

Smith, E. T. (1990). The greening of corporate America. *Business Week*, (3156), 96-103.

Solomon, R. C., & Greene, J. K. (1999). *Morality and the Good Life: An Introduction to Ethics through Classical Sources*. New York: McGraw-Hill.

Thauer, C. R. (2014). *The Managerial Sources of Corporate Social Responsibility. The Spread of Global Standards*. Cambridge, UK: Cambridge University Press. doi:10.1017/CBO9781107588950

Trevino, L., Weaver, G., Gibson, D., & Toffler, B. (1999). Managing ethics and legal compliance: What works and what hurts. *California Management Review*, *41*(2), 131–151. doi:10.2307/41165990

Trevino, L. K., & Youngblood, S. A. (1990). Bad apples in bad barrels: A causal analysis of ethical decision-making behaviour. *The Journal of Applied Psychology*, *75*(4), 378–385. doi:10.1037/0021-9010.75.4.378

Turban, D., & Greening, D. (1996). Corporate social performance and organizational attractiveness to prospective employees. *Academy of Management Journal*, *40*, 658–672.

Van de Ven, B., & Jeurissen, R. (2005). Competing responsibly. *Business Ethics Quarterly*, *15*(2), 299–317. doi:10.5840/beq200515216

Victor, B., & Cullen, J. B. (1988). The organizational bases of ethical work climates. *Administrative Science Quarterly*, *33*(1), 101–125. doi:10.2307/2392857

Vincent, O. M. (2012). *The Impact of Corporate Environmental Responsibility on Financial Performance: Extractive Sector Perspective* (Unpublished Doctoral Thesis). Brunel University.

Waldman, D., Siegel, D., & Javidan, M. (2006). Components of CEO transformational leadership and corporate social responsibility. *Journal of Management Studies*, *43*(8), 1703–1725. doi:10.1111/j.1467-6486.2006.00642.x

Wheeler, D., Fabig, H., & Boele, R. (2002). Paradoxes and Dilemmas for Stakeholder Responsive Firms in the Extractive Sector: Lessons from the Case of Shell and the Ogoni. *Journal of Business Ethics*, *39*(3), 297–318. doi:10.1023/A:1016542207069

Windsor, D. (2001). The Future of Corporate Social Responsibility. *The International Journal of Organizational Analysis*, *9*(3), 225–256. doi:10.1108/eb028934

Wood, D. J. (1991). Corporate social performance revisited. *Academy of Management Review*, *16*(4), 691–718. doi:10.5465/amr.1991.4279616

Chapter 12
How Credit Portfolio Diversification Affects the Profitability of Vietnamese Commercial Banks

Huynh Viet Khai
https://orcid.org/0000-0001-8969-5387
Can Tho University, Vietnam

Phan Thi Anh Nguyet
Can Tho University, Vietnam

Phan Dinh Khoi
Can Tho University, Vietnam

Chu Van Nam
Can Tho University, Vietnam

ABSTRACT

This study analyzed the impact of credit portfolio diversification on the profitability by using the data of 20 Vietnam commercial banks from 2009 to 2015. The results from feasible generalized least squares (FGLS) estimation show that the strategy of diversifying the credit portfolio increased the profitability of commercial banks. In addition, the study also indicates that the positive correlation of the ratio of owners' equity, credit growth, liquidity, assets, inflation rate with the profitability while the increase in non-performing loan decreased the profitability of these commercial banks.

DOI: 10.4018/978-1-5225-9607-3.ch012

INTRODUCTION

Since Vietnam became a member of the World Trade Organization, the country's economy has welcomed many opportunities as well as challenges to various economic sectors, including banking sector. On the one hand, opening the country's financial market creates many opportunities for Vietnamese commercial banks to attract foreign investment as well as to gain experience and advanced management capacity from several countries around the world. Increasing penetration of foreign banks also provides strong financial potential and professional management capabilities as well as raises pressure on domestic banks. Hence, all domestic commercial banks have to face the challenge of competitiveness and sustainable development or bankruptcy.

Credit supply plays an important role in private economic development. Along with the nation's development orientation, commercial banks have been developing a market share strategy to improve their competitiveness and serve the industrialization and modernization. On the other hand, due to high level of credit monopoly market, lending always account for a large proportion on the portfolio of Vietnamese commercial banks. In addition, the bank's main source of income mainly comes from lending activities. Therefore, the key issue for the banks in order to get high profits depends largely on lending accounts.

The above facts require a new research approach to detect and evaluate the impact of the structure of the credit portfolio on the operation of commercial banks. Various theoretical and empirical researches indicate that structure of credit portfolio by different economic sectors directly impacts on commercial banks' profitability. In particular, Bebczuk & Galindo (2008) and Rossi et al. (2009) showed that banks pursuit credit portfolio diversification strategy were able to increase profitability by taking advantage of economies of scale, minimizing operating costs, and targeting a wide range of customers. In addition, commercial banks were able to increase income from cross-selling operations such as salary payment, ATM card issuance, selling insurance, consulting and service fees. These products and services helped not only increasing banks' income but also achieving non-economic goals such as building and developing brands. Finally, allocating credit to a wide range of economic sectors less interdependent economic sectors helped commercial banks to be less interdependent and hence minimize losses and maintain stable profit for the commercial banks (Diamond, 1984).

However, many studies deny the benefits of bank's credit portfolio diversification strategy. According to Winton (1999), credit diversification increased the level of competition as well as caused serious consequences if commercial banks were not able to control portfolio risks. While Jensen (1986) and Denis et al. (1997) argued that there was no benefit from a diversification strategy, Acharya et al. (2006) articulated that expanding credit market share increased management costs and decreased the profitability of commercial banks. Therefore, commercial banks were encouraged to focus their credit portfolio on fewer areas of expertise.

The above review provides evidence of the relationship between the structure of the credit portfolio and commercial banks' profitability. This relationship may be different depending on the economic characteristics of each country and the specific characteristics of commercial banks. Particular empirical results may not apply to commercial banks in different countries. As numerous contradictions exist in the above studies, this paper focuses on the relationship between credit portfolio and profitability of commercial banks since it is a relatively new and important topic in banking sector in Vietnam.

The remain of this study is organized as follows. Section two concentrates on the theories on the impact of credit portfolio diversification to commercial bank profitability and section three reviews empirical studies in the literature. All the data used, and research models are described in section four. All results and discussion of the analysis are presented and discussed in section five. The final section presents some main conclusions and policy implications.

THEORIES ON THE IMPACT OF DIVERSIFYING CREDIT PORTFOLIO ON THE PROFIT OF COMMERCIAL BANKS

Previous studies show that there is no consensus between traditional banking theory and corporate finance theory on the impact of diversification of the credit portfolio on the profitability of commercial banks. Basically, banks manage credit portfolio by two criteria: Diversification and Centralization. According to traditional banking theory, banks should maintain their credit portfolio by diversifying the credit fields and sectors. Taking economic advantage of scale, reducing operating costs, serving a diverse range of customers, and gaining market share help the banks not only becoming more efficient but also achieving non-economic goals such as building and promoting their brands. Additionally, these strategies create opportunities for commercial banks to cross-sell products to various customers. In fact, the business environment of the commercial banks is under great competitive pressure while market share is gradually shrinking. With the trend of extending the scope of credit to spatial development, the bank can increase the number of customers and sales, thus help to increase profitability. Finally, with the existence of asymmetric information in the credit market, diversification strategies help to spread the risks in the whole portfolio of credit and contribute to reducing losses for commercial banks.

There are many previous studies supporting the view of credit portfolio diversification such as Baele et al. (2007), Rossi et al. (2009) and Chen & Chang (2015). In particular, Baele et al. (2007) provided evidence of diversification that increased the brand value and reduced the specific risk of most banks in the 15 EU countries, Norway and Switzerland in the period from 1989 to 2004. Rossi et al. (2009) indicated that diversification had a positive impact on the profitability of commercial banks. The impact was greater during the decline of the Austrian business cycle between 1997 and 2003. Later, Chen and Chang (2015) argued that, with the support of government funds, a diversified portfolio strategy could yield a higher return leverage, while centralized credit portfolio led to lower return margins.

Contrary to the above points of view, corporate finance theory suggests that businesses should focus their operations on a specific industry or group of sectors to gain a narrow technical and industry advantage. Therefore, commercial banks should concentrate on credit where they have the most comparative advantage, information and skills (Jensen, 1986; Denis et al., 1997; Acharya et al., 2006). According to Tabak et al. (2011), banks focus on large and key projects to reduce monitoring costs. Moreover, as commercial banks expand their credit activities in many areas, they will lead to increase competition with other banks. Therefore, commercial banks will not pay much attention to diversification because this strategy becomes less attractive. This encourages banks to focus on one or some industries which yield the highest return leverage, to gain higher returns than their rivals. On the other hand, banks can only benefit from diversification with low portfolio, but when the risk level of the portfolio is high, diversification leads to risk exposure in many sectors (Winton, 1999). Then just one area of recession can take the bank to bankruptcy.

Empirical studies of Acharya et al. (2006) in Italy, Norden and Szerencses (2005), Behr et al. (2007) and Hayden et al. (2007) in Germany; Mercieca et al. (2007) in Europe; Berger et al. (2010) in China supported the view of anti- diversification. More specifically, Mercieca et al. (2007) argued that there was no direct benefit from the diversification of credit portfolios for small banks in 15 EU countries between 1997 and 2003. Moreover, Hayden et al. (2007) found that diversification negatively influenced bank profitability. High risk banks did not benefit from the diversification of their credit portfolio. Based on research data from German banks, Behr et al. (2007) concluded that specialized banks (centralized) yield higher returns than other banks in sample. The studies of Elsas et al. (2010) in the United States, Canada, the United Kingdom, Australia, Italy, France, Spain, Germany, and Switzerland suggested that diversification decreased profitability and indirectly reduced the bank value. In China, Berger et al. (2010) investigated the effect of a diversification strategy on banks' profitability between 1996 and 2006, showing that diversification reduced profitability and increased the costs.

LITERATURE REVIEWS

Acharya et al. (2006) studied the effect of credit portfolio diversification strategies on commercial banks' profitability. The paper used the data from the credit portfolio structure of 105 Italian banks in the period from 1993 to 1999. Based on the Hirschman Herfindahl Index (HHI), the authors set up two indexes of diversification of credit structure by industry and type of ownership. Seemingly Unrelated Regression was used to measure the effect of diversification on the performance of commercial banks. The paper concluded that expanding lending to new industries reduced the effectiveness of commercial banks' credit portfolio monitoring. The credit diversification strategy, both in terms of industry and type of ownership, reduced the profitability of commercial banks. Acharya et al. (2006) argued that when risk occured in almost economic sectors, diversification was not effective or makes commercial banks become safer.

Behr et al. (2007) examined the impact of credit portfolio concentration on the profitability of commercial banks in Germany in the period from 1993 to 2003, to find out whether the benefits of the credit concentration strategy of commercial banks. In particular, the Hirschman Herfindahl Index (HHI) index was used to represent the industry's concentration of credit by industry. The estimation method used in this study was the Fixed Effects Model. The main conclusions of Behr et al. (2007) were that the specialized banks (centralized) achieved higher returns than diversified banks. This encouraged commercial banks to focus on one or more areas to achieve the best business results.

Hayden et al. (2007) developed three indexes of credit portfolio diversification from the Hirschman Herfindahl Index (Industry, ownership type and geographic region) to clarify as follows: Should the banks diversify their portfolio across different industries or even expand to new areas or focus on a number of key areas? In particular, Hayden et al. (2007) used data on the credit portfolio structure of 983 private banks in Germany for the period 1996-2002. The results showed that there was no benefit from the credit diversification strategy. All three forms of diversification reduced the profitability of banks in Germany.

Mercieca et al. (2007) studied the impact of diversification (income and credit portfolio) on the business performance and profitability of financial institutions in Europe. The paper used data from 15 countries, including 755 banks under 50 million Euros between 1997 and 2003. The Hirschman Herfindahl Index measured the degree of diversification of the credit portfolio as follows: $HHI_{LOAN} = (MTG/LOAN)^2 + (HPL/LOAN)^2 + (CORP/LOAN)^2 + (LTHLN/LOAN)^2$, where: *MTG* is secured loans, HPL is consumer loans and financial leasing, *CORP* is corporate loans, *LLLN* is other loans, and $LOAN = MTG + HPL + CORP + LTHLN$. The dependent variables: *ROA, ROE,* σ_{ROA}, σ_{ROE}, respectively, are business efficiency and degree of fluctuations of commercial banks' profitability. Mercieca et al. (2007) concluded that the HHI_{LOAN} index correlated positively with the profit index and correlated negatively with the level of profitability of commercial banks. This indicated that commercial banks with credit diversification strategies earned lower profits than other banks in the sample. At the same time, this strategy made profit more volatile.

Berger et al. (2010) analyzed the impact of the diversification strategies on the profitability of 88 banks in China between 1996 and 2006. The Hirschman Herfindahl Index was created based on the four main groups: Credit, deposit, property, geography. The credit rating scale was based on the classification of outstanding loans in five sectors: trade, real estate, agriculture, consumption, and other industries. The study examined the impact of restructuring the credit portfolio on banks' profitability by estimating Ordinary Least Squares. Berger et al., (2010) provided evidence of commercial banks pursuing a lower profitable diversification strategy. This conclusion is similar to the study by Acharya et al. (2006).

Tabak et al. (2011) measured the effect of concentration of credit portfolio on the profitability of 96 commercial banks in Brazil, 2003-2009. The authors used the Hirschman Herfindahl Index (*HHI*), representing the level of credit concentration by the economic sector of commercial banks. The study used Feasible Generalized Least Squares method to examine the impact of concentration of credit portfolio on the profitability of commercial banks. The results showed that the concentration of credit had a positive impact on the profitability of commercial banks. An important finding in the study by Tabak et al., (2011) showed that credit concentration strategies were the optimal choice in state owned banks, which helped commercial banks reduce the cost of supervision as well as easy to manage credit portfolio.

Bebczuk and Galindo (2008) studied the change and impact of credit portfolio diversification of commercial banks during the Argentine financial crisis in 2001-2002. Data were collected from 124 commercial banks and 930 non-financial firms in Argentina in the period 1999-2004. The article used the Hirschman Herfindahl Index to measure the impact of credit structure by industry on the business performance of commercial banks. The main conclusion from the model was as follows: i) there were no changes in the loan portfolio of commercial banks. This was a response to the crisis. Although the results from the quantitative model showed that diversification by an economic sector had a direct impact on the increase in profit margins of commercial banks. ii) Benefits from diversification depended on the size of each bank. In particular, large banks had more benefits than small banks and the benefits was more during the recession.

MAIN FOCUS OF THE CHAPTER

Empirical Model and Data Description

Based on the studies by Acharya et al. (2006), Behr et al. (2007) and Tabak et al. (2011), a model measuring the impact of credit portfolio diversification on the profits of Vietnamese commercial banks is built as follows:

$$\text{PROFIT}_{it} = \beta_0 + \beta_1\text{DIV\_IND}_{it} + \beta_2\text{NPL}_{it} + \beta_3\text{EQT}_{it} + \beta_4\text{LOAN\_G}_{it}$$

$$+ \beta_5\text{DEP}_{it} + \beta_6\text{LIQ}_{it} + \beta_7\text{SIZE}_{it} + \beta_8\text{GDP}_{it} + \beta_9\text{INF}_{it} + \varepsilon_{it}$$

where, *PROFIT* is the profitability of commercial banks, measured by Return on Assets (*ROA*) and Return on Equity (*ROE*). This measure was used in the studies of Tabak et al. (2011) and Trujillo-Ponce (2013). This variable is calculated as follows:

$$ROA = \frac{After\,Income\,Tax\,Return}{Total\,Assets}$$

$$ROE = \frac{After\,Income\,Tax\,Return}{Total\,Owners'\,Equity}$$

The explanatory factors include credit portfolio diversification (*DIV_IND*), NPL ratios (*NPL*), equity ratios (*EQT*), credit growth (*LOAN_G*), customer deposit rates (*DEP*), liquidity (*LIQ*), asset size (*SIZE*), economic growth (*GDP*) and inflation rate (*INF*).

The credit portfolio diversification (*DIV_IND*) is measured based on the classification of outstanding loans by the economic sector of commercial banks. Similar to the studies by Behr et al. (2007) and Tabak et al. (2011), this study uses the Hirshmann Herfindahl Index (*HHI*) to measure the degree of credit portfolio diversification of Vietnamese commercial banks.

$$HHI_{it} = \sum_{i=1}^{n} r_{Git}^2$$

where, *HHI* is the index of diversification of the credit portfolio, calculated by the sum of squared proportion of outstanding loans by economic sector.

$$r_{Git} = \frac{Outstanding\,loan\,of\,G\,sector\,of\,bank\,G\,in\,year\,t}{Total\,outstanding\,loans\,of\,bank\,i\,in\,year\,t}$$

The smaller the *HHI* indicator, the higher the diversification index the greater the *HHI* index, the more centralized the index, and vice versa. This implies if the coefficient $\beta_1 < 0$, the commercial banks with the higher the degree of credit portfolio diversification will have higher returns and vice versa when $\beta_1 > 0$.

High *NPLs* have reduced the profitability of commercial banks because they do not earn interest or loans, while paying interest on deposits and other costs. The studies by Acharya et al. (2006), Hayden et al. (2007) and Tabak et al. (2011) also showed that bad debt ratio was one of the main reasons for reducing the profit of commercial banks. Similar to these studies, the study expects that bad debt ratio will have adverse impact on profit targets of commercial banks. This variable is measured by the total outstanding loans from groups 3 to 5 of the total outstanding loans of the bank.

$$NPL = \frac{Total\,outstanding\,loans\,from\,groups\,3\,to\,5}{Total\,outstanding\,loans}$$

EQT is the ratio of Equity out of total assets of commercial banks. Equity often accounts for a small share of total capital but plays an important role in the bank as it provides the basis for growth, minimizing risk and maintaining public confidence. In addition, potentials in equity also affect the scale of the bank's business such as its ability to mobilize, lend, invest in finance and equip its technology. Therefore, the high equity ratio will contribute to the profitability of commercial banks (Acharya et al., 2006 and Tabak et al., 2011). This variable is expected to be positive. This ratio is calculated by dividing the owner's equity by the total assets of the bank. In the *EQT* formula, the numerator is equity while in the *ROE* formula, the denominator is equity. The correlation between *EQT* and *ROE* variability can be seen. Therefore, in order to avoid the subjective impact between the two variables which may lead to distort the results, the *EQT* variable will not be used in the model for the dependent variable of *ROE*.

$$EQT = \frac{Total\,Owners'\,Equity}{Total\,Assets}$$

As a credit intermediary, commercial banks seek to profit from the difference between interest rates and lending rates. If other factors do not change, the reasonable and quality credit growth is will contribute to the growth of profitability of commercial banks. Claeys & Vennet (2008) found evidence of credit growth positively impacting the profitability of commercial banks. However, Amador et al. (2013) argued that credit growth only affected short-term profitability, but in the long run this effect was unclear. In Vietnamese commercial banks, the main source of income comes from credit activities, so that the paper expects that credit growth has a positive impact on their profitability.

$$LOAN\_G = \frac{\left[Outstanding\,loans\,in\,year\,t - Outstanding\,loans\,in\,year\left(t-1\right)\right]}{\left[Outstanding\,loans\,in\,year\left(t-1\right)\right]}$$

Mobilized Capital has a great impact on business results of commercial banks. In particular, if banks mobilize capital at low cost, they can expand their credit activities and earn high profits. Customer deposits are said to be a more stable and cheaper source of funding than other sources of funding. As a result, higher deposit rates increase the bank's profitability. The results of Garcia-Herrero et al. (2009) also showed that deposit rates affected the business performance of commercial banks. Similarly, the study expects the positive relationship between customer deposits and commercial banks.

$$DEP = \frac{Customer\ Deposits}{Total\ Liabilities}$$

Liquidity (*LIQ)* is the ability to convert assets into cash in the shortest possible time and lowest cost. The highest liquidity assets include as follows: Cash and deposits at Central Bank, Government securities and short-term loans. Loans are often poorly liquid because the repayment can last for a period and the loan may not be sold to other investors. Bordeleau & Graham (2010) argued that holding high liquidity assets within a reasonable limit not only increased the credibility of the clients but also helped the bank to be flexible in meeting the payment needs with the lowest cost. Based on this, the topic also expects the positive relationship between liquidity and profitability of commercial banks.

$$LIQ = \frac{Liquidity\,Assets}{Total\,Assets}$$

Theoretically, large banks have the advantage of expanding their network of operations, providing more efficient products and services at lower cost while other factors unchanged. According to the studies by Acharya et al. (2006), Behr et al. (2007) and Tabak et al. (2011), in order to maximize profits, the banks need to choose the right sizes. More specifically, the scale has both a positive and a negative impact on the bank's profitability. To a certain extent, the growth of scale increases profitability, so the banks have a competitive edge in scale. However, if the banks reach such a large scale, profits may be adversely affected by an increase in the scale of negative factors such as huge, bureaucracy human resource systems, and the decrease in the productivity of employees. Similar to the relationship between *EQT* and *ROE*, *SIZE* and *ROA* variables have a negative correlation, so the *SIZE* variable is not used in the research model for *ROA*.

$$SIZE = Logarithm(Total\,Assets)$$

The GDP growth rate is used to test the correlation between the economic situation and profit targets of commercial banks. Gambacorta & Mistrulli (2004) and Kenjegalieva & Simper (2011) suggested that there was a link between the economic cycle and the bank profit. Accordingly, the difficult economic conditions, such as the cyclical risk of the economy, could exacerbate the quality of the loan portfolio, and cause credit risk and reduce the profitability of banks. In contrast, Albertazzi & Gambacorta (2009) found that in positive economic conditions, economic growth raised the demand for borrowing from households and businesses, making to increase the financial capacity of borrowers, thus having a positive impact on the income of banks. Based on that, the study expects the positive correlation between economic growth and profitability of commercial banks.

Inflation (*INF)* makes both the mobilizing and lending rates of commercial banks soar, affecting business activities of commercial banks and the economy as a whole. Perry (1992) argued that the relationship between inflation and the performance of a bank depended on whether inflation was predicted. In the case of anticipated inflation, the bank periodically changes interest rates, which increase revenue faster than costs, thus positively affected profitability.

The data source was collected from 20 commercial banks and the State Bank of Vietnam. Specifically, data on the structure of credit by an economic sector and financial indicators were collected from the financial reports, analysis reports on the performance of Vietnamese commercial banks in the period of 2009 and 2015. In addition, data on economic growth and inflation rate of Vietnam are from the websites of the General Statistics Office and the World Bank.

RESULTS AND DISCUSSION

Table 1 provides correlation between the variables in the model. According to Gujarati (2004), if the correlation coefficient between variables greater than 0.8, the model is likely to experience a serious problem of multi-co linearity. As a result, the sign of the regression coefficients may be altered, leading to the research results being biased. The results show that the absolute value of the correlation coefficients is less than 0.8. This means the model does not suffer from multi-co linearity problems.

To increase credibility, the study continues to test through the Variance Inflation Factor (VIF). As shown in Table 2, all VIF coefficients are less than 5, indicating that there is no multi-co linearity in the research model.

There are a number of models applied to analyze the impact of diversification of the credit portfolio on the profitability of Vietnamese commercial banks including the Pooled Ordinary Least Square Regression (Pooled OLS), the Fixed Effects Model (FEM), the Random Effects Model (REM) and the Feasible Generalized Least Square (FGLS) method. In order to select the appropriate model to analyze the relationship between the credit portfolio diversification and the profits of commercial banks, the study does some statistical tests. The results of F test indicate that the Pooled OLS method is not appropriate because it does not reflect the impact of individual bank differences. The results of the Breusch-Pagan test prove the REM model suitable while Hausman test shows that FEM estimation is more appropriate than REM.

Table 1. Matrix of correlation coefficient between variables.

	ROA	ROE	NPL	DIV_IND	EQT	LOAN_G	DEP	LIQ	SIZE	INF	GDP
ROA	1.0000										
ROE	0.7079	1.0000									
NPL	-0.1567	-0.2356	1.0000								
DIV_IND	-0.1997	-0.1968	-0.0079	1.0000							
EQT	0.3313	-0.2955	0.1479	-0.1259	1.0000						
LOAN_G	0.2594	0.2604	-0.0961	0.0455	-0.0416	1.0000					
DEP	-0.1810	-0.2604	-0.0171	-0.1086	0.0544	-0.1685	1.0000				
LIQ	-0.1108	0.1367	-0.0529	-0.0248	-0.2983	-0.0798	-0.0047	1.0000			
SIZE	-0.1945	0.3261	-0.1427	-0.1343	-0.7475	-0.1659	0.1230	0.2384	1.0000		
INF	0.4413	0.4157	0.0852	0.0381	0.1141	0.0117	-0.5957	-0.0900	-0.1194	1.0000	
GDP	-0.0215	0.0318	-0.1878	0.0344	-0.0739	-0.0848	-0.0003	-0.0154	0.0896	-0.0095	1.0000

Table 2. Variance inflation factor (VIF)

Variables	VIF
Credit portfolio diversification index - *DIV_IND*	1.17
Bad debt Ratio – *NPL*	1.08
Owners' Equity Ratio – *EQT*	3.06
Credit Growth - *LOAN_G*	1.16
Customers' Deposit Ratio – *DEP*	1.75
Liquidity – *LIQ*	1.12
Total Asset Size – *SIZE*	2.99
Gross Domestic Product – *GDP*	1.06
Inflation Rate – *INF*	1.66

Source: Estimated from research data

Because the results from the Wald and Wooldridge tests show the existence of heteroscedasticity and autocorrelation in FEM estimation, the FGLS method is applied to solve the problems of autocorrelation and heteroskedasticity (Tabak et al., 2011). Table 3 shows the results of the FGLS method measuring the impact of credit portfolio diversification on the profits of commercial banks.

The FGLS model shows an inverse correlation between the credit portfolio diversification index (*DIV_IND*) and the returns of Vietnamese commercial banks. Specifically, the impact factor of *DIV_IND* to *ROA* and *ROE* is -0.0092 and -0.0643, respectively, and are statistically significant. This implies that the commercial banks with higher credit portfolio diversification have higher returns. This result is consistent with the findings from Rossi et al. (2009). In addition, the independent variables which play a control role also affect the profitability of commercial banks in Vietnam. More specifically, while bad debt ratio (*NPL*) has adverse impact on the profitability of commercial banks, the other variables such as equity ratios, credit growth, liquidity, asset size, inflation rate have a positive impact on the profitability of commercial banks.

The results show that the diversification index (*DIV_IND)* has a negative impact on the profitability of commercial banks. Specifically, in the case of dependent variable of *ROA*, the coefficient of impact is -0.0092 with a statistical significance of 1% and -0.0643 for the dependent variable of *ROE* at 10% of the significant level. It can be concluded from the results that commercial banks are spreading their investment in different economic sectors to earn higher profits than just focusing on one or a specific group of economic sectors. This conclusion is consistent with previous studies such as Baele et al. (2007), Bebczuk & Galindo (2008) and Rossi et al. (2009).

Table 3. Results from the FGLS method

Variables	Model 1	Model 2
DIV_IND	-0.0092*** (0.0029)	-0.0643* (0.0364)
NPL	-0.0949*** (0.0246)	-0.4493* (0.2674)
EQT	0.0331*** (0.008)	
LOAN_G	0.0078*** (0.0012)	0.0602*** (0.0118)
DEP	0.0043 (0.0031)	0.0033 (0.0345)
LIQ	0.0026 (0.0042)	0.1251** (0.0555)
SIZE		0.0222*** (0.0035)
GDP	-0.0417 (0.0536)	-0.7027 (0.4948)
INF	0.0548*** (0.0076)	0.4916*** (0.0772)
Constant	0.0038 (0.0044)	-0.3035*** (0.0786)
Wald $chi^2(8)$	163.11***	128.57***
Observations	140	140

Notes: Dependent variables are ROA in Model 1 and ROE in Model 2; Values in parentheses are Standard Error; ***, ** and * denote significance at 1%, 5%, and 10% levels, respectively.

Source: Estimated from research data

Bad debt ratio (*NPL)* has a negative impact on the profitability of commercial banks. Specifically, in the case of dependent variable of *ROA*, the coefficient of impact is -0.0949 with a statistical significant level of 1%. Also, for the dependent variable of *ROE*, the coefficient is -0.4493 at the significant level of 10%. This result theoretically matches with the view of the relationship between bad debt ratio and profitability of commercial banks. Firstly, the failure to recover debt (principal, interest and fees) causes the capital of commercial banks to be lost, while those banks still have to pay interest for operating capital to make profits reduced. Second, when a customer owes overdue, banks are forced to set up risk provisions which would reduce profitability of commercial banks. Third, the bank's loan portfolio is stagnant. Banks' prestige and confidence in its financial strength is deteriorating due to the rising bad debt, which reduces the bank's ability to raise capital for other investments

The study also shows a positive correlation between equity ratio (*EQT*) and profitability of commercial banks. The effect coefficient of *EQT* variable to the *ROA* is 0.0331 with a statistically significant level of 1%. This means that banks holding a lot of equity are highly profitable. For empirical research in Vietnamese commercial banks, the potential of equity is a measure of bank capital strength. Banks with large size of equity are considered to be safer, avoiding liquidity risks, which is also a great concern for depositors, whereby capital-intensive banks have many advantages in terms of attracting customer deposits. This finding is consistent with previous studies in emerging economies where a high shareholding ratio is associated with high returns, such as Acharya et al. (2006) and Tabak et al. (2011).

Credit growth (*LOAN_G*) has a positive impact on the profitability of commercial banks. Specifically, in both cases the dependent variable is *ROA* and *ROE*, the coefficients of *LOAN_G* are 0.0078 and 0.0602, respectively, which are statistically significant at 1%. As a result, the profitability of Vietnamese commercial banks in the past years depends heavily on credit activities, although Vietnamese commercial banks tend to gradually reduce their dependence on credit and diversify their sources to collect fees and services. This result is consistent with the studies by Claeys & Vender (2008) and Amador et al. (2013), who argued that credit growth is one of the main factors that have a positive impact on the profitability of commercial banks.

The results show that commercial banks holding high liquidity (*LIQ*) assets have a positive impact on the profit target. Specifically, in the case of the *ROE* dependent variable, the coefficient of the *LIQ* variable is 0.1251 with a statistically significant 5%. This result is in contrast to the studies by Molyneux & Thornton (1992), Samad and Hassan (1999) and Bordeleau & Graham (2010), who argued that the banks with higher cash, deposited at other banks and stock investment proportion in their assets would be safer, but their profitability was low. However, Bordeleau & Graham (2010) also emphasized that maintaining high liquid assets did not always reduce banks' profits if the ratio was set within a reasonable limit. The research results show that in the recent time, commercial banks in Vietnam have maintained high liquidity assets within a reasonable limit. This helps commercial banks have a good liquidity position, increase the trust of customers and help banks flexible to meet the needs of payment at the lowest cost.

The result shows a positive correlation between *SIZE* and *ROE*. The coefficient is 0.0222 with a statistical significance level of 1%. It can be inferred that the larger the size of the assets, the higher the profit. This is perfectly suited to the real situation in Vietnamese commercial banks where large banks can take advantage of economies of scale, investment capacity, better management and customers' trust. At the same time, large-scale networks with extensive service networks help banks to efficiently attract customers. This conclusion is similar to previous studies, such as Acharya et al. (2006), Behr et al. (2007) and Tabak et al. (2011).

The coefficient of inflation rate (*INF*) is positive and statistically significant at 1% in both *ROA* and *ROE* models. Theoretically, inflation has had a negative impact on the operation of commercial banks. However, high inflation does not always negatively affect the profitability of commercial banks. The results show that bank administrators have predicted the inflation rate and adjusted the interest rate to achieve the best benefit. This result is consistent with studies by Demirguc-Kunt & Huizinga (1999), Pasiouras & Kosmidou (2007) and Alexiou & Sofoklis (2009).

Although previous studies have shown that there is a link between the ratio of customer deposits and the profitability of commercial banks. However, the coefficient of the *DEP* variable is not statistically significant, partly providing evidence although customer deposits are considered both stable sources of financing and main source of funds used by banks for lending, the banks actually have to pay very high interest expenses on term deposits and non-interest expenses for demanding deposits. While, commercial banks have to maintain interest rates on market signals to increase competitiveness. As a consequence, the amount of customer deposits always grows over the years but the net interest income (difference between interest income and interest expense) of banks is very low. In addition, the coefficient of the *GDP* variable is not statistically significant, meaning the economic cycle does not have much impact on the profitability of commercial banks.

CONCLUSION AND POLICY IMPLICATIONS

In order to improve profitability, commercial banks should diversify their credit portfolio by industries and economic sectors. The current situation shows that the business environment of commercial banks is now under great competitive pressure, the market share is gradually shrinking. When extending the scope of credit for space, the bank can increase the number of customers as well as credit balance. Moreover, banks, which have advantages in market share based on providing diverse products and good quality, will create a competitive position and raise brand value. On the other hand, in recent years, commercial banks had tried to increase credit to seek maximum profits, but credit activities themselves contain many risks. Expanding credit for many less interdependent industries and sectors is one of good solutions to reduce these risks and create sustainable profits for banks.

In addition to the diversification of the credit portfolio, commercial banks need to improve their financial capacity as well as increase their scale of operation through equity ratios and asset size. During examined period, the profitability of Vietnamese commercial banks depends heavily on credit activities. However, the high level of *NPLs* has partly shown the negative impact of this activity on the profitability of commercial banks. Therefore, in order to improve profitability in the coming years, commercial banks should continue to develop credit in a rational and sustainable manner, avoiding credit crunch and hot growth leading to high *NPLs*.

At the same time, commercial banks should concentrate on bad debt management because bad debts make banks' costs increase, the ability to mobilize capital and lend to the economy is reduced. In addition to focusing on dealing with bad debts arising from previous years, commercial banks also need to take measures to prevent bad debts arising in the future. Next, in order to improve profitability and good liquidity position, commercial banks should maintain high liquidity assets within a reasonable limit. This helps banks to have more stable and flexible capital to satisfy the demand of timely payment at the lowest cost. Finally, bank managers and research staff should regularly monitor the evolution of macro factors, especially the trend of inflation to have policies and solutions to respond in time.

REFERENCES

Acharya, V. V., Hasan, I., & Saunders, A. (2006). Should Banks Be Diversified? Evidence from Individual Bank Loan Portfolios. *The Journal of Business*, *79*(3), 1355–1412. doi:10.1086/500679

Albertazzi, U., & Gambacorta, L. (2009). Bank profitability and the business cycle. *Journal of Financial Stability*, *5*(4), 393–409. doi:10.1016/j.jfs.2008.10.002

Alexiou, C., & Sofoklis, V. (2009). Determinants of bank profitability: Evidence from the Greek banking sector. *Economic Annals*, *54*(182), 93-118.

Amador, J. S., Gómez-González, J. E., & Pabón, A. M. (2013). Loan growth and bank risk: New evidence. *Financial Markets and Portfolio Management*, *27*(4), 365–379. doi:10.100711408-013-0217-6

Baele, L., De Jonghe, O., & Vander Vennet, R. (2007). Does the stock market value bank diversification? *Journal of Banking & Finance*, *31*(7), 1999–2023. doi:10.1016/j.jbankfin.2006.08.003

Bebczuk, R., & Galindo, A. (2008). Financial crisis and sectoral diversification of Argentine banks, 1999–2004. *Applied Financial Economics*, *18*(3), 199–211. doi:10.1080/09603100601018773

Behr, A., Kamp, A., Memmel, C., & Pfingsten, A. (2007). *Diversification and the banks' risk-return-characteristics: evidence from loan portfolios of German banks* (No. 2007, 05). Discussion Paper, Series 2: Banking and Financial Supervision.

Berger, A. N., Hasan, I., & Zhou, M. (2010). The effects of focus versus diversification on bank performance: Evidence from Chinese banks. *Journal of Banking & Finance*, *34*(7), 1417–1435. doi:10.1016/j.jbankfin.2010.01.010

Bordeleau, É., & Graham, C. (2010). *The impact of liquidity on bank profitability* (No. 2010, 38). Bank of Canada Working Paper.

Chen, S., & Chang, C. P. (2015). Should bank loan portfolio be diversified under government capital injection and deposit insurance fund protection? *International Review of Economics & Finance*, *38*, 131–141. doi:10.1016/j.iref.2015.02.017

Claeys, S., & Vander Vennet, R. (2008). Determinants of bank interest margins in Central and Eastern Europe: A comparison with the West. *Economic Systems*, *32*(2), 197–216. doi:10.1016/j.ecosys.2007.04.001

Demirgüç-Kunt, A., & Huizinga, H. (1999). Determinants of commercial bank interest margins and profitability: Some international evidence. *The World Bank Economic Review*, *13*(2), 379–408. doi:10.1093/wber/13.2.379

Denis, D. J., Denis, D. K., & Sarin, A. (1997). Agency problems, equity ownership, and corporate diversification. *The Journal of Finance*, *52*(1), 135–160. doi:10.1111/j.1540-6261.1997.tb03811.x

Diamond, D. W. (1984). Financial intermediation and delegated monitoring. *The Review of Economic Studies*, *51*(3), 393–414. doi:10.2307/2297430

Elsas, R., Hackethal, A., & Holzhäuser, M. (2010). The anatomy of bank diversification. *Journal of Banking & Finance*, *34*(6), 1274–1287. doi:10.1016/j.jbankfin.2009.11.024

Gambacorta, L., & Mistrulli, P. E. (2004). Does bank capital affect lending behavior? *Journal of Financial Intermediation*, *13*(4), 436–457. doi:10.1016/j.jfi.2004.06.001

García-Herrero, A., Gavilá, S., & Santabárbara, D. (2009). What explains the low profitability of Chinese banks? *Journal of Banking & Finance*, *33*(11), 2080–2092. doi:10.1016/j.jbankfin.2009.05.005

Gujarati, D. N. (2004). *Basic Econometrics* (4th ed.). McGraw - Hill Irwin.

Hayden, E., Porath, D., & Westernhagen, N. V. (2007). Does diversification improve the performance of German banks? Evidence from individual bank loan portfolios. *Journal of Financial Services Research*, *32*(3), 123–140. doi:10.100710693-007-0017-0

Jensen, M. C. (1986). Agency cost of free cash flow, corporate finance, and takeovers. *Corporate Finance and Takeovers. The American Economic Review*, *76*(2).

Kenjegalieva, K. A., & Simper, R. (2011). A productivity analysis of Central and Eastern European banking taking into account risk decomposition and environmental variables. *Research in International Business and Finance*, *25*(1), 26–38. doi:10.1016/j.ribaf.2010.05.003

Mercieca, S., Schaeck, K., & Wolfe, S. (2007). Small European banks: Benefits from diversification? *Journal of Banking & Finance*, *31*(7), 1975–1998. doi:10.1016/j.jbankfin.2007.01.004

Molyneux, P., & Thornton, J. (1992). Determinants of European bank profitability: A note. *Journal of Banking & Finance*, *16*(6), 1173–1178. doi:10.1016/0378-4266(92)90065-8

Norden, L., & Szerencses, M. (2005). *Migration and concentration risks in bank lending: new evidence from credit portfolio data*. Mannheim: Department of Banking and Finance, University of Mannheim.

Pasiouras, F., & Kosmidou, K. (2007). Factors influencing the profitability of domestic and foreign commercial banks in the European Union. *Research in International Business and Finance*, *21*(2), 222–237. doi:10.1016/j.ribaf.2006.03.007

Perry, P. (1992). Do banks gain or lose from inflation? *Journal of Retail Banking*, *14*(2), 25–31.

Rossi, S. P., Schwaiger, M. S., & Winkler, G. (2009). How loan portfolio diversification affects risk, efficiency and capitalization: A managerial behavior model for Austrian banks. *Journal of Banking & Finance*, *33*(12), 2218–2226. doi:10.1016/j.jbankfin.2009.05.022

Samad, A., & Hassan, M. K. (1999). The performance of Malaysian Islamic bank during 1984-1997: An exploratory study. *International Journal of Islamic Financial Services*, *1*(3), 1–14.

Tabak, B. M., Fazio, D. M., & Cajueiro, D. O. (2011). The effects of loan portfolio concentration on Brazilian banks' return and risk. *Journal of Banking & Finance, 35*(11), 3065–3076. doi:10.1016/j.jbankfin.2011.04.006

Trujillo-Ponce, A. (2013). What determines the profitability of banks? Evidence from Spain. *Accounting and Finance, 53*(2), 561–586. doi:10.1111/j.1467-629X.2011.00466.x

Winton, A. (1999). *Don't put all your eggs in one basket? Diversification and specialization in lending*. Diversification and Specialization in Lending.

Chapter 13
System Dynamics Modelling for Policy Design:
A Case Study in Turkey

Arzu Eren Şenaras
https://orcid.org/0000-0002-3862-4551
Uludag University, Turkey

Hayrettin Kemal Sezen
Altınbaş University, Turkey

ABSTRACT

The system dynamics model was developed in the Vensim software. The model was developed based on the Yamaguchi study. The construct and behavioral validity of the model were addressed. Construct validity means that the correlations that construct the model, that is, the "rationale" of the model, are consistent with the correlations in the real system. There were five sub-models in the model. These were manufacturers and consumers sub-model, banks sub-model, central bank sub-model, balance of payments sub-model, exchange rate market sub-model. Five sub models included in the model developed with the VENSIM software are included in the appendices.

DOI: 10.4018/978-1-5225-9607-3.ch013

INTRODUCTION

System dynamics deals with how things change over time. Almost all are interested in how the past formed the present moment and how today's actions determine the future (Forrester, 1995: 16).

The concept of dynamics indicates change over time. If something is dynamic, it changes constantly. Therefore, a dynamic system is a system in which there are interactions that promote change over time. System dynamics approach is a method used to understand how the system changes over time. The elements and variables that constitute a system that changes in time are expressed as the system behavior. The aim is to understand the basic behavior system of the variables, to discover the factors that cause this mode of behavior and to improve the system behavior. Thus, it could be argued that system dynamics is a method to explain how the systems change with time. In dynamic systems, variables influence each other simultaneously (Barlas, 2005a; Ayanoğlu & Gökçe, 2007).

Dynamic complexity arises from connections and disconnections that link social and business systems. When a change occurs in one part of the system, it causes change in another part later (sooner or later). These effects could not always be observed clearly, usually they are beyond expectations (Morecroft, 2015: 21).

A BRIEF LITERATURE REVIEW

In this section, the studies conducted with system dynamic approach in the fields of economics and finance are briefly discussed.

Kameyama et al. (1997) utilized system dynamics approach to construct a national model in their study. As a result, the entire economy could be scrutinized. Although the system dynamics is one of the most useful tools available to investigate socioeconomic phenomena, it was rarely used by the policy makers. The aim of the constructed SD model was to close this gap.

Kameyama et al. (1999) investigated how the decisions made by the government and local governments affected the economy using the national accounting model they designed in their study.

Kameyama et al. (2001) reported that economic growth is closely associated with the growth of small businesses and all competitive large corporation of today once was a smaş-ll business and small businesses play a significant role in the reduction of unemployment. Thus, small businesses are important for macroeconomics. To examine the effectiveness of the support and incentives provided for small businesses, Kameyama et al. developed the SD model. Thus, they explored the long-term effects of policies, demonstrating the possibility of producing different solutions.

Kameyama et al. (2002) examined the impact of the finance sector on small businesses and its contribution to economic growth. Their model demonstrated that financial support for small businesses had a positive impact on economic growth in the long term.

Öner, Soydan and Çelebi (2003) have constructed a macro model for the Turkish economy with system dynamics method in the study they conducted. They developed a system dynamics model to examine what kind of a macroeconomic change could be experienced with which decisions until 2023 based on competitiveness, Central Bank foreign exchange reserves, national credibility, foreign investments, unemployment and economic mobility level variables.

Dwenger and Pavlov (2008) investigated the effect of speculative trading on foreign exchange markets in their study. The System Dynamics model that they developed could be used to analyze the role of speculation in foreign currency markets.

Öğüt and Şahin (2012) examined the effectiveness of policy instruments used by central banks in developing countries on financial stability based on external and internal conditions, using the system dynamics method.

Kim (1999) argued that the shortcomings of political and economic decision-makers emerge in these complex and dynamic systems when interpreting the feedback and cyclical relationships and inferring their consequences.

In a study by Lastunen (2014), new alternatives were proposed by measuring the effectiveness of post-2008 economic policies in Greece. In this study, Greek macroeconomic model was constructed and different scenarios were tested. The study argued that economic growth, a decrease in unemployment and a decrease in budget deficit would be achieved if the government postpones or cancels the austerity measures.

In a study, Utama (2014) demonstrated how a stock flow model simplified by a pedagogical and didactic approach using stocks and flows for post-Keynesian economic analysis could reflect the system dynamics model.

Yamaguchi (2001) combined economic growth with the ecological model. He demonstrated that in the long run, ecological sustainability would not be possible due to current economic growth and non-renewable resources. In another study by Yamaguchi (2003), he discussed the system dynamics approach for financial analysis of businesses and its applicability in the accounting system. After this study, Yamaguchi analyzed the macroeconomics using the system dynamics approach and after presenting a series of articles in the System Dynamics Conference, he collected his work in the book titled "Money and Macroeconomic Dynamics". In his study titled "Money Supply and Creation of Deposits" published in 2004, he reviewed formation of the Gross National Income in generation of money supply and deposits with the perspective of system dynamics. In his 2005 study titled "Total demand balance and price elasticity", he observed savings, deposits, government debt and securities and examined the gross domestic product, interest rates and price levels. By adding the price levels to the model, he analyzed market price formation, aggregate demand and enterprise capacity utilization rates. In his study, Yamaguchi (2006) combined financial and real sectors utilized in his first two studies and examined the labor market by adding population variable to the model. Balanced growth, business cycles and government debt were scrutinized. Yamaguchi studied the dynamic structure of the exchange rate balance in open market economy in 2007. The significance of that study was his pioneering work in implementing system dynamics in the international economy. Yamaguchi has combined his studies conducted in 2006 and 2007 in his article published in 2008 to obtain an open-macroeconomic model. In the study Yamaguchi conducted in 2009, he analyzed price formation based on the neoclassical economics, price formation in the real market and their basic differences, namely the concepts of rational time and real time and demonstrated that system dynamics could simulate the price mechanism that reflects the real market.

Arto et al. (2014) examined the impact of economic relations on sustainable financial policy in a two-country model. In this study, the relationship between economic growth and consumer debt was analyzed within the framework of financial policy.

Quiroga and Franco (2014) studied social and economic change in Myanmar in their study. The civil government that took the government when Myanmar was liberated from the military dictatorship wanted to open the country to the and to break free of the isolation resulting from the political and economic sanctions imposed by the Western countries for a long time. In this context, the system dynamics studies conducted by the commission mandated by the government and the results were analyzed. They concluded that the ageing population of the country, lack of educational investments, insufficient qualified workforce and highly mechanized large farms attracting the investments caused the reduction of the wages.

Oet and Pavlov (2014) studied dynamic feedback mechanisms during financial crises in their study. Several financial elements react with a delayed response to a variety of shocks. In this study, dynamic interaction in financial crises and these elements acting as shock absorbers and shock boosters was investigated.

Tasrif (2014) examined the correlation between economic growth and technological development with the system dynamics approach. In the model developed in this study, the effect of technological change on economic growth was based on macro and microeconomic theories. Thus, the study aimed to give ideas on technological policies to developing nations.

SD MODEL

The system dynamics model was developed in the Vensim software. The model was developed based on the Yamaguchi (2013) study. The construct and behavioral validity of the model were addressed. Construct validity means that the correlations that construct the model, that is, the "rationale" of the model, are consistent with the correlations in the real system. Such validity gradually evolves over a long process, from the initial phase of the model construction to the conclusion of the model. The construct validity of the developed exchange rate behavior model was also developed step by step and reached a satisfactory state. Construct validity was achieved within the framework of consistency with the economic literature. Furthermore, the unit consistency of the equations used in the model was tested. No inconsistency was found in the equations.

There were five sub-models in the model. These were manufacturers and consumers sub-model, banks sub-model, central bank sub-model, balance of payments sub-model, exchange rate market sub-model. Five sub models included in the model developed with the VENSIM software are included in the appendices.

The system dynamics model was developed in the Vensim software. The model was developed based on the Yamaguchi (2013) study. The construct and behavioral validity of the model were addressed. Construct validity means that the correlations that construct the model, that is, the "rationale" of the model, are consistent with the correlations in the real system. Such validity gradually evolves over a long process, from the initial phase of the model construction to the conclusion of the model. The construct validity of the developed exchange rate behavior model was also developed step by step and reached a satisfactory state. Construct validity was achieved within the framework of consistency with the economic literature. Furthermore, the unit consistency of the equations used in the model was tested. No inconsistency was found in the equations.

Outlier test was conducted in the study. The responses of the model to extreme values given to various parameters were examined. For example, values such as exports, imports, capital flow, etc. were assigned extreme values and the reactions of the model were examined.

In System Dynamics, it is very important to emphasize sample estimation (period, frequency, trend wave size, etc.) instead of point estimation. This is a logical consequence of the long-term tendency of system dynamics models (Barlas, 1996: 193).

The Model in Depth

There are five sub-models in the model. These are manufacturers and consumers sub-model, banks sub-model, central bank sub-model, balance of payments sub-model and exchange rate market sub-model.

Manufacturers and Consumers Sub-Model

The manufacturers and consumers sub-model in the developed model with Vensim software is presented.

Banks Sub-Model

Savings and commercial banks constitute the most powerful and common fund transfer channel in Turkish financial system (Şahin, 2014: 510).

Central Bank Sub-Model

The main function of the financial system in the economy is to mediate fund transfers. The role of the CBRT in the financial system is very significant. The CBRT influences the size of financial assets with its monetary policy tools and guides the function of the system. It is at the center of the financial system, it is the bank of banks and the last lender (Sahin, 2014: 533).

The Central Bank is basically responsible for regulating the monetary and exchange rate policies and circulation of money. Its mandate includes ensuring price stability was well as the financial stability and taking regulatory measures in monetary and foreign exchange markets. Determining the exchange rate regime to be implemented in Turkey together with the government is one of the central duties of the Central Bank. The application of the determined exchange rate regime also falls on the central bank. Since 2001, the Central Bank has been maintaining the exchange rate policy within the floating exchange rate regime. The central bank is responsible for storing and managing Turkish gold and foreign exchange reserves. The Central Bank keeps the reserves to ensure confidence in monetary and exchange rate policies and support these policies, to maintain the foreign exchange liquidity required by the Treasury to provide domestic and international foreign currency debt service, to reduce susceptibility against internal and external shocks, and to increase confidence in the country's economy in international markets. The Central Bank prioritizes the domestic interests in the administration of the reserves. The healthy, safe, risk-free and rapid operation of payment systems is among the duties of the Central Bank (CBRT).

In the central bank sub-model, while central bank foreign currency reserves increase with foreign currency purchases, it decreases with foreign currency sales. However, the Central Bank Reserve does not change. Because, against the foreign currency sales or purchases, the corresponding deposits are debited or credited to the cash account. The only variation is the increase and decrease in deposits and foreign currency in the market.

Balance of Payments Sub-Model

Balance of International Payments is a table that includes the international revenues and international payments of a country within a period of time (usually a year). A deficit in balance of international payments suggests a deterioration in the solvency of the country and the currency of the said country devaluates against foreign currencies. Balance of international payments is a determinant of monetary, fiscal and foreign trade policies that would be adopted in a country.

The receivables (positive, active) in the balance of international payments include the transactions that result in a receivable from the foreign parties. In the liability (passive, negative) section in the balance of international payments, transactions that require a payment to the foreign parties are included.

The economic relations of the country with other nations are categorized under three main groups. These are (Dinler, 2014: 589-590);

- Current accounts
- Capital and fiscal accounts
- Reserve movements

The figures in the balance of payments are related to a fiscal year, hence all the concepts are flow values. However, the concepts related to the international investment position are stock values (Seyidoğlu, 2013: 355).

Exchange Rate Market Sub-Model

The national currencies are converted in the foreign exchange market. In this market, those who demand foreign exchange and supply foreign exchange meet to create a foreign exchange price, called the foreign exchange rate. The foreign exchange market is almost a perfect competition market. In this market, goods are homogeneous, communication is full, input and entry and exit are free and there are numerous buyers and sellers.

In the foreign exchange rate model, the supply in foreign exchange is based on the value determined by the demand.

Figure 1, which shows supply and demand, describes the mechanism of formation of the market price. The price is depicted on the vertical axis and the quantity on the horizontal axis. Demand is a curve that decreases with price, while supply increases with price. Market equilibrium is the point where supply and demand curves intersect, and the corresponding price is the market price.

If the market price is higher than the equilibrium price, there is excess supply in the market. Unsold amounts increase inventory and the price attempts to decrease to attract the demand by consumers. On the other hand, if the price is below the equilibrium price, the supply shortage causes the demand surplus to increase. In both cases, the price reaches the equilibrium price at the end. Adam Smith stated that the price reaches the equilibrium price by an invisible hand. This is the price adjustment mechanism (Yamaguchi, 2013: 60).

The formation of the price as a result of supply-demand relationship is not only valid for the commodities and services market, but also for all other markets. The wage in the labor market is determined with this mechanism, the interest in the financial sector is determined the same way, and the exchange rate in the foreign exchange market is determined with this method.

Let D(P) represent the price function of demand and S (P) represent the price function of supply. The P * value that provides D (P *) = S (P *) is the equilibrium market price.

Mathematically,

$$\frac{dp(t)}{dt} = f(D(p) - S(p), \lambda) \tag{1}$$

Figure 1. Price formation mechanism
(Source: Yamaguchi, 2013: 60)

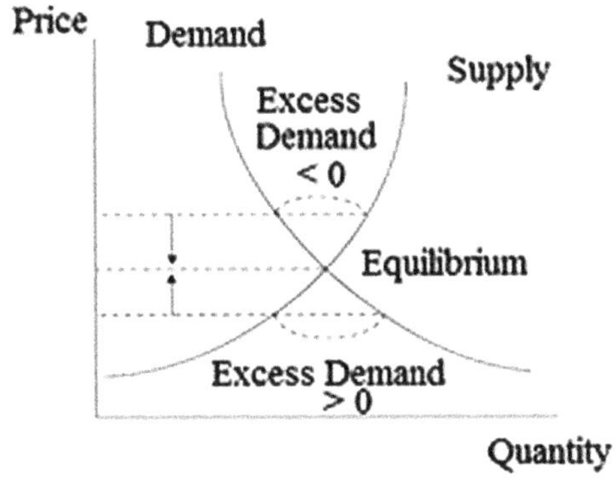

where f is the demand surplus function and λ is the correction coefficient. In the model given in Figure 2 demand surplus function could be written as follows:

$$f = \lambda \frac{D(p) - S(p)}{D(p) + S(p)} p \quad (2)$$

Selection of λ correction coefficient is important. For certain λ values cause chaos in the system and could not reach the equilibrium.

In Figure 2, $\lambda = 0.4$. In the above model, the inventory amount was not considered, which is a shortcoming. Because it was accepted that increase in inventory suppressed the prices. The following situation is achieved by adding the inventory to the model. Especially in non-equilibrium situations, calculations are performed with this method. It is impossible to obtain a P * (market equilibrium) value where there is no equilibrium without any apparent problems in the first construct (in cases such as chaos), whereas the inventory could be determined for all instances in the following case:

Another achievement here is the fact that another mechanism may be used instead of the demand surplus. This is achieved by keeping the inventory at the desired inventory level. The market price can be determined by dividing the current inventory level by the desired inventory quantity (Yamaguchi, 2013: 59-69).

Foreign currency supply includes exports, foreign investment revenues, foreign investments and foreign exchange sales by the central bank. Foreign exchange supply

Figure 2. Access equilibrium of market price (λ = 0,4)
(Source: Yamaguchi, 2013: 66)

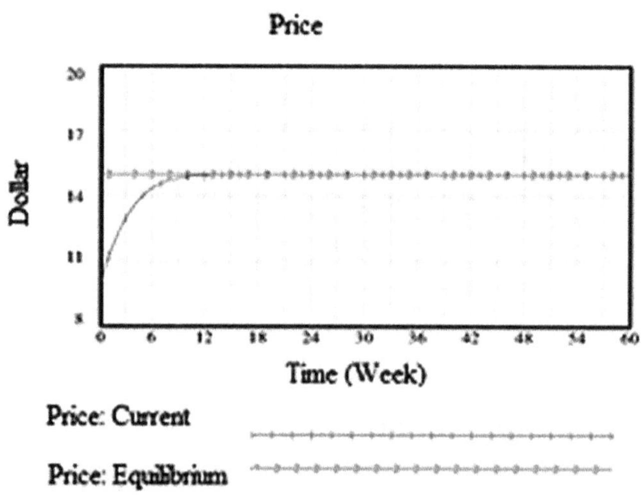

and exchange rate have a positive correlation. Thus, if the exchange rate increases, the value of export goods abroad would fall and as a result, exports would increase. A country's foreign currency demand is its demand on foreign currencies due to the payments that the country would make to foreign countries. Foreign exchange demand is the total of foreign investments, imports, foreign investment revenues and the foreign currency purchases by the central bank. Foreign currency demand and foreign exchange rate have a negative correlation. If the exchange rate increases, the foreign currency demand decreases (Dinler, 2014: 598-601).

Net exchange demand could be expressed as follows:

Net Foreign Currency Demand = Imports - Exports + International Investments

- Foreign Investments + Foreign Investment Revenues - International Investment Revenues

+ Foreign Currency Purchases - Foreign Currency Sales

Net Foreign Currency Demand = - Trading Equilibrium - Net Capital Flow - Net Investment Revenue + Net foreign currency purchases by the Central Bank (Central Bank intervention)

The exchange rate is obtained by the division of foreign exchange supply by foreign exchange demand. The revised exchange rate is added to the model to prevent excessive exchange rates, preventing the exchange rate to be less than 0.7 and over 5.5 (These values can be further reduced by testing the outliers).

Findings

One of the oldest and most widely used foreign trade policy tools is customs duties. These taxes are collected by the state during the entrance of imported goods through the country borders. A tariff means a list of tax rates to be applied to various goods. The unilateral tariffs implemented by countries are called autonomous or legal tariffs. Countries could apply lower tariffs to goods they import from each other in certain instances due to mutual treaties, thus the lower tariffs that are implemented with this method are called preferential tariffs. On the other hand, countries that participate in a customs union or free trade zone also implement zero tariffs on trade between the members. Although tariffs are generally implemented for imported goods, exports could be taxed as well. The fact that a country could apply different tariffs to the goods imported from countries with mutual agreements and to those imported from other countries means that the tariffs could vary geographically.

Increasing tariffs could be challenging due to the WTO (World Trade Organization), but other ways could be found to lower the imports.

The general objective of tariffs is to generate revenues for the treasury and to protect domestic manufacturers against the competition from foreign manufacturers. Customs tariffs help to protect domestic producers from foreign competition by increasing the domestic prices of imported goods.

In order to examine customs duties in more detail, it would be useful to examine the chart, The Developments in the Collection of General Budget Tax Revenues published by the Chair of Revenues. Thus, we could predict tax revenues better.

Tax revenues could be classified as follows:

Incomes are taxed with income and corporate taxes. 31% of all collected taxes are income and corporate taxes. The second category includes the taxes collected based on wealth. Inheritance and motor vehicles tax are included in this segment and on average constitute 2% of all tax revenues. The third category is the taxes collected on the goods and services that constitute close to the half of all tax revenues. This category includes value added tax, vehicle purchase tax, excise duties, bank and insurance transaction taxes, stamp duty, special communication tax and gambling tax. This is the largest section of all tax revenues. The next category is the taxes levied on foreign trade. This category, which includes customs duties, value added tax on imports and other foreign trade taxes, accounts for 18% of all tax revenues. The last category is the remnants of the revoked taxes and consists the lowest percentage in tax revenues.

On average, about 13% of the actual imports for the relevant year are obtained through the taxes levied on foreign trade. The tax revenues obtained with the model are presented in Figure 3.

Figure 3. Tax revenues obtained with the model

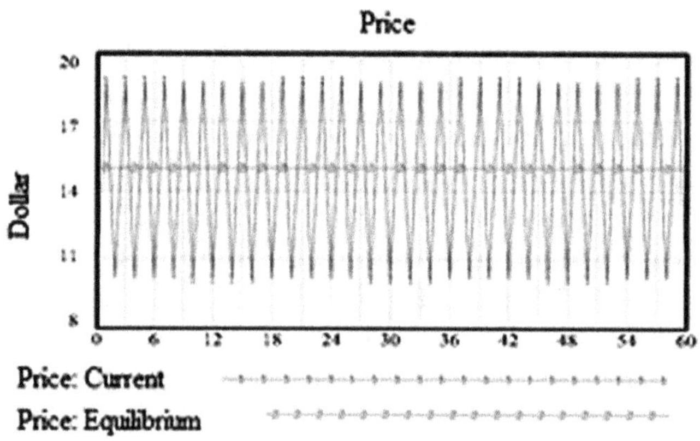

The tax revenues obtained with the model and realized are presented in Figure 4,5 and 6.

CONCLUSION

The fact that the macroeconomic structure includes several variables with complex mutual relationships and these variables function with feedback cycles reveals the dynamic structure of the system. This dynamic structure, which includes feedback cycles, also contains latency. In this context, the most adequate method to examine macroeconomic behavior would be the System Dynamics approach. Given its dynamic nature, mathematical models would be insufficient for the number of variables that are used to define the system. Furthermore, the dynamic structure resulting from

Figure 4. Taxes excluding taxes from foreign trade

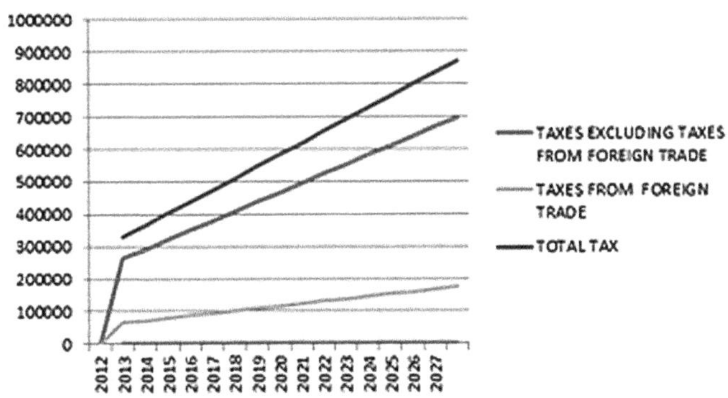

Figure 5. Taxes from foreign trade

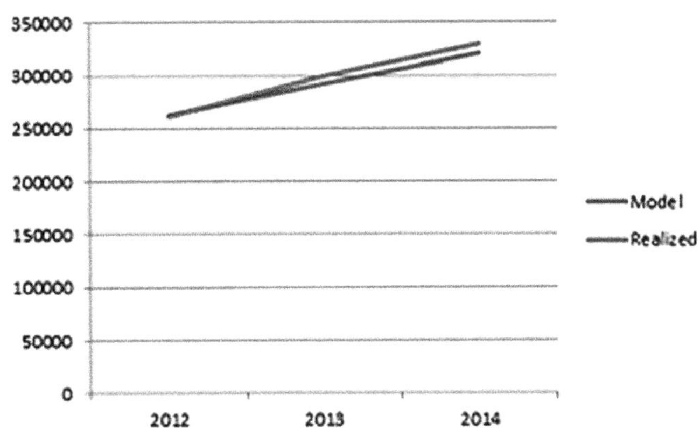

Figure 6. Total taxes

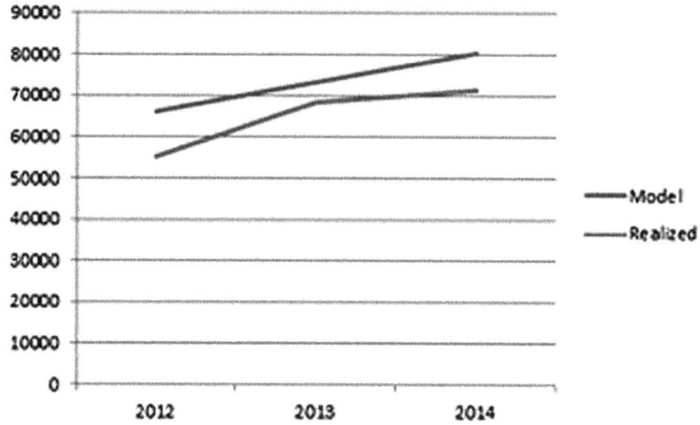

the interaction of these variables would be ignored. The system dynamics approach could have several contributions to macroeconomics. Examination of macroeconomic variables with flows and inventory, which are the basic concepts of system dynamics, would facilitate the analysis.

The macroeconomic structure was scrutinized with a holistic approach in the study. It was assumed that the developed model was an open macroeconomic structure where goods, services and capital moved freely. It was accepted that there were five industries in the economy. These were the central bank, commercial banks, consumers, manufacturers and the government.

The model developed with the VENSIM software included five sub-models. These were manufacturers and consumers sub-model, banks sub-model, central bank sub-model, balance of payments sub-model, exchange rate market sub-model. Thanks to the developed model, it was possible to examine the effects of different policies on the tax system. Effective policies could be designed by testing different scenarios. The impact of changes in macroeconomic variables on tax revenues could be examined.

REFERENCES

Abdelbari, E., & Shafi. (2015). Model Learning Using Genetic Programming Under Full And Partial System Information Conditions. *33rd International Conference of the System Dynamics Society*, Cambridge, MA.

Arto, B., & Hu, L., & Pickl. (2014). Inclusive Growth And Sustainable Finance In Connected National Economies. *Proceedings of the 32nd International Conference of the System Dynamics Society*.

Ayanoğlu, M., & Gökçe, M. (2007). Sistem Düşüncesinden Sistem Dinamiklerine. *Makine Teknolojileri Elektronik Dergisi*, (3), 29-41.

Barlas. (2005a). Dinamik Sistem Yaklaşımı: Modeller, Kurumsal Öğrenme Ve Sorun Çözme – I. *Endüstri Ve Otomasyon Dergisi,* (94).

Barlas. (2005b). Dinamik Sistem Yaklaşımı: Modeller, Kurumsal Öğrenme Ve Sorun Çözme - II. *Endüstri Ve Otomasyon Dergisi*, (95).

Başkaya. (1997). *Sistem Dinamiğinin İşletmelerde Uygulanması*. Bursa: Ekin Kitabevi Yayınları.

Campuzano, F., & Mula, J. (2011). *Supply Chain Simulation*. London: Springer-Verlag. doi:10.1007/978-0-85729-719-8

Coyle. (1996). *Systems Dynamics Modeling*. Chapman & Hall.

Dağli, H. (2005). İçme suyu kalitesi ve insan sağlığına etkileri. *Bizim İller. İller Bankası Aylık Yayın Organı*, *3*, 16–21.

Dinler. (2014). *İktisada Giriş*. Ekin Basım Yayın Dağıtım, Bursa.

Dwenger & Pavlov. (2008). *Feedback Analysis Of Speculation In A Foreign Currency Market*. The International Conference Of The System Dynamics Society, Athens, Greece.

Erkut. (1983). *Sistem Dinamiğinin Temelleri*. İTÜ Fen Edebiyat Fakültesi Ofset Atölyesi, İstanbul.

Erkut. (1995). *Sistem Yönetimi Yönetim Bilimleri Dizisi: 4*. İrfan Yayınları, İstanbul.

Ford, A. (1999). *Modeling the Environment: An Introduction to System Dynamics Modeling of Environmental Systems*. Washington, DC: Island Press.

Forrester. (1962). *Industrial Dynamics*. Waltham, MA: Pegasus Communications.

Forrester. (1969). *Urban Dynamics*. Cambridge, MA: The MIT Press.

Forrester. (1995). *Road Map 1: Counterintuitive Behaviour Of Social Systems*. MIT System Dynamics In Education Project.

Forrester. (2007a). System Dynamics: A Personal View Of The First Fifty Years. *System Dynamics Review, 23*, 345–358.

Herrera. (2014). *Integrating System Dynamics With Traditional Management Tools: A Case Study In The Apparel Industry*. 32nd International Conference of the System Dynamics Society, Delft, Netherlands.

Hesan, G., & Dignum. (2014). Using Diference Equation to Model Discrete-time Behavior in System Dynamics Modeling. *32nd International Conference of the System Dynamics Society*, Delft, Netherlands.

Kameyama, S. (1997). *A Study Of SD National Model Based On Revised SNA - Conceptual, Institutional And Operational*. 15th International System Dynamics Conference: "Systems Approach To Learning And Education İnto The 21st Century", Istanbul, Turkey.

Kameyama, S. (1999). *Government Reform İn Japan- An Application Of SD National Model Based On SNA*. 17th International Conference Of The System Dynamics Society And 5th Australian & New Zealand Systems Conference, Wellington, New Zealand.

Kameyama, S. (2001). *Model For SME Sector Development*. The 19th International Conference Of The System Dynamics Society, Atlanta, GA.

Kameyama, S. (2002). Micro-Macro Finance Structure Modeling. *20th International Conference Of The System Dynamics Society*, Palermo, Italy.

Kim. (1999). System Thinking In The Management Of Korean Economic Crisis. *Proceedings Of The 17th International System Dynamics Conference*.

Kirkwood. (1998). *System Dynamics Methods: A Quick Introduction*. College Of Business Arizona State University.

Lane & Sterman. (2011). Profiles in Operations Research: Jay Wright Forrester. In *Profiles in Operations Research: Pioners and Innovators*. New York: Springer. Retrieved from http://jsterman.scripts.mit.edu/docs/Lane2011%20Profiles%20in%20Operations%20Research.pdf

Lastunen, J. (2014). Macroeconomic Dynamics Of Greece İn The Midst Of The Eurozone Crisis – Application Of SD Modeling And Insights For Policy. *Proceedings Of The 32nd International Conference Of The System Dynamics Society.*

Maani & Cavana. (2007). *Systems Thinking And Modelling Understanding Change and Complexity*. Pearson Education.

Martin, L. A. (1997a). *Road Map 2: The First Step*. MIT System Dynamics in Education Project. Retrieved from http://sysdyn.clexchange.org/sdep/Roadmaps/RM2/D- 4694.pdf

Martin, L. A. (1997b). *Road Map 2: An Introduction To Feedback*. MIT System Dynamics In Education Project. Retrieved from http://static.clexchange.org/ftp/documents/roadmaps/RM2/D-4691.pdf

McGarvey & Hannon. (2003). *Dynamic Modelling For Business Management An Introduction*. Springer Press.

Morecroft, J. D. W., & Sterman, J. D. (1994). *Modelling For Learning Organizations*. Portland, OR: Productivity Press.

Morecroft. (2015). *Strategic Modelling And Business Dynamics:A Feedback Systems Approach*. John Wiley & Sons.

Oet & Pavlov. (2014). Feedback Mechanisms In The Financial System: A Modern View. *Proceedings Of The 32nd International Conference Of The System Dynamics Society.*

Öğüt & Şahin. (2012). *Türkiye'de Finansal İstikrar Sorununa Sistem Dinamiği Yaklaşımı*. Türkiye Ekonomi Kurumu.

Öner. (2003). *Dinamik Sistem Modelleme İle Makroekonomik Analiz: Türkiye İçin Bir Oyun Denemesi*. Çalışma Makalesi, Temmuz.

Özbayrak, M., Papadopoulou, T. C., & Akgun, M. (2007). System Dynamics Modelling of A Manufacturing Supply Chain System. *Simulation Modelling Practice and Theory*, *15*(10), 1338–1355. doi:10.1016/j.simpat.2007.09.007

Pidd. (1996). *Tools for Thinking Modelling in Management Science*. John Wiley & Sons.

Quiroga & Franco. (2014). Using System Dynamics to Analyze Social and Economic Challenges in Myanmar. *Proceedings of the 32nd International Conference of the System Dynamics Society.*

Radzicki, M. J. (2007). System Dynamics And Its Contribution To Economics And Economic Modeling. In Encyclopedia Of Complexity And System Science. Springer-Verlag.

Richardson. (1986). Problems With Causal-Loop Diagrams. *System Dynamics Review, 2*(2).

Richardson. (1999). *Feedback Throught in Social Science And Systems Theory*. Pegasus Communications, Inc.

Richmond, B. (2010). The Thinking In Systems Thinking: Eight Critical Skills. In Tracing Connections: Voices Of Systems Thinkers. Creative Learning Exchange.

Ruth & Hannon. (2012). *Modeling Dynamic Economic Systems* (2nd ed.). Springer.

Şahin. (2014). *Türkiye Ekonomisi Tarihsel Gelişimi- Bugunkü Durumu*. Bursa: Ezgi Kitabevi Yayınları.

Senge, Kleiner, Roberts, Ross, & Smith. (1994). *The Fifth Discipline Fieldbook*. Century.

Senge. (1990). *The Fifth Discipline: The Art And Practice Of The Learning Organization*. Random House.

Senge. (2002). Beşinci Disiplin, Çeviren: Ayşegül İldeniz Ve Ahmet Doğukan. *Yapı Kredi Yayınları, 16*.

Seyidoğlu. (2013). *Uluslararası İktisat*. İstanbul: Genişletilmiş Onaltıncı Baskı, Güzem CanYayınları.

Sezen & Günal. (2009). *Yöneylem Araştırmasında Benzetim*. Bursa: Ekin Yayınevi.

Sezen. (2007). *Yöneylem Araştırması*. Ekin Yayınevi, Bursa.

Soderquist, C., & Overakkers, S. (2010). Education for Sustainable Development: A Systems Thinking Approach. *Global Environmental Research, 14*, 193–202.

Sterman. (1991). *A Skeptic's Guide to Computer Models*. MIT System Dynamics In Education Project.

Sterman. (2000). *Business Dynamics Systems Thinking And Modelling In A Complex World*. McGraw-Hill.

Tang & Vijay. (2001). *System Dynamics Origins, Development And Future Prospects of a Method*. Research Seminar in Engineering Systems.

Tasrifi. (2014). System Dynamics Model Of Technology And Economic Growth: A Preliminary Study. *Proceedings Of The 32nd International Conference Of The System Dynamics Society.*

Temiz. (2008). *Türkiye'de Vergi Gelirleri ve Ekonomik Büyüme İlişkisi:1960-2006 Dönemi.* Ulusal İktisat Kongresi, İzmir.

Towil. (1996). Industrial Dynamics Modelling of Supply Chains. *Logistic Information Management, 9*(4), 43-56.

Utama, G. (2014). Old Wine İn A New Bottle: Towards A Common Language For Post-Keynesian Macroeconomics Model. *Proceedings Of The 32nd International Conference Of The System Dynamics Society.*

Vennix, J. M. (1995). Building Consensus In Strategic Decision Making: System Dynamics As A Group Support System. *Group Decision and Negotiation*, *4*(4), 335–355. doi:10.1007/BF01409778

Warren, K. (2005). Improving Strategic Management With The Fundamental Principles Of System Dynamics. *System Dynamics Review*, *21*(4), 329–350. doi:10.1002dr.325

Wheeler. (1994). *How to Get Managers To Use System Dynamics.* International System Dynamics Conference, Stirling, UK.

Wolstenholme, E. F. (1990). *Systems Enquiry: A System Dynamics Approach.* John Wiley & Sons.

Yamaguchi, K. (2001). A Step-By-Step System Dynamics Modeling Of Sustainability. *Journal Of Business Administration, Osaka Sangyo University*, *3*(1), 25–52.

Yamaguchi, K. (2003). Principle Of Accounting System Dynamics – Modeling Corporate Financial Statements. *Proceedings Of The 21st International Conference Of The System Dynamics Society.*

Yamaguchi, K. (2004). Money Supply And Creation Of Deposits: SD Macroeconomic Modeling (1). *Proceedings Of The 22nd International Conference Of The System Dynamics Society.*

Yamaguchi, K. (2005). Aggregate Demand Equilibria And Price Flexibility: Sd Macroeconomic Modeling (2). *Proceedings Of The 23nd International Conference Of The System Dynamics Society.*

Yamaguchi, K. (2006). Integration Of Real And Monetary Sectors With Labor Market: Sd Macroeconomic Modeling (3). *Proceedings Of The 24th International Conference Of The System Dynamics Society.*

Yamaguchi, K. (2007). Balance Of Payments And Foreign Exchange Dynamics: Sd Macroeconomic Modeling (4). *Proceedings Of The 25th International Conference Of The System Dynamics Society.*

Yamaguchi, K. (2008). *Open Macroeconomies As A Closed Economic System - SD Macroeconomic Modeling Completed.* International Conference Of The System Dynamics Society, Athens, Greece.

Yamaguchi, K. (2009). *Logical Vs Historical Time İn A Price Adjustment Mechanism.* International Conference Of The System Dynamics Society, Albuquerque, NM.

Yamaguchi. (2013). *Money and Macroeconomic Dynamics- Accounting System Dynamics Approach.* Awaji Island, Japan: Japan Future Research Center.

Zhu. (2001). *Beginner Modeling Exercises Section 3 Mental Simulation of Simple Negative Feedback.* MIT System Dynamics in Education Project.

Compilation of References

Abbott, L. J., Parker, S., & Peters, G. F. (2003). Audit committee characteristics and restatements: A study of the efficacy of certain Blue Ribbon Committee recommendations. *Auditing*, *23*(1), 69–87. doi:10.2308/aud.2004.23.1.69

Abbott, L. J., Park, Y., & Parker, S. (2000). The effects of audit committee activity and independence on corporate fraud. *Managerial Finance*, *26*(11), 55–67. doi:10.1108/03074350010766990

Abdallah, A. A.-N., & Ismail, A. K. (2017). Corporate governance practices, ownership structure, and corporate performance in the GCC countries. *Journal of International Financial Markets, Institutions and Money*, *46*, 98–115. doi:10.1016/j.intfin.2016.08.004

Abdelbari, E., & Shafi. (2015). Model Learning Using Genetic Programming Under Full And Partial System Information Conditions. *33rd International Conference of the System Dynamics Society*, Cambridge, MA.

Abdelghany, K. (2005). Measuring the Quality of Earnings. *Managerial Auditing Journal*, *20*(9), 1001–1015. doi:10.1108/02686900510625334

Acemoglu, D., Johnson, S., & Robinson, J. A. (2001). The colonial origins of comparative development: An empirical investigation. *The American Economic Review*, *91*(5), 1369–1401. doi:10.1257/aer.91.5.1369

Acharya, V. V., Hasan, I., & Saunders, A. (2006). Should Banks Be Diversified? Evidence from Individual Bank Loan Portfolios. *The Journal of Business*, *79*(3), 1355–1412. doi:10.1086/500679

Adams, R. B., & Mehran, H. (2012). Bank board structure and performance: Evidence for large bank holding companies. *Journal of Financial Intermediation*, *21*(2), 243–267. doi:10.1016/j.jfi.2011.09.002

Aebi, V., Sabato, G., & Schmid, M. (2012). Risk management, corporate governance, and bank performance in the financial crisis. *Journal of Banking & Finance*, *36*(12), 3213–3226. doi:10.1016/j.jbankfin.2011.10.020

Afrifa, G. A., & Tauringana, V. (2015). Corporate governance and performance of UK listed small and medium enterprises. *Corporate Governance*, *15*(5), 719–733. doi:10.1108/CG-03-2015-0029

Aggarwal, R. K., & Samwick, A. A. (1999). Executive compensation, strategic competition, and relative performance evaluation. *The Journal of Finance, 54*(6), 1999–2043. doi:10.1111/0022-1082.00180

Aggarwal, R., Bhagat, S., & Rangan, S. (2009). The impact of fundamentals on IPO valuation. *Financial Management, 38*(2), 253–284. doi:10.1111/j.1755-053X.2009.01035.x

Aggarwal, R., Erel, I., Ferreira, M., & Matos, P. (2011). Does governance travel around the world? Evidence from institutional investors. *Journal of Financial Economics, 100*(1), 154–181. doi:10.1016/j.jfineco.2010.10.018

Aggarwal, R., Prabhala, N. R., & Puri, M. (2002). Initial public offerings. *Journal of Management, 40*, 1066–1089.

Agoraki, M.-E. K., Delis, M. D., & Staikouras, P. K. (2010). The effect of board size and composition on bank efficiency. *International Journal of Banking, Accounting and Finance, 2*(4), 357–386. doi:10.1504/IJBAAF.2010.037155

Agrawal, A., & Knoeber, C. R. (1996). Firm performance and mechanisms to control agency problems between managers and shareholders. *Journal of Financial and Quantitative Analysis, 31*(3), 377–397. doi:10.2307/2331397

Aguilera, R. V., & Desender, K. A. (2012). Challenges in the measuring of comparative corporate governance: a review of the main indices. In West Meets East: Building Theoretical Bridges (pp. 289–322). Emerald Group Publishing Limited. doi:10.1108/S1479-8387(2012)0000008014

Aguilera, R. V., & Jackson, G. (2003). The cross-national diversity of corporate governance: Dimensions and determinants. *Academy of Management Review, 28*(3), 447–465. doi:10.5465/amr.2003.10196772

Agyei-Mensah, B. K., (2016b). Internal control information disclosure and corporate governance: evidence from an emerging market. *Corporate Governance: The International Journal of Business in Society, 16*(1), 79-95.

Agyei-Mensah, B. K. (2016a). Accountability and internal control in religious organisations: A study of Methodist church Ghana, *African Journal of Accounting. Auditing and Finance, 5*(2), 95–112.

Agyemang, O. S., Aboagye, E., Antwi, S., & Frimpong, J. (2014). Board of Directors and Firm Performance of Banking Institutions: A Ghanaian Experience. *European Journal of Economics, Finance and Administrative Sciences,* (67), 16.

Agyemang, O. S., & Castellini, M. (2015). Corporate governance in an emergent economy: A case of Ghana. *Corporate Governance, 15*(1), 52–84. doi:10.1108/CG-04-2013-0051

Agyemang, O. S., Gatsi, J. G., Ansong, A., & McMillan, D. (2018). Institutions structures and financial market development in Africa. *Cogent Economics & Finance, 6*(1), 1–15. doi:10.1080/23322039.2018.1488342

Agyemang, O. S., Kyeraa, M., Ansong, A., & Frimpong, S. (2017). Institutional structures and the strength of investor confidence in Africa. *International Journal of Law and Management, 59*(6), 899–915. doi:10.1108/IJLMA-03-2016-0033

Ahmed, K., Hossain, M., & Adams, M. B. (2006). The effects of board composition and board size on the informativeness of annual accounting earnings. *Corporate Governance, 14*(5), 418–431. doi:10.1111/j.1467-8683.2006.00515.x

Ajinkya, B., Bhojraj, S., & Sengupta, P. (2005). The association between outside directors, institutional investors and the properties of management earnings forecasts. *Journal of Accounting Research, 43*(3), 343–376. doi:10.1111/j.1475-679x.2005.00174.x

Aktan, B., Turen, S., Tvaronavičienė, M., Celik, S., & Alsadeh, H. (2018). Corporate governance and performance of the financial firms in Bahrain. *Polish Journal of Management Studies, 17.*

Al Daoud, K. A., Ismail, K. N. I. K., & Lode, N. A. (2015). The impact of internal corporate governance on the timeliness of financial reports of Jordanian firms: Evidence using audit and management report lags. *Mediterranean Journal of Social Sciences, 6*(1), 430.

Albertazzi, U., & Gambacorta, L. (2009). Bank profitability and the business cycle. *Journal of Financial Stability, 5*(4), 393–409. doi:10.1016/j.jfs.2008.10.002

Alchian, A. A., & Demsetz, H. (1972). Production, information cost, and economic organization. *The American Economic Review, 62*(5), 777–795.

Alexiou, C., & Sofoklis, V. (2009). Determinants of bank profitability: Evidence from the Greek banking sector. *Economic Annals, 54*(182), 93-118.

Al-Farah, A. (2001). *The effectiveness of audit committees in the Jordanian public shareholding companies: empirical study* (Unpublished Master dissertation). University of Jordan.

Alias, N., Yaacob, M., & Jaffar, N. (2017). Governance structure, corporate restructuring and performance. *Polish Journal of Management Studies, 15.*

Alimehmeti, G., & Paletta, A. (2012). Ownership concentration and effects over firm performance: Evidences from Italy. *European Scientific Journal, 8*(22).

Alix Valenti, M., Luce, R., & Mayfield, C. (2011). The effects of firm performance on corporate governance. *Management Research Review, 34*(3), 266–283. doi:10.1108/01409171111116295

Aljifri, K., & Hussainey, K. (2007). The determinants of forward-looking information in annual reports of UAE companies. *Managerial Auditing Journal, 22*(9), 881–894. doi:10.1108/02686900710829390

Alkhatib, K. (2014). The determinants of forward-looking information disclosure. *Procedia: Social and Behavioral Sciences, 109*, 858–864. doi:10.1016/j.sbspro.2013.12.554

Allam Mohammed Mousa, H., Sabri Maher Sabri, M., & Abd Almuttaleb Mohammed, A. (2013). The Audit Committee Characteristics and Earnings Quality: Evidence from Jordan. *Australasian Accounting Business & Finance Journal*, *7*(4), 51–80. doi:10.14453/aabfj.v7i4.5

Allen, F., & Faulhaber, G. (1989). Signaling by underpricing in the IPO market. *Journal of Financial Economics*, *23*(2), 303–324. doi:10.1016/0304-405X(89)90060-3

Al-Malkawi, H. A. N., Pillai, R., & Bhatti, M. I. (2014). Corporate governance practices in emerging markets: The case of GCC countries. *Economic Modelling*, *38*, 133–141. doi:10.1016/j.econmod.2013.12.019

Al-Matari, Y. A., Al-Swidi, A. K., Fadzil, F. H. B. F. H., & Al-Matari, E. M. (2012). Board of directors, audit committee characteristics and the performance of Saudi Arabia listed companies. *International Review of Management and Marketing*, *2*(4), 241–251.

Al-Najjar, B. (2013). The financial determinants of corporate cash holdings: Evidence from some emerging markets. *International Business Review*, *22*(1), 77–88. doi:10.1016/j.ibusrev.2012.02.004

Al-Najjar, B., & Belghitar, Y. (2011). Corporate cash holdings and dividend payments: Evidence from simultaneous analysis. *Managerial and Decision Economics*, *32*(4), 231–241. doi:10.1002/mde.1529

Alsaeed, K. (2006). The Association Between Firm-specific Characteristics and Disclosure. *Managerial Auditing Journal*, *21*(5), 476–496. doi:10.1108/02686900610667256

Al-Saidi, M. T., Al-Shammari, B. A., & Page, M. (2014). Corporate governance disclosure in Kuwait. *Arab Journal of Administrative Sciences*, *21*(1), 69–104.

Altamuro, J., & Beatty, A. (2006). *Do Internal Control Reforms Improve Earnings Quality?* Working Paper. Retrieved from www.ssrn.com

Al-Thuneibat, A. (2006). *Audit in the light of the international auditing standards and regulations and local laws: the theory and application* (1st ed.). Amman: Jordan University publications.

Altman, M. (2005). The ethical economy and competitive markets: Reconcilingaltruistic, moralistic, and ethical behaviour with the rational economic agent and competitive markets. *Journal of Economic Psychology*, *26*(5), 732–757. doi:10.1016/j.joep.2005.06.004

Alzoubi, E. S. S., & Selamat, M. H. (2012). The effectiveness of corporate governance mechanisms on constraining earnings management: Literature review and proposed framework. *International Journal of Global Business*, *5*(1), 17–35.

Amador, J. S., Gómez-González, J. E., & Pabón, A. M. (2013). Loan growth and bank risk: New evidence. *Financial Markets and Portfolio Management*, *27*(4), 365–379. doi:10.100711408-013-0217-6

Amaeshi, K., Adi, B. C., Ogechie, C., & Amao, O. O. (2006). Corporate SocialResponsibility in Nigeria: Indigenous practices or Western influences. *Journal of Corporate Citizenship*, *24*, 83–99. doi:10.9774/GLEAF.4700.2006.wi.00009

Amba, S. M. (2014). Corpoate governance and firms' financial performance. Journal academic and business. *Ethics*, *8*, 1–11.

Ameer, B (2013). Corporate governance – issues and challenges in Pikistan. *International Journal of Academic Research in Business and Social Sciences, 3*(4),79-96.

Ananthram, S., & Nankervis, A. R. (2014). Outcomes and Benefits of a Managerial Global Mind-set: An Exploratory Study with Senior Executives in North America and India. *Thunderbird International Business Review*, *56*(2), 193–209. doi:10.1002/tie.21611

Anderson, R. C., & Bizjak, J. M. (2003). An empirical examination of the role of the CEO and the compensation committee in structuring executive pay. *Journal of Banking & Finance*, *27*(7), 1323–1348. doi:10.1016/S0378-4266(02)00259-5

Anderson, R. C., Mansi, S. A., & Reeb, D. M. (2004). Board characteristics, accounting report integrity, and the cost of debt. *Journal of Accounting and Economics*, *37*(3), 315–342. doi:10.1016/j.jacceco.2004.01.004

Anderson, R. C., & Reeb, D. M. (2003). Founding-family ownership and firm performance: Evidence from the S&P 500. *The Journal of Finance*, *58*(3), 1301–1328. doi:10.1111/1540-6261.00567

Anderson, R. C., & Reeb, D. M. (2004). Board composition: Balancing family influence in S&P 500 firms. *Administrative Science Quarterly*, *49*, 209–237.

Andreou, P. C., Antoniou, C., Horton, J., & Louca, C. (2016). Corporate governance and firm-specific stock price crashes. *European Financial Management*, *22*(5), 916–956. doi:10.1111/eufm.12084

Andrews, K. R. (1981). Corporate strategy as a vital function of the board. *Harvard Business Review*, *59*(6), 174–184.

Aoki, M. (1984). *The cooperative game theory of the firm*. Oxford, UK: Oxford University press.

Aoki, M. (2000). *Information, corporate governance, and institutional diversity: Consequences in Japan, the USA, and the transnational economies*. Oxford, UK: Oxford University Press.

Aragón-Correa, J. A. (1998). Strategic Proactivity and Firm Approach to the Natural Environment. *Academy of Management Journal*, *41*, 556–567.

Ararat, M., Aksu, M. H., & Tansel Cetin, A. (2010). *The impact of board diversity on boards' monitoring intensity and firm performance: evidence from the Istanbul Stock Exchange*. Available at SSRN 1572283.

Ararat, M., & Orbay, H. (2006). Corporate governance in Turkey, implications for growth and investments. In *World Bank Investment Climate Assessment Report Survey for Turkey*. Washington, DC: World Bank Publications. doi:10.2139srn.2375767

Aras, G., & Crowther, D. (2008). Governance and sustainability: An investigation into the relationship between corporate governance and corporate sustainability. *Management Decision*, *46*(3), 433–448. doi:10.1108/00251740810863870

Arellano, M., & Bond, S. (1991). Some tests of specification for panel data: Monte Carlo evidence and an application to employment equations. *The Review of Economic Studies*, *58*(2), 277–297. doi:10.2307/2297968

Arellano, M., & Bover, O. (1995). Another look at the instrumental variable estimation of error-components models. *Journal of Econometrics*, *68*(1), 29–51. doi:10.1016/0304-4076(94)01642-D

Arens, A. A., Elder, R. J., & Beasley, M. S. (2009). *Auditing and Assurance Services: An Integrated Approach* (13th ed.). Prentice Hall.

Arto, B., & Hu, L., & Pickl. (2014). Inclusive Growth And Sustainable Finance In Connected National Economies. *Proceedings of the 32nd International Conference of the System Dynamics Society*.

Ashbaugh-Skaife, H., Collins, D., & Kinney, W. Jr. (2007). The discovery and reporting of internal control deficiencies prior to SOX-mandated audits. *Journal of Accounting and Economics, Vol.*, *44*(1-2), 166–192. doi:10.1016/j.jacceco.2006.10.001

Ayanoğlu, M., & Gökçe, M. (2007). Sistem Düşüncesinden Sistem Dinamiklerine. *Makine Teknolojileri Elektronik Dergisi*, (3), 29-41.

Aziz, M. A., & Dar, H. A. (2006). Predicting corporate financial Distress: Where we stand? Corporate governance. *The International Journal of Business in Society*, *6*(1), 18–33.

Azmat, F., & Ha, H. (2013). Corporate social responsibility, customer trust, and Loyalty—Perspectives from a developing country. *Thunderbird International Business Review*, *55*(3), 253–270. doi:10.1002/tie.21542

Baele, L., De Jonghe, O., & Vander Vennet, R. (2007). Does the stock market value bank diversification? *Journal of Banking & Finance*, *31*(7), 1999–2023. doi:10.1016/j.jbankfin.2006.08.003

Bahrain Bourse. (2013). *Annual Report*. Retrieved from http://www.bahrainbourse.com.bh/

Bahrain Code of Corporate Governance. (2010). Ministry of Commerce and Industry, Kingdom of Bahrain. Retrieved from http://www.moic.gov.bh/

Bahrain Code of Corporate Governance. (2010). Retrieved 14 October 2015, from http://www.moic.gov.bh/Ar/Pages/Home.aspxSmallBusiness-Chron.com

Baimwera, B., & Muriuki, A. M. (2014). Analysis of corporate financial distress determinants: A survey of non-financial firms listed in the NSE. *International Journal of Current Business and Social Sciences*, *1*(2), 58–80.

Balhaj, S. (2006). *Factors affecting the voluntary disclosure of a practical study on public companies* (Unpublished PhD dissertation). Arab Academy for Banking and Financial Sciences.

Balsam, S., Krishnan, J., & Yang, J. (2003). Auditor Industry Specialization and Earnings Quality. *Auditing*, *22*(2), 71–97. doi:10.2308/aud.2003.22.2.71

Barako, D. G., Hancock, P., & Izan, H. Y. (2006). Factors influencing voluntary corporate disclosure by Kenyan companies. *Corporate Governance*, *14*(2), 107–125. doi:10.1111/j.1467-8683.2006.00491.x

Barlas. (2005a). Dinamik Sistem Yaklaşımı: Modeller, Kurumsal Öğrenme Ve Sorun Çözme – I. *Endüstri Ve Otomasyon Dergisi*, (94).

Barlas. (2005b). Dinamik Sistem Yaklaşımı: Modeller, Kurumsal Öğrenme Ve Sorun Çözme - II. *Endüstri Ve Otomasyon Dergisi*, (95).

Barraquier, A. (2011). Ethical Behaviour in Practice: Decision Outcomes and Strategic Implications. *British Journal of Management*, *22*, 28–46. doi:10.1111/j.1467-8551.2010.00726.x

Barr, G., Gerson, J., & Kantor, B. (1997). Shareholders as agents and principals: The case for South Africa's corporate governance system. In D. H. Chew (Ed.), *Studies in international corporate finance and governance systems. A comparison of the U.S., Japan, & Europe* (pp. 297–310). Oxford, UK: Oxford University Press.

Basel Committee on Banking Supervision. (2015). *Guidelines: Corporate governance principles for banks*. Author.

Başkaya. (1997). *Sistem Dinamiğinin İşletmelerde Uygulanması*. Bursa: Ekin Kitabevi Yayınları.

Bates, T. W., Khale, K. M., & Stulz, R. M. (2009). Why do US firms hold so much more cash than they used to? *The Journal of Finance*, *64*(5), 1985–2021. doi:10.1111/j.1540-6261.2009.01492.x

Baucus, M., & Baucus, D. (1997). Paying the piper: An empirical examination of longer term financial consequences for illegal corporate behaviour. *Academy of Management Journal*, *40*, 129–151.

Bauer, M. W., Pitschel, D., & Studinger, P. (2010). *Governance Preferences of Subnational Administrative Elites in the European Union: An Empirical Analysis*. Academic Public Administration Studies Archive-APAS.

Baxter, P., & Cotter, J. (2009). Audit committees and earnings quality. *Accounting and Finance*, *49*(2), 267–290. doi:10.1111/j.1467-629X.2008.00290.x

Baysinger, B. D., & Butler, H. N. (1985). Corporate governance and the board of directors: Performance effects of changes in board composition. *Journal of Law Economics and Organization*, *1*(1), 101–124.

Beasley, M. S. (1996). An empirical analysis of the relation between the board of director composition and financial statement fraud. *The Accounting Review*, 443–465.

Bebchuk, L. A., Kraakman, R. H., & Triantis, G. G. (1999). *Stock pyramids, cross-ownership, and the dual class equity: the creation and agency costs of separating control from cash flow rights*. NBER Working Paper. No. W6951.

Bebchuk, L. A., & Cohen, A. (2005). The costs of entrenched boards. *Journal of Financial Economics*, *78*(2), 409–433. doi:10.1016/j.jfineco.2004.12.006

Bebczuk, R., & Galindo, A. (2008). Financial crisis and sectoral diversification of Argentine banks, 1999–2004. *Applied Financial Economics*, *18*(3), 199–211. doi:10.1080/09603100601018773

Bedard, J. C., Chtourou, S. M., & Courteau, L. (2004). The effect of audit committee expertise, independence, and activity on aggressive earnings management. *Auditing*, *23*(2), 13–35. doi:10.2308/aud.2004.23.2.13

Behr, A., Kamp, A., Memmel, C., & Pfingsten, A. (2007). *Diversification and the banks' risk-return-characteristics: evidence from loan portfolios of German banks* (No. 2007, 05). Discussion Paper, Series 2: Banking and Financial Supervision.

Beiner, S., Drobetz, W., Schmid, F., & Zimmermann, H. (2004). Is board size an independent corporate governance mechanism? *Kyklos*, *57*(3), 327–356. doi:10.1111/j.0023-5962.2004.00257.x

Belkhir, M. (2009). Board structure, ownership structure and firm performance: Evidence from banking. *Applied Financial Economics*, *19*(19), 1581–1593. doi:10.1080/09603100902967561

Belkhir, M., Boubaker, S., & Derouiche, I. (2014). Control–ownership wedge, board of directors, and the value of excess cash. *Economic Modelling*, *39*, 110–122. doi:10.1016/j.econmod.2014.02.026

Ben Larbi, S., & Lacroux, A. (2011). RSE et performance sociétale des entreprises: vers un renouvellement du paradigme de la valeur. In l'Alter Management. Paris: Hermès.

Bender, R. (2013). *Corporate financial strategy*. Routledge. doi:10.4324/9780203082768

Beng, W. G. (2009). Audit committees, boards of directors, and remediation of material weaknesses in internal control. *Contemporary Accounting Research, 26*(2), 7.

Bentham, J., & Harrison, W. (1945). *(edn). Introduction to the Principles of Morals and Legislation*. Oxford, UK: Hafner Press.

Bepari, M. K., & Mollik, A. T. (2015). Effect of audit quality and accounting and finance backgrounds of audit committee members on firms' compliance with IFRS for goodwill impairment testing. *Journal of Applied Accounting Research*, *16*(Issue: 2), 196–220. doi:10.1108/JAAR-05-2013-0038

Berger, A. N., Hasan, I., & Zhou, M. (2010). The effects of focus versus diversification on bank performance: Evidence from Chinese banks. *Journal of Banking & Finance*, *34*(7), 1417–1435. doi:10.1016/j.jbankfin.2010.01.010

Berger, A. N., Kick, T., & Schaeck, K. (2014). Executive board composition and bank risk taking. *Journal of Corporate Finance*, *28*, 48–65. doi:10.1016/j.jcorpfin.2013.11.006

Berger, P. G., Ofek, E., & Yermack, D. (1997). Managerial entrenchment and capital structure decisions. *The Journal of Finance, 52*(4), 1411–1438. doi:10.1111/j.1540-6261.1997.tb01115.x

Berglöf, E., & Claessens, S. (2006). Enforcement and good corporate governance in developing countries and transition economies. *The World Bank Research Observer, 21*(1), 123–150. doi:10.1093/wbro/lkj005

Berle, A. A., & Means, G. C. (1932). *The modern corporation and private property*. New York: Commerce Clearing House.

Bernile, G., Bhagwat, V., & Yonker, S. (2018). Board diversity, firm risk, and corporate policies. *Journal of Financial Economics, 127*(3), 588–612. doi:10.1016/j.jfineco.2017.12.009

Bertrand, M., & Mullainathan, S. (1998). *Executive compensation and incentives: The impact of takeover legislation* (NBER Working Paper 6830).

Bhagat, S., & Black, B. S. (2002). The non-correlation between board independence and long-term firm performance. *The Journal of Corporation Law, 27*, 231–273.

Bhagat, S., & Bolton, B. (2008). Corporate governance and firm performance. *Journal of Corporate Finance, 14*(3), 257–273. doi:10.1016/j.jcorpfin.2008.03.006

Bhatt, P. R., & Bhatt, R. R. (2017). Corporate governance and firm performance in Malaysia. *Corporate Governance: The International Journal of Business in Society, 17*(5), 896–912. doi:10.1108/CG-03-2016-0054

Bianco, M., Ciavarella, A., & Signoretti, R. (2015). Women on Corporate Boards in Italy: The Role of Family Connections. *Corporate Governance, 23*(2), 129–144. doi:10.1111/corg.12097

Bigelli, M., & Sánchez-Vidal, J. (2012). Cash holdings in private firms. *Journal of Banking & Finance, 36*(1), 26–35. doi:10.1016/j.jbankfin.2011.06.004

Bin, R. L. L., & Yi, L. S. (2015). Board mechanisms and performance of government-linked companies on Bursa Malaysia. *Procedia Economics and Finance, 31*, 399–417. doi:10.1016/S2212-5671(15)01215-0

Black, B. S., Love, I., & Rachinsky, A. (2006). Corporate Governance and Firms' Market Values: Time Series Evidence from Russia. *Emerging Markets Review, 7*(4), 361–379. doi:10.1016/j.ememar.2006.09.004

Blue Ribbon Committee (BRC). (1999). *Report and recommendations of the Blue Ribbon Committee on improving the Effectiveness of Corporate Audit Committees*. Author.

Blundell, R., & Bond, S. (1998). Initial conditions and moment restrictions in dynamic panel data models. *Journal of Econometrics, 87*(1), 115–143. doi:10.1016/S0304-4076(98)00009-8

Bordeleau, É., & Graham, C. (2010). *The impact of liquidity on bank profitability* (No. 2010, 38). Bank of Canada Working Paper.

Boubaker, S., Derouiche, I., & Hassen, M. (2015). Family Control And The Value Of Cash Holdings. *Journal of Applied Business Research, 31*(2), 647. doi:10.19030/jabr.v31i2.9159

Boubaker, S., Derouiche, I., & Nguyen, D. K. (2015). Does the board of directors affect cash holdings? A study of French listed firms. *The Journal of Management and Governance, 19*(2), 341–370. doi:10.100710997-013-9261-x

Bozec, R. (2005). Boards of directors, market discipline and firm performance. *Journal of Business Finance & Accounting, 32*(9-10), 1921–1960. doi:10.1111/j.0306-686X.2005.00652.x

Brandenburger, A. M., & Stuart, H. W. Jr. (1996). Value based business strategy. *Journal of Economics & Management Strategy, 5*(1), 5–24. doi:10.1111/j.1430-9134.1996.00005.x

Bréchet, J. P., Charreaux, G., Desreumaux, A., & de Montmorillon, B. (2015). L'entreprise, son projet, sa gouvernance: Éléments d'une vision partenariale. *Économies et sociétés*, (23): 33–65.

Brennan, N. (2006). Boards of directors and firm performance: Is there an expectations gap? *Corporate Governance, 4*(6), 577–593. doi:10.1111/j.1467-8683.2006.00534.x

Brick, I. E., & Chidambaran, N. K. (2008). Board monitoring, firm risk, and external regulation. *Journal of Regulatory Economics, 33*(1), 87–116. doi:10.100711149-007-9045-9

Brown, L. D., & Caylor, M. L. (2004). *Corporate governance and firm performance*. Academic Press.

Brown, L. D., & Caylor, M. L. (2006). Corporate governance and firm valuation. *Journal of Accounting and Public Policy, 25*(4), 409–434. doi:10.1016/j.jaccpubpol.2006.05.005

Bryan, S., & Klein, A. (2004). *Non-management director options, board characteristics, and future firm investments and performance*. Academic Press.

Buchanan, D. A., & Bryman, A. (2011). *Organisational Research Methods*. London: SAGE Publications Limited.

Bughin, C. (2004). La gouvernance par la valeur partenariale est-elle performante? *La Revue des Sciences de Gestion: Direction et Gestion, 39*(210), 89–104. doi:10.1051/larsg:2004041

Bushee, B., & Noe, C. (2003). Corporate Disclosure Practices, Institutional Investors, and Stock return Volatility. *Journal of Accounting Research, 38*(Suppl.), 171–202. doi:10.2307/2672914

Campbell, J. L. (2007). Why would corporations behave in socially responsible ways? An institutional theory of corporate social responsibility. *Academy of Management Review, 32*(3), 946–967. doi:10.5465/amr.2007.25275684

Campbell, J. Y., Hilscher, J. D., & Szilagyi, J. (2011). Predicting financial distress and the performance of distressed stocks. *Journal of Investment Management, 9*(2), 14–34.

Campbell, J. Y., Hilscher, J., & Szilagyi, J. (2008). In search of distress risk. *The Journal of Finance, 63*(6), 2899–2939. doi:10.1111/j.1540-6261.2008.01416.x

Campuzano, F., & Mula, J. (2011). *Supply Chain Simulation*. London: Springer- Verlag. doi:10.1007/978-0-85729-719-8

Caneghem, T. V. (2004). The impact of audit quality on earnings rounding-up behaviour: Some UK evidence. *European Accounting Review*, *13*(4), 771–786.

Carcello, J. V., Hollingsworth, C. W., Klein, A., & Neal, L. T. (2006). *Audit Committee Financial Expertise, Competing Corporate Governance Mechanisms, and Earnings Management*. Available at www. ssrn.com

Carcello, J. V., Hollingsworth, C. W., Klein, A., & Neal, T. L. (2006). *Audit committee financial expertise, competing corporate governance mechanisms, and earnings management*. Available at: https://ssrn.com/abstract_887512

Carcello, J. V., Hermanson, D. R., Neal, T. L., & Riley, R. A. Jr. (2002). Board characteristics and audit fees. *Contemporary Accounting Research*, *19*(3), 365–384. doi:10.1506/CHWK-GMQ0-MLKE-K03V

Carcello, J. V., Vanstraelen, A., & Willenborg, M. (2009). Rules rather than discretion in audit standards: Going-concern opinions in Belgium. *The Accounting Review*, *84*(5), 1395–1428. doi:10.2308/accr.2009.84.5.1395

Carcello, J., & Neal, T. (2003). Audit Committee Independence and Disclosure: Choice for Financially Distressed Firms. *Corporate Governance*, *11*(4), 289–299. doi:10.1111/1467-8683.00327

Carroll, A. (1991). The Pyramid of Corporate Social Responsibility: Towards the Moral Management of Organisational Stakeholder. *Business Horizons*, *34*(4), 39–49. doi:10.1016/0007-6813(91)90005-G

Carroll, A. B. (1999). Corporate Social Responsibility Evolution of a Definitional Construct. *Business & Society*, *38*(3), 268–295. doi:10.1177/000765039903800303

Carroll, A. B. (2008). A history of corporate social responsibility: concept and practices. In A. Crane, A. McWilliams, D. Matten, J. Moon, & D. S. Siegel (Eds.), *The Oxford Handbook of Corporate Social Responsibility*. Oxford, UK: Oxford University Press.

Carroll, A. B., & Shabana, K. M. (2010). The business case for corporate social responsibility: A review of concepts, research and practice. *International Journal of Management Reviews*, *12*(1), 85–105. doi:10.1111/j.1468-2370.2009.00275.x

Carroll, W. K., Carson, C., Fennema, M., Heemskerk, E., & Sapinski, J. P. (2010). *The making of a transnational capitalist class: Corporate power in the twenty-first century*. Zed books.

Celik, O., & Ecer, A., & Karabacak. (2006). Disclosure of forward-looking information: Evidence from listed companies on Istanbul stock exchange. *Investment Management and Financial Innovations*, *3*(2), 197–216.

Chancharat, N. (2008). *An empirical analysis of financially distressed Australian companies: the application of survival analysis*. A thesis submitted to University of Wollongong.

Chan, K. C., & Li, J. (2008). Audit committee and firm value: Evidence on outside top executives as expert-independent directors. *Corporate Governance*, *16*(1), 16–31. doi:10.1111/j.1467-8683.2008.00662.x

Charreaux, G. (2006). Théorie financière et stratégie financière. *Revue française de gestion*, (1), 109-137.

Charreaux, G. (2011). *Quelle théorie pour la gouvernance? De la gouvernance actionnariale à la gouvernance cognitive et comportementale*. Université de Bourgogne-CREGO EA7317 Centre de recherches en gestion des organisations.

Charreaux, G. (1997). *Le gouvernement des entreprises – Corporate Governance –Théories et Faits*. Paris: Economica.

Charreaux, G., & Desbrières, P. (1998). Gouvernance des entreprises: Valeur partenariale contre valeur actionnariale. *Finance Contrôle Stratégie*, *1*(2), 57–88.

Chatelin, C., & Trébucq, S. (2003). *Stabilité et évolution du cadre conceptuel en gouvernance d'entreprise: un essai de synthèse*. Communication pour les neuvièmes journées d'histoire de la comptabilité et du management, Jeudi, 20.

Chauhan, Y., Lakshmi, K. R., & Dey, D. K. (2016). Corporate governance practices, self-dealings, and firm performance: Evidence from India. *Journal of Contemporary Accounting & Economics*, *12*(3), 274–289. doi:10.1016/j.jcae.2016.10.002

Chen, C. J. P., & Jaggi, B. (2000). Association between independent non-executive directors, family control and financial disclosures in Hong Kong. *Journal of Accounting and Public Policy*, *19*(, 4-5), 285–310. doi:10.1016/S0278-4254(00)00015-6

Cheney, G. (2004). The Corporate Conscience and the Triple Bottom Line. *Accounting Today*.

Chen, S., & Chang, C. P. (2015). Should bank loan portfolio be diversified under government capital injection and deposit insurance fund protection? *International Review of Economics & Finance*, *38*, 131–141. doi:10.1016/j.iref.2015.02.017

Chen, S., Lin, B.-X., Wang, Y., & Wu, L. (2008). Cross-listing, corporate governance and operating performance–evidence from The Chinese market. In *Advances in Business and Management Forecasting* (pp. 19–46). Emerald Group Publishing Limited.

Chen, Z., Cheung, Y.-L., Stouraitis, A., & Wong, A. W. (2005). Ownership concentration, firm performance, and dividend policy in Hong Kong. *Pacific-Basin Finance Journal*, *13*(4), 431–449. doi:10.1016/j.pacfin.2004.12.001

Chernykh, L. (2008). Ultimate ownership and control in Russia. *Journal of Financial Economics*, *88*(1), 169–192. doi:10.1016/j.jfineco.2007.05.005

Cheung, Y., Rau, P. R., & Stouraitis, A. (2006). Tunneling, propping, and expropriation: Evidence from connected party transactions in Honk Kong. *Journal of Financial Economics*, *82*(2), 343–386. doi:10.1016/j.jfineco.2004.08.012

Chong, Y. Y. (2004). Corporate governance: Risk management starts at the top. *Balance Sheet*, *12*(5), 42–47. doi:10.1108/09657960410563586

Choy, S. L. W., Munusamy, J., Chelliah, S., & Mandari, A. (2011). Effects of financial distress condition on the company performance: A Malaysian perspective. *Review of Economics & Finance*, *1*(4), 85–99.

Chung, R., Firth, M., & Kim, J. B. (2005). Earnings management, surplus free cash flow, and external monitoring. *Journal of Business Research*, *58*(6), 766–776. doi:10.1016/j.jbusres.2003.12.002

Claessens, S. (2006). Corporate governance and development. *The World Bank Research Observer*, *21*(1), 91–122. doi:10.1093/wbro/lkj004

Claessens, S., Djankov, S., Fan, J. P. H., & Lang, L. H. P. (2002). Disentangling the incentive and entrenchment effects of large shareholdings. *The Journal of Finance*, *57*(6), 2741–2471. doi:10.1111/1540-6261.00511

Claeys, S., & Vander Vennet, R. (2008). Determinants of bank interest margins in Central and Eastern Europe: A comparison with the West. *Economic Systems*, *32*(2), 197–216. doi:10.1016/j.ecosys.2007.04.001

Clark, S. E. (1990). How to survive in the environmental jungle. *The Institutional Investor*, *24*(16), 89–91.

Clemente, A., & Labat, B. (2009). *Corporate Governance mechanism and Voluntary Disclosure. The role of independent directors in the boards of listed Spanish firms*. Retrieved from http://pendientedemigracion.ucm.es/

Coase, R. H. (1937). The nature of the firm. *Economica*, *4*(16), 386–405. doi:10.1111/j.1468-0335.1937.tb00002.x

Coffee, J. C. (2005). A theory of corporate scandals: Why the USA and Europe differ. *Oxford Review of Economic Policy*, *21*(2), 198–211. doi:10.1093/oxrep/gri012

Cohen, J., Krishnamoorthy, G., & Wright, A. (2004). The corporate governance mosaic and financial reporting quality. *Journal of Accounting Literature*, *23*, 87–152.

Coleman, L. (2011). Losses from Failure of Stakeholder Sensitive Processes: Financial Consequences for Large US Companies from Breakdowns in Product, Environmental, and Accounting Standards. *Journal of Business Ethics*, *98*(2), 247–258. doi:10.100710551-010-0544-8

Coles, J. L., Daniel, N. D., & Naveen, L. (2008). Boards: Does one size fit all? *Journal of Financial Economics*, *87*(2), 329–356. doi:10.1016/j.jfineco.2006.08.008

Coles, J. W., McWilliams, V. B., & Sen, N. (2001). An examination of the relationship of governance mechanisms to performance. *Journal of Management*, *27*(1), 23–50. doi:10.1177/014920630102700102

Conyon, M. J., & Peck, S. I. (1998). Board size and corporate performance: Evidence from European countries. *European Journal of Finance*, *4*(3), 291–304. doi:10.1080/135184798337317

Cornett, M. M., Marcus, A. J., Saunders, A., & Tehranian, H. (2007). The impact of institutional ownership on corporate operating performance. *Journal of Banking & Finance*, *31*(6), 1771–1794. doi:10.1016/j.jbankfin.2006.08.006

Cornett, M. M., McNutt, J. J., & Tehranian, H. (2009). Corporate governance and earnings management at large US bank holding companies. *Journal of Corporate Finance*, *15*(4), 412–430. doi:10.1016/j.jcorpfin.2009.04.003

COSO. (1992). *Internal Control Integrated Framework*. Retrieved June 25 2015, from http://www.coso.org/publications/executive_summary_integrated_framework.htm

Costello, A., & Wittenberg-Moerman, R. (2011). The impact of financial reporting quality on debt contracting: Evidence from internal control weakness reports. *Journal of Accounting Research*, *49*(1), 97–136. doi:10.1111/j.1475-679X.2010.00388.x

Cottrell, S. P. (2003). Influence of sociodemographics and environmental attitude on general responsible environmental behaviour among recreational boaters. *Environment and Behavior*, *33*(3), 347–375. doi:10.1177/0013916503035003003

Coyle. (1996). *Systems Dynamics Modeling*. Chapman & Hall.

Crane, A., & Matten, D. (2010). *Business Ethics* (3rd ed.). Oxford, UK: Oxford University Press.

Cremer, D. D., Dick, R., Tenbrunsel, A. E., Pillutla, M., & Murnighan, J. K. (2011). Understanding Ethical Behaviour and Decision Making in Management: A Behavioural Business Ethics Approach'. *British Journal of Management*, *22*, S1–S4. doi:10.1111/j.1467-8551.2010.00733.x

Cresswell, J. W. (1994). *Research design: quantitative and qualitative approaches*. London: SAGE Publications Limited.

Crutchley, C. E., Jensen, M. R., & Marshall, B. B. (2007). Climate for scandal: Corporate environment that contribute to accounting fraud. *Financial Review*, *42*(1), 53–73. doi:10.1111/j.1540-6288.2007.00161.x

d'Inverno, M., Luck, M., Georgeff, M., Kinny, D., & Wooldridge, M. (2004). The dMARS Architecture: A specification of the distributed multi-agent reasoning system. *Autonomous Agents and Multi-Agent Systems*, *9*(1/2), 5–53. doi:10.1023/B:AGNT.0000019688.11109.19

D'Mello, R., Krishnaswami, S., & Larkin, P. J. (2008). Determinants of corporate cash holdings: Evidence fromspin-offs. *Journal of Banking & Finance*, *32*(7), 1209–1220. doi:10.1016/j.jbankfin.2007.10.005

Dağli, H. (2005). İçme suyu kalitesi ve insan sağlığına etkileri. *Bizim İller. İller Bankası Aylık Yayın Organı*, *3*, 16–21.

Dahya, J., Dimitrov, O., & McConnell, J. J. (2008a). Dominant shareholders, corporate boards, and corporate value: A cross-country analysis. *Journal of Financial Economics*, *87*(1), 73–100. doi:10.1016/j.jfineco.2006.10.005

Darani, E. H. (2012). Corporate Governance, IPO (Initial Public Offering) Long Term Return in Malaysia. *International Conference on Economics, Business and Marketing Management*, 29.

Darko, J., Aribi, Z. A., & Uzonwanne, G. C. (2016). Corporate governance: The impact of director and board structure, ownership structure and corporate control on the performance of listed companies on the Ghana stock exchange. *Corporate Governance*, *16*(2), 259–277. doi:10.1108/CG-11-2014-0133

Darko-Mensah, A. B., & Okereke, C. (2013). 'Can environmental performance rating programmes succeed in Africa? An evaluation of Ghana's AKOBEN project'. *Management of Environmental Quality*, *24*(5), 599–618. doi:10.1108/MEQ-01-2012-0003

Dashwood, H. S. (2012). *The Rise of Global Corporate Social Responsibility:Mining and the Spread of Global Norms*. Cambridge University Press. doi:10.1017/CBO9781139058933

David, R., & Brierley, J. E. (1985). *Major legal systems in the world today. An introduction to the comparative study of law* (3rd ed.). London: Stevens & Sons.

Davis, J. H., Schoorman, F. D., & Donaldson, L. (1997). Toward a stewardship theory of management. *Academy of Management Review*, *22*(1), 20–47. doi:10.5465/amr.1997.9707180258

de Andres, P., & Vallelado, E. (2008, December). Corporate governance in banking: The role of the board of directors. *Journal of Banking & Finance*, *32*(12), 2570–2580. doi:10.1016/j.jbankfin.2008.05.008

de Oliveira Gondrige, E., Clemente, A., & Espejo, M. M. dos S. B. (2012). Composition of the board and firm value of brazilian public companies. *Brazilian Business Review (English Edition)*, *9*(3).

DeAngelo, L. (1981). Auditor size and audit quality. *Journal of Accounting and Economics*, *3*(December), 183–199. doi:10.1016/0165-4101(81)90002-1

Dechow, P., & Dichev, I. (2002). The Quality of Accruals and Earnings: The Role of Accrual Estimation Errors. *The Accounting Review*, *77*(September), 35–59. doi:10.2308/accr.2002.77.s-1.35

Dechow, P., & Schrand, C. (2004). *Earnings Quality*. The Research Foundation of CFA Institute.

Dechow, P., Sloan, R., & Sweeney, A. (1995). Detecting Earnings Management. *The Accounting Review*, *70*(2), 193–225.

Dedman, E., & Filatotchev, I. (2008). Corporate governance research: A contingency framework. *International Journal of Managerial Finance*, *4*(4), 248–258. doi:10.1108/17439130810902778

DeFond, M. L., Raghunandan, K., & Subramanyam, K. R. (2002). Do non-audit service fees impair auditor independence? Evidence from going concern audit opinions. *Journal of Accounting Research*, *40*(4), 1247–1274. doi:10.1111/1475-679X.00088

Delgado, J. B., Quevedo, E., & Fuente, J. M. (2010). The impact of ownership structure on corporate reputation: Evidence from Spain. *Corporate Governance*, *18*(6), 540–556. doi:10.1111/j.1467-8683.2010.00818.x

Demirgüç-Kunt, A., & Huizinga, H. (1999). Determinants of commercial bank interest margins and profitability: Some international evidence. *The World Bank Economic Review*, *13*(2), 379–408. doi:10.1093/wber/13.2.379

Demsetz, H. (1968). The cost of transacting. *The Quarterly Journal of Economics*, *82*(1), 33–53. doi:10.2307/1882244

Demsetz, H. (1983). The structure of ownership and the theory of the firm. *The Journal of Law & Economics*, *26*(2), 375–390. doi:10.1086/467041

Demsetz, H., & Lenh, K. (1985). The structure of corporate ownership: Causes and consequences. *Journal of Political Economy*, *93*(6), 1155–1177. doi:10.1086/261354

Denis, D. J., Denis, D. K., & Sarin, A. (1997). Agency problems, equity ownership, and corporate diversification. *The Journal of Finance*, *52*(1), 135–160. doi:10.1111/j.1540-6261.1997.tb03811.x

Des Jardins, J. R. (2001), Environmental ethics: an introduction to environmental philosophy (3rd ed.). Belmont, CA: Wadsworth/Thomson Learning.

Deumes, R. (2004). *Voluntary reporting on internal control by listed Dutch companies*. Working paper, Maastricht University, Maastricht, Faculty of economics and business administration.

Deumes, R., & Knechel, W. R. (2008). Economic incentives for voluntary reporting on internal risk management and control systems. *Auditing*, *27*(1), 35–66. doi:10.2308/aud.2008.27.1.35

Devji, S., & Suprabha, K. R. (2016). Corporate financial distress and stock return: Evidence from Indian stock market. *Nitte Management Review*, *10*(1), 34–44. doi:10.17493/nmr/2016/105514

Dezoort, F., & Salterio, S. (2001). *The Effect of Corporate Governance Experience and Financial Reporting and Audit Knowledge on Audit Committee Members Judgment*. Academic Press.

Dezoort, F., & Salterio, S. (2001). The Effect of Corporate Governance Experience and Financial Reporting and Audit Knowledge on Audit Committee Members Judgment. *Auditing*, *20*(2), 31–47. doi:10.2308/aud.2001.20.2.31

Diamond, D. W. (1984). Financial intermediation and delegated monitoring. *The Review of Economic Studies*, *51*(3), 393–414. doi:10.2307/2297430

DiMaggio, P. J., & Powell, W. W. (1983). The Iron Cage Revisited: Institutional Isomorphism and Collective Rationality in Organizational Fields. *American Sociological Review*, *48*(2), 147–160. doi:10.2307/2095101

Dimaggio, P. J., & Powell, W. W. (1991). *The New Institutionalism in Organisational Analysis*. Chicago: University of Chicago Press.

Dinler. (2014). *İktisada Giriş*. Ekin Basım Yayın Dağıtım, Bursa.

Dittmar, A., & Mahrt-Smith, J. (2007). Corporate governance and the value of cash holdings. *Journal of Financial Economics*, *83*(3), 599–634. doi:10.1016/j.jfineco.2005.12.006

Dittmar, A., Mahrt-Smith, J., & Servaes, H. (2003). International corporate governance and corporate cash holdings. *Journal of Financial and Quantitative Analysis*, *38*(01), 111–133. doi:10.2307/4126766

Djankov, S., Glaeser, E., La Porta, R., Lopez-de-Silanes, F., & Shleifer, A. (2003). The new comparative economics. *Journal of Comparative Economics*, *31*(4), 595–619. doi:10.1016/j.jce.2003.08.005

Dogan, M., Elitas, B. L., Agca, V., & Ögel, S. (2013). The impact of CEO duality on firm performance: Evidence from turkey. *International Journal of Business and Social Science*, *4*(2).

Donaldson, T., & Preston, L. E. (1995). The stakeholder theory of the corporation: Concepts, evidence, and implications. *Academy of Management Review*, *20*(1), 65–91. doi:10.5465/amr.1995.9503271992

Donnelly, R., & Mulcahy, M. (2008). Board structure, ownership and voluntary disclosure in Ireland. *Corporate Governance*, *16*(5), 416–429. doi:10.1111/j.1467-8683.2008.00692.x

Doyle, J., Ge, W., & McVay, S. (2007). Determinants of weaknesses in internal control over financial reporting. *Journal of Accounting and Economics*, *44*(1/2), 193–223. doi:10.1016/j.jacceco.2006.10.003

Drobetz, W., & Grüninger, M. C. (2007). Corporate cash holdings: Evidence from Switzerland. *Financial Markets and Portfolio Management*, *21*(3), 293–324. doi:10.100711408-007-0052-8

Dun, & Bradstreet, Inc. Business Economics Division. (1986). *The Business Failure Record*. Business Economics Division, Dun and Bradstreet.

Dunn, D. J. (1987). *Directors Arent Doing Their Jobs*. Academic Press.

Duran, N. (2012). *L'actionnaire individuel client: étude du cas français*. Toulon: Université de Toulon.

Dwenger & Pavlov. (2008). *Feedback Analysis Of Speculation In A Foreign Currency Market*. The International Conference Of The System Dynamics Society, Athens, Greece.

Eberhart, R. (2012). Corporate governance systems and firm value: Empirical evidence from Japan's natural experiment. *Journal of Asia Business Studies*, *6*(2), 176–196. doi:10.1108/15587891211254399

Eboiyehi, O. C., & Ikpesu, F. (2017). An empirical investigation of capital structure and tax shield on business distress in Nigeria: An Application of Panel Corrected Standard Error (PCSE) Approach. *Journal of Global Economics. Management and Business Research*, *8*(2), 67–75.

Eisenberg, T., Sundgren, S., & Wells, M. T. (1998). Larger board size and decreasing firm value in small firms1. *Journal of Financial Economics*, *48*(1), 35–54. doi:10.1016/S0304-405X(98)00003-8

Elkington, J. (2004). Enter the Triple Bottom Line. In A. Henriques & J. Richardson (Eds.), *The Triple Bottom Line: does it all add up*. London: EarthScan.

Elloumi, F., & Gueyie, J. P. (2001). Financial distress and corporate governance: An empirical analysis. *corporate governance. The International Journal of Business in Society*, *1*(1), 15–23.

Elouadi, S. (2014). *Analyse des effets induits par l'actionnariat salarié sur la création de valeur partenariale des entreprises du SBF 250*. Thèse de doctorat. IAE de Toulon, Université du Sud.

Elouadi, S., & Elotmani, R. (2018). Customer Shareholding as a Radical Approach to a Sustainable and Profitable Relationship. In *Marketing Techniques for Financial Inclusion and Development* (pp. 35–47). IGI Global. doi:10.4018/978-1-5225-4035-9.ch003

Elsas, R., Hackethal, A., & Holzhäuser, M. (2010). The anatomy of bank diversification. *Journal of Banking & Finance*, *34*(6), 1274–1287. doi:10.1016/j.jbankfin.2009.11.024

Eng, L., & Mak, Y. (2003). Corporate governance and voluntary disclosure. *Journal of Accounting and Public Policy*, *22*(4), 325–345. doi:10.1016/S0278-4254(03)00037-1

Erkut. (1983). *Sistem Dinamiğinin Temelleri*. İTÜ Fen Edebiyat Fakültesi Ofset Atölyesi, İstanbul.

Erkut. (1995). *Sistem Yönetimi Yönetim Bilimleri Dizisi: 4*. İrfan Yayınları, İstanbul.

European Banking Authority. (2017). *Guidelines on internal governance under Directive 2013/36/EU*. Available at https://eba.europa.eu/documents/10180/1972987/Final+Guidelines+on+Internal+Governance+%28EBA-GL-2017-11%29.pdf

European Central Bank. (2017). *Guide to fit and proper assessment*. Author.

European Commission. (2000). *Communication from the commission on promoting sustainable development in the EU non-energy extractive industry*. Brussels: The European Commission.

Evanoff, D. D., & Israilevich, P. R. (1991). Productive efficiency in banking. *Economic Perspectives*, *15*(4), 11–32.

Faleye, O. (2004). *Are large boards poor monitors? Evidence from CEO turnover*. EFMA Basel Meetings Paper.

Fama, E. F., & Jensen, M. C. (1983). Separation of ownership and control. *The Journal of Law & Economics*, *26*(2), 301–325. doi:10.1086/467037

Fama, E., & Jensen, M. (1983). Separation of Ownership and Control. *The of Law and Economics*, *26*(2), 36–67.

Fang, H., Sun, H., & Jin, Y. (2009). Corporate characteristics, external audit, and voluntary disclosure of internal control information: An empirical study based on annual reports of listed companies of Shanghai stock exchanges from 2003 to 2005. *Accountability in Research*, *10*(1), 44–95.

Fan, J. P. H., & Wong, T. J. (2005). Do external auditors perform a corporate governance role in emerging markets? Evidence from East Asia. *Journal of Accounting Research*, *43*(1), 35–72. doi:10.1111/j.1475-679x.2004.00162.x

Faraj, A. (2005). *Assess the level of disclosure in interim financial reports of public shareholding companies of Jordan in light of the disclosure requirements of the progress of local and international* (Unpublished PhD dissertation). Arab Academy for Banking and Financial Sciences.

Farinha, J., & Moreira, A. (2007). *Dividends and Earnings Quality: The Missing Link?* Working Paper, University of Porto.

Fazzari, S. M., & Petersen, B. (1993). Working capital and fixed investment: New evidence on financing constraints. *The Rand Journal of Economics*, *24*(3), 328–342. doi:10.2307/2555961

Felo, A., Krishnamurthy, F., & Solieri, S. (2003). *Audit Committee Characteristics and the Perceived Quality of Financial Reporting an Empirical Analysis*. Working Paper, School of Graduate Professional Studies, Malven. Retrieved from www.ssrn.com

Ferreira, M. A., & Vilela, A. S. (2004). Why do firms hold cash? Evidence from EMU countries. *European Financial Management*, *10*(2), 295–319. doi:10.1111/j.1354-7798.2004.00251.x

Field, A. (2009). *Discovering Statistics Using SPSS for Windows* (3rd ed.). London: Sage Publications.

Financial Times. (2006). *Rosneft IPO fails to attract big players.* Retrieved February 10, 2019 from Financial times: https://www.ft.com/content/0781b0de-1366-11db-9d6e-0000779e2340

Finkelstein, S., & Hambrick, D. (1996). *Strategic leadership.* St. Paul, MN: West Educational Publishing.

Fogel, E. M., & Geier, A. M. (2007). Strangers in the house: Rethinking Sarbanes-Oxley and the independent board of directors. *Del. J. CorP. L.*, *32*, 33.

Ford, A. (1999). *Modeling the Environment: An Introduction to System Dynamics Modeling of Environmental Systems*. Washington, DC: Island Press.

Forrester. (1962). *Industrial Dynamics*. Waltham, MA: Pegasus Communications.

Forrester. (1969). *Urban Dynamics*. Cambridge, MA: The MIT Press.

Forrester. (1995). *Road Map 1: Counterintuitive Behaviour Of Social Systems.* MIT System Dynamics In Education Project.

Forrester. (2007a). System Dynamics: A Personal View Of The First Fifty Years. *System Dynamics Review, 23*, 345–358.

Forsyth, D. R. (1980). A taxonomy of ethical ideologies. *Journal of Personality and Social Psychology*, *39*(1), 175–184. doi:10.1037/0022-3514.39.1.175

Francis, J., Khurana, I., & Pereira, R. (2001). *Investor protection laws, accounting and auditing around the world.* SSRN Electronic Library, Working Paper Series.

Franks, J. R., & Mayer, C. (1997). Corporate ownership and control in the U.K., Germany and France. In D. Chew (Ed.), *Studies in international corporate finance and governance systems. A comparison of the U.S., Japan, & Europe* (pp. 281–296). Oxford, UK: Oxford University Press. doi:10.1111/j.1745-6622.1997.tb00622.x

Freeman, R. E. (1984). *Strategic management: A stakeholder approach.* Boston: Pitman.

Freeman, R. E. (1984). *Strategic Management: A Stakeholder Approach.* Boston: Pitman.

Freeman, R. E., & Evan, W. M. (1990). Corporate governance: A stakeholder interpretation. *The Journal of Behavioral Economics*, *19*(4), 337–359. doi:10.1016/0090-5720(90)90022-Y

Friedman, M. (1970). The Social Responsibility of Business is to Increase Its Profits. *The New York Times Magazine, 13*, 32–33.

Friedman, M. (1962). *Capitalism and Freedom.* Chicago: University of Chicago Press.

Funchal, B., & Pinto, J. P. (2018). Corporate events' performance and corporate governance: The Brazilian evidence. *Corporate Governance: The International Journal of Business in Society*, *18*(1), 14–34. doi:10.1108/CG-11-2016-0219

Gambacorta, L., & Mistrulli, P. E. (2004). Does bank capital affect lending behavior? *Journal of Financial Intermediation*, *13*(4), 436–457. doi:10.1016/j.jfi.2004.06.001

García-Herrero, A., Gavilá, S., & Santabárbara, D. (2009). What explains the low profitability of Chinese banks? *Journal of Banking & Finance*, *33*(11), 2080–2092. doi:10.1016/j.jbankfin.2009.05.005

García-Olalla, M., & Clifton, J. (2018). *Contemporary Issues in Banking: Regulation, Governance and Performance*. Palgrave Macmillan Studies in Banking and Financial Institutions. doi:10.1007/978-3-319-90294-4

García-Teruel, P., & Martínez-Solano, P. (2008). On the determinants of SME cash holdings: Evidence from Spain. *Journal of Business Finance & Accounting*, *35*(1-2), 127–149. doi:10.1111/j.1468-5957.2007.02022.x

Garfatta, R. (2010). *Actionnariat salarié et création de valeur dans le cadre d'une gouvernance actionnariale et partenariale: application au contexte français*. Doctorat en sciences de gestion, Bourgogne: Université de Bourgogne.

Garriga, E., & Mele, D. (2004). Corporate Social Responsibility Theories: Mapping the Territory. *Journal of Business Ethics*, *53*(1/2), 51–71. doi:10.1023/B:BUSI.0000039399.90587.34

Gathecha, J. W. (2016). *Effect of firm characteristics on financial distress of non-financial listed firms at Nairobi Securities Exchange* (Doctoral dissertation). Kenyatta University.

Ghabayen, M. A. (2012). Board characteristics and firm performance: Case of Saudi Arabia. *International Journal of Accounting and Financial Reporting*, *2*(2), 168–200. doi:10.5296/ijafr.v2i2.2145

Gill, A., Biger, N., & Mathur, N. (2011). The effect of capital structure on profitability: Evidence from the United States. *International Journal of Management*, *28*(4), 3.

Gilligan, C. (1993). Concepts of the Self and of Morality. Harvard Educational Review, 481–517.

Givoly, D., Hayn, C., & Katz, S. (2010). Does Public Ownership of Equity Improve Earnings Quality? *The Accounting Review*, *85*(1), 195–225. doi:10.2308/accr.2010.85.1.195

Goksen, N. S., & Usdiken, B. (2001). Uniformity and diversity in Turkish business groups: Effects of scale and time of founding. *British Journal of Management*, *12*(4), 325–340. doi:10.1111/1467-8551.00213

Gomez-Mejia, L. R., Cruz, C., Berrone, P., & De Castro, J. (2011). The bind that ties: Socioemotional wealth preservation in family firms. *The Academy of Management Annals*, *5*(1), 653–707. doi:10.1080/19416520.2011.593320

Gompers, P., Ishii, J., & Metrick, A. (2003). Corporate governance and equity prices. *The Quarterly Journal of Economics*, *118*(1), 107–156. doi:10.1162/00335530360535162

Gonenc, H., & Hermes, N. (2008). Propping: Evidence from new share issues of Turkish business group firms. *Journal of Multinational Financial Management*, *18*(3), 261–275. doi:10.1016/j.mulfin.2007.11.002

Goodstein, J., Gautam, K., & Boeker, W. (1994). The effects of board size and diversity on strategic change. *Strategic Management Journal*, *15*(3), 241–250. doi:10.1002mj.4250150305

Gowthorpe, C., & Amat, O. (2005). Creative accounting: some ethical issues of macro- and micromanipulation. *Journal of Economic Literature Classification, 41*(1), 1-22.

Graham, J. H., Harveya, C. R., & Rajgopal, S. (2005). The economic implications of corporate financial reporting. *Journal of Accounting and Economics*, *40*(1-3), 3–73. doi:10.1016/j.jacceco.2005.01.002

Griffin, J. P. (1995). Consequentialism. In T. Honderich (Ed.), *The Oxford Companion to Philosophy* (pp. 154–156). New York: Oxford University Press.

Grinblatt, M., & Hwang, C. Y. (1989). Signalling and the Pricing of New Issues. *The Journal of Finance*, *44*(2), 393–420. doi:10.1111/j.1540-6261.1989.tb05063.x

Grougiou, V., Leventis, S., Dedoulis, E., & Owusu-Ansah, S. (2014). Corporate Social Responsibility and Earnings Management in U.S. Banks. *Accounting Forum*, *38*(3), 155–169. doi:10.1016/j.accfor.2014.05.003

Guest, P. M. (2009). The impact of board size on firm performance: Evidence from the UK. *European Journal of Finance*, *15*(4), 385–404. doi:10.1080/13518470802466121

Gujarati, D. (2003). *Basic Econometrics*. New York: McGraw Hill Book Co.

Gul, F. A., & Leung, S. (2004). Board leadership, outside directors' expertise and voluntary corporate disclosures. *Journal of Accounting and Public Policy*, *23*(5), 351–379. doi:10.1016/j.jaccpubpol.2004.07.001

Guney, Y., Ozkan, A., & Ozkan, N. (2007). International evidence on the non-linear impact of leverage on corporate cash holdings. *Journal of Multinational Financial Management*, *17*(1), 45–60. doi:10.1016/j.mulfin.2006.03.003

Gupta, P., & Sharma, A. M. (2014). A study of the impact of corporate governance practices on firm performance in Indian and South Korean companies. *Procedia: Social and Behavioral Sciences*, *133*, 4–11. doi:10.1016/j.sbspro.2014.04.163

Hallock, K. (1997). Reciprocally interlocking boards of directors and executive compensation. *Journal of Financial and Quantitative Analysis*, *32*(3), 331–344. doi:10.2307/2331203

Hamdan, A., & Abu Ijela, I. (2010). Auditing Quality in Jordan and its Impact on Earnings Management and Earnings Quality. *The Arab Journal of Accounting*. Retrieved from http://www.bahrainedb.com/en/about/Documents/index.html#.VjcX8bzYpPN

Hamdan, A., & Mudshtaha, S. (2011). The Relationship Between Audit Committee Characteristics and Type of Auditor's Report: An Empirical Study on the Public Shareholding Industrial Companies Listed at Amman Bourse. *The Arab Journal of Accounting*, *14*(1), 109–163. doi:10.12785/aja/140104

Hancock, J. (2005). Introduction: Why this subject? Why this book? In *Investing in corporate social responsibility: A guide to best practice, business planning and the UK's leading companies*. London: Kogan Page.

Haniffa, R. M., & Cooke, T. E. (2005). The impact of culture and governance on corporate social reporting. *Journal of Accounting and Public Policy*, *24*(5), 391–430. doi:10.1016/j.jaccpubpol.2005.06.001

Hardin, W. G., Highfield, M. J., Hill, M. D., & Kelly, W. (2009). The determinants of REIT cash holdings. *The Journal of Real Estate Finance and Economics*, *39*(1), 39–57. doi:10.100711146-007-9103-1

Harrison, J. R. (1987). The strategic use of corporate board committees. *California Management Review*, *30*(1), 109–125. doi:10.2307/41165269

Hart, O. D. (1995). *Firms, contracts, and financial structure*. London: Oxford University Press. doi:10.1093/0198288816.001.0001

Hart, S. L. (1995). A Natural-Resource-Based View of the Firm. *Academy of Management Review*, *20*(4), 986–1012. doi:10.5465/amr.1995.9512280033

Haslam, P. A. (2004). *The Corporate social responsibility system in Latin American and the Caribbean*. Ottawa: FOCAL.

Hau, H., & Thum, M. (2009). *Subprime Crisis and Board (In-)Competence: Private vs. Public Banks in Germany*. CESifo Working Paper Series No. 2640; ECGI - Finance Working Paper No. 247/2009. Available at SSRN: https://ssrn.com/abstract=1360698

Hayden, E., Porath, D., & Westernhagen, N. V. (2007). Does diversification improve the performance of German banks? Evidence from individual bank loan portfolios. *Journal of Financial Services Research*, *32*(3), 123–140. doi:10.100710693-007-0017-0

Hellenic Financial Stability Fund. (2018). *Guidelines on the Board of Directors' selection and appointment process in Greek Systemic Banks*. Author.

He, M., & Chen, J. (2009). Sustainable development and corporate environmental responsibility: Evidence from Chinese corporations. *Journal of Agricultural & Environmental Ethics*, *22*(4), 323–339. doi:10.100710806-009-9147-8

Hermalin, B. E., & Weisbach, M. S. (1988). The determinants of board composition. *The Rand Journal of Economics*, *19*(4), 589–606. doi:10.2307/2555459

Hermalin, B. E., & Weisbach, M. S. (1991). The effects of board composition and direct incentives on firm performance. *Financial Management*, *20*(4), 101–112. doi:10.2307/3665716

Hermalin, B. E., & Weisbach, M. S. (2003). Boards of directors as an endogenously determined institution: A survey of the economic literature. *Economic Policy Review*, *9*, 7–26.

Hermanson, H. M. (2000). An analysis of the demand for reporting on internal control. *Accounting Horizons*, *14*(3), 325–341. doi:10.2308/acch.2000.14.3.325

Herrera. (2014). *Integrating System Dynamics With Traditional Management Tools: A Case Study In The Apparel Industry*. 32nd International Conference of the System Dynamics Society, Delft, Netherlands.

Hesan, G., & Dignum. (2014). Using Diference Equation to Model Discrete-time Behavior in System Dynamics Modeling. *32nd International Conference of the System Dynamics Society*, Delft, Netherlands.

Hill, C. W. L., & Jones, M. T. (1992). Stakeholder-agency theory. *Journal of Management Studies*, *29*(2), 131–154. doi:10.1111/j.1467-6486.1992.tb00657.x

Hirshleifer, D., & Thakor, A. V. (1994). Managerial performance, boards of directors and takeover bidding. *Journal of Corporate Finance*, *1*(1), 63–90. doi:10.1016/0929-1199(94)90010-8

Hoffman, A. (1993). The importance of fit between individual values and organizational culture in the greening of industry. *Business Strategy and the Environment*, *2*(4), 10–18. doi:10.1002/bse.3280020402

Hoffman, A. J. (2001). *Competitive environmental strategy*. Washington, DC: Island Press.

Honjo, Y. (2000). Business failure of new firms: An empirical analysis using a multiplicative hazards model. *International Journal of Industrial Organization, 18*(4), 557–574. doi:10.1016/S0167-7187(98)00035-6

Hooghiemstra, R., & Van Manen, J. (2002). Supervisory directors and ethical dilemmas: Exit or voice. *European Management Journal, 20*(1), 1–9. doi:10.1016/S0263-2373(01)00104-9

Ho, S. M. S., & Wong, K. R. (2001). A Study of the Relationship Between Corporate Governance Structures and the Extent of voluntary Disclosure. *Journal of International Accounting, Auditing & Taxation, Vol., 10*(2), 139–156. doi:10.1016/S1061-9518(01)00041-6

Huang, H. (2005). *The Effects of Audit Committee Characteristics on Investors Perception of Financial Reporting*. Working Paper, Florida International University.

Huang, X., & Staples, W. (2017). Do Chinese corporations take their governance practices abroad? Evidence from Chinese mining subsidiaries in Australia. *Thunderbird International Business Review*.

Humayun, K., & Adelepo, I. (2012). Corporate governance disclosure practices by Swaziland public enterprises. *African Journal of Business Management, 6*(24), 7136–7148.

Hunziker, S. (2013). Efficiency of internal control: Evidence from Swiss non-financial companies. *The Journal of Management and Governance*, 401–433.

Hussain, S., & Millan, C. (2002). Corporate Governance in Bahrain. *Corporate Governance: An International Review, 10*(3), 197-210.

Ibbotson, R. (1975). Price performance of common stock new issues. *Journal of Financial Economics, 2*(3), 235–272. doi:10.1016/0304-405X(75)90015-X

Idemudia, U. (2008). Conceptualising the CSR – Development Debate: Bridging Existing Analytical Gaps. *Journal of Corporate Citizenship, 29*(29), 91–110. doi:10.9774/GLEAF.4700.2008.sp.00011

Idemudia, U. (2011). Corporate social responsibility and developing countries moving the critical CSR research agenda in Africa forward. *Progress in Development Studies, 11*(1), 1–18. doi:10.1177/146499341001100101

Idrees, S., & Qayyum, A. (2018). *The impact of financial distress risk on equity returns: A case study of non-financial firms of Pakistan stock exchange*. Retrieved from https://mpra.ub.uni-muenchen.de/85346/1/MPRA_paper_85346.pdf

Ikpesu, F., & Eboiyehi, O. C. (2018). Capital structure and corporate financial distress of manufacturing firms in Nigeria. *Journal of Accounting and Taxation, 10*(7), 78–84. doi:10.5897/JAT2018.0309

Investing. (2019a). *NK Rosneft PAO (ROSN)*. Retrieved March 25, 2019 from https://www.investing.com/equities/rosneft_rts

Investing. (2019b). *Sberbank Rossii PAO (SBER)*. Retrieved March 25, 2019 from https://www.investing.com/equities/sberbank_rts

Investing. (2019c). *VTB (VTBR)*. Retrieved March 25, 2019 from https://www.investing.com/equities/vtb_rts

Irac, D., & Lopez, J. (2015). Euro area structural convergence? A multi-criterion cluster analysis. *International Economics*, *143*, 1–22. doi:10.1016/j.inteco.2015.01.005

Isukul, A. C., & Chizea, J. J. (2016). A comparative analysis of corporate governance disclosure in Nigerian and South African banks. *Asian Journal of Economics. Business and Accounting*, *1*(3), 1–15.

Ite, U. E. (2004). Multinationals and Corporate Social Responsibility in DevelopingCountries: A Case Study of Shell in Nigeria. *Corporate Social Responsibility and Environmental Management*, *11*, 1–11. doi:10.1002/csr.49

Ite, U. E. (2005). Poverty reduction in resource-rich developing countries: What have multinational corporations got to do with it? *Journal of International Development*, *17*(7), 913–929. doi:10.1002/jid.1177

Jaafar, A., & El-Shawa, M. (2009). Ownership concentration, board characteristics and performance: evidence from Jordan. In *Accounting in Emerging Economies* (pp. 73–95). Emerald Group Publishing Limited. doi:10.1108/S1479-3563(2009)0000009005

Jamali, D., & Karam, C. (2016). CSR in developing countries as an emerging field of Study. *International Journal of Management Reviews*, 1–30. doi:10.1111/ijmr.12112

Jamali, D., & Mirshak, R. (2007). Corporate Social Responsibility (CSR): Theory and Practice in a Developing Country Context. *Journal of Business Ethics*, *72*(3), 243–262. doi:10.100710551-006-9168-4

Jara, B. M., & López, F. J. (2007). Earnings management and internal control mechanisms: Evidence from Chilean firms. In L. W. Cornwall (Ed.), *New developments in banking and finance* (pp. 159–178). Hauppauge, NJ: Nova Science Publishers.

Jensen, M. C. (1993). The modern industrial revolution, exit, and the failure of internal control systems. *The Journal of Finance, 48*(3), 831-880.

Jensen, M. C. (1986). Agency cost of free cash flow, corporate finance, and takeovers. *Corporate Finance and Takeovers. The American Economic Review*, *76*(2).

Jensen, M. C. (1986). Agency cost of free cash flow, corporate finance, and takeovers. *Corporate Finance, and Takeovers. The American Economic Review*, *76*(2).

Jensen, M. C. (1993). The modern industrial revolution, exit, and the failure of internal control systems. *The Journal of Finance*, *48*(3), 831–880. doi:10.1111/j.1540-6261.1993.tb04022.x

Jensen, M. C., & Meckling, W. H. (1976). Theory of the firm: Managerial behavior, agency costs and ownership structure. *Journal of Financial Economics*, *3*(4), 305–360. doi:10.1016/0304-405X(76)90026-X

Jiang, F., & Kim, K. A. (2015). Corporate governance in China: A modern perspective. *Journal of Corporate Finance*, *32*, 190–216. doi:10.1016/j.jcorpfin.2014.10.010

Jiang, G., Lee, C. M., & Yue, H. (2010). Tunneling through intercorporate loans: The China experience. *Journal of Financial Economics*, *98*(1), 1–20. doi:10.1016/j.jfineco.2010.05.002

Jim, C. (2011). Leadership the Triumph Of Humility and Fierce Resolve. *Harvard Business Review*.

Johl, S., Jubb, C., & Houghton, K. (2007). Earning Management and the Audit Opinion: Evidence from Malaysia. *Managerial Auditing Journal, 22*(7), 688-715. doi:10.1108/02686900710772591

Johl, S. K., Johl, S. K., Subramaniam, N., & Cooper, B. (2013). Internal audit function, board quality and financial reporting quality: Evidence from Malaysia. *Managerial Auditing Journal*, *28*(9), 780–814. doi:10.1108/MAJ-06-2013-0886

John, K., & Kedia, S. (2006). *Design of corporate governance: Role of ownership structure, takeovers, and bank debt* (NYU Working Paper FIN-00-048). New York: Stern School of Business.

John, K., & Senbet, L. W. (1998). Corporate governance and board effectiveness1. *Journal of Banking & Finance*, *22*(4), 371–403. doi:10.1016/S0378-4266(98)00005-3

Johnson, S., La Porta, R., López-de-Silanes, F., & Shleifer, A. (2000). Tunneling. *The American Economic Review*, *90*(2), 22–27. doi:10.1257/aer.90.2.22 PMID:11031284

Jones, T. (1991). Ethical decision making by individuals in organizations: An issue contingent model. *Academy of Management Review*, *16*(2), 366–395. doi:10.5465/amr.1991.4278958

Joyner, B. E., & Payne, D. (2002). Evolution and implementation: A study of values, business ethics and corporate social responsibility. *Journal of Business Ethics*, *41*(4), 297–311. doi:10.1023/A:1021237420663

Judge, W. Q., Naoumova, I., & Koutzevol, N. (2003). Corporate governance and firm performance in Russia: An empirical study. *Journal of World Business*, *38*(4), 385–396. doi:10.1016/j.jwb.2003.08.023

Kameyama, S. (1997). *A Study Of SD National Model Based On Revised SNA - Conceptual, Institutional And Operational*. 15th International System Dynamics Conference: "Systems Approach To Learning And Education İnto The 21st Century", Istanbul, Turkey.

Kameyama, S. (1999). *Government Reform İn Japan- An Application Of SD National Model Based On SNA*. 17th International Conference Of The System Dynamics Society And 5th Australian & New Zealand Systems Conference, Wellington, New Zealand.

Kameyama, S. (2001). *Model For SME Sector Development*. The 19th International Conference Of The System Dynamics Society, Atlanta, GA.

Kameyama, S. (2002). Micro-Macro Finance Structure Modeling. *20th International Conference Of The System Dynamics Society*, Palermo, Italy.

Kant, I. (1981). *Grounding of the Metaphysics of Morals* (J. W. Ellington, Trans.). Indianapolis: Hackett Publishing Company. (Original work published 1785)

Kaptein, M. (2003). The diamond of managerial integrity. *European Management Journal*, *21*(1), 99–108. doi:10.1016/S0263-2373(02)00157-3

Kenjegalieva, K. A., & Simper, R. (2011). A productivity analysis of Central and Eastern European banking taking into account risk decomposition and environmental variables. *Research in International Business and Finance*, *25*(1), 26–38. doi:10.1016/j.ribaf.2010.05.003

Kent Baker, H., & Powell, G. E. (2009). Management views on corporate governance and firm performance. In *Corporate Governance and Firm Performance* (pp. 83–118). Emerald Group Publishing Limited. doi:10.1108/S1569-3732(2009)0000013006

Khanal, A. R., & Mishra, A. K. (2017). Stock price reactions to stock dividend announcements: A case from a sluggish economic period. *The North American Journal of Economics and Finance*, *42*, 338–345. doi:10.1016/j.najef.2017.08.002

Khan, M. (2015). *Program governance*. Boca Raton, FL: CRC Press.

Khanna, T., & Palepu, K. (2005). The evolution of concentrated ownership in India: Broad patterns and a history of the Indian software industry. In R. Mork (Ed.), *A history of corporate governance around the world: Family business groups to professional managers* (pp. 283–324). Chicago: National Bureau of Economic Research, The University of Chicago Press.

Khlif, H., & Samaha, K. (2016). Audit committee activity and internal control quality in Egypt: Does external auditor's size matter? *Managerial Auditing Journal*, *31*(3), 269–289. doi:10.1108/MAJ-08-2014-1084

Kiel, G. C., & Nicholson, G. J. (2003). Board composition and corporate performance: How the Australian experience informs contrasting theories of corporate governance. *Corporate Governance*, *11*(3), 189–205. doi:10.1111/1467-8683.00318

Kim. (1999). System Thinking In The Management Of Korean Economic Crisis. *Proceedings Of The 17th International System Dynamics Conference.*

Kim, C. S., Mauer, D. C., & Sherman, A. E. (1998). The determinants of corporate liquidity: Theory and evidence. *Journal of Financial and Quantitative Analysis*, *33*(3), 305–334. doi:10.2307/2331099

Kim, J. B., Chung, R., & Firth, M. (2003). Auditor conservatism, asymmetric monitoring, and earnings management. *Contemporary Accounting Research*, *20*(2), 323–359. doi:10.1506/J29K-MRUA-0APP-YJ6V

King, T., Srivastav, A., & Williams, J. (2016). What's in an education? Implications of CEO education for bank performance. *Journal of Corporate Finance*, *37*, 287–308. doi:10.1016/j.jcorpfin.2016.01.003

Kini, O., Kracaw, W., & Mian, S. (1995). Corporate takeovers, firm performance, and board composition. *Journal of Corporate Finance*, *1*(3-4), 383–412. doi:10.1016/0929-1199(94)00011-I

Kirkwood. (1998). *System Dynamics Methods: A Quick Introduction*. College Of Business Arizona State University.

Klein, A. (2002). Audit committee, board of director characteristics, and earnings management. *Journal of Accounting and Economics*, *33*(3), 375–400. doi:10.1016/S0165-4101(02)00059-9

Klien, A. (2002). Economic determinants of audit committee. *The Accounting Review*, *77*(2), 30–56.

Knechel, W. R., Krishnan, G. V., Pevzner, M. B., Stefchik, L., & Velury, U. (2013). Audit quality: Insights from the academic literature. *Auditing*, *32*(1), 385–421. doi:10.2308/ajpt-50350

Kohlberg, L. (1969). Stage and sequence: the cognitive-developmental approach to socialization. In *Handbook of Socialization Theory and Research* (pp. 347–480). D.A. Goslin.

Kolk, A. (2016). The social responsibility of international business: From ethics and the environment to CSR and sustainable development. *Journal of World Business*, *51*(1), 23–34. doi:10.1016/j.jwb.2015.08.010

Kolk, A., & Lenfant, F. (2009). MNCS reporting on CSR and conflict in CentralAfrica. *Journal of Business Ethics*, *93*(S2), 241–255. doi:10.100710551-009-0271-1

Krishnan, J. (2005). Audit Committee Financial Expertise and Internal Control: An Empirical Analysis. *The Accounting Review*, *80*(2), 649–675. doi:10.2308/accr.2005.80.2.649

Kristanti, F. T., Rahayu, S., & Huda, A. N. (2016). The determinant of financial distress on Indonesian family firm. *Procedia: Social and Behavioral Sciences*, *219*, 440–447.

Kuada, J., & Hinson, R. E. (2012). Corporate social responsibility (CSR) practices offoreign and local companies in Ghana. *Thunderbird International Business Review*, *54*(4), 521–536. doi:10.1002/tie.21481

Kuan, H. T., Li, C. S., & Chu, S. H. (2011). Cash Holdings and Corporate Governance in Family-Controlled Firms. *Journal of Business Research*, *64*(7), 757–764. doi:10.1016/j.jbusres.2010.07.004

Kukreja, G. (2013). Impact of new corporate governance on disclosure: Evidence from Bahrain Listed commercial Banks. *Advance in Management and Applied Economics*, *3*(3), 171–191.

Kupor, S. (2013). *The US can battle wealth inequality by letting startups IPO earlier.* Retrieved February 10, 2019 from Quartz: https://qz.com/66371/us-can-battle-wealth-inequality-by-letting-startups-ipo-earlier/

Küskü, F. (2007). From Necessity to Responsibility: Evidence for Corporate Environmental Citizenship Activities from a Developing Country Perspective. *Corporate Social Responsibility and Environmental Management*, *14*(2), 74–87. doi:10.1002/csr.119

La Porta, R., Lopez-de-Silanes, F., & Shleifer, A. (1999). Corporate ownership around the world. *The Journal of Finance*, *52*(2), 471–517. doi:10.1111/0022-1082.00115

La Porta, R., López-de-Silanes, F., Shleifer, A., & Vishny, R. (1997). Legal determinants of external finance. *The Journal of Finance*, *52*(3), 1131–1150. doi:10.1111/j.1540-6261.1997.tb02727.x

La Porta, R., López-de-Silanes, F., Shleifer, A., & Vishny, R. (1998). Law and finance. *Journal of Political Economy*, *106*(6), 1113–1155. doi:10.1086/250042

La Porta, R., López-de-Silanes, F., Shleifer, A., & Vishny, R. (2000). Investor protection and corporate governance. *Journal of Financial Economics*, *58*(1-2), 3–27. doi:10.1016/S0304-405X(00)00065-9

Lane & Sterman. (2011). Profiles in Operations Research: Jay Wright Forrester. In *Profiles in Operations Research: Pioners and Innovators*. New York: Springer. Retrieved from http://jsterman.scripts.mit.edu/docs/Lane2011%20Profiles%20in%20Operations%20Research.pdf

Lary, A. M., & Taylor, D. W. (2012). Governance characteristics and role effectiveness of audit committees. *Managerial Auditing Journal*, *27*(4), 336–354. doi:10.1108/02686901211217969

Lastunen, J. (2014). Macroeconomic Dynamics Of Greece İn The Midst Of The Eurozone Crisis – Application Of SD Modeling And Insights For Policy. *Proceedings Of The 32nd International Conference Of The System Dynamics Society*.

Lautenschläger, S. (2018). *Good governance and the role of supervisory boards*. Member of the Executive Board of the ECB and Vice-Chair of the Supervisory Board of the ECB, Speech at the Luncheon of Chairs of Supervisory Boards of banks in Germany. Retrieved from https://www.ecb.europa.eu/press/key/date/2018/html/ecb.sp181106.en.html

Le Breton-Miller, I., & Miller, D. (2006). Why do some family businesses outcompete? Governance, long-term orientations and sustainable capability. *Entrepreneurship Theory and Practice*, *30*(6), 731–746. doi:10.1111/j.1540-6520.2006.00147.x

LeClere, M. J. (2005). Time-dependent and time-invariant covariates within a proportional hazards model: A financial distress application. *Review of Accounting and Finance*, *4*(4), 91–109. doi:10.1108/eb043439

Leech, D., & Leahy, J. (1991). Ownership structure, control type classifications and the performance of large British companies. *Economic Journal (London)*, *101*(409), 1418–1437. doi:10.2307/2234893

Lee, P. (2015). Problems of Implementing Audit Committee and Supervisory Board Simultaneously in China. *Journal of Accounting, Auditing & Finance*, *30*(4), 509–528. doi:10.1177/0148558X15587649

Lehmann, D. R., Gupta, S., & Steckel, J. (1988). *Marketing research*. Reading, MA: Addison-Wesley.

Levin, M. R. (2015). *What is private ordering?* Retrieved from http://www.theactivistinvestor.com/The_Activist_Investor/Blog/Entries/2015/9/29_What_is_Private_Ordering.html

Liang, Q., Xu, P., & Jiraporn, P. (2013). Board characteristics and Chinese bank performance. *Journal of Banking & Finance*, *37*(8), 2953–2968. doi:10.1016/j.jbankfin.2013.04.018

Lichtenberg, F. R., & Pushner, G. M. (1994). Ownership structure and corporate performance in Japan. *Japan and the World Economy*, *6*(3), 239–261. doi:10.1016/0922-1425(94)90014-0

Lim, S., Matolcsy, Z., & Chow, D. (2007). The association between board composition and different types of voluntary disclosure. *European Accounting Review*, *16*(3), 555–583. doi:10.1080/09638180701507155

Lin, J. W., Li, J. F., & Yang, J. S. (2006). The effect of audit committee performance on earning quality. *Managerial Auditing Journal*, *21*(9), 921–933. doi:10.1108/02686900610705019

Lipton, M., & Lorsch, J. W. (1992). A modest proposal for improved corporate governance. *Business Lawyer*, 59–77.

Lisic, L., Neal, T., & Zhang, Y. (2011). *Audit committee financial expertise and restatements: The moderating effect of CEO power*. Fairfax, VA: School of Management, George Mason University.

Liu, Q., Luo, T. & Tian, G. (2015). Family control and corporate cash holdings: evidence from China. *Journal of Corporate Finance, 31*, 220-245.

Liu, Y., Miletkov, M. K., Wei, Z., & Yang, T. (2015). Board independence and firm performance in China. *Journal of Corporate Finance*, *30*, 223–244. doi:10.1016/j.jcorpfin.2014.12.004

Lorino, P. (1998). Valeur pour l'actionnaire: Une mode à risques. *Alternatives Economiques*, *162*, 55.

Loughran, T., & Ritter, J. (2000). Uniformly least powerful tests of market efficiency. *Journal of Financial Economics*, *55*(3), 361–389. doi:10.1016/S0304-405X(99)00054-9

Lubatkin, M., Schulze, W., Ling, Y., & Dino, R. (2005). The effects of parental altruism on the governance of family-managed firms. *Journal of Organizational Behavior*, *26*(3), 313–330. doi:10.1002/job.307

Maani & Cavana. (2007). *Systems Thinking And Modelling Understanding Change and Complexity*. Pearson Education.

Makower, J. (1993). *The E factor: The Bottomline Approach to Environmentally Responsible Business*. New York: Random House.

Mamatzakis, E., & Bermpei, T. (2015). The effect of corporate governance on the performance of US investment banks. *Financial Markets, Institutions & Instruments*, *24*(2-3), 191-239.

Marcos, S., & Castrillo, L. A. (2018, June). *Equilibrium in corporate governance*. Paper presented at the XXVIII meeting of the Asociación Científica de Economía y Dirección de la Empresa, Valladolid, Spain.

Marilen, P., & Ana-Cristina, N. (2013). Corporate governance codes of best practice of top romanian banks. *Annals of the University of Oradea. Economic Science Series*, *22*(2), 390–397.

Marshall, R. S., Akoore, M. E. M., Hamann, R., & Sinha, P. (2009). Environmental Practices in the wine industry: An empirical application of the theory of reasoned action and stakeholder theory in the United States and New Zealand. *Journal of World Business*, *45*(4), 405–414. doi:10.1016/j.jwb.2009.08.009

Marsh, H. L., & Powell, T. E. (1989). The audit committee charter: Rx for fraud prevention. *Journal of Accountancy*, *167*(2), 55.

Martin, L. A. (1997a). *Road Map 2: The First Step*. MIT System Dynamics in Education Project. Retrieved from http://sysdyn.clexchange.org/sdep/Roadmaps/RM2/D- 4694.pdf

Martin, L. A. (1997b). *Road Map 2: An Introduction To Feedback*. MIT System Dynamics In Education Project. Retrieved from http://static.clexchange.org/ftp/documents/roadmaps/RM2/D-4691.pdf

Matar, M. (2006). Recent trends in financial and credit analysis, methods, tools and practical uses (2nd ed.). Amman: Darwael for publication and distribution.

Matten, D., & Moon, J. (2008). "Implicit" and "Explicit" CSR: A Conceptual Framework for a Comparative Understanding of Corporate Social Responsibility. *Academy of Management Review*, *33*(2), 404–424. doi:10.5465/amr.2008.31193458

McGarvey & Hannon. (2003). *Dynamic Modelling For Business Management An Introduction*. Springer Press.

McMullen, D. A. (1996). Audit committee performance: An investigation of the consequences associated with audit committees. *Auditing*, *15*(1), 87.

McMullen, D., & Raghunandan, K. (1996). Enhancing Audit Committee Effectiveness. *Journal of Accountancy*, *182*(2), 79–81.

McWilliams, A., Siegel, D. S., & Wright, P. M. (2000). Corporate Social Responsibility: Strategic Implications. *Journal of Management Studies, 43*(1).

McWilliams, A., & Siegel, D. S. (2000). 'Corporate Social Responsibility and Financial Performance: Correlation or Misspecification'? *Strategic Management Journal*, *21*(4), 603–609. doi:10.1002/(SICI)1097-0266(200005)21:5<603::AID-SMJ101>3.0.CO;2-3

McWilliams, A., & Siegel, D. S. (2001). A Theory of the Firm Perspective. *Academy of Management Review*, *26*(1), 117–127. doi:10.5465/amr.2001.4011987

Mehran, H. (1995). Executive compensation structure, ownership, and firm performance. *Journal of Financial Economics*, *38*(2), 163–184. doi:10.1016/0304-405X(94)00809-F

Mercieca, S., Schaeck, K., & Wolfe, S. (2007). Small European banks: Benefits from diversification? *Journal of Banking & Finance*, *31*(7), 1975–1998. doi:10.1016/j.jbankfin.2007.01.004

Mersland, R., & Strøm, R. Ø. (2009). Performance and governance in microfinance institutions. *Journal of Banking & Finance*, *33*(4), 662–669. doi:10.1016/j.jbankfin.2008.11.009

Michaely, R., & Shaw, W. H. (1995). Does the choice of auditor convey quality in an initial public offering? *Financial Management*, *24*(4), 15–30. doi:10.2307/3665948

Milfont, T. L., & Duckitt, J. (2010). The environmental attitudes inventory: A valid and reliable measure to assess the structure of environmental attitudes. *Journal of Environmental Psychology*, *30*(1), 80–94. doi:10.1016/j.jenvp.2009.09.001

Milgrom, P. (1988). Employment contracts, influence activities, and efficient organization design. *Journal of Political Economy*, *42*(1), 42–61. doi:10.1086/261523

Miller, M., & Orr, D. (1966). A model of the demand for money by firms. *The Quarterly Journal of Economics*, *80*(3), 413–435. doi:10.2307/1880728

Miller, T., Kim, A. B., & Roberts, J. M. (2018). *Index of economic freedom*. Washington, DC: The Heritage Foundation.

Mínguez, A., & Martín, J. F. (2003). *El consejo de administración como mecanismo de control: Evidencia para el mercado español* (Working Paper). Instituto Valenciano de Investigaciones Económicas. (WP-EC 2003-02)

Mitchell, R. K., Agle, B. R., & Wood, D. J. (1997). Toward a theory of stakeholder identification and salience: Defining the principle of who and what really counts. *Academy of Management Review*, *22*(4), 853–886. doi:10.5465/amr.1997.9711022105

Mitchell, V. Z., Singh, H., & Singh, I. (2008). Association between independent audit committee members' human-resource features and underpricing. The case of Singapore IPOs from 1997-2006. *Journal of Human Resource Costing & Accounting*, *12*(3), 179–212. doi:10.1108/14013380810919840

Miteva, E. (2005). *Improving Corporate Governance in the Middle East and North Africa*. Paper presented at the MENA and OECD's Initiative on Governance for Investment and Development, MENA Regional Corporate Governance Forum, Amman, Jordan.

Mitton, T. (2002). A cross-firm analysis of the impact of corporate governance on the East Asian financial crisis. *Journal of Financial Economics*, *64*(2), 215–241. doi:10.1016/S0304-405X(02)00076-4

Modigliani, F., & Miller, M. H. (1963). Corporate income taxes and the cost of capital: A correction. *The American Economic Review*, *53*(3), 433–443.

Mollah, S., & Talukdar, B. (2007). *Ownership Structure, Corporate Governance, and Firm's Performance in Emerging Markets: Evidence from Bangaldesh*. Academic Press.

Mollah, S., & Zaman, M. (2015). Shari'ah supervision, corporate governance and performance: Conventional vs. Islamic banks. *Journal of Banking & Finance*, *58*, 418–435. doi:10.1016/j.jbankfin.2015.04.030

Molyneux, P., & Thornton, J. (1992). Determinants of European bank profitability: A note. *Journal of Banking & Finance*, *16*(6), 1173–1178. doi:10.1016/0378-4266(92)90065-8

Mongalo, T. (2004). South Africanizing company law for a modern, competitive global economy. *South African Law Journal*, *121*(1), 93–116.

Morck, R., Shleifer, A., & Vishny, R. (1988). Management ownership and market valuation: An empirical analysis. *Journal of Financial Economics*, *20*, 293–315. doi:10.1016/0304-405X(88)90048-7

Morecroft. (2015). *Strategic Modelling And Business Dynamics:A Feedback Systems Approach*. John Wiley & Sons.

Morecroft, J. D. W., & Sterman, J. D. (1994). *Modelling For Learning Organizations*. Portland, OR: Productivity Press.

Muigai, R. G. (2016). *Effect of capital structure on financial distress of non-financial companies listed in Nairobi securities exchange* (Doctoral dissertation). COHRED, Finance, JKUAT.

Mushtaha, S. (2009). *The Extent to Which the Characteristics of The Audit Committee Improves the Quality of Financial Reporting*. PHD Research.

Muth, M. M., & Donaldson, L. (1998). Stewardship theory and board structure: A contingency Approach. *Corporate Governance*, *6*(1), 5–28. doi:10.1111/1467-8683.00076

Myers, S. C. (1984). The capital structure puzzle. *The Journal of Finance*, *39*(3), 575–592. doi:10.2307/2327916

Myers, S. C., & Majluf, N. S. (1984). Corporate financing and investment decisions when firms have information that investors do not have. *Journal of Financial Economics*, *13*(2), 187–221. doi:10.1016/0304-405X(84)90023-0

Nahar Abdullah, S. (2006). Directors' remuneration, firm's performance and corporate governance in Malaysia among distressed companies. c*orporate governance: The International. Journal of Business and Society*, *6*(2), 162–174.

Neri, L., D'Agostino, A., Regoli, A., Pulselli, F. M., & Coscieme, L. (2017). Evaluating dynamics of national economies through cluster analysis within the input-state-output sustainability framework. *Ecological Indicators*, *72*, 77–90. doi:10.1016/j.ecolind.2016.08.016

Ngare, E., Nyamongo, E. M., & Misati, R. N. (2014). Stock market development and economic growth in Africa. *Journal of Economics and Business*, *74*, 24–39. doi:10.1016/j.jeconbus.2014.03.002

Nimer, K., Warrad, L., & Khuraisat, O. (2012). The effect of audit committee's effectiveness on dividend payout policy: Evidence from the Jordanian firms. *International Journal of Business and Management, 7*(7), 172–179. doi:10.5539/ijbm.v7n7p172

Norden, L., & Szerencses, M. (2005). *Migration and concentration risks in bank lending: new evidence from credit portfolio data*. Mannheim: Department of Banking and Finance, University of Mannheim.

Norton, G. (2007). *Russia: VTB puts on a good show with $8 billion IPO.* Retrieved March 12, 2019 from Euromoney: https://www.euromoney.com/article/b13222cnkc8y08/russia-vtb-puts-on-a-good-show-with-$8-billion-ipo?copyrightInfo=true

Norwani, N., Mohamad, Z. Z., & Chek, I. A. (2011). Corporate governance failure and its impact on financial reporting within selected companies. *International Journal of Business and Social Science, 2*, 205 – 213.

Nouy, D. (2018). *Good governance for good decisions*. Chair of the Supervisory Board of the ECB, Second banking supervision conference, "Governance expectations for banks in a changing financial environment", Frankfurt, Germany. Retrieved from https://www.bankingsupervision.europa.eu/press/speeches/date/2018/html/ssm.sp180322_1.en.html

Nwagbara, U. (2013). The effects of social media on environmental sustainability activities of oil and gas multinationals in Nigeria. *Thunderbird International Business Review, 55*(6), 689–697. doi:10.1002/tie.21584

Oba, B., Tigrel, E., & Sener, P. (2014). Board structure in listed firms: Evidence from an emerging economy. *Corporate Governance: The International Journal of Business in Society, 14*(3), 382–394. doi:10.1108/CG-05-2012-0044

Obay, L. A. (2009). Corporate governance & business ethics: A Dubai-based survey. *Journal of Legal. Ethical & Regulatory Issues, 12*(2), 29–47.

OECD Policy Brief. (2004). *The OECD Principles of Corporate Governance*. Available: http://www.oecd.org/corporate/corporateaffairs/corporategovern

OECD. (2013). *Supervision and enforcement in corporate governance. Corporate Governance*. OECD Publishing. doi:10.1787/9789264203334-

Oet & Pavlov. (2014). Feedback Mechanisms In The Financial System: A Modern View. *Proceedings Of The 32nd International Conference Of The System Dynamics Society*.

Ogundipe, L. O., Ogundipe, S. E., & Ajao, S. K. (2012). Cash holding and firm characteristics: Evidence from Nigerian emerging market. *Journal of Business Economics and Finance, 1*(2), 45–58.

Öğüt & Şahin. (2012). *Türkiye'de Finansal İstikrar Sorununa Sistem Dinamiği Yaklaşımı*. Türkiye Ekonomi Kurumu.

Ohlson, J., & Feltham, J. (1995). Valuation and clean surplus accounting for operating and financial activities. *Contemporary Accounting Research*, *11*(2), 689–731. doi:10.1111/j.1911-3846.1995.tb00462.x

Ojeka, S., Iyoha, F., & Obigbemi, I. F. (2014). effectiveness of audit committee and firm financial performance in Nigeria: an empirical analysis. *Journal of Accounting and Auditing: Research & Practice*.

Okereke,, C., & Vincent,, O. (2018). Determinants of Nigerian managers' environmental attitude: Africa's Ubuntu ethics versus global capitalism. *Thunderbird International Business Review*, *2018*, 1–14.

Okereke, C., & Küng, K. (2013). Climate policy and business climate strategies: EUcement companies' response to climate change and barriers against action. *Management of Environmental Quality*, *24*(3), 286–310. doi:10.1108/14777831311322622

Okpara, J. O., & Wynn, P. M. (2012). Stakeholders' perceptions about corporate social responsibility: Implications for poverty alleviation. *Thunderbird International Business Review*, *54*(1), 91–103. doi:10.1002/tie.21441

Okutan-Nilsson, G. (2007). Corporate governance in Turkey. *European Business Organization Law Review*, *8*(2), 196–236.

Oliff, M. D., & Vandermerwe, S. (1990). Customers drive corporations green. *Long Range Planning*, *23*(6), 10–17. doi:10.1016/0024-6301(90)90096-M

Omran, M. M., Bolbol, A., & Fatheldin, A. (2008). Corporate governance and firm performance in Arab equity markets: Does ownership concentration matter? *International Review of Law and Economics*, *28*(1), 32–45. doi:10.1016/j.irle.2007.12.001

Önder, A. Ö., Deliktas, E. R., & Lenger, A. (2003). Efficiency in the manufacturing industry of selected provinces in Turkey: A stochastic frontier analysis. *Emerging Markets Finance & Trade*, *39*(2), 98–113. doi:10.1080/1540496X.2003.11052537

Öner. (2003). *Dinamik Sistem Modelleme İle Makroekonomik Analiz: Türkiye İçin Bir Oyun Denemesi*. Çalışma Makalesi, Temmuz.

Opler, T., Pinkowitz, L., & Stulz, R. (1999). The determinants and implications of corporate cash holdings. *Journal of Financial Economics*, *52*(1), 3–46. doi:10.1016/S0304-405X(99)00003-3

Organization for Economic Co-operation and Development. (2004). *Corporate Governance: A Survey of OECD Countries*. OECD Publishing.

Orpen, C. (1987). The Attitudes of United States and South African Managers to Corporate Social Responsibility. *Journal of Business Ethics*, *6*(2), 89–96. doi:10.1007/BF00382022

Özbayrak, M., Papadopoulou, T. C., & Akgun, M. (2007). System Dynamics Modelling of A Manufacturing Supply Chain System. *Simulation Modelling Practice and Theory*, *15*(10), 1338–1355. doi:10.1016/j.simpat.2007.09.007

Ozen, S., & Kusku, F. (2009). Corporate Environmental Citizenship Variation inDeveloping Countries: An Institutional Framework. *Journal of Business Ethics, 89*(2), 297–313. doi:10.100710551-008-0001-0

Ozkan, A., & Ozkan, N. (2004). Corporate cash holdings: An empirical investigation of UK companies. *Journal of Banking & Finance, 28*(9), 2103–2134. doi:10.1016/j.jbankfin.2003.08.003

Pallant, Y. (2011). *SPSS Survival Manual: A Step by Step Guide to Data Analysis using SPSS for Windows* (3rd ed.). McGraw Hill Open University Press.

Parker, S., Peters, G. F., & Turetsky, H. F. (2002). Corporate governance and corporate failure: a survival analysis. *Corporate Governance: The International Journal of Business in Society, 2*(2), 4-12.

Pasiouras, F., & Kosmidou, K. (2007). Factors influencing the profitability of domestic and foreign commercial banks in the European Union. *Research in International Business and Finance, 21*(2), 222–237. doi:10.1016/j.ribaf.2006.03.007

Paskelian, O. G., Bell, S., & Nguyen, C. V. (2010). Corporate governance and cash holdings: A comparative analysis of Chinese and Indian Firms. *The International Journal of Business and Finance Research, 4*, 59–73.

Pathan, S., & Faff, R. (2013). Does board structure in banks really affect their performance? *Journal of Banking & Finance, 37*(5), 1573–1589. doi:10.1016/j.jbankfin.2012.12.016

Patteli, L., & Prencipe, A. (2007). The Relationship Between Voluntary Disclosure and Independent Directors in the Presence of a Dominant Shareholder. *European Accounting Review, 16*(1), 5–33. doi:10.1080/09638180701265820

Patton, A., & Baker, J. C. (1987). Why wont directors rock the boat. *Harvard Business Review, 65*(6), 10.

Pearce, J. A., & Zahra, S. A. (1992). Board composition from a strategic contingency perspective. *Journal of Management Studies, 29*(4), 411–438. doi:10.1111/j.1467-6486.1992.tb00672.x

Peng, K. C., Wei, Z., & Yang, Z. (2011). Yang, (2011). Tunneling or propping: Evidence from connected transactions in China. *Journal of Corporate Finance, 17*(2), 306–325. doi:10.1016/j.jcorpfin.2010.08.002

Peng, M. W., & Jiang, Y. (2010). Institutions behind family ownership and control in large firms. *Journal of Management Studies, 47*(2), 253–273. doi:10.1111/j.1467-6486.2009.00890.x

Peng, T.-C. M., Bartholomae, S., Fox, J. J., & Cravener, G. (2007). The impact of personal finance education delivered in high school and college courses. *Journal of Family and Economic Issues, 28*(2), 265–284. doi:10.100710834-007-9058-7

Perry, P. (1992). Do banks gain or lose from inflation? *Journal of Retail Banking, 14*(2), 25–31.

Pfeffer, J. (1972). Sizc and composition of corporatc boards of directors: The organization and its environment. *Administrative Science Quarterly*, *17*(2), 218–228. doi:10.2307/2393956

Pfeffer, J., & Salancik, G. R. (1978). *The external control of organizations: A resource dependence approach.* Harper and Row Publishers.

Pidd. (1996). *Tools for Thinking Modelling in Management Science*. John Wiley & Sons.

Pilkington, E. (2009). Shell pays out $15.5 million over Saro-Wiwa Killing. *The Guardian.* Available at: http://www.guardian.co.uk/world/2009/jun/08/nigeria-usa

Pinkowitz, L., Stulz, R. S., & Williamson, R. (2012). *Multinationals and the high cash holdings puzzle*. National Bureau of Economic Research (NBER) Working Paper No. 18120.

Pinkowitz, L., Stulz, R. M., & Williamson, R. (2003). *Do firms in countries with poor protection of investor rights hold more cash? (No. w10188).* National Bureau of Economic Research. doi:10.3386/w10188

Poulain-Rehm, T. (2006). *L'actionnariat salarié en France, un facteur de création de valeur? Woking paper*. Université Montesquieu-Bordeaux IV.

Prakash, A., & Potoski, M. (2007). Investing Up: FDI and the Cross-Country Diffusion of Iso 14001 Management Systems. *International Studies Quarterly*, *51*(3), 723–744. doi:10.1111/j.1468-2478.2007.00471.x

Pranowo, K., Achsani, N. A., Manurung, A. H., & Nuryartono, N. (2010). Determinant of corporate financial distress in an emerging market economy: Empirical evidence from the Indonesian stock exchange 2004-2008. *International Research Journal of Finance and Economics*, *52*(1), 81–90.

Pucheta-Martínez, M. C., & De Fuentes, C. (2007). The Impact of Audit Committee Characteristics on the Enhancement of the Quality of Financial Reporting: An empirical study in the Spanish context. *Corporate Governance*, *15*(6), 1394–1412. doi:10.1111/j.1467-8683.2007.00653.x

Puffer, S. M., & McCarthy, D. J. (2012). Corporate governance and initial public offerings in Russia. In A. Zattoni & W. Q. Judge Jr., (Eds.), *Corporate Governance and Initial Public Offerings* (pp. 354–377). Cambridge, UK: Cambridge University Press. doi:10.1017/CBO9781139061513.016

Qaraqish, S. (2009). *The Effect of Audit Committee Characteristics on Earnings Quality An Empirical Study on the Industrial Sector Firms Listed at Amman Stock Exchange* (Unpublished dissertation). Arab Academy for Banking and Financial Sciences.

Quiroga & Franco. (2014). Using System Dynamics to Analyze Social and Economic Challenges in Myanmar. *Proceedings of the 32nd International Conference of the System Dynamics Society.*

Radzicki, M. J. (2007). System Dynamics And Its Contribution To Economics And Economic Modeling. In Encyclopedia Of Complexity And System Science. Springer-Verlag.

Rajan, R. G., & Zingales, L. (1995). What do we know about capital structure? Some evidence from international data. *The Journal of Finance*, *50*(5), 1421–1460. doi:10.1111/j.1540-6261.1995.tb05184.x

Rajan, R. G., & Zingales, L. (2000). The governance of the new enterprise. In X. Vives (Ed.), *Corporate governance* (pp. 201–232). Cambridge, UK: Cambridge University Press. doi:10.1017/CBO9781139175333.007

Rappaport, A. (1998). *Creating shareholder value*. New York: Free Press.

Rashid, A. (2018). Board independence and firm performance: Evidence from Bangladesh. *Future Business Journal*, *4*(1), 34–49. doi:10.1016/j.fbj.2017.11.003

Rawls, J. (1971). *A Theory of Justice*. Cambridge, MA: Harvard University Press.

Ray, S. (2011). Assessing corporate financial distress in automobile industry of India: An application of Altman's model. *Research Journal of Finance and Accounting, 2*(3), 155-168.

Razman, S. R., & Iskandar, M. (2004). The effectiveness of audit committee in monitoring the quality of corporate reporting. In *Corporate Governance: An International Perspective* (pp. 154–175). Kuala Lumpur: Malaysian Institute of Corporate Governance.

Reddy, K., Locke, S., & Scrimgeour, F. (2010). The efficacy of principle-based corporate governance practices and firm financial performance: An empirical investigation. *International Journal of Managerial Finance*, *6*(3), 190–219. doi:10.1108/17439131011056224

Rediker, K. J., & Seth, A. (1995). Boards of directors and substitution effects of alternative governance mechanisms. *Strategic Management Journal*, *16*(2), 85–99. doi:10.1002mj.4250160202

Reed, M. I. (2002). New managerialism, professional power and organisational governance in UK universities: A review and assessment. In *Governing higher education: National perspectives on institutional governance* (pp. 163–185). Springer. doi:10.1007/978-94-015-9946-7_9

Reuters. (2007). *Russia's VTB Raises $8 Billion in IPO, Shares Surge*. Retrieved March 13, 2019 from: https://www.cnbc.com/id/18607910

Richardson. (1986). Problems With Causal-Loop Diagrams. *System Dynamics Review, 2*(2).

Richardson. (1999). *Feedback Throught in Social Science And Systems Theory*. Pegasus Communications, Inc.

Richmond, B. (2010). The Thinking In Systems Thinking: Eight Critical Skills. In Tracing Connections: Voices Of Systems Thinkers. Creative Learning Exchange.

Riddick, L. A., & Whited, T. M. (2009). The corporate propensity to save. *The Journal of Finance*, *64*(4), 1729–1766. doi:10.1111/j.1540-6261.2009.01478.x

Ridley, A. (1998). *Beginning Bioethics*. New York: St. Martin's Press.

Roberts, M. R., & Whited, T. M. (2013). Endogeneity in empirical corporate finance. In G. M. Constantinides, M. Harris, & R. M. Stulz (Eds.), Handbook of the economics of finance (vol. 2, Part A, pp. 493-572). Amsterdam: North Holland.

Robinson, W. I. (2005). Gramsci and Globalization: From Nation-State to Transnational Hegemony. *Critical Review of International Social and Political Philosophy*, *8*(4), 1–16. doi:10.1080/13698230500205243

Rodriguez, F. J. G., & Cruz, Y. M. A. (2007). Relationship between social-environmental responsibility and performance in hotel firms. *Hospital Management*, *26*(4), 824–839. doi:10.1016/j.ijhm.2006.08.003

Romero, E. J. (2004). Hispanic identity and acculturation: Implications formanagement. *Cross Cultural Management*, *11*(1), 62–71. doi:10.1108/13527600410797756

Rondinelli, D. A., & Berry, M. A. (2000). Environmental citizenship in multinational corporations: Social responsibility and sustainable development. *European Management Journal*, *18*(1), 70–84. doi:10.1016/S0263-2373(99)00070-5

Rosen, S. (1990). *Contracts and the Market for Executives (No. w3542)*. National Bureau of Economic Research. doi:10.3386/w3542

Rosenstein, S., & Wyatt, J. G. (1990). Outside directors, board independence, and shareholder wealth. *Journal of Financial Economics*, *26*(2), 175–191. doi:10.1016/0304-405X(90)90002-H

Rossi, S. P., Schwaiger, M. S., & Winkler, G. (2009). How loan portfolio diversification affects risk, efficiency and capitalization: A managerial behavior model for Austrian banks. *Journal of Banking & Finance*, *33*(12), 2218–2226. doi:10.1016/j.jbankfin.2009.05.022

Ruigrok, W., Peck, S. I., & Keller, H. (2006). Board characteristics and involvement in strategic decision making: Evidence from Swiss companies. *Journal of Management Studies*, *43*(5), 1201–1226. doi:10.1111/j.1467-6486.2006.00634.x

Russo, M. V., & Fouts, P. A. (1997). A resource-based perspective on corporate environmental performance and profitability. *Academy of Management Journal*, *40*(3), 534–559.

Ruth & Hannon. (2012). *Modeling Dynamic Economic Systems* (2nd ed.). Springer.

Şahin. (2014). *Türkiye Ekonomisi Tarihsel Gelişimi- Bugunkü Durumu*. Bursa: Ezgi Kitabevi Yayınları.

Saleh, N., Iskandar, T., & Rahmat, M. (2007). Audit Committee Characteristics and Earning Management: Evidence from Malaysia. *Asian Review of Accounting*, *15*(2), 147–163. doi:10.1108/13217340710823369

Salim, R., Arjomandi, A., & Seufert, J. H. (2016). Does corporate governance affect Australian banks' performance? *Journal of International Financial Markets, Institutions and Money*, *43*, 113–125. doi:10.1016/j.intfin.2016.04.006

Samad, A., & Hassan, M. K. (1999). The performance of Malaysian Islamic bank during 1984-1997: An exploratory study. *International Journal of Islamic Financial Services*, *1*(3), 1–14.

Samaha, K., & Dahawy, K. (2010). Factors influencing corporate disclosure transparency in the active share trading firms: An explanatory study. *Research in Accounting in Emerging Economies*, *10*, 87–118. doi:10.1108/S1479-3563(2010)0000010009

Samaha, K., Dahawy, K., Hussainey, K., & Stapleton, P. (2012). The extent of corporate governance disclosure and its determinants in a developing market: The case of Egypt. *Advances in Accounting*, *28*(1), 168–178. doi:10.1016/j.adiac.2011.12.001

Sánchez, J. M., & Yurdagul, E. (2013). Why are corporations holding so much cash? *The Regional Economist*, *21*(1), 4–8.

Schipper, K., & Vincent, L. (2003). Earnings Quality. *Accounting Horizons*, *17*(s-1), 97–110. doi:10.2308/acch.2003.17.s-1.97

Schultz, E. L., Tan, D. T., & Walsh, K. D. (2010). Endogeneity and the corporate governance-performance relation. *Australian Journal of Management*, *35*(2), 145–163. doi:10.1177/0312896210370079

Schwarcz, S. T. (2002). Private ordering. *Northwestern University Law Review*, *97*(1), 319–350.

Scott, W. R. (1992). *Organisational: Rational, Natural, and Open Systems*. Englewood Cliffs, NJ: Prentice-Hall.

Securities and Exchange Commission. (2003). Final Rule: Standards Related to Listed Company Audit Committees (SEC Release Nos. 33-8330; 34-47654). Washington, DC: Author.

Senge, Kleiner, Roberts, Ross, & Smith. (1994). *The Fifth Discipline Fieldbook*. Century.

Senge. (1990). *The Fifth Discipline: The Art And Practice Of The Learning Organization*. Random House.

Senge. (2002). Beşinci Disiplin, Çeviren: Ayşegül İldeniz Ve Ahmet Doğukan. *Yapı Kredi Yayınları, 16*.

Sergaev, S. (2019). Placement of shares of banks: Sberbank and VTB. *Banking*, *6*, 40–43.

Seyidoğlu. (2013). *Uluslararası İktisat*. İstanbul: Genişletilmiş Onaltıncı Baskı, Güzem CanYayınları.

Sezen & Günal. (2009). *Yöneylem Araştırmasında Benzetim*. Bursa: Ekin Yayınevi.

Sezen. (2007). *Yöneylem Araştırması*. Ekin Yayınevi, Bursa.

Shah, A. S. Z., & Butt, S. A. (2009). The impact of corporate governance on the cost of equity: Empirical evidence from Pakistani listed companies. *The Lahore Journal of Economics*, *14*(1), 139–171. doi:10.35536/lje.2009.v14.i1.a6

Sharma, S. (2000). Managerial interpretations and organizational context as predictors of corporate choice of environmental strategy. *Academy of Management Journal*, *43*, 681–697.

Shivdasani, A., & Yermack, D. (1999). CEO involvement in the selection of new board members: An empirical analysis. *The Journal of Finance*, *54*(5), 1829–1853. doi:10.1111/0022-1082.00168

Shleifer, A., & Vishny, R. (1986). Large shareholders and corporate control. *Journal of Political Economy*, *94*(3), 461–488. doi:10.1086/261385

Shleifer, A., & Vishny, R. (1997). A survey of corporate governance. *The Journal of Finance*, *52*(2), 737–783. doi:10.1111/j.1540-6261.1997.tb04820.x

Shleifer, A., & Vishny, R. W. (1988). Value maximization and the acquisition process. *The Journal of Economic Perspectives*, *2*(1), 7–20. doi:10.1257/jep.2.1.7

Simon, J. (1997). *Endangered Mexico*. San Francisco, CA: Sierra Club Books.

Singh, R. K., Murty, H. R., Gupta, S. K., & Dikshit, A. K. (2007). Development of composite sustainability performance index for steel industry. *Ecological Indicators*, *7*(3), 565–588. doi:10.1016/j.ecolind.2006.06.004

Sklair, L. (2001). *The Transnational Capitalist Class*. Oxford, UK: Blackwell.

Slatter, S. (2011). *Leading corporate turnaround: How leaders fix troubled companies*. John Wiley & Sons.

Slatter, S., & Lovett, D. (1999). *Corporate turnaround*. Penguin, UK.

Smith, A. (1776). *An inquiry into the nature and causes of the wealth of nations* (vol. 1). London: Printed for W. Strahan; and T. Cadell, 1776.

Smith, E. T. (1990). The greening of corporate America. *Business Week*, (3156), 96-103.

Soderquist, C., & Overakkers, S. (2010). Education for Sustainable Development: A Systems Thinking Approach. *Global Environmental Research*, *14*, 193–202.

Solomon, R. C., & Greene, J. K. (1999). *Morality and the Good Life: An Introduction to Ethics through Classical Sources*. New York: McGraw-Hill.

Stančić, P., Čupić, M., & Obradović, V. (2014). Influence of board and ownership structure on bank profitability: Evidence from South East Europe. *Economic Research-Ekonomska Istraživanja*, *27*(1), 573–589. doi:10.1080/1331677X.2014.970450

Steiner, I. D. (1972). *Group processes and group productivity*. New York: Academic.

Sterman. (1991). *A Skeptic's Guide to Computer Models*. MIT System Dynamics In Education Project.

Sterman. (2000). *Business Dynamics Systems Thinking And Modelling In A Complex World*. McGraw-Hill.

Stewart, J., & Munro, L. (2007). The Impact Of Audit Committee Existence and Audit Committee Meeting Frequency on the External Audit: Perceptions of Australian Auditors. *International Journal of Auditing*, *11*(1), 51–69. doi:10.1111/j.1099-1123.2007.00356.x

Stiles, P., & Taylor, B. (2001). *Boards at work: How directors view their roles and responsibilities: How directors view their roles and responsibilities*. OUP Oxford.

Sun, F., Wei, X., & Xu, Y. (2012). Audit committee characteristics and loss reserve error. *Managerial Auditing Journal*, *27*(4), 355–377. doi:10.1108/02686901211217978

Sun, J., & Cahan, S. F. (2012). The economic determinants of compensation committee quality. *Managerial Finance*, *38*(2), 188–205. doi:10.1108/03074351211193721

Sun, J., Cahan, S. F., & Emanuel, D. (2009). Compensation committee governance quality, chief executive officer stock option grants, and future firm performance. *Journal of Banking & Finance*, *33*(8), 1507–1519. doi:10.1016/j.jbankfin.2009.02.015

Tabak, B. M., Fazio, D. M., & Cajueiro, D. O. (2011). The effects of loan portfolio concentration on Brazilian banks' return and risk. *Journal of Banking & Finance*, *35*(11), 3065–3076. doi:10.1016/j.jbankfin.2011.04.006

Taffler, R. J. (1983). The assessment of company solvency and performance using a statistical model. *Accounting and Business Research*, *13*(52), 295–308. doi:10.1080/00014788.1983.9729767

Tang & Vijay. (2001). *System Dynamics Origins, Development And Future Prospects of a Method*. Research Seminar in Engineering Systems.

Tanna, S., Pasiouras, F., & Nnadi, M. (2011). The effect of board size and composition on the efficiency of UK banks. *International Journal of the Economics of Business*, *18*(3), 441–462. doi:10.1080/13571516.2011.618617

Tasrifi. (2014). System Dynamics Model Of Technology And Economic Growth: A Preliminary Study. *Proceedings Of The 32nd International Conference Of The System Dynamics Society*.

TBB. (2009). *The financial system and banking sector in Turkey*. Retrieved from http://www.tbb.org.tr/Dosyalar/Arastirma_ve_Raporlar/The_Financial_System_and_Bankin g_Sector_in_Turkey.pdf

Teitel, K., & Machuga, S. (2010). The Interaction of Audit Firm Quality and the Mexican Code Of Best Corporate Practices On Earnings Quality. *Review of Business Research*, *10*(1), 32–40.

Temiz. (2008). *Türkiye'de Vergi Gelirleri ve Ekonomik Büyüme İlişkisi:1960-2006 Dönemi*. Ulusal İktisat Kongresi, İzmir.

Tesfamariam, Y. (2014). *The determinants of financial distress in the case of manufacturing share companies in Addis Ababa-Ethiopia*. A Thesis in the Department of Accounting and Finance Addis Ababa University.

Thakor, A. V. (2014). Bank capital and financial stability: An economic trade-off or a Faustian bargain? *Annual Review of Financial Economics*, *6*(1), 185–223. doi:10.1146/annurev-financial-110613-034531

Thauer, C. R. (2014). *The Managerial Sources of Corporate Social Responsibility. The Spread of Global Standards*. Cambridge, UK: Cambridge University Press. doi:10.1017/CBO9781107588950

The World Bank. (2011). *Sustaining high growth: The role of domestic savings: Turkey country economic memorandum* (World Bank Report No. 66301-TR). Retrieved from http://wwwwds.20121128233319/Rendered/PDF/NonAsciiFileName0.pdf

Thim, C. K., Choong, Y. V., & Nee, C. S. (2011). Factors affecting financial distress: The case of Malaysian public listed firms. *Corporate Ownership and Control*, *8*(4), 345–351. doi:10.22495/cocv8i4c3art3

Thomson, C. (2009). *Knowledge Center for Students: Corporate governance theories and issues*. Retrieved 13 October 2016, from http://knowledgecenterforstudents.blogspot.com/2011/10/corporate-governance-theories-and.html

Tinic, S. (1988). Anatomy of initial public offerings of common stock. *The Journal of Finance*, *43*(4), 789–822. doi:10.1111/j.1540-6261.1988.tb02606.x

Tiras, S., Ruf, B., & Brown, R. (1998). The Relation Between Stakeholders. *Implicit Claims and Firm Value', National American Accounting Association Meeting*.

Tirole, J. (2001). Corporate governance. *Econometrica*, *69*(1), 2–18. doi:10.1111/1468-0262.00177

Titman, S., & Wessels, R. (1988). The determinants of capital structure choice. *The Journal of Finance*, *43*(1), 1–19. doi:10.1111/j.1540-6261.1988.tb02585.x

Towil. (1996). Industrial Dynamics Modelling of Supply Chains. *Logistic Information Management*, *9*(4), 43-56.

Tradingview. (2019a). *Rosneft Oil Co MOEX:ROSN*. Retrieved March 15, 2019 from https://www.tradingview.com/symbols/MOEX-ROSN/

Tradingview. (2019b). *Sberbank Co MOEX:SBER*. Retrieved March 15, 2019 from https://www.tradingview.com/symbols/MOEX-SBER/

Tradingview. (2019c). *VTB Co MOEX:VTB*. Retrieved March 15, 2019 from https://www.tradingview.com/symbols/MOEX-VTBR/

Trevino, L. K., & Youngblood, S. A. (1990). Bad apples in bad barrels: A causal analysis of ethical decision-making behaviour. *The Journal of Applied Psychology*, *75*(4), 378–385. doi:10.1037/0021-9010.75.4.378

Trevino, L., Weaver, G., Gibson, D., & Toffler, B. (1999). Managing ethics and legal compliance: What works and what hurts. *California Management Review*, *41*(2), 131–151. doi:10.2307/41165990

Trujillo-Ponce, A. (2013). What determines the profitability of banks? Evidence from Spain. *Accounting and Finance*, *53*(2), 561–586. doi:10.1111/j.1467-629X.2011.00466.x

Turban, D., & Greening, D. (1996). Corporate social performance and organizational attractiveness to prospective employees. *Academy of Management Journal*, *40*, 658–672.

Turetsky, H. F., & McEwen, R. A. (2001). An empirical investigation of firm longevity: A model of the ex ante predictors of financial distress. *Review of Quantitative Finance and Accounting*, *16*(4), 323–343. doi:10.1023/A:1011291425075

Turley, S., & Zaman, M. (2004). The corporate governance effects of audit committees. *The Journal of Management and Governance*, *8*(3), 305–332. doi:10.100710997-004-1110-5

Ugur, M., & Ararat, M. (2006). Does macroeconomic performance affect corporate governance: Evidence from Turkey. *Corporate Governance*, *14*(4), 325–348. doi:10.1111/j.1467-8683.2006.00510.x

Ujunwa, A., Salami, P., & Umar, A. (2013). CEO duality and firm performance: An integration of institutional perceptive with agency theory. *International Journal of Social, Behavioral, Educational, Economic. Business and Industrial Engineering*, *7*(1), 180–186.

Utama, G. (2014). Old Wine İn A New Bottle: Towards A Common Language For Post-Keynesian Macroeconomics Model. *Proceedings Of The 32nd International Conference Of The System Dynamics Society*.

Uyar, K., & Kuzey, C. (2014). Determinants of corporate cash holdings: Evidence from the emerging market of Turkey. *Applied Economics*, *46*(9), 1035–1048. doi:10.1080/00036846.2013.866203

Vafeas, N. (1999). Board meeting frequency and firm performance. *Journal of Financial Economics*, *53*(1), 113–142. doi:10.1016/S0304-405X(99)00018-5

Van de Ven, B., & Jeurissen, R. (2005). Competing responsibly. *Business Ethics Quarterly*, *15*(2), 299–317. doi:10.5840/beq200515216

Veaco, K., & Sorokin, C. (2014). Corporate Governance Consultants: What to Look for When Hiring. *Corporate Governance Advisor*, *22*(4), 1–5.

Vennix, J. M. (1995). Building Consensus In Strategic Decision Making: System Dynamics As A Group Support System. *Group Decision and Negotiation*, *4*(4), 335–355. doi:10.1007/BF01409778

Vermaelen, T. (1981). Common stock repurchases and market signaling: An empirical study. *Journal of Financial Economics*, *9*(2), 139–183. doi:10.1016/0304-405X(81)90011-8

Verschoor, C. C. (2002). Reflections on the audit committee's role. *Internal Auditor*, *59*(April), 26–35.

Vicknair, D., Hickman, K., & Carnes, K. C. (1993). A note on audit committee independence: Evidence from the NYSE on" grey" area directors. *Accounting Horizons*, *7*(1), 53.

Victor, B., & Cullen, J. B. (1988). The organizational bases of ethical work climates. *Administrative Science Quarterly*, *33*(1), 101–125. doi:10.2307/2392857

Vig, S., & Datta, M. (2018). Corporate governance and value creation: A study of selected Indian companies. *International Journal of Indian Culture and Business Management*, *17*(3), 259–282. doi:10.1504/IJICBM.2018.094582

Villalonga, B., & Amit, R. (2006). How do family ownership, control and management affect firm value? *Journal of Financial Economics*, *80*(2), 385–417. doi:10.1016/j.jfineco.2004.12.005

Vincent, O. M. (2012). *The Impact of Corporate Environmental Responsibility on Financial Performance: Extractive Sector Perspective* (Unpublished Doctoral Thesis). Brunel University.

Vintilă, G., & Gherghina, Ş. C. (2014). The impact of ownership concentration on firm value. Empirical study of the Bucharest stock exchange listed companies. *Procedia Economics and Finance*, *15*, 271–279. doi:10.1016/S2212-5671(14)00500-0

Wahab, E. A., Mat Zain, M., & James, K. (2011). Political connections, corporate governance and audit fees in Malaysia. *Managerial Auditing Journal*, *26*(5), 393–418. doi:10.1108/02686901111129562

Waldman, D., Siegel, D., & Javidan, M. (2006). Components of CEO transformational leadership and corporate social responsibility. *Journal of Management Studies*, *43*(8), 1703–1725. doi:10.1111/j.1467-6486.2006.00642.x

Wang, K., Sewon, O., & Claiborne, M. C. (2008). Determinants and consequences of voluntary disclosure in an emerging market: Evidence from China. *Journal of International Accounting, Auditing & Taxation*, *17*(1), 14–30. doi:10.1016/j.intaccaudtax.2008.01.001

Warren, K. (2005). Improving Strategic Management With The Fundamental Principles Of System Dynamics. *System Dynamics Review*, *21*(4), 329–350. doi:10.1002dr.325

Welch, I. (1989). Seasoned offerings, imitation costs, and the underpricing of initial public offerings. *The Journal of Finance*, *44*(2), 421–450. doi:10.1111/j.1540-6261.1989.tb05064.x

Wesa, E. W., & Otinga, H. N. (2018). Determinants of financial distress among listed firms at the Nairobi securities exchange. *The Strategic Journal of Business & Change Management*, *5*(4), 1057–1073.

Westman, H. (2011). The impact of management and board ownership on profitability in banks with different strategies. *Journal of Banking & Finance*, *35*(12), 3300-3318. doi:10.1016/j.jbankfin.2011.05.013

Wheeler. (1994). *How to Get Managers To Use System Dynamics*. International System Dynamics Conference, Stirling, UK.

Wheeler, D., Fabig, H., & Boele, R. (2002). Paradoxes and Dilemmas for Stakeholder Responsive Firms in the Extractive Sector: Lessons from the Case of Shell and the Ogoni. *Journal of Business Ethics*, *39*(3), 297–318. doi:10.1023/A:1016542207069

Williamson, O. E. (1983). Organizational form, residual claimants, and corporate control. *The Journal of Law & Economics*, *26*(2), 351–366. doi:10.1086/467039

Williamson, O. E. (1984). Corporate Governance. *The Yale Law Journal*, *93*(7), 1197–1230. https://digitalcommons.law.yale.edu/fss_papers/4392. doi:10.2307/796256

Windsor, D. (2001). The Future of Corporate Social Responsibility. *The International Journal of Organizational Analysis*, *9*(3), 225–256. doi:10.1108/eb028934

Wintoki, M. B., Linck, J. S., & Netter, J. M. (2012). Endogeneity and the dynamics of internal corporate governance. *Journal of Financial Economics*, *105*(3), 581–606. doi:10.1016/j.jfineco.2012.03.005

Winton, A. (1999). *Don't put all your eggs in one basket? Diversification and specialization in lending.* Diversification and Specialization in Lending.

Wolstenholme, E. F. (1990). *Systems Enquiry: A System Dynamics Approach.* John Wiley & Sons.

Wood, D. J. (1991). Corporate social performance revisited. *Academy of Management Review*, *16*(4), 691–718. doi:10.5465/amr.1991.4279616

World Bank. (2019). *GINI index (World Bank estimate).* Retrieved March 17, 2019 from World Bank: https://data.worldbank.org/indicator/SI.POV.GINI?locations=RU

World Economic Forum. (2018). *The Inclusive Development Index 2018.* Retrieved February 10, 2019 from World Economic Forum: http://www3.weforum.org/docs/WEF_Forum_IncGrwth_2018.pdf

Xiaowen, S. (2013). Corporate characteristics and internal control information disclosure – evidence from annual reports in 2009 of listed companies in Shenzhen stock exchange. *Physics Procedia*, *25*(1), 630–635.

Xie, B., Davidson, W. III, & DaDalt, P. (2003). Earnings management and corporate governance: The role of the board and the audit committee. *Journal of Corporate Finance*, *9*(3), 295–316. doi:10.1016/S0929-1199(02)00006-8

Yamaguchi, K. (2008). *Open Macroeconomies As A Closed Economic System - SD Macroeconomic Modeling Completed.* International Conference Of The System Dynamics Society, Athens, Greece.

Yamaguchi, K. (2009). *Logical Vs Historical Time İn A Price Adjustment Mechanism.* International Conference Of The System Dynamics Society, Albuquerque, NM.

Yamaguchi. (2013). *Money and Macroeconomic Dynamics- Accounting System Dynamics Approach.* Awaji Island, Japan: Japan Future Research Center.

Yamaguchi, K. (2001). A Step-By-Step System Dynamics Modeling Of Sustainability. *Journal Of Business Administration, Osaka Sangyo University*, *3*(1), 25–52.

Yamaguchi, K. (2003). Principle Of Accounting System Dynamics – Modeling Corporate Financial Statements. *Proceedings Of The 21st International Conference Of The System Dynamics Society.*

Yamaguchi, K. (2004). Money Supply And Creation Of Deposits: SD Macroeconomic Modeling (1). *Proceedings Of The 22nd International Conference Of The System Dynamics Society.*

Yamaguchi, K. (2005). Aggregate Demand Equilibria And Price Flexibility: Sd Macroeconomic Modeling (2). *Proceedings Of The 23nd International Conference Of The System Dynamics Society.*

Yamaguchi, K. (2006). Integration Of Real And Monetary Sectors With Labor Market: Sd Macroeconomic Modeling (3). *Proceedings Of The 24th International Conference Of The System Dynamics Society.*

Yamaguchi, K. (2007). Balance Of Payments And Foreign Exchange Dynamics: Sd Macroeconomic Modeling (4). *Proceedings Of The 25th International Conference Of The System Dynamics Society.*

Yang, J., & Krishnan, J. (2005). Audit Committee and Quarterly Earning Management. *International Journal of Auditing, 9*(3), 201–219. doi:10.1111/j.1099-1123.2005.00278.x

Yermack, D. (1996). Higher valuation of companies with a small board of directors. *Journal of Financial Economics, 40*(2), 185–212. doi:10.1016/0304-405X(95)00844-5

Yermack, D. (2004). Remuneration, retention, and reputation incentives for outside directors. *The Journal of Finance, 59*(5), 2281–2308. doi:10.1111/j.1540-6261.2004.00699.x

Yermack, D. (2015). Is Bitcoin a real currency? An economic appraisal. In *Handbook of digital currency* (pp. 31–43). Elsevier. doi:10.1016/B978-0-12-802117-0.00002-3

Yoshikawa, T., & Rasheed, A. A. (2009). Convergence of Corporate Governance: CriticalReview and Future Directions. *Corporate Governance, 17*(3), 388–404. doi:10.1111/j.1467-8683.2009.00745.x

Young, M. N., Peng, M. W., Ahlstrom, D., Bruton, G. D., & Jiang, Y. (2008). Corporate governance in emerging economies: A review of the principal–principal perspective. *Journal of Management Studies, 45*(1), 196–220. doi:10.1111/j.1467-6486.2007.00752.x

Zabri, S. M., Ahmad, K., & Wah, K. K. (2016). Corporate governance practices and firm performance: Evidence from top 100 public listed companies in Malaysia. *Procedia Economics and Finance, 35*, 287–296. doi:10.1016/S2212-5671(16)00036-8

Zagorchev, A., & Gao, L. (2015). Corporate governance and performance of financial institutions. *Journal of Economics and Business, 82*, 17–41. doi:10.1016/j.jeconbus.2015.04.004

Zahra, S. A., & Pearce, J. A. II. (1989). Boards of directors and corporate financial performance: A review and integrative model. *Journal of Management, 15*(2), 291–334. doi:10.1177/014920638901500208

Zeitoun, H., Osterloh, M., & Frey, B. S. (2015). Learning from ancient Athens: Demarchy and corporate governance. *Academy of Management Perspectives, 3015*(1), 4-18. doi:10.5465/amp.2012.0105.test

Zhang, Y., Zhou, J., & Zhou, N. (2007). Audit Committee Quality, Auditor Independence, and Internal Control Weaknesses. *Journal of Accounting and Public Policy*, *26*(3), 300–327. doi:10.1016/j.jaccpubpol.2007.03.001

Zhu. (2001). *Beginner Modeling Exercises Section 3 Mental Simulation of Simple Negative Feedback*. MIT System Dynamics in Education Project.

Zingales, L. (1998). Corporate governance. In P. Newman (Ed.), *The New Palgrave Dictionary of Economics and the Law*. London: Palgrave Macmillan.

Zureigat, Q. (2010). The Effect of Modified Auditors Opinions on Shares Prices: Evidence from Amman Stock Exchange. *Jordan Journal of Business Administration.*, *6*(2), 210–224.

About the Contributors

Otuo Serebour Agyemang is a Senior Lecturer in the Department of Finance, School of Business, University of Cape Coast. He received his PhD from the University of Ferrara, Italy. He has presented and discussed research papers at several international conferences. In addition, he has chaired conference sessions on corporate governance in emerging economies. He is a member of the European Corporate Governance Institute and the Academy of African Management. His research interests are in the areas of Corporate Governance, Institutions, CSR and Business Ethics, and Financial markets. Some of his works have been published in reputable journals such as Society and Business Review, Corporate Governance, Management Research Review, Social Responsibility Journal, Journal of Global Responsibility, Journal of African Business, Accounting Research Journal, International Journal of Law and Management, Population Health Management among others. Further, he is an editorial board member of the African Journal of Corporate Governance and an ad hoc reviewer for several reputable journals. He has served on a number of committees and boards at the University of Cape Coast, Ghana. Areas of his teaching interests are Business Economics, Managerial Economics, Corporate Governance, Business Ethics and CSR, Financial Markets and Institutions, and International Finance. He has consulted for some rural banks in Ghana in the area of corporate governance.

Abraham Ansong holds a PhD from the University of Cape Coast, Ghana. He is presently the Head of the Department of Management at the same university. His research interests focus on corporate governance, business management, corporate social responsibility and entrepreneurship. He has published in several renowned journals such as Journal of African Business, Management Research Review, African Journal of Business Management, Social Responsibility Journal, among others. He is a member of the Institute of Directors-Ghana.

Ben Agyei-Mensah is a Chartered Management Accountant and member of the Chartered Institute of Management Accountants, (CIMA) U.K Currently an Associate Professor at SolBridge International School of Business, Daejeon, South Korea. Research areas are: Financial Accounting, Corporate Governance, Management Accounting and Performance Management.

* * *

Elif Akben-Selçuk is an Associate Professor of Finance at the Department of Business Administration, Faculty of Management at Kadir Has University in Istanbul, Turkey. She teaches undergraduate and graduate courses in accounting and financial management. Professor Akben-Selçuk's research interests include corporate finance, mergers and acquisitions, corporate governance, emerging markets, personal finance and financial literacy. Her research has appeared in such outlets as Managerial Finance, International Journal of Bank Marketing, International Journal of Emerging Markets, Economics Bulletin, Psychological Reports among others. Professor Akben-Selçuk received a PhD in Finance, an MA in Economics, and a BA in Business Administration from Bogazici University in Istanbul, Turkey.

Iustina Alina Boitan is an Associate Professor, Ph.D. at the Faculty of Finance and Banking from the Bucharest University of Economic Studies (Romania). She is member of several professional bodies, such as the Center of Financial and Monetary Research, within the Bucharest University of Economic Studies, Romania (since 2008) and the Monetary Research Center within the University of National and World Economy, Bulgaria (research fellow since 2015). She has been granted the Georgescu Roegen award for excellence in scientific research, concretized in papers published in journals indexed Thomson Reuters (Bucharest University of Economic Studies, 2014). Her research interests focus on banking systems' efficiency and competition, assessment of banking systems' distress, quantitative supervisory tools (such as the development of early warning systems), ethical or socially responsible banks. She holds in-depth expertise in quantitative methods applied to financial system.

Luis A. Castrillo is a Full Professor in Financial Economics and Accounting at the University of Burgos, where he was Head of the Department of Business Administration. He studied Business Administration in Valladolid (Spain) and received her PhD in Business Administration at the University of Valladolid. Her main research focuses on financial accounting and corporate governance.

Şaban Çelik is Assistant Professor of Finance in the department of Business Administration at Izmir Katip Çelebi University. His primary research interests are corporate finance, investment analysis, portfolio management in general and asset pricing, bankruptcy prediction, corporate governance and intellectual capital in particular.

Olamitunji Dakare is presently a senior lecturer at the prestigious Pan-Atlantic University, School of Management and Social Sciences (SMSS). Prior to joining PAU, Dr Dakare was a lecturer in Department of Business Administration, University of Lagos, where he had taught both undergraduate and post-graduate students. He is also a management consultant. His research interests include Competitive Strategy, Corporate Strategy and Entrepreneurship.

Manipadma Datta is a Professor in the Department of Business and Sustainability at TERI School of Advanced Studies (TERISAS), New Delhi, the pioneer in sustainability research.He has been in management teaching, training and research for more than three decades in India and abroad. His areas of expertise are - Sustainable Development, Climate Finance, Responsible Investments, Integrated Reporting, Circular Economy Finance, Weather Derivative, Public Management, CSR, Strategic Management, Sustainability and Creativity, Valuation of Intangibles.

Sara Elouadi is a research professor at Hassan II University, teaches finance and accounting and author of several articles on governance.

Arzu Eren Şenaras graduated from Uludağ University in 2007. She took her master and Phd degree in the Deparment of Econometrics at Uludag University.

Tuna Can Güleç is a Research Assistant in the department of Banking and Finance at Manisa Celal Bayar University. His primary research interests are cryptocurrency valuation, investment analysis and portfolio management in particular, and corporate governance and behavioral finance, in general.

Allam Mohammed Mousa Hamdan is a Professor and Dean of College of Business and Financet, Ahlia University. He has many papers published in regional and international journals that discussed several accounting, financial and economic issues concerning the Arab world. In addition, he has interests in educational related issues in the Arab world universities like educational governance, investment in education and its relation with economic growth. He was awarded the first prize of Al-Owais Creative Award, UAE, 2019 and 2017; the second prize of Rashid bin Humaid Award for Culture and Science, UAE, 2016; the third prize of Arab Prize for the Social Sciences and Humanities, Qatar, 2015, and the first prize of 'Durrat watan', UAE, 2013. He is a member of National Qualifications Framework (NQF) – Validation Panel.

Ikpesu Fredrick is a lecturer currently at Pan-Atlantic University, Lagos Nigeria. His experience cut across the industry and educational sector. Prior to joining PAU he has occupied the position of the Group Head of Finance/Administration. His research interests include international and corporate finance.

Huynh Viet Khai received his Ph.D from Kyushu University, Japan. Currently, he is the head of Department of Environmental and Resource Economics at College of Economics, Can Tho University, Vietnam. His research involves productive efficiency of agricultural production, water pollution, the demand of agricultural insurance, the solution of poverty reduction, organic production, biodiversity conservation, as well as economic valuation of non-market goods such as externality of agriculture and forest, waste management, environmental policy, the applications of contingent valuation and choice modeling methods.

Phan Dinh Khoi is an Assistant Professor of Finance and Chair of the Department of Finance and Banking at the College of Economics, Can Tho University, Vietnam. He earned a PhD in Finance from Lincoln University in New Zealand. He published a few papers and book chapters in international peer-reviewed journals including Journal of Asian Economics, the Journal of Asia- Pacific Economy, Journal of Eastern European and Central Asian Research and World Scientific Publishing. He is currently a member of the editorial board for the Southeast Asia Review of Economics and Business. His research interest focuses on development finance, development economics, corporate finance, stock market and banking.

Sonia Marcos studied Business Administration in Alcalá de Henares (Spain). She received her PhD in Business Administration at the University of Burgos. She is assistant professor of Business Administration at the University of Burgos and her main research focuses on corporate governance.

Parmenas Njoroge is a Ph.D. student at Southern Federal University in the faculty of Economics. Holds a Masters degree in Finance and credit from Southern Federal University, Russia. His academic research fields of interest include Event studies, Financial economics, and financial markets.

Pinar Sener is an Associate Professor of Finance and Accounting in EDC Paris Business School which she joined in September 2016. She teaches undergraduate and graduate courses in accounting and financial management. Professor Sener's research interests include corporate governance, family businesses and corporate finance with a special focus on emerging markets. Her research has appeared in such outlets as Managerial Finance, international Entrepreneurship and Management Journal, Economics Bulletin, Corporate Governance: The International Journal of Business in Society among others. Professor Sener received a PhD in Management from Sorbonne Business School, IAE de Paris and an MA in Economics from Marmara University in Istanbul.

Hayrettin Sezen is professor at the School of Applied Science at Altınbaş University in İstanbul.

Dmitry Shevchenko currently works at the Department of Finance and Credit, Southern Federal University (Rostov on Don, Russia). Associate Professor, PhD, Director of the Master's degree program "Financial Institutions and Financial Instruments", Mobility Coordinator on the Faculty of Economics. Research interests are Financial Economics, Corporate Finance, Financial Markets and Behavioral Finance.

Shinu Vig is a research scholar in the Department of Business and Sustainability at TERI School of Advanced Studies, New Delhi, India.She is also working with IMS Ghaziabad, India. Her areas of interest are corporate governance, business ethics, CSR and business sustainability.

Olusegun Vincent is a Senior Lecturer in School of Management and Social Sciences at Pan Atlantic University in Nigeria. Prior to academic life he worked as a chartered accountant in Ernst & Young, few financial institutions and one time Director of Economic Intelligence Unit in Lagos State, Nigeria. His research interests include sustainability, strategy, corporate governance and corporate finance.

Qasim Zureigat is a professor of accounting with 15 years of teaching experiences for graduate and under graduate programs. In addition to his teaching responsibilities he has served in various quality improvements tasks and projects including founding faculty at Sulaiman AlRajhi School of Business, Director of Accounting Program, CBE's Steering Committee for Quality and Accreditation, Strategic Planning, and curriculum development. Since 2012, he served as director of AACSB accreditation project and then as Assistant Dean for Accreditation since January 2014 at College of Business and Economics (AACSB and NCAAA Accredited). His research interests are mainly focused on auditing and audit quality, and include corporate governance, internal auditing, performance measurement, and business education, and he published papers in SCOPUS, Thomson Reuters indexed journals, ABDC and ERA ranked journals. He serves as an editor and reviewer in many international journals. At the meanwhile, Prof Zureigat believes of interactive and skills based learning strategies that could engage students in real life business cases and applications to enhance their long-life learning experiences.

Index

Ensure Quality Research is Introduced to the Academic Community

Become an IGI Global Reviewer for Authored Book Projects

The overall success of an authored book project is dependent on quality and timely reviews.

In this competitive age of scholarly publishing, constructive and timely feedback significantly expedites the turnaround time of manuscripts from submission to acceptance, allowing the publication and discovery of forward-thinking research at a much more expeditious rate. Several IGI Global authored book projects are currently seeking highly-qualified experts in the field to fill vacancies on their respective editorial review boards:

Applications and Inquiries may be sent to:
development@igi-global.com

Applicants must have a doctorate (or an equivalent degree) as well as publishing and reviewing experience. Reviewers are asked to complete the open-ended evaluation questions with as much detail as possible in a timely, collegial, and constructive manner. All reviewers' tenures run for one-year terms on the editorial review boards and are expected to complete at least three reviews per term. Upon successful completion of this term, reviewers can be considered for an additional term.

If you have a colleague that may be interested in this opportunity, we encourage you to share this information with them.

www.ingramcontent.com/pod-product-compliance
Lightning Source LLC
LaVergne TN
LVHW080557300926
849162LV00005B/976